NEWCOMER'S HANDBOOK®

FOR MOVING TO

San Francisco
and the Bay Area

Including San Jose, Oakland, Berkeley, and Palo Alto

2nd Edition

D0062818

6750 SW Franklin
Portland, OR 97223
503-968-6777
www.firstbooks.com

FIRST BOOKS

S

© Copyright 2001 by First Books. All rights reserved.

2nd Edition

Newcomer's Handbook® is a registered trademark of First Books.

Reproduction of the contents of this book in any form whatsoever is not permissible without written permission from the publisher, First Books, 6750 SW Franklin, Portland, OR 97223, 503-968-6777.

First Books is not legally responsible for any change in the value of any enterprises by reason of their inclusion or exclusion from this work. Contents are based on information believed to be accurate at the time of publication.

First Books has not accepted payment from any individuals, firms or organizations for inclusion in this book.

Authors: Ruth Rayle and Michael Bower
Publisher: Jeremy Solomon
Series Editor: Bernadette Duperron
Copy Editor: Karen Freed
Contributors: Holly Erickson, Alexandra D'Italia, Luba Golburt, Rebecca Field, Susan Anderson
Cover/Interior Design, Production: Erin Johnson
Cartographer: Scott Lockheed
Chapter Icons: Matt Brownson

Transit map courtesy of Bay Area Rapid Transit

ISBN: 0-912301-46-5
ISSN: 1533-5100

Printed in the USA on recycled paper.

Published by First Books, 6750 SW Franklin, Portland, OR 97223.

TABLE OF CONTENTS

CONTENTS *(continued)*

CONTENTS *(continued)*

REMINISCENT OF THE MID-19TH CENTURY GOLD RUSH, THE BAY AREA today is experiencing a gold rush of a different sort—microprocessor chips and anything to do with computers, the internet or wireless communications. The nine-county San Francisco Bay Area is Oz to computer programmers, software and hardware designers, internet junkies, inventors, entrepreneurs, and venture capitalists. Located south of San Francisco, Silicon Valley hosts big name computer and software companies like Intel, Cisco, Oracle, and Apple, as well as hundreds of other technological giants in the making. To the north of San Francisco, in Marin County, you'll find small but burgeoning communities with dramatic landscapes and stunning vistas; head east toward Sonoma and Napa counties for charming vineyards tucked in among rolling hills.

Most newcomers come to the Bay Area for work. Ask anyone why they stay and most likely you'll hear about the area's endless opportunities, whether professional, recreational or educational—not to mention the great weather. The Bay Area is the only place in America where you can ride a moving national landmark (cable cars) while taking in some of the world's most beautiful scenery, including the

> THE BAY AREA IS THE ONLY PLACE IN AMERICA WHERE YOU CAN RIDE A MOVING NATIONAL LANDMARK, WHILE TAKING IN SOME OF THE WORLD'S MOST BEAUTIFUL SCENERY...

Bay, Alcatraz Island, Golden Gate Bridge, Golden Gate Park, and the city skyline itself. Because of its proximity to the Pacific Ocean and the accompanying steady winds that move any smog away, San Francisco and its environs have some of the cleanest big-city air in the country. All you get are lovely, blue shimmering skies. Many would agree that Bay Area meteorologists have one of the easiest jobs around. The weather forecast is consistently "low clouds and fog overnight, clearing by mid-morning, giving way to afternoon sunshine," with the temperature rarely dipping below 40° or above 80° Fahrenheit. The one exception to that rule comes with the much anticipated Indian Summer months of September and October, when it can get into the 80s and on extremely rare occasions, over 100° Fahrenheit. The fall and winter rainy seasons begin with a few drizzles in October that become outright downpours by November, and continue intermittently through April. Communities located away from the ocean, particularly those in the South and East Bay, are, as a general rule, likely to have weather that is drier, warmer, and has more smog.

This *Newcomer's Handbook®* is intended to help make your move here as seamless and enjoyable as possible. It describes San Francisco and surrounding Bay Area neighborhoods/communities in detail, and provides lists of neighborhood resources, including neighborhood web sites, police stations, post offices, libraries, hospitals, public schools, and community groups. Transportation routes are also covered. In addition to profiling area neighborhoods and communities, this guide will assist you with the biggest of Bay Area challenges: finding a place to live, as well as getting your belongings here **(Moving and Storage)**, setting up your bank accounts **(Money Matters)** and utilities **(Getting Settled)**, where to go to buy a shower curtain, area rug, or mop and broom **(Shopping for the Home)**, and places to go to kick back and relax in a welcoming patch of green **(Greenspace and Beaches)**. It's all here, and much more.

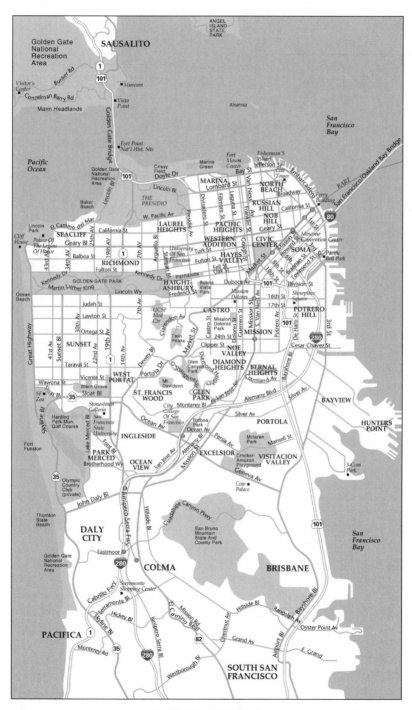

SAN FRANCISCO

CITY OF SAN FRANCISCO

WELCOME TO SAN FRANCISCO KNOWN AS "THE CITY" WITH A capital "C" (never call it "Frisco" or everyone will know you are not from here). More than six million people live in the Bay Area, yet only 800,000 people live in San Francisco proper. The City's population almost doubles during weekdays when hundreds of thousands arrive for work, clogging the local freeways. Traffic also flows out of San Francisco and sometimes that passage is even worse than the commute into the City. In fact, some of the nation's worst morning and evening commutes are here, despite the existence of the sleek, clean, and usually efficient Bay Area Rapid Transit (BART) system. Where the BART trains don't go, more than two dozen other transit systems do, including buses, trolleys, cable cars, commuter trains, shuttles, and ferryboats.

Only 48 square miles in size, San Francisco is compact when compared to cities like New York City, Los Angeles or Chicago. Every inch of the City teems with activity, from roller-blading, hiking and biking in Golden Gate Park, surfing or hang gliding at Ocean Beach, dining or shopping at Chinatown or North Beach, and the list goes on.

One of the dominant features of San Francisco life is fog. London is perhaps the only city more famous for its fog than San Francisco. Locals call it "Mother Nature's air conditioner" and it's especially prevalent during the Indian Summer months of September and October. Neighborhoods are defined by the amount of sun that shines there, or lack thereof. There are some areas of the City which get less fog than others, such as the Mission, Potrero Hill, Noe Valley, and the Castro, but you won't be able to avoid it entirely. After you've been here for a while, chances are you'll grow to love the fog, if you don't already. For those six to eight weeks of Indian Summer residents wake up in homes blanketed by a mist so thick it almost looks solid. It usually burns away by noon, giving way to clear blue skies and temperatures into the 90's. Then, just when you can't take the heat anymore, the fog tumbles into the Bay Area from the Pacific Ocean to the west, cooling temperatures down to the 40s and 50s.

There are areas of the City blessed by certain smells. Fresh brewed, dark Italian and French roast coffee and baking focaccia are the scents of North Beach; steamed crab and freshly baked sourdough permeate the Northpoint/Fisherman's Wharf area; and the smell of yeasty bagels wafts through the air in the Richmond. There is a salty ocean bite along the western edge of the Sunset, and the sometimes-disturbing odor of cable car brakes as you descend some of the City's steepest slopes on Russian Hill and Nob Hill. Go to Chinatown for the smell of exotic herbs intermingled with fresh dumplings; and throughout the City's parks you'll learn to savor the unforgettable aroma of wet eucalyptus.

> THERE ARE AREAS OF THE CITY BLESSED BY CERTAIN SMELLS. FRESH BREWED, DARK ITALIAN AND FRENCH ROAST COFFEE AND BAKING FOCACCIA ARE THE SCENTS OF NORTH BEACH; STEAMED CRAB AND FRESHLY BAKED SOURDOUGH PERMEATE THE NORTHPOINT/FISHERMAN'S WHARF AREA; AND THE SMELL OF YEASTY BAGELS WAFTS THROUGH THE AIR IN THE RICHMOND.

Aside from its stunning physical beauty, much of San Francisco's charm and vitality is due to its ethnic diversity. The earliest non-native settlers came from Russia, Italy, Ireland, Germany, China, Japan, and the Philippines, all of them establishing their own neighborhoods at first, and then branching out. That intra-city migration continues today, most notably the Chinatown population spreading out into formerly Italian-dominated North Beach. Historical areas of interest include the rowdy Barbary Coast days in the 19th century, the 1950s Beat Generation of North Beach, and the 1960s "make love not war" counter culture of Haight-Ashbury. Today the City is home to a large, politically active gay and lesbian population, many of whom reside in the Castro and Upper Market districts. At the other end of Market Street stand the towering temples of capitalism and economic power that make up the compact downtown Financial District, home to the largest concentration of banks and financial service companies west of the Mississippi, the Pacific Stock Exchange, and a number of high-tech companies.

All of this makes the City a vibrant and stimulating locale to call home. San Francisco has more than two dozen neighborhoods or districts, each of which can be clearly defined, despite the fact that some of them meld into one another at the edges. The following neighborhood profiles focus on the general characteristics and histories of each neighborhood, and provides information about neighborhood housing, weather, public transit, post office locations, emergency services, hospitals, public safety agencies, local attractions, and restaurant suggestions. Speaking of food, you certainly won't go hungry in San Francisco. There are more restaurants per capita here than in any other US city, offering every cuisine imaginable and, according to the *San Francisco Chronicle*, a majority of San Franciscans eat out almost five nights a week! With so many restaurants, there's some stiff competition between the eateries, many of which fail every year, but don't worry if your favorite spot shuts down, something equally good will most likely replace it.

You can expect varied types of housing in San Francisco. The famous and oft-depicted Victorians are wood-framed buildings, which range from relatively simple cottages to extremely ornate gingerbread-style mansions. There are Italianate Victorians, Queen-Anne Victorians, and others, which you might enjoy learning to identify once you live here. Built between the 1870s and the 1910s, Victorians have inner features as distinctive as their external features. Very high ceilings are the norm along with elaborate ceiling fixtures. The wainscoting can range from simple wooded slats to ornate carvings. The rooms tend to be rather small, but they generally have double doors which, when opened, create one large room out of two smaller rooms; great for creating a cozy home office. Often the rooms are entered from a railway hall, which runs from the front of the house or flat to the kitchen in the back. The grander Victorians still have fireplaces and marble fixtures; and the front rooms nearly all have bay windows. Also common here are Edwardians, built in the 1900s and 1910s. Some are wooden and similar to Victorians although less ornate. They often have bay windows, but gone are the Victorian styled railway halls and the odd little rooms. Many have double doors between bedroom and living room and many have closets that originally had or still have Murphy beds in them. They usually offer built-in cupboards in the dining room. The apartments, many of which were built in the 1920s, are generally of stucco and brown brick. They often sport a web of fire escapes in front and/or back, and typically are steam-heated via radiators. Some have Murphy beds or large closets that once housed Murphy beds. Often the kitchen has some built-in glass cupboards, and maybe a table and ironing board.

> ASIDE FROM ITS STUNNING PHYSICAL BEAUTY, MUCH OF SAN FRANCISCO'S CHARM AND VITALITY IS DUE TO ITS ETHNIC DIVERSITY.

Many of the homes of the Richmond and Sunset districts were built during the Depression. Places built during this time are snug and comfortable. They often have fireplaces, hardwood floors, and built-in book cabinets. Housing from the 1950s, '60s and '70s, which is scattered throughout the City, tends to be a little boxy. Rooms are smaller, walls, and ceilings without adornment; bathrooms and kitchens sometimes are without windows. There are no entire neighborhoods made up completely of this more contemporary style until you get to South San Francisco and Daly City.

There is a building boom taking place in San Francisco. New housing borrows features from the City's past and incorporates these into modern designs. Bay windows are the norm. New condos and apartments tend to be colorful, sometimes asymmetrical, with special attention paid to natural lighting.

About two-thirds of San Francisco residents are renters, paying a high monthly rate as, surely you've heard, rents here are expensive! Unless otherwise indicated, rental information provided in this book is from Metro-Rent, www.metrorent.com. Check their web site for more up to date pricing and trends.

Those considering buying a home should prepare for even more sticker shock. To give an indication of the upward trending housing market, according to the California Association of Realtors the median home price for a San Francisco home in October 2000 was $483,824—up 23.6% from the previous year. As long as the economy continues to flourish this trend will most likely continue. Unless otherwise noted, housing stats, particularly for surrounding Bay Areas, were supplied by the California Association of Realtors. See www.car.org for the latest information on Bay Area homes.

NORTH BEACH, TELEGRAPH HILL

Boundaries: **East**: The Embarcadero; **West**: Columbus Avenue; **North**: Fisherman's Wharf; **South**: Broadway (Telegraph Hill is at the east corner of North Beach, with Stockton Street as the border).

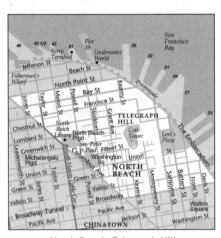

North Beach, Telegraph Hill

Don't bring your bathing suit to **North Beach,** just an appreciation for fine Italian food and a loaded wallet. North Beach is famous for its mouth-watering aromas of olive oil, garlic, and espresso, as well as its vibrant nightlife. These perks, coupled with its close proximity to downtown, make it a favorite neighborhood for young professionals, so called "empty-nesters" (older couples with grown children), and a burgeoning Chinese-American population, many of whom are moving over from nearby Chinatown.

Perhaps what is most famous about North Beach is its 1950s and '60s beat generation history. The area became a gathering place for poets, writers, and critical thinkers, who were coined "beatniks" by *San Francisco Chronicle* columnist Herb Caen. Adorned in sandals, berets and dark glasses, beatniks opposed mainstream beliefs and spoke out against complacency. The most famous of the bunch included poet Lawrence Ferlinghetti, who opened the City Lights Bookstore at 261 Columbus, Jack Kerouac, Allen Ginsberg, and Gary Snyder. Right across the alley from City Lights is Vesuvio's, 255 Columbus at Jack Kerouac Alley, a funky bar that hosted many of the beatniks, and Specs' Twelve Adler Museum Cafe, 12 Adler Place, was another hot spot. Tosca Cafe, 242 Columbus, with its brandy-laced cappuccinos, Irish coffee, and jukebox opera remains a popular place for artists and actors meet.

Another piece of San Francisco history visible from City Lights, is Broadway's red light district, which is where many a bachelor party take place. On the corner of Broadway and Columbus, you'll find the world famous Condor Club, which used to feature Carol Doda who sparked Broadway's topless scene in the 1960s when she exposed her enormous silicon-enhanced breasts. Retired from the stripping days, Doda now is appropriately in the lingerie business and owns a shop on Union Street. The Condor has become a sports bar.

The nightlife here is hopping, and it's not just about sex. Voted by the *San Francisco Bay Guardian* as the best place to swing, the High-Ball Lounge, 473 Broadway, is a fun and happening place. For blues, try the Grant and Green Blues Club, 1371 Grant Avenue. Down the street, The Saloon, 1232 Grant Avenue, hosts blues bands every night. Bimbos 365 Club, 1025 Columbus Avenue, features bigger bands in a much bigger place. For a true San Franciscan experience and the City's longest running musical, Beach Blanket Babylon at Club Fugazi, 678 Beach Blanket Boulevard, sports huge hats and great wit. On the same street, grab some Guinness at O'Reilly's, 655 Beach Blanket Boulevard.

Locals take a break from the food and frenzy of their neighborhood at Washington Square Park, one of the City's oldest parks. In the early morning, you can see Chinese-Americans moving their limbs at glacial like speed as they practice tai chi. At the same hour you can smell the focaccia being baked across the street at Liguria's Bakery, 1700 Stockton Street, which has been baking bread here since 1911. Then as the day progresses, neighbors, sunbathers, and artists congregate at the Square. Some locals also play ball at the North Beach playground on Lombard and Mason streets. This playground is where baseball hall of famer Joe DiMaggio swung the bat around with his kid brothers. The City recently renamed the playground after Joe DiMaggio, though DiMaggio's estate lawyer unsuccessfully put up a fight, arguing that the playground isn't sophisticated enough for Joe. It's too bad Joe could not be here to tell us himself.

The neo-gothic St. Peter and Paul's Cathedral, 666 Filbert Street, looms over the park. The church is famous for its midnight Easter services. In 1954, DiMaggio wanted to marry sex goddess Marilyn Monroe here, in his hometown church but, because this was a second marriage for both, he was only allowed to have wedding pictures taken on the steps. They were married at city hall.

Upper Grant Street is home to low-end blues and rock and roll bars, trendy clothing shops, vintage clothing stores, and houseware shops. Because of increased rents, some merchants are being replaced by expensive boutiques, but no chain stores thanks to the neighborhood groups that have fought vehemently to keep the neighborhood's character intact. Fortunately, many of the owners of the North Beach shops don't have to pay rent because they own the store property. This may allow North Beach to retain its colorful local charm.

There used to be a long beach along the area's northern edge, between Telegraph Hill on the east and Russian Hill on the west. Shortly after the 1906 Earthquake, the City dumped debris from the earthquake and built a series of breakwaters and piers that is now home to the tourist mecca of Fisherman's Wharf and Pier 39. Here, at the northern end of the Embarcadero, you'll find dozens of seafood restaurants. The Embarcadero thoroughfare runs along the bayside edge of the City, from the South of Market Area to the Fisherman's Wharf. Ghirardelli Square Shopping Center is a former chocolate factory that still serves the dark confection in various forms, perhaps most notably, hot chocolate sauce on top of ice cream. Stroll along Fisherman's Wharf, take a look at the still-active fishing fleet moored here, buy a steamed crab to take home for dinner, and view the rich sights of this bustling visitor's delight. Then pause for a moment, and savor the fact that you're no longer a tourist.

Most North Beach residents live in three-story Edwardian apartments, flats or condos built on the ashes of the 1906 earthquake fires. North Beach still is home to many Italian families (though that number has diminished significantly over the years), and Chinese-Americans. Young, mostly single, professionals enjoy North Beach for its food and nightlife, and because it's an easy commute downtown. Vacancies here are rare. According to Metro-Rent, in 2000 a studio apartment set you back about $1,050 per month, a one-bedroom about $2,500.

Once you have your North Beach pad, you may never want to leave. It's a short walk to most any kind of shopping, and to the Financial District. If you work downtown you may decide not to own a car, as parking is difficult and sometimes downright impossible, plus buses and cable cars are frequent. If you do have a car, you'll need to get a parking permit. Remember to curb your wheels when parking on a hill. If the car is facing downhill, your front wheels must turn in towards the curb. If the car faces uphill, the front wheels should turn out from the curb. And, set that parking brake! Parking control officers will ticket you for not obeying the curbing rule. If your apartment doesn't come with a garage (most here don't) and you have the money, check the newspaper's rental section and you may be able to rent a garage.

If you choose to make North Beach your home, undoubtedly you will find your own favorite restaurant. Here is just a smattering of the fine choices: Michaelangelo's at 579 Columbus Avenue is a local favorite for family style pasta. Just up the street is a little more intimate Northern Italian restaurant called L'Osteria del Forno, 519 Columbus Avenue. North Beach Pizza, 1499 Grant Avenue, serves some of the best pizza in town. For focaccia sandwiches and fritattas, try Mario's Bohemian Cigar Store, 1715 Union. Fior d'Italia, 601 Union Street, which overlooks Washington Square Park, and The North Beach Restaurant, 1512 Stockton Street, seem to be where the old-timers hang out. Enrico's, 504 Broadway, might also fit in that category. Gira Pollio, 659 Union Street, serves the best roasted chicken in town. The House, 1230 Grant Avenue, knows how to prepare fusion food, a mixture of Asian food with California cuisine. Tommaso, 1042 Kearny, and Rose Pistola, 532 Columbus Avenue, are some of the upscale eateries in the neighborhood. For even finer dining, try Moose's, 1652 Stockton Avenue, with its California cuisine. Francis Ford Coppola opened a restaurant just underneath his Zoetrope Production Company, in the historic Sentinel Building on Columbus and Kearny—Cafe Niebaum-Coppola, 916 Kearny Street. With the Italian waiters in their tuxedos, it feels like the godfather may just be eating at the next table. For breakfast, lunch or dinner, you'll find espressos and cappuccinos available on every block. If you want to mix opera with your coffee, try Cafe Trieste, 609 Vallejo, one of the oldest coffeehouses in the neighborhood. If the opera's not live it's being played on the jukebox.

Neighborhood activities for hearty souls include swimming the chilly waters at Aquatic Park, directly in front of Ghirdelli Square. The Dolphin Club, 502 Jefferson Street, 415-441-9329, and the South End Rowing Club, 500 Jefferson Street, 415-776-7372, both provide facilities and encouragement for your plunge into the cold water.

Another desirable place to live, and not as hectic as North Beach, is **Telegraph Hill**. Formerly called Goat Hill, it became Telegraph Hill in 1853 because it was the site of the West Coast's first telegraph station. Here spotters scouted for ships entering San Francisco Bay through the Golden Gate. After sighting a ship, spotters used Morse code to notify port officials of the ship's impending arrival. The "Hill," as locals call the area, features breathtaking bay views, including Alcatraz Island, the former home of the notorious prison and convicts, such as Al Capone and the "Birdman of Alcatraz" (who actually never kept birds there). Here you'll find narrow streets lined with quaint cottages and picture-windowed condominiums, beautiful gardens and even fewer rental vacancies than the rest of North Beach. Many residents must walk up tiny stair-ways and paths to their compact homes (compact due to the City's 40-foot height limit here). You'll also find two picturesque and delicious restaurants, Julius Castle, 1541 Montgomery, and Dalla Torre at 1349 Montgomery.

Coit Tower, the most prominent feature of this area, rises 210-feet from the top of Telegraph Hill. A monument to the City's firefighters, Coit Tower was built in 1934, funded by the private contribution of Lillie Hitchcock Coit, an eccentric San Franciscan known for going against the grain (when she was

15 she served as a volunteer fire fighter). The area around the tower is a romantic spot to bring a bottle of wine and watch the sunset or the boats on the Bay beneath you. If romance isn't in your cards, try climbing the 377 Filbert Street steps to Coit Tower for exercise. Listen carefully for the neighborhood parrots up in the trees; legend has it that a few escaped their cage around 1989 and since then have multiplied. For daily sightings, check their web page, www.wildparrots.com.

Web Site: www.ci.sf.ca.us
Area Code: 415
Zip Code: 94133
Post Office: North Beach Station, 1640 Stockton Street, 800-275-8777
Police Station: Central Police Station, 766 Vallejo Street, 415-553-1532; Community Police On Patrol, 415-362-4349
Emergency Hospitals: California Pacific Medical Center, 2333 Buchanan, 415-923-3333; St. Francis Memorial Hospital, 900 Hyde Street, 415-353-6000
Library: North Beach Library, 2000 Mason, 415-274-0270
Public Schools: San Francisco Unified School, District, 135 Van Ness Avenue, San Francisco, 94102, 415-241-6000, www.sfusd.k12.ca.us
Community Publication: *North Beach Now*, 415-391-1043
Community Resources: Telegraph Hill Dwellers, P.O. Box 330159, 415-255-6799; North Beach Neighbors P.O. Box 330115, 415-928-4044; Telegraph Hill Neighborhood Center, 660 Lombard Street/555 Chestnut Street, 415-421-6443 (offers medical offices, a basketball court, daycare, and eldercare, a community garden, playground and community meeting space); North Beach Museum, 1435 Stockton Street, 415-626-7070
Public Transportation: *MUNI buses*: 15 Third, 30 Stockton, 41 Union, 39 Coit, 32 Embarcadero, 42 Downtown Loop; *Cable Car* access to Hyde Street line at Ghirardelli Square area and to Mason Street line at Bay and Taylor streets. MUNI bus and Cable Car connections to BART and Light Rail stations along Market Street

RUSSIAN HILL, NOB HILL

LOWER NOB HILL

Boundaries: *Russian Hill*: **East**: Columbus Avenue; **North**: Aquatic Park; **West**: Van Ness Avenue; **South**: Broadway; *Nob Hill*: **East**: Kearny Street; **North**: Broadway; **West**: Van Ness Avenue; **South**: California Street

You won't come across *samovars*, *piroshki* or *borscht* on **Russian Hill**, nor will you find the graves of the Russian sailors buried here before the Gold Rush. What you will find is one of San Francisco's most charming and exclusive neighborhoods, dotted with tiny gardens and parks known only to the locals. The top of the hill is crowded with high-rise condominiums and apartment buildings, serviced by brass-buttoned doormen. These buildings stand interspersed with Victorian mansions, a few converted firehouses, relatively humble Edwardian flats, and numerous dolled-up "earthquake cottages" built originally as temporary housing following the 1906 earthquake. As in much of the City, housing here is difficult to find and expensive. Rents will set you back about $2,200 for a one-bedroom and $1,300 for a studio.

Russian Hill, Nob Hill

Tucked into the neighborhood, you'll find several small playgrounds for children, including the delightful Michelangelo Park on Greenwich Street and Ina Coolbrith Park off of Taylor. Sterling Park has public tennis courts with a stunning view of the Bay that might take an opponent's mind off the ball.

The streets are steep or winding, or both. And just when you're tired of asphalt, you'll find a surprising patch of green. Sometimes-rickety staircases assure access to these public spaces. The architectural and green patchwork that makes up Russian Hill is embroidered with cable car lines, invented by Andrew Hallidie back in 1873. It's said that Hallidie's pity for the horses strenuously pulling wagons up the hills is what inspired him to invent the cable cars. At its peak, the cable car system ran eight lines and more than 100 miles of track throughout the City. Today three lines remain, two of which serve both Russian Hill and Nob Hill (the Mason and Hyde lines), the third rumbles through Nob Hill and the Financial District along California Street.

Some of San Francisco's oldest homes keep watch from a lovely enclave between Taylor and Jones. And while neither claim happens to be true, Russian Hill boasts both the crookedest (Lombard) and the steepest (Filbert between Hyde and Leavenworth) streets in the City. (Actually you'll find the crookedest street in the Potrero District, but don't tell the hordes of tourists.)

The twisting Lombard Street is situated on the eastern slope of Russian Hill, between Hyde and Leavenworth streets. Local residents, who pay a pretty penny for the honor of living here, are privy to the near-constant click of camera shutters and vehicle fumes, as gleeful motorists navigate the eight near-hairpin turns in just one block.

On the north side of Russian Hill, you'll find the San Francisco Art Institute, 800 Chestnut, with its public exhibitions and Diego Rivera murals. Although the Art Institute schools many budding artists, most of Russian Hill is not the bohemian enclave it was in the early 1900s when poets, painters, and photographers such as Ina Coolbrith, Maynard Dixon, and Dorothea Lange populated the area. Today, bankers, suited professionals, and the so-called San Francisco elite live here.

Russian Hill's commercial area is to the west, on upper Polk and Hyde streets, though many locals also walk down the hill to North Beach. You'll find excellent restaurants in Russian Hill, including The Hyde Street Bistro at 1521 Hyde Street, Frascati at 1901 Hyde Street, and the always-crowded Zarzuela at 2000 Hyde Street. Locals rave about the gourmet pizza at Za Pizza, 1919 Hyde Street. For less expensive fare try one of the many hole-in-the-wall Chinese food places where owners still charge non-elite prices. Opened in 1948, Swenson's Ice Cream store, at the corner of Union and Hyde, is a classic San Francisco establishment. Upper Polk is home to small coffee shops, boutique stores selling vintage furniture and antiques, upscale consignment shops, and used bookstores. The lower half of Polk Street is still somewhat sleazy and contains places to eat, along with bars, liquor stores, leather shops, and adult entertainment outlets. Drugs and teen-runaways are components of street life along this stretch of Polk. However, as with much of San Francisco's fringe areas, lower Polk is being revitalized with art galleries, vintage stores, restaurants, and cafes.

Named after the well to do of the post Gold Rush era who built their enormous mansions here, **Nob Hill** is perhaps the most famous of San Francisco's hills. In 19th century San Francisco, the newly rich were known as nobs or more derogatorily as nabobs, which was used interchangeably with the word snob. Ask around, and you'll find no one seems to mind the slightly unflattering origination of the neighborhood's name. Area residents are quite content to call Nob Hill home. Located south of Russian Hill and only minutes from downtown, Nob Hill is slightly less expensive with rents in the summer of 2000 averaging $2,223 for a one-bedroom apartment, according to Metro-Rent.

Architecturally, you'll find several eyesore, 1960s high rises mixed in with stately older buildings at the top of the Hill, where lucky tenants enjoy a panoramic view of the city. There are some humbler apartment buildings and garden apartment "bargains" that turn up on the market from time to time. The original mansions went up in smoke following the 1906 earthquake and fire, and in their stead are the City's grand hotels: the Fairmont, the Mark Hopkins, the Stanford Court, the Clift. They all have excellent restaurants and bars, many with spectacular city- and bay-views. James Clair Flood, who made his millions in mining stocks, built an impressive brownstone mansion at 1000 California Street. The Flood Mansion is the only survivor of the grand houses of the 19th century and today is the home of the exclusive Pacific-Union Club. Because its exterior is made of sandstone, the shell of the building survived the 1906 fire.

Huntington Park, at the apex of Nob Hill, with its flowerbeds, bubbling fountains, and church bell serenades is a lovely place to while away a Sunday afternoon (as long as you don't have to find parking). On Wednesday evenings, locals gather at the park with their dogs for a little wine and social bantering. Across the street from the park is the Episcopalian Grace Cathedral, home to the Cathedral's Men and Boys Choir, and host of world-renowned musicians. For interesting lectures or big performances check out the Masonic Auditorium at 1111 California Street.

Close to the City's downtown shopping, theater, and hotel district, **Lower Nob Hill** lies between California Street on the north, Powell Street to the east, Geary Boulevard to the south, and Polk Street to the west. Called Lower Nob Hill by realtors, some refer to it as "Tenderloin Heights," due to its proximity to the Tenderloin, San Francisco's seediest part of town. Lower Nob Hill is home to posh hotels, exclusive restaurants, and all of the leading private clubs. There are plenty of apartment buildings here, some with art deco masterpieces like Egyptian-styled foyers or gilt caged elevators, as well as cheap youth hostels. Views also run the gamut, ranging from brick walls to breathtaking urban panoramas. Many of the buildings have hidden gardens, complete with goldfish ponds and loquat trees. Some consider Lower Nob Hill to be the most urban of San Francisco's neighborhoods, "like Manhattan with hills" claim homesick New Yorkers. Yet oddly and fortunately, in a region of pigeons, taxi whistles, and "un-trendified" diners, there is a definite neighborhood feel here. The corner store may extend credit, the cafe remembers your usual, and the dry cleaner doesn't have to ask your name. Parking is impossible, although monthly rentals at commercial garages are available. The Hill is traversed with bus and cable cars, but most people who live here walk to work, either to the Financial District, South of Market, or Union Square. Generally safe, centrally located, bustling, and well serviced, Lower Nob Hill is worth looking into for newcomers comfortable in such teeming surroundings.

Web Site: www.rhn.org
Area Code: 415
Zip Codes: Russian Hill, 94109; Nob Hill, 94108 and 94109
Post Office: Pine Street Station, 1400 Pine Street, 800-275-8777
Police Station: Central Station, 766 Vallejo Street, 415-553-1532
Emergency Hospitals: St. Francis Memorial, 900 Hyde Street, 415-353-6000; California Pacific Medical Center, 2333 Buchanan, 415-923-3333

Library: North Beach Branch, 2000 Mason Street, 415-274-0270; The Main Branch, 100 Larkin Street, 415-557-4400; Chinatown Branch, 1135 Powell, 415-274-0275

Public Schools: San Francisco Unified School, District, 135 Van Ness Avenue, San Francisco, 94102, 415-241-6000, www.sfusd.k12.ca.us

Community Publication: *Nob Hill Gazette*, 53rd Street, Suite #222, 415-227-0190

Community Resources: Russian Hill Neighbors, 2040 Polk Street, Suite 221, 94109, 415-267-0575, www.rhn.org; Nob Hill Association, 1177 California Street, 415-346-8720; Cable Car Museum, 1201 Mason Street, 415-474-1887; Huntington Square Park; Russian Hill Park, Bay at Larkin Streets, Alice Marble Park, Hyde and Lombard

Public Transportation: Russian Hill, *MUNI* buses: 1 California, 27 Bryant, 19 Polk, 41 Union, 45 Union-Stockton, 30 Stockton, 83 Pacific; *Cable Cars*: Hyde, Mason and California Street lines (MUNI bus and Cable Cars provide access to BART and MUNI Light Rail stations along Market Street). Nob Hill, *MUNI* buses: 1 California, 3 Jackson, 4 Sutter; *Cable Cars*: California, Mason and Hyde lines; all Market Street lines

TENDERLOIN

East: Powell Street; **West**: Van Ness Avenue; **South**: Market Street; **North**: California Street

Long considered San Francisco's seediest neighborhood, the **Tenderloin** is experiencing some improvement, with new construction and new faces. Used by many recently arrived immigrants as a kind of gateway neighborhood, you'll also find young urbanites and students living here. Located just a few blocks from Union Square, the Tenderloin is named for the time when the neighborhood had a number of butcher shops. Others refer to it as the "Theater District" with the Orpheum at 1192 Market; George Coates Performance Works at 110 McAllister; and the Golden Gate Theatre at 1 Taylor, all within its boundaries.

According to the Tenderloin Task Force, the police heavily patrol the area because it is a rough neighborhood, home to drug addicts and prostitutes, street people, and the just plain down and out. Amenities are sparse—there is no large supermarket, nor even a bank in the neighborhood. Take a drive through and you will see that the streets are full of liquor stores, saloons, X-rated movie houses, and many boarded storefronts. The recently constructed neighborhood school, Tenderloin Elementary, 627 Turk Street, was a much needed addition in this neighborhood of 4,000 plus children. According to the Bay Area Women's and Children's Center, new playgrounds and parks are also in the works, and there are a number of new community resources to assist area residents.

After the devastation brought on by the 1906 earthquake and fire, the Tenderloin had to rebuild itself. In preparation for the 1915 Panama Pacific International Exposition, small hotels with unique and ornate architecture were constructed. In addition to these smaller hotels, many of which still remain, you'll find huge hotels, like the Hilton at 333 O'Farrell, and The Nikko, 222 Mason Street. During World War II, when San Francisco served as a military logistics center, many shipyard and other employees of the military lived in the single room hotels. Later these hotels served new immigrants. Dozens of inexpensive Vietnamese and Chinese restaurants dot the neighborhood. In addition, you'll find more upscale restaurants, including Stars, 555 Golden Gate Avenue, and Backflip, 601 Eddy. On Sunday mornings and Wednesday afternoons, the Civic Center hosts a market of the old world variety, where you can buy live chickens, fresh fish, and vegetables.

Interspersed throughout the neighborhood are a number of government buildings, including the Federal Courthouse, the State Courthouse, the Main Library, City Hall and the University of California Hastings Law School. If

Tenderloin

you're lucky, you can hear singing emanating from Glide Memorial Church, 330 Ellis Street. Run by Reverend Cecil Williams and his wife, poet Janice Mirikitani, the Glide Church is considered a Tenderloin institution, offering help to the homeless. Glide has more than fifty different social service programs, including its food program, which serves over one and a half million free meals each year. Many volunteers offer their services to the church throughout the year, particularly during Thanksgiving and Christmas.

As you might expect, rents in the Tenderloin are much lower than in the rest of the City, and landlords may not even require the first and last month's rent when signing a lease. In spite of the area's downtrodden reputation, you may be able to find a studio or one-bedroom apartment in a semi-secure art-deco building, with an elevator, and if you are really lucky, a doorman and great City views. However, like the rest of the City, rents and property values have increased significantly in the past few years. According to Metro-Rent, during the summer of 2000, the average rent for a studio ran $1,039 and a one-bedroom apartment was $1,385. Locals know that gentrification is coming to the Tenderloin and though they applaud the cleaner and safer streets, they are concerned that they will no longer be able to afford living here.

Because of its recent start toward gentrification and its proximity to downtown, the Tenderloin might be a realistic housing option for those comfortable with urban life. In addition, transportation is top notch as many MUNI lines pass straight down Market Street, and Bart stops at the Civic Center.

Web Site: www.tndc.org, www.ci.sf.ca.us
Area Code: 415
Zip Code: 94103
Post Office: 390 Main Street Lobby; 101 Hyde Street, 800-275-8777
Police Station: Tenderloin Task Force, 1 Jones, 415-557-6700; Community Police on Patrol, 415-362-4349
Emergency Hospitals: St. Francis Memorial, 900 Hyde Street, 415-353-6000; California Pacific Medical Center, 2333 Buchanan, 415-923-3333; San Francisco General Hospital, 1001 Potrero Avenue, 415-206-8111
Library: Main Branch, 100 Larkin Street, 415-557-4400
Public Schools: San Francisco Unified School, District, 135 Van Ness Avenue, San Francisco, 94102, 415-241-6000, www.sfusd.k12.ca.us
Community Resources: North of Market Planning Coalition, 375 Eddy Street, 415-474-2164, Tenderloin Neighborhood Development Corporation, 201 Eddy Street, 415-776-2151; Tenderloin Children's Playground, 570 Ellis Street, 415-292-2162; Bay Area Women's and Children's Center, 318 Leavenworth Street, 415-474-2400; Glide Memorial Church, 330 Ellis Street, 415-674-6040, www.glide.org
Public Transportation: MUNI buses: Polk 19, 27 Bryant, 31, 38 Geary, 76, 16; all Market Street buses

PACIFIC HEIGHTS, MARINA DISTRICT, COW HOLLOW

PRESIDIO
PRESIDIO HEIGHTS
LAUREL HEIGHTS

Boundaries: *Pacific Heights*: **East**: Van Ness Avenue; **North**: Broadway; **West**: Arguello Boulevard; **South**: California Street; *Marina*: **East**: Van Ness Avenue; **North**: Marina Boulevard; **West**: Lyon Street; **South**: Lombard; *Cow Hollow*: **East:** Laguna Street; **North**: Greenwich Street; **West**: Divisadero Street; **South**: Vallejo Street

With its sweeping bay views, eucalyptus and cypress groves, hidden staircases and grand mansions, many consider **Pacific Heights** to be one of San Francisco's most beautiful neighborhoods. Some of the mansions were rebuilt in the wake of the 1906 earthquake and fire that decimated much of the City, while others are glorious survivors of that conflagration. This area is home to lawyers, doctors, entertainment-industry moguls, corporate big-wigs, movie stars, and rock legends who enjoy the relative anonymity that San Francisco affords them. International consulates, private schools, and graceful art-deco high-rises add to the aura of privilege. While the houses have hidden gardens and exquisite interiors, there is no gated com

Pacific Heights, Marina District, Cow Hollow

munity feel here or any star maps for sale. Residents retain their privacy and, unlike other parts of the City, you will not see many people walking the streets— except on Halloween. With a reputation for quality treats, elaborately decorated mansions, and a carnival-like atmosphere, Pacific Heights is where children from all over the City beg their parents to take them for trick-or-treating.

Corner grocers are within walking distance from any point in the neighborhood. Both Sacramento and Fillmore streets have coffee shops, restaurants, and pricey boutiques. Fillmore Street has a number of used clothing stores, such as Junior League's Next to New Shop, 2226 Fillmore, and San Francisco Symphony's Repeat Performance, 2436 Fillmore Street. For delicious dining around Sacramento Street, locals love Garibaldi at 347 Presidio Avenue, and Osteria at 3277 Sacramento. Breakfast at Ella's, 500 Presidio Avenue, is popular. Perhaps the best-kept secret here is the French bakery, Boulangerie on Pine Street, where the croissants and baguettes rival those made in France. Larger grocery stores are close by with Whole Foods on Franklin and California, and Molly Stones and Laurel Village down on California Street.

For exercise, the Lyon Street stairs serve as an outdoor Stairmaster (certainly if the breathtaking views don't steal your breath away, the steep stairs will). Locals also use the nearby Presidio for running, hiking, biking, and golfing. Down the hill is San Francisco Bay, where you'll find world class sailing and windsurfing.

Houses in Pacific Heights can cost as much as $10 million; expect to pay at least $1 million. The so-called "affordable rental units" in Pacific Heights may look downright dowdy next to their elegant neighbors, but those lucky enough to track down a vacancy are not bothered by this in the least. Victorians, Edwardian flats, sturdy one-bedroom apartments from the 1920s, and some 1960s buildings rent for about $2,300 a month, according to Metro-Rent's summer 2000 averages. Farther down the hill, either toward Cow Hollow to the north or the Western Addition to the south, the rents decrease, and the supply of apartments increase, though only slightly. In 2000, average rents in Cow Hollow were $2,193 for a one-bedroom; the Western Addition ran significantly less at $1,677 a month.

In the middle of Pacific Heights, at the corner of Jackson and Steiner streets, is Alta Plaza Park, which features stunning views of Alcatraz Island and Marin County to the north, and Mount Davidson to the south. Tennis courts are available, and a children's playground. If you have a dog, visit in the morning before work and you'll be sure to meet your canine-loving neighbors. Lafayette Park on Washington Street, just across from the Spreckels Mansion, 2080 Washington Street, is another popular hangout for dogs and kids—and sunbathers when the sun comes out.

Just north of Pacific Heights, **Cow Hollow**, so-named for the herds of cattle that grazed here in the 1860s, is another pleasant place to live. One of the area's most interesting landmarks is the Octagon House at Gough and Union. This 19th century oddity was built based on the belief, outlined in the book *A Home for All* by Orson Fowler, that eight-sided houses were somehow healthier to live in—similar perhaps to today's Feng Shui. It is open to the public, but only a few days each month.

Once the cows were moved out of Cow Hollow, the neighborhood became exclusively residential, and it wasn't until the late 1950s that the ground floor apartments on Union Street became storefronts and restaurants. Today, Union is crammed with clothing boutiques, jewelry stores, bars, and restaurants. Area restaurants range from Indian (Pasand) to Italian (Prego) to Cajun (Blue Light) or Asian (Betelnut), with micro-brewed ales and upscale pub food available at Union Street Ale House. If you're looking for a date, check out Perry's, between Laguna and Buchanan. It's a longtime favorite pick-up place, and the food's pretty good too. Parking, especially along Union Street, between Fillmore, and Van Ness, is a challenge at best, particularly on the weekends when visitors flock to the area.

After the 1906 earthquake and fire, San Franciscans brushed off the ash and rubble and rebuilt their city with astonishing speed. They were so proud of what they had accomplished that they leapt at the opportunity to show off to the world and hosted the 1915 Panama-Pacific Exposition at the west end of the **Marina District**. Although the official purpose of the expo was to mark the opening of the Panama Canal, San Francisco also used the Expo to clean house—there's nothing like a party to get things done. The City took all the rubble from the earthquake and dumped it in the Marina. Architect Bernard Maybeck designed the Palace of Fine Arts on Lyon Street, between Bay and Jefferson, for the expo, which today houses one of the Bay Area's most popular attractions, the Exploratorium. Much more than just a "hands on" science museum, the Exploratorium is a place where you can get your whole body involved in many of the more than 600 exhibits and demonstrations. Call ahead to reserve space at the Tactile Dome (415-397-5673), a huge darkened sphere. Groups have even been known to reserve the Dome privately and explore in the buff!

Prior to the exposition, the land around the Marina was created by landfill, mostly from the debris caused by the earthquake and fire. Hundreds of mostly Mediterranean-style homes were resurrected here in the 1920s and '30s. If you caught any of the television coverage of the fires that followed the 1989 Loma Prieta earthquake then you've seen the Marina District from the air. The 7.1 magnitude temblor did the most damage to the Marina — along Marina Boulevard, scores of the most desirable homes and apartment buildings in the City were destroyed. Before this quake the neighborhood was a quiet area occupied by long-time residents, many of them older and of Italian descent. Following the disaster, many old-timers high-tailed it away from the landfill and young people, perhaps less cognizant of their own mortality, moved in, creating a vibrant area along Chestnut Street which is now chock full of cafes, restaurants, and clothing stores. It seems that many people have forgotten the Marina is mostly landfill and real estate as well as rental prices reflect this. Metro-Rent's summer 2000 rental averages for the Marina were $2,285 for a one-bedroom and $1,581 for a studio.

Chestnut Street is one of the liveliest and perhaps trendiest shopping streets in the City. Like Union Street in Cow Hollow (which is just a few blocks south of the Marina), Chestnut bustles every day of the week with a similar mix of shops, though a bit more chain stores than Union, eateries and parking problems to match. When not shopping or eating, locals head north to the Marina Greens and the Presidio for outdoor fun. Marina Greens is optimum for kite flying as well as informal soccer and football matches. Running, biking, and rollerblading are also popular along the waterfront.

The eastern end of the Marina District is home to Fort Mason, a former military facility that now houses museums, bookstores, art galleries, public service organizations and one of the world's best vegetarian restaurants, Greens (Building A in Fort Mason). Reservations are highly recommended here, otherwise the wait might force you to go looking for something else to eat, even meat! The Fort Mason Center is home to a number of non-profit groups, as well as a theater and an art gallery. It's a great place to take classes ranging from yoga to photography to driver's education. If interested, stop by Fort Mason to grab a monthly newsletter and calendar or call the center at 415-441-3400, www.fortmason.org.

At the Western end of the Marina District sits the **Presidio**, the former military base, which is now an art, history, and cultural center, national park and shorebird lagoon, among other things. Unique in the national parks system, the Presidio is run jointly by the National Park Service and the Presidio Trust, an independent federal agency. The US Congress mandated that the Presidio be completely self-sufficient by the year 2013, and to that end, the Presidio Trust has had to be quite creative about how to keep afloat. Finding big business tenants seems to be the way the Trust has decided to go, and in May 2000 George Lucas was approved to move his Lucas Enterprises to the Presidio, much to the dismay of area environmentalists. Other projects may include a theater built by Robert Redford's Sundance Institute. Regardless of the politics, the Presidio is a San Francisco treasure, offering trails for hiking, biking and walking. Area organizations/businesses have offices here, including nonprofits and some dot.coms, and the Presidio is also a residential area with houses and apartments available primarily to those who work in the area.

The area called **Presidio Heights** sits between the Presidio, Presidio Avenue, Arguello Boulevard, and California Street, and differs little from Pacific Heights except for the view. Many of the homes here overlook cypress and eucalyptus groves, the golf course of the Presidio or Julius Kahn Park. Sacramento Street, from Divisadero to Walnut, offers antique stores, chic clothing for men, women, and children, high-end consignment shops, gift shops, housewares stores, hair and nail salons, and a smattering of restaurants with outdoor seating (bring a sweater).

Laurel Heights, which extends to Laurel Village a little farther to the south of Pacific Heights, is served by the accessible shopping area called Laurel Village. Retailers include gourmet food and wine shops, well-stocked grocery stores, including Cal-Mart and Bryans, which has a locally famous meat market, plus several children's stores, an independent bookshop, a stationery store, a clothing boutique, a classic five and dime, and an old-fashioned diner. There are many ornate single family homes, but some apartments, flats, and even brand new condos are also available. Rent for a basic one-bedroom unit will put you back about $1,800.

With their access to the Presidio, Marin County and downtown, many people find the Pacific Heights, Cow Hollow and Marina neighborhoods desirable. Marina and Cow Hollow attract a significant number of single professionals. For the more settled/family-oriented, Pacific, Presidio and Laurel Heights might be your best choice.

Web Site: www.ci.sf.ca.us
Area Code: 415
Zip Codes: Pacific Heights, 94115, Marina, 94123, Presidio, 94129, Laurel and Presidio Heights, 94118
Post Office: Marina Station, 2055 Lombard Street, 800-275-8777
Police Station: Northern Station, 1125 Fillmore Street, 415-553-1563; Community Police on Patrol, 415-923-1604

Emergency Hospitals: California Pacific Medical Center, 2333 Buchanan, 415-923-3333; California Pacific Medical Center Standby Urgent Care, 3700 California Street, 415-387-8700; St. Francis Memorial Hospital, 900 Hyde Street, 415-353-6000

Libraries: Presidio Branch, 3150 Sacramento, 415-292-2155; Golden Gate Valley Branch, 1801 Green Street, 415-292-2195; Marina Branch, 1890 Chestnut, 415-292-2150

Public Schools: San Francisco Unified School District, 135 Van Ness Avenue, San Francisco, CA 94102, 415-241-6000, www.sfusd.k12.ca.us

Community Publications: *New Fillmore*, 2443 Fillmore Street, #343, 94115, 415-931-0515; *Marina Times*, 2269 Chestnut Street, #620, 94123-2600, 415-928-1307

Community Resources: Marina Neighborhood Association, 3727 Fillmore Street, #201, 415-771-8662; Cow Hollow Association, 2867 Green Street, 415-567-8611; Cow Hollow Neighbors in Action, 2742 Baker Street, 415-776-3191; Golden Gate Valley Neighborhood Association, Box 29086, Presidio, 94129, 415-931-3438; San Francisco Recreation Harbor Tenants Association, P.O. Box 470428, 94147, 415-441-0650; Marina Merchants Association, 2269 Chestnut Street, 415-776-3191; Union Street Association, 1686 Union Street, 415-441-7055; Presidio Homeowners' Association 650 Presidio Avenue; Pacific Heights Residents Association, 2585 Pacific, 415-922-3572; the Exploratorium, 3601 Lyon Street, 415-397-5673; Fort Mason Center, 415-441-3400; Presidio National Park, 415-561-4323; Palace of Fine Arts, 415-750-3600, Jewish Community Center, 3200 California Street, 415-346-6040

Public Transportation: Pacific Heights, *MUNI* buses: 1 California, 24 Divisadero, 41 Union, 45 Union-Stockton, 83 Pacific; Marina, *MUNI* buses: 22 Fillmore, 30 Stockton, 41 Union, 45 Union-Stockton

THE RICHMOND, SEACLIFF

WEST CLAY PARK

Boundaries: **West**: *Richmond*: The Great Highway/Pacific Ocean; **North**: Lincoln Park and the Presidio; **East**: Arguello Boulevard; **South**: Fulton Street and Golden Gate Park; *Seacliff*: **West**: Lincoln Park/Legion of Honor; **North**: Sea Cliff Avenue/Pacific Ocean; **East**: 27th Avenue; **South**: California Street

After Mark Twain visited San Francisco's Richmond district, he declared the coldest winter he ever experienced, was the summer he spent in San Francisco. Located on the edge of the Pacific, this is the part of the City that is first to greet the wind and fog blowing in from the ocean. There are many days when the

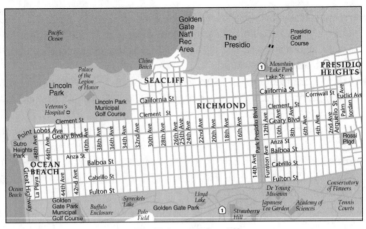

The Richmond, Seacliff

rest of the City is clear and sunny, while the Richmond is blanketed in fog—something to keep in mind if you are thinking about setting up house here. It's a great zone for people who like sweater weather; and, because of San Francisco's microclimates, you can drive just a few blocks or miles to find the sun.

In the 1860s when Twain lived in the City, the Richmond was mostly sand. Today, however, this sandy area consists primarily of single family, middle-class homes. There are some enclaves, such as West Clay Park and Seacliff, where the homes are larger; many are mansions with spectacular Golden Gate Bridge and ocean views. Sandwiched between Lincoln Park to the west and the Presidio to the east, **Seacliff** is a gorgeous neighborhood with, wouldn't you know it, sea cliffs, cypress trees, winding streets, and views of the Golden Gate Bridge. There are three-bedroom homes listed with multi-million dollar price tags. The private and luxurious Katherine Del Mar Burke's School for Girls, from kindergarten to eighth grade, is located at the edge of Seacliff.

West Clay Park, hiding between 22nd and 24th avenues, is another unique San Francisco neighborhood, full of children and lovely houses. Legendary photographer Ansel Adams used to live here. On Easter, kids from all over the City come here to eat chocolate and hunt for eggs.

When the fog is not so thick and the sun is shining, check out Baker Beach where the pounding waves swirl the smell of salt into the air. Swimsuits are optional at the beach closest to the Bridge, one of the City's nude beaches. Other nude beaches are at a small rocky beach in Land's End and south of the City at Fort Funston with the paragliders and horseback riders. Swimming at Baker Beach is another matter, suit or no suit, fog or no fog; the ocean is cold—hovering at around 56° Fahrenheit. China Beach, which is farther south, is a little more protected from the wind, smaller and family-friendly.

Another outdoor favorite is Land's End on El Camino Del Mar and 32nd Avenue, just below Lincoln Golf Course. Part of the Golden Gate Recreation

Area, Land's End overlooks the Golden Gate Bridge to the right. Jefferson Starship's Paul Kantner and Grace Slick used to live in the wooden house perched on the cliff at the beginning of the Land's End trail. When walking the trail, beware of flying golf balls from the not-so-talented golfers enjoying nearby Lincoln Park Golf Course. The trail winds along the coast just below the picturesque Palace of the Legion of Honor Museum, culminating at the concrete ruins of Sutro Baths. Built in 1863 but later destroyed by a fire, Sutro Baths was once the world's largest public swimming hole.

If you like hiking Land's End, you'll also enjoy San Francisco's newest treasure, the Presidio, located north of the Richmond. Formerly an army base, the Presidio is now a national park, complete with a world-class golf course, numerous hiking and biking trails and superb access to the beach. The base is prime real estate, and thanks to the fact that it is now federally protected, it won't be sold off to developers. Today, a number of non-profit organizations work in the Presidio. Private businesses are also calling the Presidio home, including George Lucas who is in the process of building and designing a huge multimedia complex.

Hungry souls should venture to Clement Street. With a Chinese restaurant on just about every block, from Argeullo to Presidio Boulevard, and again from 20th to 25th avenues, this area is known as the "New Chinatown." However, in this ethnically diverse neighborhood Chinese food isn't your only choice. Here you can also sample Russian *piroshki*, Japanese sushi, Italian raviolis, Spanish paella, Thai curries, or Indian tandoori. Clement Street is hopping every day of the week as residents choose their fresh vegetables, spices, herbs, fruit, meats, poultry, and fish at the markets. Tourists, college students, and residents alike drop by hoping to find a literary treasure at Green Apple Used Books, 506 Clement Street, or to visit area coffee bars and Irish pubs, including The Plough & The Stars at 116 Clement Street. Clement Street is also one of the few neighborhoods left that has fabric and sewing stores for people who still sew. Parking here is atrocious; if you're not buying so much that you'll need the car to taxi it home, it's best to walk, bike, or take the bus.

One street south of Clement is Geary Street, Richmond's other main shopping street. While not as attractive as Clement Street, it is a practical locale where you will find everything from car repair shops, computers stores, florists, furniture and imports stores, as well as Irish pubs, Russian bakeries and delicatessens, and perhaps the best dim sum in town at Ton Kiang, 5821 Geary Boulevard.

It's possible to find an affordable (by Bay Area standards) rental property in the Richmond, although you may wear yourself out unearthing such a gem. In fact, the Richmond, and the Sunset, on the southern side of Golden Gate Park, are two of the few San Francisco locales where you're most likely to strike residential gold at silver prices. According to Metro-Rent, in July 2000 the average rent for a one-bedroom flat in the Richmond was $1,456. If you have a pot of gold, buying a house would cost you between $600,000 and several million dollars depending on the location.

Though the Richmond is often socked-in with fog, the beaches, coastal views, scrumptious food, and neighborhood cafes make it one of San Francisco's coziest neighborhoods. Move here and you'll get to know your neighbors, the butcher at the local grocery store, and many of the restaurant proprietors on a first name basis. Just remember to dress warmly.

Web Site: www.richmondsf.org
Area Code: 415
Zip Codes: 94118, 94121
Post Office: Geary Station, 5654 Geary Boulevard, 800-275-8777
Police Station: Richmond Station, 461 6th Avenue, 415-553-1385; Community Police on Patrol, 415-752-0664
Emergency Hospitals: California Pacific Medical Center, 2333 Buchanan, 415-923-3333; California Pacific Medical Center Standby Urgent Care, 3700 California Street, 415-387-8700; UCSF Medical Center, 505 Parnassus, 415-476-1037; St. Mary's Medical Center, 450 Stanyan, 415-750-5700
Library: Richmond Branch, 351 9th Avenue, 415-666-7165
Public Schools: San Francisco Unified School, District, 135 Van Ness Avenue, San Francisco, 94102, 415-241-6000, www.sfusd.k12.ca.us
Community Publication: *Richmond ReView* is a neighborhood monthly, 415-831-0461
Community Resources: Richmond Neighborhood Coalition, 3626 Balboa Street, 415-668-5955; Planning Association for the Richmond 415-974-9332; Palace of the Legion of Honor, Lincoln Park, 415-750-3600; Lincoln Park Golf Course, 415-221-9911
Public Transportation: *MUNI buses*: 1 California, 2 Clement, 3 Jackson, 4 Sutter, 5 Fulton, 6 Parnassus, 18 46th Avenue, 21 Hayes, 29 Sunset, 31 Balboa, 33 Stanyan, 38 Geary

SUNSET, PARKSIDE

GOLDEN GATE HEIGHTS
ST. FRANCIS WOOD
FOREST HILL

Boundaries: *Sunset*: **North**: Golden Gate Park and Lincoln Way; **West**: Great Highway/Pacific Ocean; **East**: Stanyan Street; **South**: Ortega Street; *Parkside*: **North**: Ortega; **West**: Great Highway; **East**: Dewey, Laguna Honda boulevards; **South**: Sloat Boulevard

If you choose to make the Sunset District your home, be prepared with some cozy, thick sweaters, even in the summer, and know that it may be days before

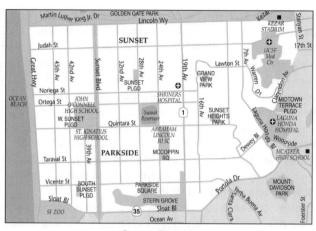

Sunset, Parkside

you actually watch a sunset here, as the neighborhood frequently is encased in fog. Rest assured, however, the skies do clear, offering a fabulous view of the ocean and the sunset. The weather in the Sunset actually acts as a housing market deterrent, keeping values here slightly less than in many other parts of the City. In addition, the Sunset's low crime rate, decent public schools and manageable street parking, make it an ideal family neighborhood. It is also home to students and professionals, particularly those attending classes or working at the University of California at San Francisco (UCSF) Medical Center—a premier research and teaching hospital.

Residents here are privy to one of San Francisco's greatest treasures, Golden Gate Park, right in their backyard! (See **Greenspace and Beaches** for more details.) Access to outdoor activities is easy, including endless running and bike trails, museums galore, horseback riding, rowing on Stow Lake, and soccer, polo or lacrosse at the polo fields. You can even learn to fly fish in the park. Ocean Beach beckons from the west, where daring souls swim or surf in the cold Pacific—beware of the strong undertow. And for the more daring, Fort Funston, on the Great Highway, is a popular place to hang glide. If your fear of heights dissuades you from the sport, you can still enjoy it as a spectator from the viewing area.

The Sunset is comprised of the **inner Sunset** (west from UCSF Medical Center to 19th Avenue) and the **outer Sunset** (west of 19th Avenue to the Great Highway). And, while many locals consider the entire area the Sunset, technically the homes to the south of Ortega Street and all the way to Sloat Boulevard are actually in **Parkside**. The hilly area around Lomita and 16th avenues is known as **Golden Gate Heights**, but considered by many as the Sunset. When the fog lifts, the views from Golden Gate Heights are stunning.

Architecturally, the inner Sunset area is comprised of a number of Victorians and Edwardians, while the Outer Sunset is predominantly

Mediterranean- and Spanish-style stuccos. Some of the homes along the hilly, tree-lined, streets have spectacular views of the ocean and the park. Others, especially those west of 19th Avenue, are just plain unoriginal. Designed by Henry Doelger in the 1930s, they were built quickly and sold for about $5,000. While uninspiring, these "white cliffs of Doelger" usually have a small garden, and street parking is not a problem, unlike most of the City.

Two upscale neighborhoods border the Sunset on the east, **St. Francis Wood** and **Forest Hill**, where you'll find some of the loveliest, best-tended homes in the City with prices to match. A review of the multiple listing service of homes sold from 1999 to 2000 show property prices ranging from $600,000 to well over a million dollars and often several million dollars. The lots are large, giving these exquisite homes substantial space.

The main north-south artery in the Sunset is 19th Avenue, which slices through the neighborhood. (It's easy to keep track of direction here, as the streets along 19th Avenue are alphabetical from Judah Street south to Wawona Street.) Nineteenth Avenue is frequently crammed with vehicles, as it links Highway 280, coming up from San Mateo County, with Highway 1, heading north toward the Golden Gate Bridge and Marin County. (Be aware that 19th Avenue changes to Park Presidio Boulevard when it crosses Fulton Street, just north of Golden Gate Park.)

Residents of the Sunset happily boast that they can find just about everything they need within their neighborhood—from daily staples to exotic food, coin-operated laundries, electronics stores, and clothing outlets. In the inner Sunset, the commercial areas run along Irving and Judah streets. More upscale shopping, including clothing boutiques, coffeehouses, and ethnic eateries, is centered along 9th Avenue and Irving. Local favorites include cajun seafood from PJs Oysterhouse, 737 Irving Street, and for fusion food try The House at 1269 9th Avenue. Yummas, 721 Irving Street, is reputed to make the best falafel in the area, and Hotei serves filling Japanese noodles. Go west on Irving to about 20th Avenue for the neighborhood Chinatown, which is chock full of produce markets and Asian delicacies.

One block south of Irving is Judah Street, which offers easy access to the Light Rail Vehicles (LRV). Called the Muni Metro or Metrolines, they will take you quickly to the Financial District's Embarcadero station. A number of regular bus lines also go that way, but the LRV is the most popular choice for those headed downtown.

At the southern end of 19th Avenue, near the Stonestown neighborhood, you'll find San Francisco State University (SFSU). With more than 26,000 students, it is one of the biggest schools in the California State University System. The San Francisco Conservatory of Music is located at 19th Avenue and Ortega Street, though it has plans to move closer to the Opera House in downtown San Francisco. Obviously, with these two schools located in the immediate vicinity come lots of students, particularly in the outer Sunset/Parkside environs. The best time to find a place here is early summer, when many of the students take a year's worth of laundry home to mom and dad's house, vacating their San Francisco digs.

The Sigmund Stern Grove, located on Sloat Avenue, is a natural amphitheater, surrounded by giant eucalyptus groves, redwoods, and firs. Since 1938, Stern Grove has hosted Sunday afternoon concerts for all types of music lovers. The Midsummer Music Festival features opera, operetta, symphonic, choral, jazz, rock and roll, and Broadway music ... and it's all free! For the best seats, arrive early, otherwise you'll have to settle for lounging on the hillside lawn on your blanket. The crowds are mixed and that means you could end up sitting between a spike-haired, nose-ringed, bike messenger and a corporate CEO, each equally enraptured by what's happening on the outdoor stage.

With its proximity to the airport and Interstate 280, many newcomers are choosing to live in the Sunset and commute to Silicon Valley. In addition, transportation to downtown is quick, making it an optimum choice for professionals who work in the City. And, unlike most of the rest of the City, parking here is not too difficult.

Web Site: www.ci.sf.ca.us
Area Code: 415
Zip Codes: Sunset: 94122; Parkside, 94116
Post Offices: Sunset Station, 1314 22nd Avenue; Parkside Station, 1800 Taraval Street, 800-275-8777
Police Station: Taraval Station, 2345 24th Avenue, 415-553-1612, Community Police on Patrol, 415-731-0502
Libraries: Merced Branch, 155 Winston Drive, 415-337-4780, Parkside Branch, 1200 Taraval Street, 415-753-7125
Public Schools: San Francisco Unified School, District, 135 Van Ness Avenue, San Francisco, 94102, 415-241-6000, www.sfusd.k12.ca.us
Community Publication: *Sunset Beacon*, a neighborhood monthly, 415-831-0461
Community Resources: Sunset Neighborhood Beacon Center, 3151 Ortega Street, 415-759-2770; Inner Sunset Merchants Association, 1032 Irving Street, 415-731-2884; Golden Gate Park Visitors Center, 415-831-7200, www.parks.sfgov.org
Public Transportation: Sunset, *MUNI buses*: 6 Parnassus, 18 46th Avenue, 29 Sunset, 66 Quintara, 71 Haight/Noriega; *LRV*: N-Judah; Parkside, *MUNI buses*: 18 46th Avenue, 23 Monterey, 28 19th Avenue, 29 Sunset, 35 Eureka, 48 Quintara/24th Street, 66 Quintara; *LRV*: L Taraval, K Ingleside, M Oceanview

HAIGHT ASHBURY

COLE VALLEY
BUENA VISTA PARK
PARNASSUS/ASHBURY HEIGHTS

Boundaries: *Haight Ashbury*: **North**: Oak Street; **East**: Divisadero Street; **West**: Stanyan Street, **South**: Parnassus Street; *Buena Vista Park*: **North**: Haight Street; **East**: Divisadero; **West**: Masonic Avenue; **South**: Roosevelt Way; *Parnassus/Ashbury Heights*: **North**: Parnassus Avenue; **East**: Buena Vista Avenue and Roosevelt Way; **West**: UC Medical Center; **South**: Clarendon Avenue and Tank Hill Park

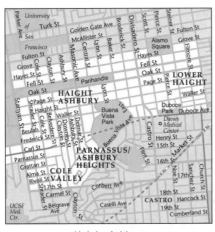

Haight Ashbury

Known for its glory days of the 1960s, this neighborhood of free love, psychedelic drugs and the Grateful Dead certainly has changed from what it was back then. Today the Haight, named for the intersection of Haight and Ashbury streets, has moved far beyond its counterculture and anti-Vietnam war days, and has become an established and desirable neighborhood. The Haight consists primarily of a busy commercial zone surrounded by restored Victorian houses, flats, and apartments. The unique mansions set on tree-lined hills that rock-and-roll bands once bought for a song and painted purple and orange are now tastefully restored and worth a fortune. Had you lived here in the Haight's heyday your neighbors could have been people such as Janis Joplin, members of bands like the Grateful Dead and Jefferson Airplane as well as members of Charles Manson's band of a different type. Today, professional types, as well as students and employees of nearby UCSF Medical Center and University of San Francisco call the Haight home. Life is a tad more like it was in the 1960s the closer you get to Haight Street itself. Here, the apartments, often Victorian or Edwardian with hardwood floors, fireplaces, views of Golden Gate Park, and even cupolas, often still are lived in by groups of young people who have to share rooms to make ends meet.

Haight Street itself is lined with popular chains, trendy boutiques selling vintage clothing, fetish shoes, used-furniture, and toys for grown-ups. Not surprisingly, there are still plenty of stores that sell used records (remember them?), clothes, books, comics, vintage rock-and-roll posters (even some of the "black light" variety), and new age and hippie paraphernalia, including incense, body oils and Tarot cards. Throughout the Haight vestiges of hip-piedom remain, including folks with flowers in their hair wearing tie-dyes and sandals, and coffee bars frequented by angry young writers with detailed man-ifestos on how to change all that's wrong with the world. It's also common-place to be approached on the street by folks selling all manner of illegal drugs. There are still plenty of panhandlers, some neo-hippie, some neo-punk, and some just plain annoying.

Those considering making their home here may want to "try the neighbor-hood out" first with a stay at The Red Victorian bed and breakfast, 1665 Haight Street, 415-864-1978, www.redvic.com. The Red Victorian Movie House, just down the street at 1727 Haight, features alternative films. For dinner, Spanish tapas can be had at the favorite Cha! Cha! Cha! at 1801 Haight Street, and locals rave about the Indian food at Ganges Restaurant, 775 Frederick Street.

Outdoor recreation is nearby, with the Golden Gate Park "panhandle" between Oak and Fell streets from Stanyan to Baker. The panhandle is a finger-like extension of the 1,000-plus-acre park that stretches all the way out to Ocean Beach. The park, which was once nothing but sand dunes, is laced with walking trails and contains sports fields, playground equipment, an antique carousel, a science museum, an art museum, a riding stable, polo fields, an angling pond, Dutch windmills, and much more.

Cole Valley is a small neighborhood located on the southern edge of Haight-Ashbury, bounded by Carl and Cole streets. It's quieter than the Haight and home to doctors and medical students from the nearby UCSF Medical Center. The local shopping area on Cole Street is packed with cafes, bakeries, bars, and restaurants, ranging from low cost creperies at Zazie, 941 Cole, to elegant dining at Eos, 901 Cole. Hardware stores, flower shops, health-food stores, and dry cleaners are also available. The neighborhood pub, The Kezar Bar and Restaurant, 900 Cole, may be a good place to snoop for any unadver-tised rentals. According to Metro-Rent, in the summer of 2000 rent for a studio averaged $1,210, a one-bedroom apartment, $1,827. The commute to down-town is convenient, just hop on the MUNI LRV N Judah and you'll get there in less than ten minutes.

The **Buena Vista Park** neighborhood, which surrounds the 36-acre Buena Vista Park, has curvy, hilly streets, magnificent homes, and plenty of wealthy occupants. In fact, this neighborhood has a history of well-to-do resi-dents, including the members of the Spreckels family who made a sweet living in the sugar refining industry. One of two Spreckels homes in the City is at the west end of the Haight, overlooking Buena Vista Park. Built in 1887 and locat-ed at 737 Buena Vista Avenue West, this mansion is exquisite, and typical of some of the other homes lining the avenue. If you think this place is grand, take a trip over to the second Spreckels palace at 2080 Washington Street in Pacific Heights. Kind of makes one wonder if there are any openings in the sugar refinery biz.

Visit the lookout at the top of the Buena Vista Park and you'll find a vast panorama that includes the San Bruno mountains in the south, Mount Diablo in the east, Mount Tamalpais and the Golden Gate Bridge in the north, and the Farrallon islands to the west. Though right in the midst of the City, this park with its eucalyptus groves and stately pines, makes you feel like you've left the City behind entirely.

For more charming neighborhoods with old, refurbished homes, check nearby **Parnassus** and **Ashbury Heights** located south of Haight Street. These neighborhoods have plenty of ornate Victorians and Edwardians, as well as a few apartment buildings and large homes converted into apartments. Residents here claim that the wild parrots of Telegraph Hill come to visit, often in flocks of twenty or more. (To learn about these notorious birds and daily sightings, check their web page at www.wildparrots.com.) Rents and house prices in this area and in Buena Vista Park are slightly higher than in the rest of the upper Haight.

Web Site: www.ci.sf.ca.us
Area Code: 415
Zip Code: 94117
Post Office: Clayton Street Branch, 554 Clayton Street, 800-275-8777
Police Station: Park Station, Stanyan and Waller streets, 415-553-1061; Community Police on Patrol, 415-252-0305
Emergency Hospitals: St. Mary's Medical Center, 450 Stanyan, 415-750-5700; UCSF Medical Center, 505 Parnassus, 415-476-1037
Library: Park Branch, 1833 Page Street, 415-666-7155
Public Schools: San Francisco Unified School, District, 135 Van Ness Avenue, San Francisco, 94102, 415-241-6000, www.sfusd.k12.ca.us
Community Resources: The Haight-Ashbury Free Medical Clinic (offers free medical help to uninsured or underinsured people), 558 Clayton Street, 415-487-5632; Haight Ashbury Neighborhood Council, P.O. Box 170518, 94117, 415-331-1500, ext 105; Haight Ashbury Neighborhood Council Recycling Center, 780 Frederick, 415-753-0932; Cole Valley Improvement Association, P.O. Box 170611, 94117; John Adams Community College, 1860 Hayes Street, 415-561-1900
Public Transportation: *MUNI buses*: 5 Fulton, 6 Parnassus, 7 Haight, 33 Stanyan, 37 Corbett, 43 Masonic, 21 Hayes, 24 Divisadero, 66 Quintara, 71 Haight-Noriega: *MUNI LRV*: N-Judah

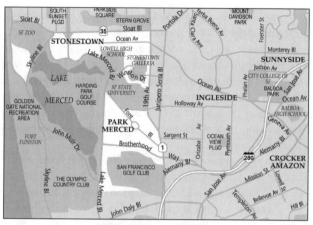

Stonestown, Park Merced

STONESTOWN, PARK MERCED

LAKESHORE

Boundaries: *Stonestown*: **North**: Sloat Boulevard; **West**: Lake Merced Boulevard; **East**: 19th Avenue; **South**: Brotherhood Way; *Lakeshore*: **North**: Sloat Boulevard; **West**: Great Highway/Pacific Ocean; **East**: Lake Merced Boulevard; **South**: San Francisco/San Mateo County Line

The neighborhoods of Stonestown, Park Merced, and Lakeshore meld together and surround the compact campus of San Francisco State University (SFSU) which serves some 28,000 students. Today the school is known for its Education, Business and Creative Arts departments. In the 1960s, however, it was one of the flash points of the student protests. Well known alumnae include actress Annette Benning, pianist Vince Guaraldi (he did the music for the "You're a Good Man, Charlie Brown" cartoons), singer Johnny Mathis (rumor has it Mathis quit at SFSU after being told he'd never sing), and author Anne Rice.

The **Stonestown** area, which is often fog-bound, is simply a southern extension of the Parkside district that comes with its own mall, the Stonestown Galleria. This is a shopping destination for people from near and far that boasts major department stores, upscale boutiques, restaurants and coffee shops, a supermarket, movie theaters, medical offices and, perhaps most important in this city, oodles of free parking.

Stonestown is also the name of a pleasant collection of apartments adjacent to the Galleria. Here, you'll find scores of units, many of which are occupied by middle aged and older residents who've lived here for years, and by students of nearby San Francisco State University. Just south of the campus is an even larger residential complex known as **Park Merced**. Metropolitan Life Insurance Company developed the 200-acre project in 1948 to house San Francisco's elderly. Today, it is a haven for SFSU students, especially if mom and dad are paying the rent for their garden or tower apartment that's just a five-minute walk to campus. Park Merced is also home to many families and older residents.

Across Lake Merced Boulevard, to the west of Park Merced, is Lake Merced, one of San Francisco's main reservoirs, which is surrounded by a wooded park and the 18-hole Harding Park golf course. Paddle boats and rowboats are available for rent.

The western edge of Lake Merced is known as **Lakeshore**, where few San Franciscans ever visit, unless they're hang-gliders destined for the cliffs of Fort Funston, or they're lucky and well off enough to have scored one of the luxury apartments or condominiums lining John Muir Drive. Rents here are steep, amenities exceptional, and the atmosphere serene, but vacancies are rare. If you can afford it and if living this far away from the hustle and bustle is for you, keep checking, someone's bound to move out eventually.

Web Site: www.ci.sf.ca.us
Area Code: 415
Zip Codes: 94132
Post Offices: Stonestown Station, 565 Buckingham Way, 800-275-8777
Police Station: Taraval Police Station, 2345 24th Avenue, 415-553-1612; Ingleside Station, 1 Sergeant John V. Young Lane, 415-553-1603
Emergency Hospital: UCSF Medical Center, 505 Parnassus, 415-476-1037
Libraries: Merced Branch, 155 Winston Drive, 415-337-4780
Public Schools: San Francisco Unified School, District, 135 Van Ness Avenue, San Francisco, 94102, 415-241-6000, www.sfusd.k12.ca.us
Community Resources: Harding Park, Harding Drive at Skyline Boulevard; San Francisco Zoo, Sloat Boulevard at 45th, 415-753-7080; San Francisco State University, 1600 Holloway Drive, 415-338-1111; Oceanview, Merced, Ingleside District (OMI), 2530 Ocean Avenue, 415-239-2510
Public Transportation: Stonestown, *MUNI buses*: 17 Park Merced, 18 46th Avenue, 23 Monterey, 26 Valencia, 28 19th Avenue, 29 Sunset; *MUNI Metro*, M Oceanview; *MUNI*: K Ingleside, M Oceanview; Lake Merced, *MUNI buses*: 18 46th Avenue, 88 BART shuttle (to nearby Daly City BART station).

GLEN PARK, DIAMOND HEIGHTS

Boundaries: **North**: Clipper Street; **West**: O'Shaughnessy Boulevard; **East**: Dolores Street/San Jose Avenue; **South**: Bosworth Street.

Affordable property (by San Francisco standards) and a cozy neighborhood feel make **Glen Park** worth exploring. A rural community at the turn of the century, Glen Park replaced Cow Hollow, which suffered from a cholera outbreak, as the dairy capital of the area. Shortly thereafter, San Francisco bought Glen Canyon Park in 1922 and sold residential lots. Today, this hilly area located south of Noe Valley is made up of a quaint collection of single-family homes, Victorian flats, and apartments that run along narrow, curvy streets. In fact, for a moment you may wonder if you've detoured into a small, twisting mountain village. The main shopping area around Chenery and Diamond streets is nestled in the hillside surrounding the Glen Park BART Station. Close to the station you'll find a handful of coffee shops and restaurants. Recently a few small businesses, including an architectural firm and a photographer, moved their businesses out of downtown to Glen Park. For newcomers particularly concerned about temblors, this neighborhood survived last century's two great earthquakes relatively unscathed. In summer 2000, average rent for a one-bedroom apartment was $1,529, according to Metro-Rent. Public transit to and from downtown San Francisco is easy.

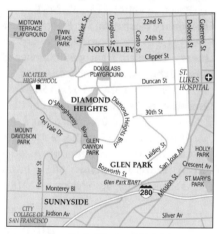

Glen Park, Diamond Heights

The neighborhood is named for the lovely Glen Canyon Park, San Francisco's second largest park, located on the sunny bayside slopes of Mt. Davidson. Because this 70-acre park is off the beaten path, few people who live in San Francisco even know this eucalyptus-rich area exists. Many locals walk their dogs in the canyon. In addition to hiking trails there are tennis courts, a children's playground, baseball field, and an 80-foot band of sandstone for beginner climbers. Beware of poison oak! The recreation center in the park has a basketball court and offers dance and art classes. (See listings below.)

The hilltop residential area of **Diamond Heights** was one of the last areas settled in San Francisco. Overlooking Glen Park to the north, it contains row upon row of sizable apartment complexes, at least one major shopping center, and some superb views of the City and the Bay below. Parking is not a problem and affordable rental housing can be found here, despite the general rule of thumb that the higher the elevation the higher the price. One drawback to living here is the fog and the wind, both of which will send you scurrying for cover. Across Market Street, to the north of Diamond Heights sit the famous Twin Peaks. Climb up here on clear days to view the snow-capped Sierra Nevada mountain range 200 miles to the east. Nearby Sutro Tower is a strange looking structure, and many would call it an eyesore, but it's an accepted part of the San Francisco skyline. Used by television and radio stations to beam their signals to the masses below, at 981 feet, it is actually the tallest structure in the City.

Web Site: www.ci.sf.ca.us
Area Code: 415
Zip Code: 94131
Post Office: Diamond Heights Station, 5262 Diamond Heights Boulevard, 800-275-8777
Police Station: Ingleside Station, Balboa Park, 415-553-1603; Community Police on Patrol, 415-333-3433
Emergency Hospitals: San Francisco General, 1001 Potrero Avenue, 415-206-8111; St. Luke's Hospital, Cesar Chavez and Valencia Streets, 415-647-8600
Library: Glen Park Branch; 653 Chenery Street, 415-337-4740
Public Schools: San Francisco Unified School District, 135 Van Ness Avenue, San Francisco, CA 94102, 415-241-6000, www.sfusd.k12.ca.us
Community Resources: Friends of Glen Canyon Park, 140 Turquoise Way, 94131, 415-648-0862; Glen Park Association, P.O. Box 31292, 94131, 415-908-6728; Glen Park Recreation Center, 70 Elk Street, 415-337-4705; Diamond Heights Community Association, P.O. Box 31529, 415-826-3867
Public Transportation: *MUNI buses*: 23 Monterey, 26 Valencia, 44 O'Shaughnessy, 52 Excelsior; *MUNI LRV*: J Church line; *BART*: Glen Park Station

THE CASTRO

CORONA HEIGHTS

Boundaries: *Castro*: **North** and **West**: Market Street; **East**: Dolores Street; **South**: 22nd Street; *Corona Heights*: **North** and **West**: Roosevelt Way, **East**: Divisadero Street; **South**: Market Street

The Castro, technically known as Eureka Valley, occupies a small but vibrant area of the City that spills across Market Street into the Upper Market area. Since the 1970s, the Castro has been the center of San Francisco's dynamic and politically powerful gay community. For a number of years Castro Street hosted one of the nation's largest and most ribald Halloween celebrations. Tens of thousands of people dressed to the nines, if dressed at all, crammed into the blocked-off street to stand cheek to cheek, to cheek to cheek, as a near-solid block of humanity. Although attempts have been made to move the party to the Civic Center where there is live music, dancing, and several stages, many still congregate in the Castro each Halloween.

Due to AIDS which has claimed many lives in this tight-knit community, the freewheeling days of the Castro seem to be over. Naturally, community leaders have been in the vanguard of the effort to convince the government and corporate America to increase AIDS/HIV research funding. These days the neighborhood is tamer and more health conscious; you'll no longer hear disco music booming out of every bar or see people spilling out into the street, drinking and cruising all hours of the day. Keep in mind,

The Castro

it's not only AIDS that changed the neighborhood, but age as well. In the Castro, rainbow flags bedeck the windows as gay tenants go about their daily lives—shepherding their children to school, going to work, etc.

Housing in the Castro consists of dozens of Victorian and Edwardian cottages, rows of two- and three-story Edwardian apartments, and a smattering of 1920s stucco flats. Streets here are often tree-lined and many of the houses have been recently renovated. In 2000, rent for a studio averaged $1,260, a one-bedroom, $2,058.

For area shopping, Castro Street offers a variety of boutiques selling everything from jewelry, clothing, leather goods, sexual aids, health foods, hamburgers, and coffees, teas, and pastries. Some stores have catchy names to go with their products. For greeting cards, try Does Your Mother Know? at 4079 18th Street, and for hamburgers go to Hot N' Hunky, 4039 18th Street. Castro Street also is where you'll find more mundane needs, with drug, hardware, and grocery stores scattered throughout. Locals consider Cliff's Variety Store, 479 Castro, a neighborhood fixture, offering more than just hardware. Taking in a show is easy at the beautiful 1930s Spanish Colonial style Castro Theatre, 429 Castro, with its huge organ and live organist. It's one of the City's cultural landmarks. If you like old movies, including musicals and art flicks, this is the place to go. It is also one of the venues for many local film festivals. Each June the Castro plays host to the annual Gay Pride Parade—truly an event to behold.

Walk across Market Street, the northern boundary of the Castro, and you'll find yourself in the so-called **Corona Heights** area. Almost like a bedroom community for the Castro, Corona Heights has well-tended Victorian homes along steep and narrow streets. You'll also find a good selection of contemporary apartments in this area, many of which offer sweeping views of the southeastern section of the City and the Bay. Rentals are rare in this upscale section. Twin Peaks shelters both Upper Market and the Castro, keeping much of the fog away, and many of these homes have sun decks in the back or on the roofs. Some even have small swimming pools. There's plenty of tight, tanned skin here, and few residents are shy about showing it off.

On Museum Way in Corona Heights, children come from all over the City to visit the Randall Junior Museum, which features an earthquake exhibit, live animals, art and science programs, films, lectures, concerts, and plays.

Web Site: www.ci.sf.ca.us
Area Code: 415
Zip Code: 94114
Post Office: 18th Street Station, 4304 18th Street, 800-275-8777
Police Station: Mission Station, 1240 Valencia, 415-553-1544; Community Police on Patrol, 415-647-2767
Emergency Hospitals: San Francisco General, 1001 Potrero Avenue, 415-206-8111; Davies Medical Center, Castro at Duboce, 415-565-6060
Library: Noe Valley Branch, 451 Jersey Street, 415-695-5095
Public Schools: San Francisco Unified School District, 135 Van Ness Avenue, San Francisco, CA 94102, 415-241-6000, www.sfusd.k12.ca.us
Community Resources: NAMES Project Foundation, 2362A Market Street, 415-882-5500; Metropolitan Community Church, 150 Eureka Street, 415-863-4434; Randall Junior Museum, 199 Museum Way, 415-554-9600; Eureka Valley Promotion Association, P.O. Box 14137, 94114, 415-255-3624; Castro Theater, 429 Castro Street, 415-621-6120
Public Transportation: *MUNI buses*: 24 Divisadero, 33 Stanyan, 35 Eureka, 48 Quintara-24th; *MUNI LRV*: J Church, K Ingleside, M Oceanview; *BART*: 24th Street Station

NOE VALLEY

Boundaries: North: 22nd Street; **South**: 30th Street; **East**: Dolores Street; **West**: Diamond Heights Boulevard

Surrounded by hills, Noe Valley is geographically separate from the rest of the City, yet still easily accessible to downtown and the South Bay. A mix of well-to-do families and singles of all persuasions and from virtually every corner of the globe inhabit Noe Valley. Local comic Marga Gomez characterizes the area as ambitious and spiritual, sort of a "yuppie Tibet." Indeed, Noe has a progressive ambiance, similar to Berkeley, but completely unlike its boisterous neighbor, the Castro. Residents of Noe Valley, named after Jose Noe, San Francisco's last Mexican *alcalde* (town administrator), are proud of their quiet neighborhood, their homes, and their colorful gardens.

Architecturally, you'll find rows of two-story Victorian homes accompanied by a smattering of Edwardians and Tudors. And, with many homeowners busily renovating their houses, it seems there's always at least one construction project happening on every block. Some even opt to tear out an existing house and build from scratch. The array of large, single-family homes with gardens is impressive; add to this the many strollers bobbing up and down the steep hills, and you'll quickly realize you've come

Noe Valley

to a family-focused neighborhood. Children and infants are everywhere, especially at the playgrounds. Local residents designed the popular Douglass Playground, nestled underneath Twin Peaks and shaded by looming pine trees.

Twenty-fourth Street, from Castro to Church, is the local shopping area, and is jam packed with coffee shops, restaurants, Irish pubs, mom and pop markets, and one-of-a-kind clothing stores. Locals rave about the food at Firefly Restaurant, 4288 24th Street. You'll find a number of bookshops and vintage clothing stores as well. A quick drive east on 24th Street, and you'll end up in the heart of the Mission, where taquerias, and Mexican bakeries replace the coffee shops and boutique clothing stores of Noe. Church Street, from about 24th to 30th streets, is another commercial area dotted with neighborhood stores. Drewes Natural Meat at 1706 Church has been in the neighborhood since 1889, and Star Bakery, 1701 Church, which bakes Irish soda bread everyday, are local favorites. Chloes Cafe, 1339 Church, is a hot spot for breakfast; Eric's, 1500 Church, serves tasty Chinese; and if the long line means a good review, people like Hamano Sushi at 1332 Church.

Like much of the City, Noe's housing market, both in terms of buying and renting, is active and pricey. According to BJ Droubi & Company, home prices have soared in Noe Valley; in 2000 prices ranged from $700,000 to well over one million dollars. Renting a one-bedroom apartment cost around $2,000, and a studio about $1,250, according to Metro-Rent's summer 2000 averages. However, while it costs a bundle to live here, it hasn't a trace of chic about it. In the mornings tie-dyed t-shirt wearing kids who attend local public schools abound, mixing in with the uniformed kids being carpooled around the city to attend private schools. There's a small town feel to this community and overall it's a place where you'd have little to complain about. The Noe Valley Ministry, 1021 Sanchez Street, is a Presbyterian Church that also hosts community groups, classes, and concerts. Concerts vary from religious (it is a church, after all) to jazz, folk, and classical. Classes range from belly dancing to ecology. Another neighborhood center for those who are expecting or are new parents is Natural Resources, 1307 Castro, 415-550-2611, located one block up from 24th Street. Here, you can enroll in pregnancy, childbirth, CPR, and early parenting classes or peruse their library.

Noe Valley offers easy access to public transit, including buses and BART. For those making the commute to the South Bay, Interstate 280 is accessible from Dolores Street/San Jose Avenue, only a few minutes away. You can access CalTrain at the 22nd and Pennsylvania station.

Web Site: www.noevalley.com
Area Code: 415
Zip Codes: 94114, 94131
Post Office: Noe Valley Station, 4083 24th Street, 800-275-8777
Police Station: Mission Station, 1240 Valencia, 415-553-1544; Community Police on Patrol, 415-647-2767
Emergency Hospitals: San Francisco General, 1001 Potrero Avenue, 415-206-8111; Davies Medical Center, Castro at Duboce, 415-565-6060
Library: Noe Valley/Sally Brunn Branch, 451 Jersey Street, 415-695-5095
Public Schools: San Francisco Unified School District, 135 Van Ness Avenue, San Francisco, CA 94102, 415-241-6000, www.sfusd.k12.ca.us
Community Resources: Noe Valley Ministry, 1021 Sanchez, 415-282-2317, www.noevalleyministry.org; Noe Valley Voice, 1021 Sanchez Street, 415-821-3324, www.noevalleyvoice.com; Friends of Noe Valley, 327 Jersey Street, 415-826-2044; Noe Valley Democratic Club, 167 Valley Street, 415-821-4087; Upper Noe Neighbors, 169 Valley Street, 415-285-0473; East and West of Castro Street, 492 Douglass Street, 415-647-3753; Noe Courts Coalition, P.O. Box 460520, 94146, 415-675-0110; Douglass Park San Francisco Recreation & Parks Department, 25th & Douglass streets, 415-695-5017; Natural Resources, 1307 Castro Street, 415-550-2611; East and West Castro Street Improvement Club, 492 Douglass Street, 415-647-3753
Public Transportation: *MUNI buses*: 24 Divisadero, 33 Stanyan, 35 Eureka, 48 Quintara 24th; *MUNI LRV*: J Church, K Ingleside, M Oceanview; *BART*: 24th Street Station

---

MISSION DISTRICT

MISSION DOLORES

Boundaries: *Mission District*: **North** and **East**: Highway 101; **West**: Valencia Street; **South**: Cesar Chavez (formerly Army) Street

The **Mission District** is one of San Francisco's most dynamic neighborhoods, with locals filling up the restaurants, nightclubs, and outdoor markets at all hours of the day and night. Residents here live in San Francisco's sunniest environs. In fact, folks in the Mission are often basking in sunshine when other neighborhoods are enshrouded in fog. Add to this warmth the heat from the local Latin beat and spicy food and you can be nowhere else but the Mission.

Mission District

Indeed, many from throughout the Bay Area come to this neighborhood for handmade tortillas, mouth-watering margaritas, and scrumptious chicken moles. The Mission District is the venue for the City's annual Cinco de Mayo and Carnaval celebration, a colorful, musically rich event, attended by thousands of people.

While it's not cheap to live anywhere in San Francisco, the Mission remains relatively affordable compared to the rest of the City, though rents have increased dramatically in recent years. According to Metro-Rent, in one year rents here increased between 17% and 25%, with the average price for a studio rising from about $800 in 1999 to $1,100 by 2000.

Recent gentrification around 24th Street, particularly by those from the "dot.com" world, has made locals a bit hot under the collar. However, the recent influx of money to this area has helped to clean up the streets and parks, and many of the homes have been rehabbed. In addition, new shops and gourmet restaurants have been added. The Mission's biggest park, Mission Dolores Park (bordered by 18th and 20th streets, and Church and Dolores) was also cleaned up. Area residents come here to enjoy the stunning City views, sunbathe, barbecue and chase their kids at the playground. On the lower side of the park you'll find six tennis courts, competitive soccer matches, and dogs chasing frisbees.

On the east side of Mission Dolores Park is Dolores Street, one of San Francisco's most attractive boulevards, which runs south from Market Street until it merges with San Jose Avenue. Unlike many of the other streets in the neighborhood, Dolores Street is a wide, divided residential boulevard with an oasis of leafy palms. Housing along Dolores Street is a mixture of traditional Mediterranean stucco houses and apartments; some of the homes are quite ornate, while others are more box-like and modern.

The **Mission Dolores** area (a rectangular neighborhood with Market

Street to the north, 20th Street to the south, Church Street to the west and Valencia Street on the east) is a quiet enclave in this often-boisterous neighborhood. It consists of classic, single-family Victorian and Edwardian houses and some contemporary apartment buildings. Rents here are higher than in the rest of the Mission, but still lower when compared to most of the City.

On Dolores and 16th streets stands San Francisco's oldest building, Mission Dolores. Completed in 1795, Mission Dolores is the sixth California mission founded by Spanish missionary Father Junipero Serra. The ceiling, covered by a mural with Indian basket designs, is spectacular. Today, Roman Catholics from all over the City congregate for mass at Mission Dolores. The noon mass is conducted in Spanish. From its inception as a mission, various ethnic groups have settled this area. By the 1850s, the neighborhood was filled with German and Scandinavian immigrants, with the Italians and Irish moving here *en masse* after the 1906 earthquake and fire displaced them from their North Beach and South of Market homes. In fact, the three-day fire following the 8.3 Richter earthquake leveled much of San Francisco but stopped across the street from Mission Dolores. In the 1950s, many from Mexico and Central America found the Mission an attractive place to call home, and since then there's been a steady influx of Latinos moving into the neighborhood. By the 1980s, artists, activists, and students began populating the area. And today, with the Mission's convenient proximity to downtown and I-80, young professionals are beginning to make their homes here.

Valencia Street, bordering the Mission to the west, has trendy herbal shops, restaurants and bars, vintage clothing shops, and art galleries. You'll find the progressive New College here whose motto is "Education and Social Change." Nightlife in the Mission centers around 16th and Valencia. Roxie Cinema at 3117 16th Street is an old movie house that features alternative films and documentaries. Many of the bookstores, coffeehouses, and restaurants are open late and the proprietors won't rush you as you nurse your latte or espresso. Locals like to browse books at Modern Times Bookstore, 888 Valencia, and then sip coffee at one of the numerous coffee shops, particularly Muddy's Coffee House, 1304 Valencia. For a quick, inexpensive bite try Pancho Villa Taqueria, 3071 16th Street. Ti Couz, 3108 16th Street, serves authentic French crepes, and for Vietnamese try Saigon, Saigon at 1134 Valencia or the more upscale, Slanted Door at 584 Valencia Street. Other local eateries abound.

Leaving Valencia and heading south to 24th Street brings you to the heart of the Mission, where Spanish is the dominant language and Mexican taquerias and Salvadoran bakeries dot the street. Twenty Fourth Street hosts the greatest concentration of colorful murals, particularly at Balmy Alley, between 24th and 25th streets, and Folsom and Harrison, where every garage door and backyard fence sports a mural. The Precita Eyes Mural Arts and Visitor Center, 2981 24th Street, sponsors an art walk which features 75 murals in six blocks.

Roughly between Potrero, on the east, South Van Ness to the west, and

16th and 20th streets to the north and south you'll find an artist's enclave where graphic artists, computer firms, animation, and film arts companies work in their bougainvillea decked offices. Cafes, pubs, and restaurants thrive near these businesses. In addition, Theater Artaud, 450 Florida, and Theater Rhinoceros, 2926 16th Street, present contemporary performances.

Transportation in the Mission is top notch with both MUNI buses and BART easily available.

Web Site: www.ci.sf.ca.us
Area Code: 415
Zip Code: 94110
Post Office: Mission Station, 1198 South Van Ness Avenue, 800-275-8777
Police Station: Mission Station, 1240 Valencia Street, 415-553-1544; Community Police on Patrol, 415-657-2767
Emergency Hospital: San Francisco General, 1001 Potrero Avenue, 415-206-8111
Library: Mission Branch, 300 Bartlett Street, 415-695-5090
Public Schools: San Francisco Unified School District, 135 Van Ness Avenue, San Francisco, CA 94102, 415-241-6000, www.sfusd.k12.ca.us
Community Publication: *New Mission News*, 3288 21st Street, 415-695-8702
Community Resources: Mission Neighborhood Center, 415-206-7747, Mission Cultural Center, 2868 Mission Street, 415-821-1155 (offers classes in dance, art, and more); Women's Building, 3543 18th Street, 415-861-8969; Inner Mission Neighbors, 415-826-7319; Mission Economic Cultural Association, 415-826-1401; Precita Eyes Mural Arts and Visitor Center, 2981 24th Street, 415-285-2287; New College, 777 Valencia, 888-437-3460, www.newcollege.edu
Public Transportation: *MUNI buses*: 12 Folsom, 14 Mission, 22 Fillmore, 27 Bryant, 33 Stanyan; BART: 16th Street Station

BERNAL HEIGHTS

North: Cesar Chavez Street; **East**: Highway 101; **West**: San Jose Avenue; **South**: Interstate 280/Alemany Boulevard

Formerly a rough, working class neighborhood, Bernal Heights, located in the southeast section of the City, is now considerably safer than it used to be and, at the time of this writing, still more affordable than much of the rest of the City. Indeed, because of its off-the-beaten-path location and affordable prices, many artists, musicians and writers have made Bernal Heights their home. And the view from atop the brown bald hill (brown in the summer and green in the winter) offers a spectacular panorama of the City below.

Named for a Mexican soldier, Juan Francisco Bernal, who moved to the area in the late 1770s, Bernal Heights was originally a grazing area for cows, goats, and other livestock. By the 1860s small plots had been sold to Irish and Italian immigrants, and farming continued, giving the area the nickname "nanny goat hill." Bernal Heights was basically unscathed after the 1906 earthquake, and this is where many displaced Italians from North Beach came.

Today, Bernal Heights is an intimate community where neighbors know each other's names and come together to fight for area causes, including safer streets and improved playgrounds. Each August, residents host a hill-wide garage sale. Visit the newly renovated playground behind the public library on 500 Cortland Avenue and you'll quickly realize you've arrived in a melting pot. Residents here hail from Japan, China, Italy, Mexico and other countries. Many seem to have a furry friend with them and quite a few spend their free time tilling their gardens.

Many of the streets are narrow, lined with small, Victorian cottages and some contemporary (1960s and '70s) box-like homes. Today, some of the smaller homes are being torn down and replaced by larger structures. Though the streets are narrow, parking is usually not a challenge. In 2000, rent for a studio averaged $980; a one-bedroom $1,650. An August/September 2000 sales report listed by Bernal Hill Realty shows property prices ranging from a low of $322,000 to a high of $875,000.

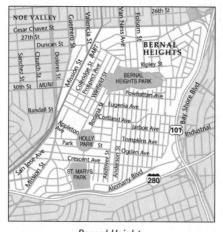

Bernal Heights

Besides sushi at Moki's Sushi and Pacific Grill, 830 Cortland, you'll find that Cortland Avenue offers a number of shopping options, from a classic barber shop, to coffee shops, a bookstore, produce stands, and pet shops. Liberty Cafe, 410 Courtland, is a local favorite for basic fare. The menu changes every month, but whether its chicken pot pie, eggs benedict or Cornish game hen, it's almost guaranteed to be delicious. Progressive Grounds at 400 Cortland Avenue hosts poetry readings in the back room with a fireplace, and Bernal Books, 401 Cortland Avenue, is one of the few independent bookstores left. For bigger shopping needs, head to the Saturday morning farmers' market at 100 Alemany Boulevard (near the 101-280 interchange). The oldest farmers' market in the City, many consider this one to be the most affordable. Produce selections and other goods come in from all over the state. Bargain hunters should return on Sunday mornings when the site hosts a flea market.

To learn more about the neighborhood, stop by the Bernal Heights Neighborhood Association at 515 Cortland Avenue, where you may bump into Supervisor Tom Ammiano. In 1999 Ammiano entered the San Francisco mayoral race just two weeks before the election. Hundreds of grassroots activists helped Ammiano's write-in campaign and their work paid off. Ammiano garnered 25% of the votes and ended up second out of fifteen candidates. This meant a run-off election against Mayor Willie Brown, who ultimately won with 60% of the votes. You can also catch up with the locals at Liberty Cafe.

Web Site: www.ci.sf.ca.us
Area Code: 415
Zip Code: 94110
Post Office: Bernal Station: 30-29th Street, 800-275-8777
Police Station: Ingleside Station: 1 Sergeant John Young Lane, 415-553-1603
Hospitals: St. Luke's Hospital, 3555 Cesar Chavez Street, 415-647-8600; San Francisco General, 1001 Potrero Avenue, 415-206-8111
Library: Bernal Heights Branch Library, 500 Cortland Avenue, 415-695-5160
Public Schools: San Francisco United School District, 135 Van Ness Avenue, San Francisco, 94102, 415-241-6000, www.sfusd.k12.ca.us
Community Resources: Bernal Heights Neighborhood Center, 515 Cortland Avenue, 415-206-2140; Bernal Heights Recreation Center, 500 Moultrie, 415-695-5007; farmers' market, 100 Alemany Boulevard, 415-647-9423; Writing Salon, for creative writing instruction, www.writingsalons.com
Public Transportation: *MUNI buses*: 9X-San Bruno, 12 Folsom, 14 Mission, 14X Mission, 23 Monterey, 24 Divisadero, 27 Bryant, 49 VanNess Mission, 67 Bernal Heights

POTRERO HILL

Boundaries: **North**: 15th Street; **South**: Cesar Chavez Street; **East**: San Francisco Bay; **West**: Highway 101

Much like the Mission, its neighbor to the west, Potrero Hill is one of the sunniest areas of the City as the fog seldom makes it way this far south. Atop Potrero Hill you'll experience some of the best views of the Bay and downtown. Because of its proximity to Highway 101 on the east and 280 on the west, the Potrero district is now considered a choice place to live by those working in the South Bay or South of Market Area.

If you want to live in the Potrero, make sure you're ready to climb. The surrounding hills are what inspired the name Potrero, which means "pasture" in Spanish, and nicknamed "Billy Goat Hill." Back around the turn of the century, goats spent their days scrambling up the hillside. These hills also gave rise to the most crooked street in San Francisco, which is located on the slope of 20th and Vermont. Unlike Lombard Street, Vermont Street, with its six hairpin turns and 14.3% grade, does not have the tourists waiting to experience the ride, nor is it as photogenic. Nearby you'll find a small, windswept playground at McKinley Square Park.

Housing in Potrero is varied and includes many recently renovated Victorians, dark-shingled Edwardians, 1920s art-deco stucco apartment buildings, and not so attractive apartments from the 1960s and '70s, as well as recently constructed high-tech loft spaces. To the south lie the housing projects where O.J. Simpson was raised. Once a predominantly working class neighborhood and home to many recently arrived immigrants, the neighborhood is now suffering the pains of rapid gentrification. Construction and renovation projects are occurring all over the neighborhood, and many homes are being torn down and replaced. In 2000, a review of the Multiple Listing Service showed housing prices here ranged considerably, from $150,000 for a condominium to more than one million dollars for a large house on the hill. In 2000 rents averaged $1,251 for a studio to $4,220 for a three-bedroom house.

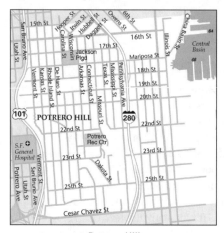

Potrero Hill

Local establishments—coffee shops, restaurants, grocers, etc.—are adequate and rather slow paced compared to many of San Francisco's more frenetic neighborhoods. Comfortable coffeehouses, like Farleys at 1315 18th Street, dot the neighborhood making it easy for you to grab a cup of joe on your way out in the morning or to sit down and visit. There are also friendly neighborhood bars, including Bloom's Saloon, 1318 18th Street, and restaurants along 18th Street and Connecticut. To hear popular music in an intimate setting, try the Bottom of the Hill Club on 17th Street and Missouri; the Anchor Steam Brewery Company is at 1705 Mariposa Street. Gardeners will be interested to know about the community gardens located at San Bruno and 20th Street, and Connecticut and 22nd streets. Newcomers looking to learn how to dance the tango, swing or lindy hop, should check out The Metronome, 1830 17th Street, which was voted by the *San Francisco Bay Guardian* as the best place to learn to dance.

Outside of those searching for a good view or a taste of fine beer, not many venture into Potrero Hill. Consider this a bonus, particularly on those gloriously clear mornings when you can relax on your hilltop perch and pat yourself on the back for moving to the City that's spread out before you.

Web Site: www.ci.sf.ca.us
Area Code: 415
Zip Code: 94107
Post Office: Brannan Street Station, 460 Brannan Street, 800-275-8777
Police Station: Potrero Station, 201 Williams, 415-553-1021
Emergency Hospital: San Francisco General, 1001 Potrero Avenue, 415-206-8111
Library: Potrero Branch, 1616 20th Street, 415-695-6640
Public Schools: San Francisco Unified School District, 135 Van Ness Avenue, San Francisco, CA 94102, 415-241-6000, www.sfusd.k12.ca.us
Community Publication: *The Potrero View Newspaper*, 953 DeHaro Street, 415-824-7516
Community Resources: Potrero Hill Neighborhood House, 953 DeHaro Street, 415-826-8080; Potrero Hill Family Resource Center, 415-206-2121; Potrero Hill Health Center, 1050 Wisconsin Street, 415-648-3022
Public Transportation: *MUNI buses*: 15 3rd Street, 19 Polk, 22 Fillmore, 48 Quintara 24th Street, 53 Southern Heights; *CalTrain*: 22nd Street Station

SOUTH OF MARKET AREA (SOMA)

SOUTH PARK
SOUTH BEACH

Boundaries: **North** and **West**: Market Street; **South**: 16th Street; **East**: San Francisco Bay

Back in the 1980s only the brave ventured down to the South of Market Area, not so today. Now it's *the* hip place to live and work, and the center of San Francisco's dot.com world. Commonly called "SOMA," its old industrial warehouses have been transformed into internet businesses, nightclubs, restaurants, hotels, museums, and New York-type loft/work spaces. Residents are "techies," artists and young professionals, many of whom can roll out of bed after a night at the clubs and walk to the office. The Moscone Convention Center (named for Mayor George Moscone who was assassinated along with Supervisor Harvey Milk in 1978) attracts thousands of people to SOMA for conventions and conferences. The art scene is flourishing with the Yerba Buena Center for the Performing Arts, and the $87 million Museum of Modern Art. People also come here to visit the Mexican Museum, the Jewish Museum, and the Sony Metreon, a gigantic urban playground, which includes a merry-go-round, a bowling alley, the Zeum chil-

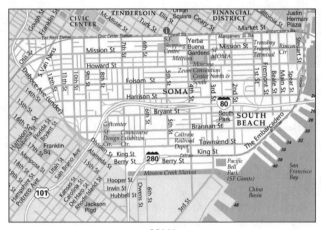

SOMA

dren's museum, shops, restaurants, and an ice skating rink

The **South Park** section of SOMA originated as an upscale residential area with elegant English style townhouses. It surrounds an oval, European style park between 2nd and 3rd streets, and Bryant and Brannan streets, and was the first posh neighborhood in San Francisco. Built in 1854 by Englishman George Gordon, the park remains, but the mansions do not. Wealthy San Franciscans moved to newer neighborhoods after the 1906 earthquake and fires ruined their homes, and in the years that followed, SOMA became decidedly more industrial than residential. By the late 1970s photographers, graphic designers, and artists, attracted by cheap rents, moved into the neighborhood. In the 1980s a couple of restaurants tested the waters, and the rest is history. Some multi-media star-tups rented space in warehouses that had been converted into live-work spaces and almost overnight South Park became "Multimedia Gulch." Bordering the park, you'll find cafes and elegant restaurants including the South Park Cafe, 108 South Park, Ecco, 101 South Park, and the Infusion Bar and Restaurant, 555 2nd Street, as well as housewares and clothing shops, and architect and design firms.

A number of waterfront condominium and apartment complexes have been built in what is now called **South Beach** near the west-end of the Bay Bridge, along the Embarcadero from Market Street to 3rd Street. In addition, many of the old red brick buildings built during the area's industrial days, including the former Hills Brothers Coffee building, have been or are being strengthened against earthquakes and turned into offices, restaurants, and hotels. The apartments and lofts here are all new, the terrain flat, and the prices high. Residents can walk to work in the nearby Financial District, downtown, or Multimedia Gulch. In 1986, the old harbor was retrofitted into a huge 700-berth marina. Numerous top-name clothing and furniture outlet stores in SOMA attract shoppers from all over the City, including the Gunne Sacks Outlet, 35 Stanford, North Face Outlet, 1325 Howard Street, and Georgiou

Outlet Clothing at 925 Bryant. Like much of the City, restaurant choices here are endless, and further west on 11th Street you'll find an enclave of bars and dance clubs, including Slim's, 333 11th Street, owned by singer Boz Skaggs. In fact, there are more dance clubs in SOMA than in any other part of the City.

SOMA's housing options are varied, ranging from newly built lofts, small Edwardian apartments in wood framed buildings on tiny alleyways, to residential high-rise units in the bayfront areas. In 2000, according to San Francisco Marketing, the price of a one-bedroom loft ranged considerably, from $350,000 to more than one million dollars. In South Beach you can expect to add an additional hundred thousand dollars. According to Metro-Rent, in July 2000 the average rental price for a one-bedroom apartment was $2,407, a studio $1,194.

Because much of the area was an empty industrial zone not too long ago, you'll find services like laundromats and grocery stores lacking—although you can grab a bite to eat, see a live performance, and do your laundry all in one sitting at Brainwash, 1122 Folsom. Kitchen items, bath towels, office supplies or cases of canned goods are available at the nearby discount stores like Bed Bath and Beyond, Trader Joe's, or Costco, but it's not easy to find a fresh pork chop or a head of romaine at your corner store, yet.

Home to two of the City's main transit centers, the Transbay bus terminal (Fremont and Mission streets) and the CalTrain station on 4th and King streets, makes taking public transportation a cinch. BART stations line Market Street, SOMA's northern boundary.

Web Site: www.ci.sf.ca.us
Area Code: 415
Zip Codes: 94103, 94105, 94107
Post Offices: Bell Bazaar Station, 3030 16th Street; Bryant Station, 1600 Bryant Street; Rincon Finance Station, 180 Steuart Street; Brannan Street Station, 460 Brannan Street, 800-275-8777
Police Station: Southern Station, 850 Bryant, 553-1373; Community Police on Patrol, 415-553-9191
Emergency Hospital: San Francisco General, 1001 Potrero Avenue, 415-206-8111
Library: 100 Larkin Street, 415-557-4400
Public Schools: San Francisco Unified School District, 135 Van Ness Avenue, San Francisco, CA 94102, 415-241-6000, www.sfusd.k12.ca.us
Community Resources: South of Market Cultural Center, 415-552-2131; San Francisco Museum of Modern Art, 415-357-4000; Yerba Buena Center for the Arts, 415-978-2787, 701 Mission Street, 415-978-2787; Ansel Adams Center for Photography, 250 4th Street, 415-495-7000; Cartoon Art Museum, 415-227-8666; Jewish Museum, 415-543-8880; Mexican Museum, 415-441-0404; South of Market Recreational Center, 6th at Folsom, 415-554-9532; SOMA Literary Review, www.somalit.com

Public Transportation: *MUNI buses*: 9 San Bruno, 12 Folsom, 14 Mission, 15 3rd Street, 26 Valencia, 27 Bryant, 30 Stockton; *MUNI LRV*, all routes along Market Street; BART: all trains along Market Street; Trans Bay Bus Terminal for *AC Transit* and *Sam Trans buses*, on Mission Street, between 1st and Fremont streets; *CalTrain Station* on 4th and King streets

EXCELSIOR, MISSION TERRACE/OUTER MISSION, CROCKER AMAZON, INGLESIDE, VISITACION VALLEY, PORTOLA

Boundaries: *Excelsior*: **West**: Mission Street; **South**: Geneva Avenue; **North**, Alemany Boulevard; **East**: McLaren Park; *Mission Terrace/Outer Mission*: **North** and **West**: Interstate 280; **South**: San Mateo County Line; **East**: Mission Street; *Crocker Amazon*: **North** and **West**, Mission Street; **North** and **East**: Geneva Avenue; **South**: San Mateo County Line; *Ingleside*: **North**: Monterey Boulevard; **West**: 19th Avenue; **East**: Interstate 280; **South**: San Mateo County Line; *Visitacion Valley*: **West**: John McLaren Park; **East**: Bayshore Boulevard; **South**: San Mateo County Line; **North**: Mansell Street; *Portola*: **North**: Interstate 280; **South**: Mansell Street; **West**: Cambridge to Silver to Madison; **East**: Highway 101

These neighborhoods are all primarily residential and located in the southern section of San Francisco, near San Mateo. They are predominantly foggy and windy areas, relatively inexpensive, and are considered middle-income, working class neighborhoods. A true melting pot, home to a variety of ethnic groups, especially Asian, Latino, and African-American. A number of residents attend San Francisco City College, which is north of Ingleside in Sunnyside.

Visit the **Excelsior** and **Outer Mission** neighborhoods and you'll find row upon row of single-family stucco homes, flats, apartment complexes, duplexes and townhouses. These homes vary from immaculate to in need of serious renovation. Look for housing here and you may find a hidden treasure in the form of an affordable, mother-in-law rental unit tucked away in a sun-baked backyard garden. Residents here have an easy commute into downtown San Francisco to the north or into the shopping mall-rich suburbia of San Mateo County to the south. Buses run frequently along Mission Street, and the two nearby BART Stations are Glen Park and Balboa Park. Mission and Geneva streets are where you'll find a number of inexpensive yet tasty Asian and Latin restaurants.

The triangular shaped **Crocker Amazon** lies directly south of Excelsior. These homes and the ones in Daly City supposedly served as the inspiration for the Malvina Reynolds song (made famous by folk singer Pete Seeger) that refers to "the little boxes, on a hilltop and they're all made out of ticky tacky." The Crocker Amazon Playground is the biggest playground in the City. It's a great place, but it's been neglected by the City over the past few years and needs a bit of sprucing up. Residents have been known to mow the park's lawn themselves.

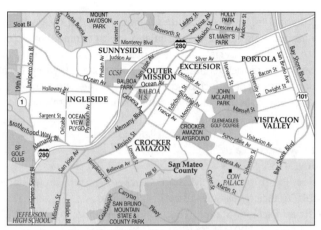

Excelsior, Mission Terrace/Outer Mission,
Crocker Amazon, Ingleside, Visitacion Valley, Portola

Situated west of Outer Mission and east of San Francisco, the **Ingleside** district is a not-unpleasant but lackluster hodgepodge of single-family homes built in the 1920s and '30s. Ingleside used to be home to one of the City's first racetracks and today's Urbano Drive traces the old racecourse. While not the safest area of San Francisco, Ingleside is far from being the most dangerous.

Visitacion Valley is perhaps a bit more lively than Crocker Amazon, but it's by no means exciting. What may be exciting to home seekers is that some of the least expensive homes in the City are here, both for purchase and to rent. Housing includes single stuccos, wood-framed apartments, Victorian flats, town-houses, and duplexes. There are also two public housing projects, Sunnydale and Geneva Towers. The area was named in 1777 by Franciscan priests who came across the land on July 2, the day of the annual Catholic feast commemorating the visitation ("visitacion" in Spanish) of the Virgin Mary to her cousin Elizabeth.

McLaren Park, which comes with its own golf course, makes up Visitacion Valley's western border with Excelsior. The world-famous Cow Palace sits a bit to the south of McLaren Park, along Geneva Avenue. The Beatles played at the Cow Palace, as have hundreds of other big-name acts over the years. The arena also hosts sports and boat shows, dog and cat exhibitions, consumer electronics auctions, car auctions, professional tennis tournaments, motorcycle races, and tractor-pulls.

Just across Highway 101 sits 3COM Park, previously known as Candlestick Park, the current home of the National Football League's 49ers. This is a cold and windy place, except for a few days in the summer, which was one of the reasons the Giants built their own facility in the City's China Basin/Mission Bay area. The 49ers are working on building a new stadium as well, but they want to stay at Candlestick Point.

Just north of Visitacion Valley, south of Bernal Heights, is **Portola**, an area similar to Bernal Heights when it comes to housing options, climate, and residential makeup. It also has a rich Italian and Jewish heritage, much of which survives to this day, especially in the thriving commercial zone along San Bruno Avenue, the district's southern border with Visitacion Valley. Local shopping options are practical, including an Italian butcher shop, mom and pop grocers, and flower shops. With McLaren Park nearby, there's plenty of open space for recreational activities.

Web Site: www.ci.sf.ca.us
Area Code: 415
Zip Codes: Excelsior, Outer Mission, Crocker Amazon, Ingleside: 94112; Portola/Visitacion Valley: 94134
Post Offices: Excelsior Station, 15 Onondaga Avenue; Visitacion Valley, 68 Leland Avenue, 800-275-8777
Police Stations: Ingleside Station, 1 Sergeant John V. Young Lane, 415-553-1603; Community Police on Patrol, 415-333-3433; Potrero Station, 2300 3rd Street, 415-553-1021; Community Police on Patrol, 415-255-6297
Emergency Hospital: San Francisco General, 1001 Potrero Avenue, 415-206-8111
Libraries: Excelsior Branch, 4400 Mission Street, 415-337-4735; Visitacion Valley, 45 Leland Avenue, 415-337-4790; Portola, 2450 San Bruno Avenue, 415-715-4090; Ingleside Branch, 387 Ashton, 415-337-4745
Public Schools: San Francisco Unified School District, 135 Van Ness Avenue, San Francisco, CA 94102, 415-241-6000, www.sfusd.k12.ca.us
Public Transportation: Excelsior, *MUNI buses*: 14 Mission, 29 Sunset, 52 Excelsior, 54 Felton; Crocker Amazon, *MUNI buses*: 14 Mission, 43 Masonic, 88 BART shuttle; Visitacion Valley, *MUNI buses*: 9 San Bruno, 15 3rd Street, 29 Sunset, 56 Rutland

WESTERN ADDITION, CIVIC CENTER

THE FILLMORE
JAPANTOWN
LOWER HAIGHT
ALAMO SQUARE
HAYES VALLEY
LOWER PACIFIC HEIGHTS

Boundaries: Western Addition: **North**: Pine Street and Pacific Heights; **East**: Polk Street and The Tenderloin; **South**: Haight Street and The Lower Haight; **West**: Masonic and Richmond; Civic Center: **North**: Turk Street; **West**: Gough Street; **East**: Larkin Street; **South**: Market Street

Nestled between the upscale neighborhood of Pacific Heights and the colorful Haight Ashbury, the Western Addition is one of the most ethnically and economically diverse neighborhoods in the City. It boasts rows of restored Victorians, ritzy bed and breakfasts, and tony restaurants as well as auto repair shops and thrift stores. Housing choices are varied, including apartments, railway flats, colorful mansions, single-family Victorians, brand new condos, and public housing. Although the economic boom of the past decade has driven San Francisco housing costs through the roof, affordable housing can still be found in this part of the City, and young professionals are flocking to the neighborhood, bringing commercial development with them. In July 2000, Craig's List, a community bulletin board on the internet, www.craigslist.org, listed a basic, one-bedroom apartment in the Western Addition for $2,000. A three-bedroom in Lower Pacific Heights with ideal amenities— high ceilings, oversized kitchen, decorative fireplace, formal dining room—listed at $3,600.

This large area, covering what is now the center of San Francisco, was a wasteland of sand dunes until it was developed in the 1850s. Located west of the already settled section of the City, officials aptly named the expansion the Western Addition. The neighborhood survived the 1906

Western Addition, Civic Center

earthquake and fire without much damage; the buildings, many of which were built on top of bedrock, did not topple, and it was beyond the downtown fire zone. After the great fire many Japanese-Americans sought refuge here. Then, during WW II, African-Americans flooded into the vacancies left by the interred Japanese population. It is during this era that the jazz scene flourished on Fillmore Street. As late as the 1940s much of the housing in the Western Addition remained true to its original form. In the decades following WW II this neighborhood was hit with suburban flight and the introduction of public housing, which spiraled the area into urban decay. Shortly after WW II San Francisco declared the Western Addition a slum area and created an urban renewal plan, which was largely unsuccessful. Eventually many of the longstanding Victorians were either demolished or removed to other areas of town, and for years vacant lots scarred the once vibrant Fillmore Street. It took the real estate crunch of the 1980s and '90s to get developers, real estate agents, and more affluent residents to rediscover the area.

Fillmore Street, shared by both Pacific Heights and the Western Addition, now caters to the chic as well as practical shoppers. Upper Fillmore, part of neighboring Pacific Heights, is lined with exclusive clothing and home stores, vintage clothing shops, trendy restaurants, and an art film house. Upscale chain stores are ever-present. Lower Fillmore is home to a multiplex theater, cheap restaurants, and dozens of stores meeting more everyday needs. Remnants of the Fillmore District's 1940s music scene continue today with the famous Fillmore Auditorium, John Lee Hooker's Boom Boom Room, and Rassela's Jazz Club.

Japantown is also part of the Lower Fillmore area, sporting sushi bars, specialty stores, and cultural events. Of particular note is the Japan Center, with the Kabuki Theater Cinema Complex and the relaxing Kabuki Baths. Japanese necessities, from stationery and books, to kimonos and cosmetics, to fresh seafood and wasabi, are all available here. As you would expect, there are a number of sushi palaces, noodle shops, and yes, karaoke bars. The Cherry Blossom Festival takes place here in late winter. A high-rise apartment complex attracts a wide variety of people, from students to professionals, although the retail space below still suffers from frequent turnovers. Old Victorians and newly built public housing also surround this part of the Western Addition.

More urban and slightly gritty, Divisadero Street is the less gentrified artery of the Western Addition. Divisadero Street separates the **Lower Haight** from the Upper Haight or Haight-Ashbury. The Lower Haight has a distinctly different feel from its more famous sister. For the last fifteen to twenty years, artists, musicians, herbalists, and the like have lived here in the cheap cavernous railway flats. Now these places are being snapped up, remodeled, and re-sold for a tidy profit. Garages and gas stations hinder the cohesiveness of the street's commercial center, but independent and imaginative business owners maintain a stronghold in the neighborhood. A barbecue restaurant, karate studio, game store, hubcap store, vinyl record shop, and used cookingware store are testament to the street's diversity. Divisadero Street is also home to several independently owned cafes, one of which has an adjoining international magazine and newspaper stand. The recent influx of young professionals seeking their fortune in the internet gold rush is bringing new vitality to Divisadero Street. Housing around Divisadero Street is composed mostly of Victorians split into flats and small bay-windowed apartment buildings. Street crime in the Lower Haight is still considered a problem by many, but long-time residents say it is getting better each year.

A breath of fresh air for residents and tourists alike, Alamo Square Park (between Fulton, Scott, Hayes, and Steiner streets) is a full city block of greenery with spectacular views of the City. The park, with its seventeen underground springs that bubble over onto sidewalks, its rarely used tennis court, and its windswept evergreens and weeping willows is often too windy to enjoy as a picnic site or sunbathing area. But, each evening after work, packs of dog owners led by eager pets converge here. Visible from the park are the Painted

Ladies, a row of six beautifully restored Victorians that were moved to this site during the 1940s urban renewal. Other small parks freckle the neighborhood offering respites from the largely urban area.

As picturesque as the famous row of Painted Ladies is, they literally pale in comparison to many other bright glories of the Western Addition. Some of the homes, decorated in rich Victorian colors with hints of gold, resemble Gustav Klimt's paintings; other rows of delicate pastel painted houses look as sweet and creamy as a bag of saltwater taffies; a few are painted in hippie regalia of purple, orange and green. A few of these houses are still owned by families who bought them for a song in the mid-1940s. Others have been broken up into flats and several do service as bed and breakfasts.

With a frenzy of buying and refurbishing going on here, the **Alamo Square** neighborhood, like the rest of the Western Addition, is considerably less dangerous than it was fifteen years ago. It is probably no coincidence that many New Yorkers love the neighborhood. They feel safer than they did back east and can rent a beautiful apartment that they could never have afforded back home. The area is still under-serviced as far as groceries go. You won't find any sports bars, boutique food shops, or chic clothing stores—yet. But you can find old-time butchers, stores selling African and Jamaican apparel, and Country Cheese, 415 Divisadero, 415-621-8130, a discount cheese, canned goods, and bulk food store. And one of the few places you can get your car washed in the entire city is here at Divisadero and Oak streets.

Hayes Valley was a little like a mole coming into the sunlight after the Central Freeway was demolished, following the 1989 earthquake. Freed from the shadow of the freeway, the area has become a hip neighborhood, with gourmet cuisine and boutique stores. Housing includes an assortment of Victorian mansions, Edwardian flats and apartments, hidden-away cottages, and dozens of brand new condos. The area is littered with cafes along Hayes, Laguna, and Franklin streets. Here you can graze among Brazilian, German, Italian, French, Mexican, and Thai restaurants. In keeping with the *tres-chic* atmosphere, there are galleries and performance spaces as well as trendy shoe, clothing, jewelry, and houseware shops. The popular wine bar, Hayes and Vine, 377 Hayes, 415-626-5301, serves tidbits to complement its libations. Merchants in the Hayes Valley throw variously themed afternoon or early evening street parties a few times a year. Depending on the theme, you can have your hands tattooed with henna, dance the polka to an accordion band, watch belly dancers and firebreathers, have your tarot cards read, hear live music, eat homemade cookies, or drink sangria.

Lower Pacific Heights, located roughly between California Street, Presidio Avenue, Van Ness Avenue, and Geary Boulevard, was previously considered to be part of the Western Addition until realtors tagged it with the catchier name of Lower Pacific Heights. The area does differ from the bulk of the Western Addition in that it is hilly and the rents are high. Sturdy and comfortable apartments from the 1920s with brick fronts, Murphy beds, and kitchen built-ins abound in this region, running side by side with Victorian houses and mansions, as well as smaller places built in the 1960s and '70s. Neighborhood shopping can be found in Pacific Heights at the upscale Sacramento Street and Fillmore Street shopping districts. According to Metro Rent, the median rental price for a studio in lower Pacific Heights in summer 2000 was $1,195, up 17% from 1999; a one-bedroom apartment averaged $1,500, an increase of 11%.

Civic Center feels like an area that is not necessarily a neighborhood, though it does have modern condos to rent or buy, and 1920s era apartments with studios, and efficiencies. The area is busy and urban but is centrally located and has public transportation galore. Area amenities include the ballet, the opera, the symphony, art openings or lectures, and expensive restaurants. Also, the newly renovated City Hall is here with its glowing tower and marbled halls. You'll have to travel a bit for groceries and laundry, but rents are generally lower here compared to more established San Francisco neighborhoods.

Web Site: www.ci.sf.ca.us
Area Code: 415
Zip Codes: 94115, 94117, 94102
Post Offices: Steiner Street Station, 1849 Geary Street, 800-275-8777; Clayton Street Station, 554 Clayton Street, 800-275-8777
Police Stations: east of Steiner Street: Northern Station, 1125 Fillmore Street, 415-553-1563; west of Steiner Street: Park Station, 1899 Waller Street, 415-242-3000
Emergency Hospitals: California Pacific Medical Center, Pacific Campus, 2333 Buchanan Street, 415-600-0600; California Pacific Medical Center, Davies Campus, 45 Castro Street, 415-600-3333; St. Francis Memorial Hospital, 900 Hyde Street, 415-353-6300
Library: Western Addition Branch, 1550 Scott Street, 415-292-2160
Public Schools: San Francisco Unified School District, 135 Van Ness Avenue, San Francisco, 415-241-6000, www.sfusd.k12.ca.us
Community Resources: 848 Community Space, 848 Divisadero Street, 415-922-2385; Alliance Française de San Francisco, 1345 Bush Street, 415-775-7755; Audium (a theater for audiophiles), 1616 Bush Street, 415-771-1616; Fillmore Auditorium, 1805 Geary Boulevard, 415-346-6000; San Francisco Fire Department Pioneer Memorial Museum, 655 Presidio Avenue, 415-861-8000; San Francisco Performing Arts Library and Museum, 399 Grove Street, 415-255-4800; Ella Hill Hutch Community Center, 415-921-6276, 1050 McAllister Street; War Memorial Opera House; 199 Grove Street: Opera, 415-864-3330, Ballet, 415-865-2000; Louise M. Davies Symphony Hall, 415-864-6000; Bill Graham Civic Auditorium, 99 Grove Street, 415-974-4060; Alamo Square Neighbors Association, P.O. Box 15372; Western Addition Neighborhood Association, 1948 Sutter Street

Public Transportation: *MUNI buses*: east-west: 38 Geary, 2 Clement, 3 Jackson, 4 Sutter, 5 Fulton; north-south: 22 Fillmore, 24 Divisadero, 43 Masonic, 42 Downtown Loop, 49 Van Ness/Mission, 47 Van Ness; inter-city: 76 Marin/Headlands; *Golden Gate Transit buses* (to and from Marin County): 10, 20, 60, 70, 80, 90

MISSION BAY, BAYVIEW, HUNTERS POINT

BAYVIEW HEIGHTS

Boundaries: *Bayview/Hunter's Point*: **West**: Bayshore Boulevard; **South** and **East**: the Bay; **North**: Highway 280; *Mission Bay*: **West**: Highway 280; **South**: Mariposa Street; **East**: the Bay; **North**: Townsend Street

Located at the sunny southeastern tip of San Francisco, the Bayview/Hunter's Point and Mission Bay area is ripe for development, mostly due to San Francisco's continuing prosperity and unremitting housing shortage. Home to the City's largest African-American neighborhood, many long-time locals fear displacement as the neighborhood goes through gentrification. While locals are eager to improve their neighborhood they want to make sure that they don't get priced out of their own homes.

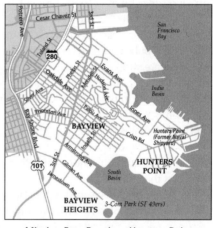

Mission Bay, Bayview, Hunters Point

Despite these concerns, property prices have increased dramatically over the last few years and are expected to continue to climb.

Mission Bay, which borders South Beach and South of Market Area, is literally a neighborhood in the making. Formerly a duck hunting blind, then a dump, later a railway yard, today, it is mainly an industrial area. Obvious harbingers of new development include the newly built Pacific Bell Park, the Giants' new stadium, and the huge Mission Bay project, which broke ground in 1999. When complete, this project will include 6,000 new housing units, a 43-acre research center for UCSF, a library, offices, retail space, entertainment space, a hotel and a light rail line along 3rd Street to Hunter's Point. Architects predict that the entire project will take about fifteen years to finish.

Those considering looking for housing here may find Mission Bay's proximity to downtown and Multimedia Gulch ideal, although currently much of Mission Bay seems uninhabited. Businesses here include only a few restaurants, a boatyard, and two Yacht Clubs, the Bayview Boat Club and the Mariposa Hunters Point Yacht Club. The Ramp, 855 China Basin, is a lunch favorite for locals, and on Friday and Saturday nights live music takes center stage with people from all over San Francisco coming here to unwind. There are also a number of industrial buildings, including The Esprit Outlet, 499 Illinois, which specializes in children's clothing.

Third Street is the main thoroughfare here. Head south on it to get to the **Bayview/Hunters Point** area. In 1867, Hunters Point was the first permanent dry-dock on the Pacific Coast. In 1939 the US Navy purchased the land for use as a dry-dock and shipbuilding operation, and by 1974 the shipyards were closed. Shortly thereafter, the naval station itself became home to more than 250 artists who converted the barracks and administration buildings into art studios. Overlooking the Bay and the decaying shipyards, the views provide inspiring subject matter to the resident artists.

Architecturally, the Bayview/Hunters Point area is comprised of a variety of homes, some ramshackle and some exquisite Victorians, mixed in with box-like stuccos and public housing projects. Unlike the rest of the city, the stores along 3rd Street are struggling to stay open. Many residents go to the Bayview Plaza for general shopping needs. According to the Bayview Police Department, criminal activity in this neighborhood is among the highest in the city. What's more, after WW II, the US Navy dumped quantities of toxic waste, some of which still remains. To date, the Navy has spent more than $162 million cleaning up the area, but according to Bayview/Hunters Point community advocates, the cleanup job is not complete and the community continually meets to discuss this issue.

With lots of undeveloped space, Hunter's Point has a surprising amount of wildlife including blue herons, possums, barn owls, seals, jackrabbits, foxes, raccoons, falcons and red tailed hawks. Locals boast that the weather is better here compared to much of the rest of the City. Views of downtown San Francisco are incredible; rents are low, houses are affordable, and reasonably priced condominiums are being built—all located within a ten-minute drive of downtown San Francisco. Hunter's Point, with its bait and tackle shops, soul-food restaurants, and traffic free roads has almost a country feel. There are few parks, however, down by the Bay, you can find tranquil places to view the peaceful waters. Because of the convenient location and the low housing costs, a number of artists and architects have moved here.

Bayview Heights near the San Mateo County Line is the home of Candlestick Park ('The Stick") also known as 3Com Park, where the 49ers play. There is talk about rebuilding the stadium or moving closer to San Francisco, but no concrete plans are underway.

Web Site: www.ci.sf.ca.us
Area Code: 415
Zip Code: 94124, 94134, 94107
Emergency Hospital: San Francisco General, 1001 Potrero Avenue, 415-206-8111
Post Office: Bayview Station, 2111 Lane Street; Hunter's Point: San Francisco Manual Processing Facility; 180 Napoleon Street, 800-275-8777
Police: Bayview Station, 201 Williams, 415-671-2300
Library: Bayview Branch, 5075 3rd Street, 415-715-4100
Public Schools: San Francisco Unified School District, 135 Van Ness Avenue, San Francisco, 415-241-6000, www.sfusd.k12.ca.us
Community Resources: Bayview Opera House, 4705 3rd Street, 415-824-0386 (theater, dance, African-American center, aftercare and arts programs; Burnett Child Development Center, 1520 Oakdale, 415-695-5660; Hunter's Point Naval Station, east end of Evans Street; Shipyard Trust for the Arts, Building 101-1317; Hunters Point Naval Shipyard, 415-822-0922; Southeast Community Facility, 1800 Oakdale, 415-821-1534; India Basin Neighborhood Association; Joseph Lee Recreation Center, 1395 Mendell Street
Public Transportation: *MUNI buses*: 9 San Bruno, 15 3rd, 19 Polk, 23 Monterey, 24 Divisadero, 29 Sunset, 44 O'Shaughnessey, 54 Felton

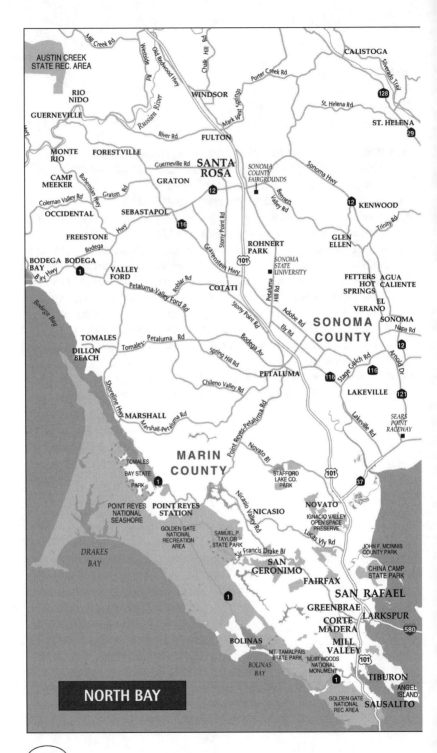

NORTH BAY

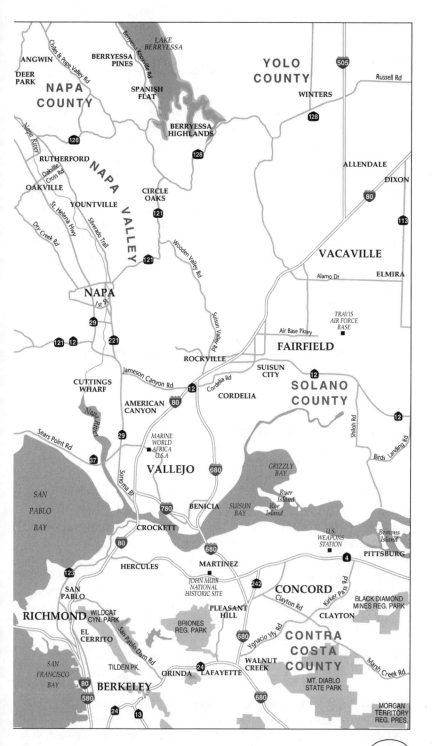

SURROUNDING AREAS

Many coming to the Bay Area choose to live outside of San Francisco proper. The reasons are varied—perhaps the City is too expensive, too congested, too foggy, some want to live in the country or suburbs, and many are looking to set up house near their office, which very often is outside of San Francisco. More than six million people live in the nine Bay Area counties of Alameda, Contra Costa, Marin, Sonoma, San Mateo, Napa, Solano, Santa Clara, and San Francisco, and the numbers continue to increase. What follows is an overview of these counties, divided into four regions, the **North Bay**, **East Bay**, **Peninsula**, and **South Bay**. The following profiles are by no means comprehensive, but intended as a launch to your exploration of the greater Bay Area. Unless otherwise noted, housing stats were supplied by the California Association of Realtors. See www.car.org for the latest information on Bay Area homes.

NORTH BAY
(MARIN, SONOMA, NAPA, SOLANO COUNTIES)

MARIN COUNTY

SAUSALITO, MILL VALLEY, TIBURON
SAN RAFAEL
CORTE MADERA, NOVATO, FAIRFAX

Just north of San Francisco, across the Golden Gate Bridge, the weather is warmer and life more relaxed. Encased by the Bay on the east and the Pacific Ocean on the west, Marin County's terrain is hilly and full of oak trees, eucalyptus groves, redwoods, and other evergreens. The Coastal Miwok Indians inhabited Marin first, followed by the Spaniards, the seafarers, and eventually San Franciscans, who became especially numerous after the Golden Gate Bridge opened in 1937. With easy access to San Francisco, Marin County was no longer a hidden, hard to get to enclave. Today 44% of Marin County consists of natural preserves and public lands.

Home to CEOs, CFOs, old money, new money, and a few remaining artists, writers, and musicians, Marin County once elicited hedonistic images of hot tubs and peacock feathers. The 1980 movie made from the book, *The Serial: A Year in the Life of Marin County*, parodied this milieu, and although the book was intended to poke fun at the hot-tubbing, peacock-feather waving, affair-having, therapizing, divorcing stereotypes of the locals, some believe it did not stray far from the truth. These days you'll find life in Marin pretty mainstream, although vestiges of the past still can be found, particularly in the sixties-era Volkswagen mini-buses decorated with peace signs and batiked curtains, and the occasional hitch-hiker waving her thumb along the roadside.

Most of the western part of Marin is dramatic, with wooded mountains and hills bordering the Pacific Ocean. California's stunning North Coast offers a visual feast, from Sausalito all the way up to the Oregon border. In the sum-mer sun worshippers flock to Muir Beach and Stinson Beach on the frequently glorious weekends, clogging Highway 1 and turning the coastal highway into the proverbial "parking lot," one of the Bay Area's most frustrating traffic prob-lems. Residents of Marin have one of the grandest views of the entire Bay Area made especially photogenic when the fog hovers on the bay or around the bridge. From Mount Tamalpais' wooded vantage point, you can often see for over 100 miles in any direction.

The southwestern end of Marin County encompasses the 1,000-acre Golden Gate National Recreation Area, which includes the remains of wartime batteries and bunkers of Fort Cronkite. During WW II, twelve-foot guns sat aimed toward the sea in the expectation of enemies invading the US from the Pacific. Thankfully these invaders never materialized. If you enjoy hiking or camping, you may want to make the 90-minute drive from San Francisco to the 66,000-acre Point Reyes National Seashore, north of Stinson Beach. The seashore curls gracefully around Drake's Bay, so named for the explorer Sir Francis Drake who is credited with "discovering" San Francisco Bay in 1579.

A recent report issued by the National Low-Income Housing Coalition ranks Marin, San Francisco, and San Mateo counties as the least affordable places to live in the nation. According to the California Association of Realtors, the median price for a home in Marin County increased 38.9% ($400,000 to $555,500) between August 1999 and August 2000. Sausalito, Mill Valley, Tiburon, and Belvedere are the most expensive cities in the county. The towns located farther north of San Francisco, such as San Rafael, Corte Madera and Novato, are more affordable, and the most affordable towns here are the West Marin towns of San Geronimo Valley, Inverness, Tomales, and Marshall.

MARIN COUNTY
Web Sites: www.co.marin.ca.us, www.marin.org
Zip Codes: 94965, 94941, 94920, 94901, 94925, 94945, 94930
Area Code: 415
Sheriff: Marin County Sheriff Department, 3501 Civic Center Drive, #167, San Rafael, 415-499-7250
Emergency Hospital: Marin General Hospital, 250 Bon Air Road, Greenbrae, 415-925-7000
Library: Main, 3501 Civic Center Drive, San Rafael, 415-499-6056
Public Schools: Marin County Office of Education, 415-472-4110, http://marin.k12.ca.us

Community Publications: *Marin Independent Journal*, 150 Alameda del Prado, Novato, 415-883-8600; *The Ark Newspaper*, 1550 Tiburon Boulevard, Tiburon, 415-435-2652; *The Coastal Post*, P.O. Box 31, Bolinas, 415-868-0502; Marin Scope Community Newspapers *(Mill Valley Herald, Ross Valley Reporter, Twin Cities Times, San Rafael News Pointer, Ebbtide*, and *Marin Scope)*, P.O. Box 1689, Sausalito, 415-332-3778; *Novato Advance*, P.O. Box 8, Novato, 415-898-7084; *Pacific Sun*, P.O. Box 5553, Mill Valley, 415-383-4500; *Point Reyes Light*, P.O. Box 210, Point Reyes Station, 415-663-8404; *San Rafael/Terra Linda News Pointer*, 415-289-4040

Community Resources: Marin Community Resource/New Perspectives, 415-924-8500; Marin Services for Women, 415-924-5995; Falkirk Cultural Center, 1408 Mission Avenue, San Rafael, 415-485-3435; Bay Area Discovery Museum, Fort Baker, 557 McReynolds Road, Sausalito, 415-487-4398; Marin Civic Center, Avenue of the Flags, San Rafael; Golden Gate National Recreation Area, Fort Mason, Building 201, 415-556-0560; Point Reyes National Seashore, Point Reyes, 415-663-1092; Muir Woods National Monument, 415-388-2595; Mount Tamalpais State Park, 801 Panoramic Highway, Mill Valley, 415-388-2070; City of San Rafael Community Center, 618 B Street, San Rafael, 415-485-3333; County Park and Recreation Department, 415-435-4355

Public Transportation: *Golden Gate Transit*, 415-455-2000; *Blue & Gold Fleet*, 415-705-5555 (advance tickets), 415-773-1188 (recorded schedule); *Angel Island Ferry*, 415-435-2131; *RIDES for Bay Area Commuters*, 800-755-7665

SAUSALITO, MILL VALLEY, TIBURON

Just across the Golden Gate Bridge, where the weather is always warmer, you'll find the upscale and highly desirable communities of Sausalito, Mill Valley, and Tiburon. **Sausalito** (population 7,500), which means "little willow" in Spanish, hosts splendid mansions with views of the Bay and City. Down on the water, the Sausalito Harbor shelters thousands of boats and houseboats, including the Taj Majal, a replica of the Indian monument, only this one is smaller and floats. Tourists flock to Sausalito via the ferry from San Francisco and on weekends they virtually take over Bridgeway, the main street. To avoid the crowds and the overabundance of t-shirt shops and art galleries on Bridgeway, locals prefer to gather on Caledonia Street, one block east from the Bay. Away from the clicking cameras, residents of Sausalito have an active community, from the Sausalito Women's Club, which works to improve the city, to the yachties putzing on their boats, to resident artists inspired by their surroundings. The Sausalito Arts Festival, held every Labor Day, brings people from all over the Bay Area in search of good art and live music.

Once a bohemian, hippie-type enclave, Sausalito is now joining the rank and file of the rest of the Bay Area with a wealthy population, soaring housing costs, and a number of high-tech businesses. The hills above downtown Sausalito are peppered with a broad range of abodes, from artist cabin/studios, craftsman homes, ranch-style houses, condos and apartments to Victorians and contemporary mansions. Many of the homes have exquisite bay views and gardens, and garage space is at a premium, especially on the hillside. Rental vacancies are rare and generally costly. According to Marin Rentals, in 2000 a studio averaged about $1,000, a one-bedroom $1,400, and a two-bedroom apartment $1,700 per month.

Those commuting to San Francisco generally rely on the Sausalito Ferry or Golden Gate Transit.

Formerly a lumber town, **Mill Valley** (14,000) has more rentals and available property than Sausalito, and it is not as touristy. Located northwest of Sausalito at the foot of Mount Tamalpais, Mill Valley has a popular downtown with charming restaurants, a coffee shop, and other stores. The famous Book Depot Bookstore is here, located smack center in the town square where people play chess, hacky sack, or chat with their neighbors. The square gives the city a real community feel, somewhat reminiscent of town squares in Mexico. The Village Grocery is another landmark, featuring a gourmet deli that's ideal for hungry bikers or hikers. With Mount Tamalpais as a backdrop, many Mill Valley residents spend their free time hiking, biking or just walking trails. Since 1905 runners have gathered to race the 7-mile rigorous Dipsea Race, which starts in Mill Valley and ends at Stinson Beach. The Mill Valley Film Festival, held each fall, is gaining worldwide respect.

Many of the homes here were built during Mill Valley's lumber days and are Craftsman types, built with exquisite redwood. You'll also find many traditional homes, some Victorians, and a number of apartments, townhouses and condominiums. According to the California Association of Realtors, the average selling price for a home in Mill Valley in October 2000 was $720,000, a 19% increase from the previous year.

Located 18 miles north of San Francisco, nearby **Tiburon** (8,650), which means "shark" in Spanish, is even more upscale than Mill Valley and Sausalito, with homes averaging more than one million dollars. Many homes are either on the water or up in the hills. Downtown Tiburon is where you can catch the ferry to San Francisco, or better yet, to Angel Island—a delightful 750-acre state park in San Francisco Bay that is part wilderness and part former army base. In the early 1900s Asian immigrants came here first for government processing; later in the century nuclear Titan missiles were based here. Parts of the immigration station remain; you can still find graffiti, names, and even a poem etched into the walls of the buildings where the immigrants were held.

Restaurants on Tiburon's Main Street, notably Guaymas at 5 Main Street, and Sam's Anchor Cafe, 27 Main Street, are popular, though pricey. The

Sweden House Bakery, 35 Main Street, bakes some of the best éclairs and cookies, not to mention delicious Swedish pancakes. Views of the Bay from the shops and restaurants on Main Street are lovely. The Tiburon Playhouse movie theater, 40 Main Street, 415-435-3585, has a soundproof private viewing booth, ideal for infants. Boat owners can take their pick from one of three yacht clubs: San Francisco Yacht Club (in nearby Belvedere), and Corinthian and Tiburon Yacht clubs. Bikers enjoy the scenic ride on Paradise loop or the path by Blackie's Pasture along Tiburon Boulevard. The Belvedere Peninsula sports some of the most upscale homes in Marin County. Many of these stately mansions were built more than a hundred years ago, and some have their own docks.

SAUSALITO
Web Site: www.ci.sausalito.ca.us
Area Code: 415
Zip Codes: 94965, 94966
Post Office: 150 Harbor Drive, 800-275-8777
Police Station: 29 Caledonia, 415-289-4170
Library: 420 Litho Street, 415-289-4100, ext.121

MILL VALLEY
Web Site: www.cityofmillvalley.org, www.gomillvalley.com
Area Code: 415
Zip Codes: 94941, 94942
Post Office: 751 East Blithedale Avenue, 800-275-8777
Police Station: One Hamilton Lane, 415-388-4142
Library: Mill Valley Public Library, 375 Throckmorton Avenue, 415-389-4292

TIBURON
Web Site: www.tiburon.org
Area Code: 415
Zip Code: 94920
Post Office: 6 Beach Road, Tiburon, 800-275-8777
Police Station: 1155 Tiburon Boulevard, 415-435-7360
Library: 1501 Tiburon Boulevard, Tiburon, 415-789-2665

SAN RAFAEL

Situated north of Tiburon, San Rafael is the largest city in Marin County and the oldest. Founded in 1817 as a mission, San Rafael (population 54,000) is home to both blue-and white-collar populations. Compared to Sausalito and Mill Valley, rental housing here is plentiful and quite a bit more affordable. In

2000, according to Marin Rentals, the average rent for a studio was $900, a one-bedroom $1,100 and a two-bedroom about $1,400 per month. The median October 2000 price for a home in San Rafael was $553,500, up seven percent from the previous year, according to the California Association of Realtors. Architecturally, homes range from apartments to ranch style homes, cottages and Mediterranean-style villas.

Nestled beneath wooded mountains, San Rafael's claim to fame is the Marin County Civic Center, a national historic landmark, designed in the early 1960s by Frank Lloyd Wright. With its salmon-colored arches and a blue domed roof, the building's colors are intended to merge with the colors of nature. It was featured in George Lucas' first feature film, *THX-1138*, (look for the golden escalator). Speaking of George Lucas, his Skywalker Ranch is located nearby, though plans are in place to move part of Lucas studios to the San Francisco Presidio. Fourth Street, San Rafael's main drag, also found its way onto the cinematic map, as the place to cruise in your big Buick or Chevrolet in Lucas' *American Graffiti*. Throckmorton is another shopping street, home to chic clothing stores and quaint one-of-a-kind boutiques. Down by Highway 101 is the large Strawberry Shopping Center where you'll find a Safeway, cafes, restaurants, bookstores, boutiques, and galleries. In addition to the unique Civic Center, the Falkirk Cultural Center, 1408 Mission Avenue, is a historic Queen Anne Victorian built in 1888. The Falkirk hosts contemporary art exhibits, art classes, and poetry readings.

The San Rafael to San Francisco commute via Highway 101 can be frustrating. Many locals prefer to take the Ferry or Golden Gate Transit. The ferry service is fast and scenic—board at the Larkspur Ferry Terminal. On the way out of Larkspur, the ferry passes San Quentin State Prison, still in operation, as well as Alcatraz Island, which has been closed since the mid-1960s. Drinks and snacks are served on the ride.

SAN RAFAEL
Web Site: www.cityofsanrafael.org
Area Code: 415
Zip Codes: 94901, 94902, 94903
Post Office: 40 Bellam Boulevard, San Rafael, 800-275-8777
Police Station: 1400 5th Avenue, 415-485-3000
Library: 1100 East Street, San Rafael, 415-485-3323

CORTE MADERA, NOVATO, FAIRFAX

Corte Madera (8,300) is a less expensive part of the Bay Area where, according to the California Association of Realtors, you can expect to pay in the $600,000 range for a family home. The city boasts two shopping centers, the

Village at Corte Madera, and the Corte Madera Shopping Center. The best way to commute to the City is via the Larkspur Ferry. A little farther north, homes in **Novato** (47,085) are even more affordable, averaging just under $400,000. Novato quickly outgrew its dairy and fruit orchard days when developers built condominiums and inexpensive tract homes, but you will also find large estates hidden in the hills. Novato has the ingredients of classic suburbia, with sprawling malls, theaters, fast food eateries, and family restaurants. Saxophone giant Clarence Clemons lives here, and the $100 million Buck Center for Research in Aging set up its facilities in Novato. Perhaps the biggest challenge about taking up residence in sunny Novato is the commute to San Francisco. It's even longer and more arduous than the San Francisco commute from San Rafael, although the Larkspur Ferry is an excellent option. Away from busy Highway 101, **Fairfax** is a charming small town with a quaint downtown and plenty of open space for hiking, biking, horseback riding, and pondering life. The Fairfax-Bolinas Road is not only scenic, but provides access to the coast. Fairfax's claim to fame is being home of the mountain bike, which was "invented" here in 1974. Other than the long commute to the City, the only other negative Fairfax residents must contend with is the risk of flooding from the creeks each winter.

CORTE MADERA
Web Site: www.ci.corte-madera.ca.us
Area Code: 415
Zip Codes: 94925
Post Office: Main, 7 Pixely Avenue, Corte Madera, 800-275-8777
Police Station: 950 Doherty Drive, Larkspur, 415-927-5150
Library: 707 Meadowsweet Drive, Corte Madera, 415-924-4844

NOVATO
Web Site: www.ci.novato.ca.us
Area Code: 415
Zip Codes: 94945, 94948, 94949
Post Office: 1537 South Novato Boulevard, 800-275-8777
Police Station: 908 Sherman Avenue, 415-897-4378
Library: 1720 Novato Boulevard, 415-898-4623

FAIRFAX
Web Site: www.mo.com/fairfax
Area Code: 415
Zip Codes: 94930
Post Office: 773 Center Boulevard, 800-275-8777
Police Station: 144 Bolinas Road, 415-453-5330
Library: 2097 Sir Francis Drake Boulevard

WEST MARIN COUNTY

Though much of Marin County is super expensive, many of the homes in West Marin, which includes the coastal communities of **Muir Beach**, **Stinson Beach**, **Bolinas**, **San Geronimo Valley** (www.sgvalley.marin.ca.us), **Nicasio**, **Olema**, **Inverness**, **Point Reyes Station** (www.pointreyes.net), **Tomales** (http://tomales.com) **Marshall**, and **Dillon Beach**, are more affordable. To discourage tourists, residents of Bolinas have been known to tear down the town's street sign, indicating the turn-off. Point Reyes National Seashore is the area's crown jewel, as well as Tomales Bay, which is famous for its oysters. Filmmaker George Lucas (Star Wars) has his ranch and headquarters in Nicasio along Lucas Valley Road. Up in Marshall, the Strauss family pioneered organic milk. In addition to Strauss milk, they also make butter and yogurt. Check your local health food store for the "skinny." Throughout many of these towns you'll find homes, complete with redwoods and acreage, that can still be purchased for under $350,000. Recently, about 800 new homes were built around San Geronimo and its golf course. In addition to hiking, biking, and horseback riding, introspective residents of San Geronimo may meditate at the Spirit Rock Meditation Center, 6360 Sir Francis Drake Boulevard.

SONOMA COUNTY

SANTA ROSA
SONOMA

Adjacent to Marin County, Sonoma County consists of rolling, green, tree- or vineyard-covered hills, dramatic coastline, seamless skies, glorious weather (most of the time), and some of the world's top chefs. Derived from the Indian word meaning "many moons," Sonoma County along with neighboring Napa County, is internationally known for the wines produced in this region. Hundreds of wineries dot the countryside, most offering free tastings. Visitors from around the country come to the wine country to sample the fare and learn about the fine art of making wine. Architecturally, the housing options range from apartments and condominiums to single-family homes and stately Victorians. You'll also find farms and ranches, mobile home parks, and summer cottages.

SONOMA COUNTY
Web Site: www.sonoma-county.org
Area Code: 707
Zip Codes: 95403, 95404, 95405, 95406, 95476

Sheriff: 600 Administration Drive, Santa Rosa, 707-565-2650

Emergency Hospitals: Community Hospital, 3325 Chanate Road, Santa Rosa, 707-576-4000; Palm Drive Hospital, 501 Petaluma Avenue, Sebastopol, 707-823-8511; Santa Rosa Memorial, 1165 Montgomery Drive, Santa Rosa, 707-546-3210; Sonoma Valley Hospital, 347 Andrieux Street, Sonoma, 707-935-5000

Libraries: Sonoma County Library, Petaluma Branch, 100 Fairgrounds Drive, 707-763-9801

Public Schools: Sonoma County Office of Education, 5340 Skylane Boulevard, Santa Rosa, www.sonoma.k12.ca.us, 707-524-2600

Community Publications: *Santa Rosa Press Democrat*, 427 Mendocino Avenue, Santa Rosa, 707-546-2020, www.pressdemocrat.com; *Marin Independent Journal*, 150 Alameda Del Prado, Novato, 415-883-8600, www.marinij.com

Community Resources: Sonoma Valley Chamber of Commerce, 651-A Broadway, Sonoma, 707-996-1033; Sonoma Community Center, 707-938-4626; Sonoma Valley Jazz Society, 707-769-4635; Sonoma Valley Chorale, 707-996-4200; Sonoma County Farm Trails, 800-207-9464, www.farmtrails.org; Sonoma County Regional Parks, 707-565-2041

Public Transportation: *Sonoma County Transit*, 800-345-7433, www.transitinfo.org

SANTA ROSA

Santa Rosa is the county seat, located 50 miles north of San Francisco in central Sonoma County. City officials here are picky about the look of new buildings and businesses, so you'll find Santa Rosa easy on the eyes. Despite the close tabs kept on development, Santa Rosa is growing, as is traffic congestion, especially going "cross-town" from east to west or vice versa. Highway 101, which splits the city in two going north and south is probably too narrow for the enormous number of vehicles it must handle on a daily basis. Highway officials were not prepared for the influx of people. According to the California Association of Realtors, the October 2000 median price for a home in this picturesque town was $275,000.

SANTA ROSA

Web Site: www.ci.santa-rosa.ca.us

Zip Codes: 95403, 95404, 95405, 95406

Area Code: 707

Post Office: 730 2nd Street, 800-275-8777

Police: 965 Sonoma Avenue, 707-543-3600

Library: Santa Rosa Branch of the Sonoma County Library, 3rd & E streets, 707-545-0831

SONOMA

The City of Sonoma, to the southeast of Santa Rosa, is a prime spot in Northern California for just plain good living and excellent wine tasting near-by. A picture-postcard community, rich in history, culinary treasures, and health resorts, Sonoma is a wonderful corner of the world. If you have to tran-sit to San Francisco though, plan on at least one hour each way in the car, longer by bus. Architecturally, the single-family homes are predominantly ranch and traditional style, built between 1950 and 1970. The median price for a home here in October 2000 was $367,500, an increase of 42.2% from the previous year.

SONOMA
Web Site: www.sonomacity.org
Area Code: 707
Zip Codes: 95476
Post Office: 617 Broadway, 800-275-8777
Police: 171 1st Street West, 707-996-3602
Library: Sonoma Branch of the Sonoma County Library, 755 Napa Street, 707-996-5217

NAPA COUNTY

ST. HELENA, RUTHERFORD, YOUNTVILLE, NAPA, CALISTOGA

East of Sonoma County, lies Napa Valley, a place where you can indulge your taste buds with fine wine and gourmet meals. With a mild, Mediterranean-like climate, Napa Valley produces hundreds of thousands of gallons of wine includ-ing zinfandel, merlot, cabernet, pinot noir, and chardonnay. Here in the valley, premier grapes are grown on the vine, then aged in the casks, and finally bot-tled and corked with an end result rivaling the best in France. On weekends, thousands of wine lovers take to Highway 29, the road that runs north-south through Napa County, stopping along the way at the vineyards, wineries, and picturesque small towns, such as **St. Helena**, **Rutherford**, and **Yountville**. A typical day visit might begin with one or two tastings in the cool basement of a winery, followed by a picnic lunch break in a park, then a few more wineries before dinner. If you enjoy wine and bucolic hills, it's a delightful way to spend a day. Better yet, it might be an ideal place to call home.

The city of **Napa** is the center of county government. If the hot air from the politicians is too much, try hot air ballooning, an ideal way to soar in Napa's often-sunny skies fanned by gentle breezes. Set up house here, and you can sample the wine year round. Average price in October 2000 was $240,000.

Calistoga, at the northern end of the Napa Valley, attracts people ready to be pampered with a mud bath, herbal wrap, mineral bath, and/or a massage. (For more see the **Quick Getaways** chapter.) There's also a natural geyser, called the Old Faithful (not to be confused with Yellowstone's Old Faithful) that shoots 350°-water sixty feet into the air. The owner claims Old Faithful acts erratically about 2 to 14 days before the area's about to experience a significant earthquake. It's not yet conclusive whether Old Faithful predicted the September 2000, 5.2 magnitude earthquake that struck Napa County. The quake, the epicenter of which was in the town of Yountville, about 6 miles northwest of Napa, caused millions of dollars worth of damage to buildings and hospitalized one person.

NAPA COUNTY

Web Site: www.co.napa.ca.us
Area Code: 707
Zip Codes: 94558, 94559, 94574, 94508
Sheriff: 1125 Third Street, Napa, 707-253-4440
Libraries: Napa City-County Library, 580 Coombs Street, 707-253-4241
Public Schools: Napa Valley Unified School District, 2425 Jefferson Street, Napa, 707-253-3715, www.nvusd.k12.ca.us
Community Publications: *The Napa Valley Register*, 1615 Second Street, Napa, 707-226-3711; *St. Helena Star*, 1328 Main Street, St. Helena, 707-967-5167
Community Resources: Community Resources for Children, 5 Financial Plaza #224, Napa, 707-253-0366; Napa Walk-In Center, 3295 Claremont Way, Napa, 707-224-4309; NCRIMS (Rental Mediation), 1714 Jefferson Street, Napa, 707-253-2700; Wildlife Rescue, P.O. Box 2571, 707-224-4295; The Petrified Forest, 707-942-6667; Old Faithful Geyser, 707-942-6463; Bothe-Napa Valley State Park, 800-444-7275; Napa County Historical Society, 1219 First Street, 707-224-1739; Napa Valley Museum, 55 Presidents Circle, Yountville, 707-944-0500; Napa Community Resources Department, 1100 West Street, 707-257-9529
Public Transportation: *CalTrain*, 800-660-4287; *Napa Valley Transit*, 800-696-6443, www.transitinfo.org; *Napa Valley Wine Train*, 800-427-4124, www.winetrain.com

SOLANO COUNTY

FAIRFIELD, VACAVILLE
VALLEJO

East of Napa County, Solano County is one of the fastest growing counties in the Bay Area, with housing developments and new businesses springing up, from Vallejo in the southwestern corner of the county to Vacaville and Fairfield farther inland. So called "refugees from the big city" seem to be arriving en masse and are snatching up many of the new homes. From October 1999 to October 2000, home prices in Solano County increased 23% (from $158,000 to $195,000), which gives certain indication of where things are headed. Crime rates are relatively low here and schools, in general, are better than their counterparts in San Francisco and Oakland.

SOLANO COUNTY
Web Site: www.co.solano.ca.us
Area Code: 707
Zip Codes: 94533, 94587, 95687, 95688, 94589, 94590
Sheriff: 530 Union Avenue, Suite 100, Fairfield, 707-421-7040
Libraries: Solano County Library, 1150 Kentucky Street, Fairfield, 707-421-6500
Public Schools: Solano County Office of Education, Superintendent's Office, 5100 Business Center Drive, Fairfield, 707-399-4402, www.solanoco.k12.ca.us
Community Publications: *Vallejo Times Herald*, 440 Curtola Parkway, Vallejo, 707-644-1141; *Daily Republic*, 1250 Texas Street, 707-425-4646; *Vacaville Reporter*, 318 Main Street, Vacaville, 707-448-6401; *Benicia Herald*, P.O. Box 65, Benicia, 707-745-0733; *Dixon Tribune*, 145 East A Street, Dixon, 916-678-5594; *River News Herald and Journal*, P.O. Box 786, Rio Vista, 707-374-6431
Community Resources: Six Flags Marine World, 2001 Marine World Parkway, 707-643-6722, www.sixflags.com; Solano County Fair, 707-644-4401; Solano County Family and Children Services, 100 Cement Hill Road, Suite 500, Fairfield, 707-427-6600
Public Transportation: *Vallejo Baylink Ferry*, 800-640-2877; *Vallejo Transit Buses*, 800-640-2877; *Vacaville City Coach*, 707-449-6000; *Fairfield-Suisun Transit*, 707-422-2877; *RIDES*, 800-755-POOL, www.rides.org

FAIRFIELD, VACAVILLE

Fairfield and Vacaville are typical American towns, with tract homes, apartment complexes, duplexes, townhouses, strip malls, and shopping centers. They are located northeast of San Francisco along Interstate 80 and offer easy access to

University of California at Davis and the state capital in Sacramento. Fairfield plays happy host to Travis Air Force Base, one of the few military installations left open in California. Vacaville's claim to fame is the local state prison that cares for mentally ill inmates.

FAIRFIELD
Web Site: www.fairfieldcity.com
Area Code: 707
Zip Codes: 94533, 94587
Post Office: 600 Kentucky Street, 800-275-8777
Police: 1000 Webster, 707-428-7307
Library: Fairfield Branch, 1150 Kentucky Street, 707-421-6510

VACAVILLE
Web Site: www.ci.vacaville.ca.us
Area Code: 707
Zip Codes: 95688, 95687
Post Office: 98 Cernon Street,
Police: 630 Merchant Street, 707-449-5200
Library: Vacaville Branch, 1020 Ulatis Drive, 707-449-6290

VALLEJO

In January 1999, the *San Francisco Chronicle* listed housing in Vallejo as among the lowest priced housing in the Bay Area, with the median price range near $159,000. Because of its affordability, many people are moving to Vallejo and commuting the 32 miles to San Francisco. The high-speed Vallejo Catamaran can cross the Bay, from Vallejo to the San Francisco Ferry Building, in 55 minutes. Commuting by car would take you almost double the time due to traffic.

Founded by General Mariano G. Vallejo in 1844, Vallejo originated as an important shipping and naval center. Around that time, a temporary capital building was built in Vallejo in 1852, but because of the area's lack of housing the legislature moved up to Sacramento. In 1853 a devastating flood then brought the legislature back to Vallejo, but they were still dissatisfied, and moved on to Benicia, and then later returned to Sacramento.

Today, Vallejo (population 118,700) is the largest city in Solano County. It is best known for being home to Six Flags Marine World, a large outdoor theme and animal park. In addition to Marine World, Vallejo has an outside farmer's market, a golf course (rated by the *Examiner* as the third best in the state), a yacht club, and California Maritime Academy, a California State University School. In 1996, the Mare Island Shipyards closed, and the city is now in the process of converting the 5,460 acres to civilian use. Part of the conversion includes an estimated $81 million environmental cleanup of lead-based paint, petroleum waste and other toxic remnants left in the shipyard.

Architecturally, you'll find an eclectic mix of homes, from beautifully restored Victorians to tract homes. In the Northgate, Mare Island, and Hiddenbrooke Golf Course neighborhoods, more than 3,300 units are being built, in addition to the already completed 1,000. The City of Vallejo is at a crossroads, with new plans and developments in the making. Many fleeing San Francisco's high prices and congestion are settling here.

VALLEJO
Web Site: www.ci.vallejo.ca.us
Area Code: 707
Zip Codes: 94589, 94590, 94591
Post Office: 485 Santa Clara Street, 800-275-8777
Police: 111 Amador Street, 707-648-4553
Library: John F. Kennedy Library, 505 Santa Clara Street, 707-553-5568

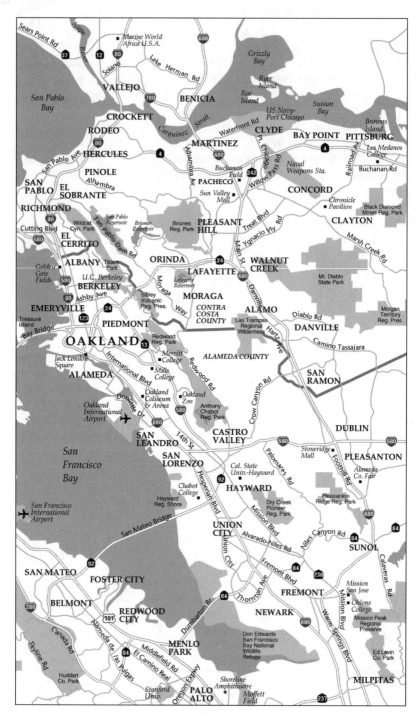

EAST BAY

EAST BAY
(ALAMEDA AND CONTRA COSTA COUNTIES)

ALAMEDA COUNTY

HAYWARD, FREMONT, NEWARK, UNION CITY
ALAMEDA
EMERYVILLE
ALBANY
PIEDMONT
OAKLAND
BERKELEY

The East Bay is the most densely populated region of the Bay Area, from Crockett and Hercules at the northern end; through Pinole, Richmond, El Cerrito, Albany, Berkeley, Oakland, and Alameda in the center; to San Leandro, Castro Valley, Hayward, Union City, and Fremont on the southern end; and Livermore, Pleasanton, Dublin, Concord, Walnut Creek, Martinez, Pittsburg, and Antioch out east. In fact, the East Bay contains so many enclaves it's difficult to generalize about life here, except to say that it's not San Francisco. For the most part, you'll find parking the car is not as arduous a task compared to the City, rents are somewhat lower, rental property is more available, and the weather is generally clearer and warmer than in San Francisco. However, the biggest drawback to living in the East Bay is commuting into the City by car. Fortunately, the entire area is served, and served well, by an extensive criss-crossing network of public transit systems, including buses, trains, and BART. Another asset is the Oakland International Airport, one of the friendliest airports you're likely to find anywhere in the United States. While officials at both San Francisco International Airport and San Jose International Airport often warn passengers about overflowing parking lots, their Oakland counterpart generally can proclaim hassle free parking at its gates.

Many fleeing San Francisco's exorbitant prices look to cities in the East Bay to call home. And the East Bay has a lot to offer. The lush parks offer hiking, biking, boating, picnicking, swimming and more. Berkeley's Tilden Park, the crown jewel of the park system, has hiking and biking trails, a swimming hole, a carousel, a petting zoo, a steam train and much more. Another escape to the outdoors is Mount Diablo State Park, located in eastern Contra Costa County. Not only is Mount Diablo the highest peak in the Bay Area, but it is also a popular weekend destination for hikers, campers, and families. Oakland's 122-acre saltwater Lake Merritt, spread out beneath the downtown Oakland skyline, hosts joggers, walkers, and bikers at all times of the day. You can even hire an authentic Venetian gondola to chauffeur you on a romantic glide across the lake. Lakeside Park, the park adjacent to Lake Merritt, hosts several public events, most notably the annual June Festival. This annual celebration includes live music, food booths, environmental education, arts and entertainment booths, as well as theatrical performances.

The East Bay contains several colleges and universities, most prominent of which is the University of California, Berkeley, or "Cal" (the only school in the University of California system so called). The California State University system has a campus in Hayward. Other private colleges and universities in the East Bay include Saint Mary's in the densely wooded community of Moraga, John F. Kennedy University in Orinda, and Mills College in Oakland. The northern environs of the East Bay are a stone's-throw away, if you've got a strong arm, from the University of California at Davis, Sacramento State University in Sacramento and the University of the Pacific in Stockton.

ALAMEDA COUNTY

Web Site: www.co.alameda.ca.us

Area Code: 510

Sheriff: 1401 Lakeside Drive, 12th Floor, 510-271-5198

Emergency Hospitals: Alameda Hospital, 2070 Clinton Avenue, 510-522-3700; Alameda County Medical Centers: Fairmont Hospital, 15400 Foothill Boulevard, San Leandro; Highland Hospital, 1411 East 31st. Street, Oakland, 510-534-8055; St. Rose Hospital, 27200 Calarogh Avenue, Hayward, 510-264-4000, Kaiser Medical Center, 27400 Hesperian Boulevard, Hayward, 510-784-4000; Alta Bates Medical Center, 2450 Ashby Avenue, Berkeley, 510-204-4444; Children's Hospital Oakland, 747 52nd Street, 510-428-3000

Library: 2450 Stevenson Boulevard, Fremont, 510-745-1500, www.aclibrary.org

Public Schools: Alameda County Unified School District, 510-887-0152, www.alameda-coe.k12.ca.us

Community Publications: *Oakland Tribune*, 510-208-6300; *East Bay Express*, 510-540-7400; Hills Newspapers, Incorporated, 510-339-8777, publications include: *The Berkeley Voice, El Cerrito Journal, The Montclarion, The Piedmonter*, and *Alameda Journal; The (East Bay) Monthly*, 510-658-9811; *East Bay Express*, 510-540-7400, *The Berkeley Daily Planet*, 510-841-5600; *The Daily Californian*, 510-548-8300

Community Resources: Alameda One-Stop Career Center, 510-748-2208; Bananas (information for child-care referrals) 510-658-0381; East Bay Regional Park District, 510-562-7275; Alameda County Children and Family Services, 510-259-1800; Eden Information and Referral for Social Services, 510-537-2552

Public Transportation: *AC (Alameda-Contra Costa) Transit*, 510-891-4777; *BART*, 510-465-2278; *Alameda-Oakland Ferry*, 510-522-3300; *Emery-Go-Round*, 510-451-3862; *RIDES*, 800-755-7665; *Amtrak*, 800-872-7245; *Greyhound*, 2103 San Pablo, Oakland, 510-832-4730

HAYWARD, FREMONT, NEWARK, UNION CITY

A sprawling, often hot, expanse of suburbia, **Hayward** (population 123,000) is complete with a standard fare of strip malls, shopping centers, gigantic car dealerships, and fast food restaurants. This family-oriented city includes a large Hispanic and Asian population. In the eastern part of the city, California State University at Hayward perches high atop a hill, offering dynamic views of the Bay Area below. Hayward is feeling the effects of the continuing tight housing market and is in the midst of a building frenzy. Many new residents are opting to live in Hayward and commute the 25 miles northeast to San Francisco or the 26 miles south to Silicon Valley.

The cities of **Fremont**, **Newark**, and **Union City** all lie to the south of Hayward, and are similar in appearance, socio-economic components, housing options and the like. According to the *San Francisco Chronicle*, in 1999 the National Public Health and Hospital Institute ranked Fremont as the number one city in America for overall child welfare. Contributing to the ranking were Fremont's low rates of infant mortality, teen pregnancy, and childhood poverty.

Area residents frequent Lake Elizabeth for boating, walking, and picnics. For local shopping, the New Park Mall in Newark is one of the busiest malls in the Bay Area, and Union City has a new shopping center on Alvarado-Niles Street with a gigantic theater.

HAYWARD
Web Site: www.ci.hayward.ca.us
Area Code: 510
Zip Codes: 94538, 94541, 94542, 94544, 94545
Post Offices: 822 C Street; 24438 Santa Clara Street; 2163 Aldengate Way, 800-275-8777
Police: Hayward Police Department, 300 West Winton Avenue, 510-293-7272
Library: Hayward Main Library, 835 C Street, 510-293-8685; Weekes Branch, 27300 Patrick Avenue, 510-782-2155

FREMONT
Web Site: www.ci.fremont.ca.us
Area Code: 510
Zip Codes: 94536, 94538, 94539, 94555
Post Offices: Fremont: 37010 Dusterberry Way; 160 J Street; 41041 Trimboli Way; 43456 Ellsworth Street; 240 Francisco Lane, 800-275-8777
Library: Fremont Main Library, 2400 Stevenson Boulevard, 510-745-1400

NEWARK
Web Site: www.ci.newark.ca.us
Area Code: 510
Zip Code: 94560
Post Office: Newark Post Office, 6250 Thornton Avenue, 800-275-8777
Library: 6300 Civic Terrace Avenue, 510-795-2627

UNION CITY
Web Site: www.ci.union-city.ca.us
Area Code: 510
Zip Code: 94587
Post Office: Main Post Office, 33170 Alvarado-Niles Road, 800-275-8777
Library: 34007 Alvarado-Niles Road, 510-745-7464

ALAMEDA

Located just south of Oakland, the City of Alameda (population 80,000) is mostly an island, tucked alongside the East Bay. Flat as a pancake with one long beach, a number of bridges and tunnels connect Alameda to the mainland. In the late 1800s Alameda was a popular resort for San Franciscans and Oaklanders who sought its mild climate and comfortable sand. The seawater was even heated to accommodate nighttime swimmers, and, until 1961, folks could play at an amusement park. During WW II, the Navy built the Alameda Naval Air Station, creating a bustling Naval Base. However, in 1997, Congress decommissioned the base, and today it is slowly being converted into a business and entertainment center, home to several software and entertainment companies, including Manex Entertainment, and Bladium Sports. Lucent Technologies and Chevron have also set up shop in Alameda. Another recent addition to the base is the terminal for the Alameda to San Francisco Ferry. Alameda hasn't fully recovered from its button-down Navy days as is evidenced by the downtown area, which still feels small and unpolished, as though from another era. Compared to the frenzy of much of the rest of the Bay Area, it seems local residents appreciate the calm, unsophisticated environment. Alameda has all your basic shopping needs, though not generally in the form of chain stores, and it is centrally located.

Crown Memorial Beach, equipped with picnic tables and showers, is a mile-and-a-half beach, good for beginning windsurfers and kite boarders (you'll have to see it to believe it). Washington Park, just before Crown Memorial Beach, has a number of tennis courts, a baseball field, and a new dog park. Don't take your dogs to the beach as you may receive a big fine. Butting right up next to the Oakland International Airport, you can play golf at the Chuck Corica Golf Complex, on Harbor Bay Island, One Clubhouse Memorial Road, 510 864-3424.

Architecturally, Alameda has some of the most beautifully restored Victorians in the Bay Area. You'll also find a few that haven't yet been renovated, and you may be lucky enough to find one at a decent price. Late in 2000 the vacancy rate in Alameda was under five percent. According to the California Association of Realtors, in October 2000, the average family home ran about $397,000, but that is quickly rising. Certainly, as Alameda dusts off its old navy image, it will become a more sought after locale with higher prices to match.

ALAMEDA

Web Site: www.ci.alameda.ca.us
Area Code: 510
Zip Codes: 94501, 94502
Post Offices: 2201 Shoreline Drive; 1333 Park Avenue, #A; 1415 Webster Street, 800-275-8777
Police: Alameda Police Department, 1555 Oak Street, 510-748-4508
Library: Alameda Main Library, 2200 A Central Avenue, 510-748-4660
Public Schools: Alameda County Unified School District, 313 West Winton Avenue, Hayward 94544, 510-887-0152, www.alameda-coe.k12.ca.us.
Community Resources: Alameda Park and Recreation Department, 1327 Oak Street, 510-748-4565; Alameda Chamber of Commerce, 2447 Santa Clara Avenue, Suite 302, 51-521-8677; Altarena Playhouse, 1409 Hyde Street, 510-523-1553; Bill Osborne Model Airplane Field on Doolittle Street, 510-522-3128; Alameda Historical Museum, 2324 Alameda Avenue, 510-521-1233; USS Hornet Museum, Alameda Point, Pier 3, 510-521-8448; Alameda Civic Light Opera, 2200 Central Avenue, 510-864-2256

EMERYVILLE

Sandwiched between Oakland and Berkeley and virtually at the foot of the Bay Bridge, Emeryville was originally an industrial area, with not much else happening. By the late 1980s and early 1990s, the 1.2 square-mile city decided to change. The city converted old industrial sites into huge shopping centers, warehouses became loft-style apartments and offices, and new apartments and condominiums were constructed. Today about 8,000 people call Emeryville home, and about 25,000 commute here to work for businesses such as Chiron (biotech), Sybase (software), and Pixar (the computer animation company that created *Toy Story* and *A Bug's Life*). Ongoing construction includes two new hotels, 1,000 more housing units, and the Bay Street development project which, when complete, will be a retail and entertainment center.

To help the 25,000 employees get to and from the BART station, Emeryville has a free shuttle, the Emery-Go-Round, which transports people to BART and around the city. Others do their daily commute via the new Amtrak

Station, 5885 Landregan Street, 510-450-1080. In addition, bike paths wind throughout the city. Another progressive attribute of Emeryville is a city-run daycare facility, known as the Child Development Center, 1220 53rd Street, 510-596-4343. The Center operates year-round and provides childcare services for 90 infants and toddlers whose parents are working, in training, or in school. In 1999 Ex'pressions, www.xnewmedia.com, 877-833-8800, a college devoted exclusively to digital visual media and sound arts technology, opened its doors. Many of its students plan future careers in the entertainment industries or in high-tech companies.

Most Emeryville residents live in some kind of rental situation, with apartment complexes, condominiums or loft warehouses the most common housing types here. There are some single-family detached homes in "the triangle" area, on San Pablo Avenue. Here, you'll find mostly Craftsman style houses built in the early 1920s and '30s. Waterfront living is available at the 1970s era Watergate Condominiums, which have a spectacular view of the Bay and the City. Other Emeryville residents live in the 30-story Pacific Park Plaza with its 650 condominium units.

While many of Emeryville's 'original' loft residents were artists, today professionals are taking up residence in the unique spaces created in these old industrial buildings. Emeryville's population is mostly young, single, professionals and students, though a number of families are arriving. Once considered one of the last of affordable housing areas in the Bay Area, here too prices have skyrocketed. In 1999 a townhouse listed at $150,000, one year later that same unit almost doubled in price.

Numerous chain stores, such as Borders, Good Guys, Trader Joes, and Ross Dress For Less occupy space in Emeryville. Just recently, the international retailer IKEA opened a monstrous, 274,000-square-foot (equivelent to five football fields) store. People from all over the Bay Area come here in droves. For food, the Emeryville Public Market, 5800 Shellmound, is a favorite with its inexpensive ethnic dishes, from Korean BBQ to French crepes to Japanese noodles, served cafeteria style.

EMERYVILLE

Web Site: www.ci.emeryville.ca.us
Area Code: 510
Zip Code: 94608
Post Office: Emeryville Branch, 1585 62nd Street, 800-275-8777
Police: Emeryville Police Department, 2449 Powell Street, 510-596-3700
Library: Golden Gate Library, 5606 San Pablo Avenue, 510-597-5023
Public Schools: Emeryville Unified School District, 4727 San Pablo Avenue, 510-655-6936, www.emeryusd.k12.ca.us
Community Resources: Emeryville Chamber of Commerce, 5858 Horton Street, 510-652-5223; Emeryville Senior Center, 4321 Salem Street, 510-

596-3730, Emeryville Child Development Center, 1220 53rd Street, 510-596-4343; Recreation Department, 4300 San Pablo Avenue, 510-596-4395; Emery-Go-Round Free Shuttle, 510-451-3862; First Time Homebuyers Program, 2200 Powell Street, Suite 1200, 510-596-4350

ALBANY

Just north of Berkeley, Albany is one of the Bay Area's best-kept secrets. Like Emeryville, it's small—just a little over one square mile, with about 18,000 residents. Local public schools are considered better than average, and parents who live in other cities have been known to stretch the truth a tad in order to have their children attend Albany schools. The crime rate is among the lowest in the region, and Albany is located only 30 to 50 minutes from downtown San Francisco. Housing includes a number of single-family homes as well as apartments from the 1940s and '50s. The median price for a home in October 2000 was $390,500, an increase of 28% from the previous year.

The commercial strip of Solano Avenue is shared with Berkeley. Once a railroad thoroughfare, Solano Avenue now offers day-to-day services and shopping options, all within walking distance from most parts of Albany. Among the selection here are bookstores, boutique clothing stores, restaurants, cafes, a supermarket, and a movie theater. Locals rave about Rivoli Restaurant, 1539 Solano Avenue. Each fall the mile-long stretch of Solano Avenue is closed for the "Solano Avenue Stroll," a weekend festival of food, music and entertainment.

ALBANY
Web Site: www.albanyca.org
Area Code: 510
Zip Code: 94706
Post Office: 1191 Solano Avenue, 510-649-3135
Police: Albany Police Department, 1000 San Pablo Avenue, 510-525-7300
Library: Albany Main Library, 1247 Marin Avenue, 510-526-3720
Public Schools: Albany Unified School District, 904 Talbot Avenue, 510-558-3750
Community Resources: Albany Chamber of Commerce, 510-525-1771; Albany Recreation Community Services, 1249 Marin Avenue, 510-524-9283; Solano Avenue Association, 1563 Solano Avenue, #101, 510-527-5358

PIEDMONT

Surrounded by Oakland, but a city in itself, **Piedmont** is one of the wealthiest communities in the East Bay—and indeed the Bay Area. Incorporated in 1907 and only 1.8-square miles in size, Piedmont is a tiny enclave of large estates, mansions, tennis courts, immaculate wooded parks, and civility. This city is also known for its excellent school district. Don't go looking for an apartment here, you won't find one. As a matter of fact, rental property of any type is virtually non-existent here. If the name Piedmont rings a bell for you it may be because the local high school has for years been the host of a national bird-calling contest, the winners of which are invited to appear on "The Tonight Show."

PIEDMONT
Area Code: 510
Zip Codes: 94611, 94610, 94618, 94612
Post Office: (nearest one) 195 41st Street, Oakland, 800-275-8777
Police: Piedmont Police Department, 401 Highland Avenue, 510-420-3000
Community Resources: City Hall, 120 Vista Avenue, 510-420-3040;
    Recreation Department, 358 Hillside Avenue

OAKLAND

DOWNTOWN OAKLAND
LAKE MERRITT
MONTCLAIR
CLAREMONT HILLS
ROCKRIDGE

Across the Bay in Oakland is another Mayor Brown, but he's not related to San Francisco's Mayor Willie Brown. Here Mayor Jerry Brown, former Governor of California (1975-1983) and three-time presidential candidate, is making waves in Oakland. With people and companies being priced out of San Francisco, many have sought 'shelter' in Oakland, and Mayor Brown has welcomed them with open arms and business tax incentives. Housing costs are moderate here too, at least when compared to much of the rest of the Bay Area. The median home price in October 2000 was $263,000.

For sports fan, living in Oakland means you'll have a number of professional teams to root for. Oakland is home to the NFL's Raiders, Major League Baseball's Oakland Athletics (A's), and the NBA's Golden State Warriors. The A's and the Raiders play at the Oakland-Alameda County Coliseum complex known as the Oakland Coliseum, and the Warriors play at the Oakland Arena, off I-880 in southern Oakland.

In the 1930s, Oakland was a cluster of ranches, farms, and lavish summer estates. A lot has changed since then. The birthplace of the Black power movement and home to the World Series winning Oakland A's, Oakland is a happening place with all the amenities that a city of almost 400,000 can offer. Although much of Oakland is green, and middle-class, a high crime rate and

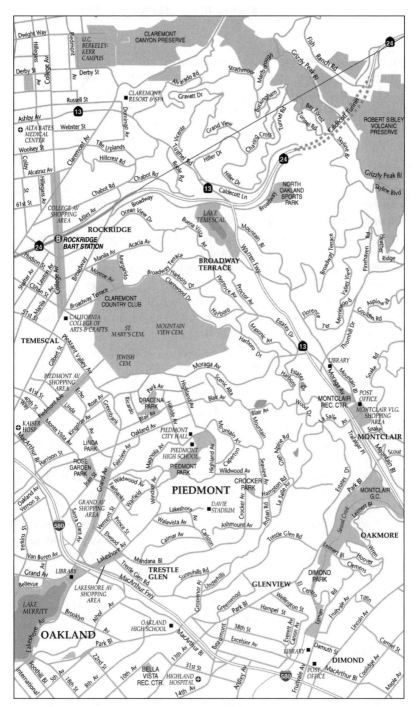

OAKLAND

impoverished areas have tarnished its reputation in the past few decades. The neighborhoods that make up Oakland are as different as water and oil. Generally speaking, the more upscale neighborhoods are found higher up on the hills, complete with Bay views; down the hills and further west are what many would consider the rougher neighborhoods. Today Oakland is certainly at a crossroads, moving away from its gritty past and diminished reputation. According to the city, between 1999 and 2000, rents throughout Oakland increased about 30%.

Under Mayor Brown, Oakland is developing quickly. The newly built federal government offices of the twin towers were just the beginning of **Downtown Oakland's** facelift. Since Brown became mayor in 1999, several new office buildings have gone up, many of which will be home to hi-tech companies. Also, about 4,600 housing units are under construction plus another 1,000 units are in the pipeline. Old Oakland, adjacent to the City Center, has a collection of vintage Victorian buildings that were spared from the bulldozer. Known as Preservation Park, this area is a commercial zone, and has a lovely fountain in the center. Paramount Theater, an art deco landmark, is another highlight of downtown Oakland.

A world-class port, Oakland's waterfront teems with activity, bringing in an estimated $25 billion dollars worth of goods each year, mostly from Asia. Situated next to the boats, Jack London Square is a destination place to dine, shop, and stroll along the waterfront, much like San Francisco's Pier 39, only not as crowded. Here, you can eat sushi and listen to jazz at the popular Yoshi's Jazz and Sushi Club, 510 Embarcadero West. Also located at the Pier is Franklin Delano Roosevelt's 165-foot USS Potomac, which was frequented by the late president, close advisors, and congressional leaders for informal strategy sessions. Every Sunday locals gather at the Pier for the farmer's market. You can also take the ferry into San Francisco. Just across the street from the square is the relatively new Amtrak Station, 245 2nd Street.

If you want to be near downtown, but also feel like you are away from the bustle of the city, Lake Merritt may be a viable option. Around **Lake Merritt** are abundant apartments in older brick buildings from the 1920s, two- and three-bedroom homes from the 1940s and '50s, and condos from the 1960s and '70s. In the early 19th century, elite estates were built around the lake. Only one home remains today, the Camron Stanford House, 1418 Lakeside. Lake Merritt residents who work downtown enjoy a quick commute.

In October 1991 a fire struck the Oakland Hills destroying more than 2,500 homes and killing 25 people. Fire investigators believe an arsonist set the fire that raged for days in the hills above the city. Responding fire trucks had a difficult time trying to navigate the narrow, winding, and tree-lined roads. As a result, Oakland implemented new fire codes and constructed roads wide enough to allow emergency vehicle accessibility to outlying areas. A mural at the Rockridge Bart Station commemorates the fire victims. One of the areas hardest hit by the fires was the upscale **Montclair** district. New construction here is evident, as many of the homes destroyed in the fire have been rebuilt. The homes immediately surrounding the main shopping area along Mountain Boulevard are wood-framed stuccos with a Mediterranean look, built shortly after the fire. Many of these pricey, Mediterranean-styled Craftsman bungalows are nearly hidden by trees and are neighbors to rambling redwood and glass homes perched atop stilts. Some of these homes are blessed with views of the Bay and San Francisco or simply an expanse of redwoods. There are a several apartment complexes in Montclair as well. Many Montclair residents commute into San Francisco which, without traffic, is only 15 to 20 minutes; with traffic it's sometimes triple that. While a pricey district for Oakland, housing here is considerably less costly than San Francisco. Even so, property values doubled between 1998 and 2000.

The **Claremont Hills** area, just north of Montclair, also suffered from the fire of 1991. These wooded environs have large dwellings mixed in with a smattering of smaller, sometimes student-occupied homes. There are few apartments in this section of town as well. Access to Interstate 24 makes commuting to San Francisco or the South Bay easier. Nearby Redwood Regional Park provides for miles of secluded serenity amidst the redwoods.

Of all the areas that make up Oakland, many would argue that **Rockridge**, located south of Berkeley, offers the quintessential "neighborhood" feel. Created after the 1906 earthquake destroyed San Francisco, this former hayfield originally was developed as a racially exclusive housing tract. Today, the area known as Lower Rockridge (between Claremont and Broadway) is an ethnically diverse and upscale area. In fact, many consider this to be one of Oakland's hippest neighborhoods. Some students and employees of UC live here, and many young professionals commuting into San Francisco or the South Bay call Rockridge home. BART's central location at College and Shafter makes the commute a breeze. Homes here are typically stucco and wood shingled Craftsman-style bungalows with small cottage gardens. Residents can stroll along tree-lined streets to the gourmet restaurants and trendy shops clustered around the strip of College Avenue, between Alcatraz and Broadway.

Upper Rockridge (above Broadway), built during the post-war housing booms of the 1920s and 1940s, extends into the hills northeast toward Lake Temescal. Many of the homes destroyed in the 1991 fire were replaced by a unique "tract" of million-dollar custom homes. As a result, housing is expensive in Rockridge, with median home prices in 2000 ranging well above the $500,000 mark. Apartments are scarce as the area has zoning restrictions on buildings with more than four units. Finding a rental here is easiest in the early summer when many UC students go home for the break. Any rentals below $1,500 are difficulty to come by.

Shopping and eating are main attractions in Rockridge. Market Hall, 5655 College Avenue, touts a European-style shopping experience with specialty grocery shops located under one open-air roof. Restaurants here reflect the ethnic diversity of Oakland and include several Mexican eateries as well as Ethiopian, Italian, Japanese, Chinese, and Irish cuisine. Specialty pizza at Zachary's, 5801 College Avenue, is always standing room only, while up the street you can dip into the sushi boats at Isobune, 5897 College Avenue. Coffee shops (Peaberry's at Market Hall, 5655 College Avenue, and the Royal, 6255 College Avenue) and comfortable pubs with well-lit pool tables cater to locals as well as UC students that filter down from Berkeley. Oakland's own Dreyer's Ice Cream Company at 5925 College Avenue is headquartered here and is complete with a sampling shop. Comfort foods—macaroni and cheese, rice crispy treats, and the like—can be had at The Red Tractor, 5634 College Avenue. Also along College Avenue are fine antique shops, art galleries, and clothing boutiques. Children's toys can be found at Rockridge Kids, 5511 College Avenue, and Cotton & Company, 5901 College Avenue. For those looking for a good book, the Sierra Club bookstore, 6014 College Avenue, Pendragon's new and used books, 5560 College Avenue, and a brand new branch library, 5366 College Avenue, should satisfy most literary tastes.

The public schools for this district are Hillcrest Elementary and Middle School (K-8, enrollment about 275) and Chabot Elementary (K-5, enrollment about 350). In both schools students' STAR achievement test scores are well into the 80th percentile for reading and math, rating them among the highest of the Oakland Unified School District.

OAKLAND
Web Site: www.ci.oakland.ca.us, www.rockridge.org
Area Code: 510
Zip Codes: 94601-94627, 94643, 94649, 94659, 94660, 94661, 94662, 94666
Main Post Office: 1675 Seventh Avenue, 800-275-8777
Police: Oakland Police Department, 455 7th Street, 510-238-3365
Libraries: Oakland Public Library, Main Branch, 125 14th Street, 510-238-3134; Cesar Chavez Branch, 1900 Fruitvale Avenue, 510-535-5620; Montclair Branch, 1687 Mountain Boulevard, 510-482-7810; Rockridge Branch, 5366 College Avenue, 510-597-5017
Public Schools: Oakland Unified School District, 1025 Second Avenue, Oakland 94606, 510-879-8100, www.ousd.k12.ca.us
Community Publications: *Oakland Tribune*, 510-208-6300; *East Bay Express*, 510-540-7400; Hills Newspapers, Incorporated, 510-339-8777, publications include: *The Berkeley Voice, El Cerrito Journal, The Montclarion, The Piedmonter*, and *Alameda Journal; The (East Bay) Monthly*, 510-658-9811
Community Resources: East Bay Regional Park District, 2950 Peralta Oaks Court, P.O. Box 5381, Oakland, 94605, 510-562-PARK, www.ebparks.org; Alameda Arts Commission, P.O. Box 29004, Oakland, 510-208-9646;

Oakland Museum of California, 510-238-2200; Oakland East Bay Symphony, 510-444-0801; Oakland Ballet, 510-465-6400; Oakland Ensemble Theatre, 510-763-7774; Museum of Children's Art, 510-465-8770; Oakland Zoo, 9777 Golf Links Road, 510-632-9525; Pro Arts, Inc., 461 Ninth Street Oakland, www.proartsgallery.org; Oakland-Alameda County Coliseum, 510-569-2121; Chabot Observatory and Science Center, 10000 Skyline Boulevard, 510-530-3480; Oakland A's Baseball, 510-638-0500; www.oaklandathletics.com; Golden State Warriors Basketball, 510-986-2222; Lake Temescal Regional Recreation Area, 510-652-1155; California College of Arts & Crafts, 5212 Broadway, 510-655-4180; Oakland DMV, 5300 Claremont Avenue, 510-450-3670; Claremont Country Club, 5295 Broadway Terrace, 510-653-6789

BERKELEY

NORTH BERKELEY
BERKELEY HILLS
SOUTH BERKELEY
CLAREMONT, ELMWOOD
DOWNTOWN/CENTRAL BERKELEY
WEST BERKELEY

Nicknamed the "The People's Republic of Berkeley" and many other more or less affectionate monikers, Berkeley conjures images of student protests, hippies, Birkenstocks, counterculture and, above all, independent thinking. This was the first city in the nation to replace Columbus Day observances with Indigenous Peoples Day, honoring the Native Americans who lived here before Columbus arrived. The uproar caused when the Reverend Jerry Falwell claimed that the purple Teletubby, Tinky Winky, was homosexual resulted in the Berkeley City Council passing a resolution in support of this diminutive television character. More recently, traffic cops in Berkeley have handed out non-alcoholic beverage coupons to those caught driving safely and courteously, part of their Good Driver Recognition Program. (Rumor has it tickets to the movies are next.) With its colorful residents and liberal leanings, Berkeley beckons the young, the politically active, and those who seek an intellectual existence. Many find it a stimulating and relaxed place to call home. According to the California Association of Realtors, the median home price in Berkeley was $436,250 in October 2000.

Berkeley is home to about 107,000 people from all walks of life. University of California at Berkeley ("Cal") and Lawrence Livermore laboratory are the city's largest employers. Founded in 1868, Cal spreads out between the downtown area and the Berkeley hills, and has more than 30,000 undergraduate and graduate students in attendance. The reputation of today's students is not as liberal it was in the 1960s when Mario Savio rallied against the university's policies, sparking the free speech movement, and when Berkeley students protested the Vietnam War. Student activism was triggered again in the early 1990s when students protested Cal's South African investments. More recent protests revolve around obtaining student diversity. In addition to the heated discussions at the coffeehouses, Berkeley's milieu of evening entertainment includes 32 movie theatres, 31 bookstores and 414 restaurants—certainly a lot of food for thought.

North Berkeley, considered to be the calmer side of town, is home to many graduate students, professors, and young families. Strollers glide past the many American Craftsman-style bungalows, rolling over to the many small parks spread throughout the area. The children here literally are from all walks of life.

North on Shattuck Avenue, from Rose until Hearst, you'll find the "Gourmet Ghetto," which is equipped with restaurants and specialty shops. It was 1971 when Alice Waters pioneered serving organic food at her restaurant, Chez Panisse, 1517 Shattuck Avenue. She has since instigated serving organic foods in Berkeley's public schools. Waters opened another less formal restaurant, Cesars, 1515 Shattuck Avenue, which serves delicious (and organic) tapas. Other gourmet delights in this area include: the Cheese Board at 1512 Shattuck Avenue, for gourmet bread and pizza; Phoenix Pastificio, 1786 Shattuck Avenue, which sells homemade pasta, ravioli and olive bread; Cha'Am, 1543 Shattuck Avenue, a local favorite for Thai food; Saul's Deli, 1475 Shattuck Avenue, which makes the best matzo-ball soup in town; and the French Hotel at 1538 Shattuck Avenue is well known for its cappuccino and morning pastries. Intimate Walnut Square, between Walnut and Shattuck, is home to the original Peet's coffee store at 2124 Vine Street. Black Oak Books at 1491 Shattuck Avenue is an established independent and features guest authors several times a week. Additional shopping is available on Hopkins Street (known as "Gourmet Ghetto West"), home to Monterrey Market, 1550 Hopkins, Acme Bread, 1601 San Pablo Avenue, and another Waters' institution, Cafe Fanny, 1603 San Pablo Avenue, named after Alice's daughter.

Up in the **Berkeley Hills**, which run from the North Campus area, east to Berkeley's magnificent Tilden Park and then north to Kensington, you'll discover magnificent views and be surrounded by the lovely smell of eucalyptus. To get to the Berkeley Hills take either Euclid Avenue north all the way to Grizzly Peak, coming through Tilden Park at its northernmost entrance, or start at the football stadium and take Centennial Drive up to Grizzly Peak. Along your drive you'll see exquisite Craftsman-style homes, some with striking bay views and fabulous gardens. If you are willing to navigate the hill every day, you may be able to rent a room in one of these homes.

Along Euclid Street, you'll find that the higher you ascend, the more spectacular the homes. The Berkeley Rose Garden on Euclid Street (between Eunice and Bayview Place) offers great bay views and lovely aromas. For a romantic sunset, the benches at the top of the garden are front row seats. Travelling up the hills via the Centennial route will bring you to the Botanical Gardens in Strawberry Canyon. Considered one of the world's leading gardens in terms of plant variety and quality, the Botanical Gardens are home to Chinese medicinal herbs and soaring redwoods. Also on the hill is the Lawrence Hall of Science, which sports one of the best views of the city, not to mention a first rate public science center for people of all ages.

Visitors come from all over to enjoy the 2,065 acres of open meadows and forests of Tilden Park. There are 30 miles of hiking and horse trails, an 18-hole public golf course, swimming at Anza Lake, pony rides, a petting farm, carousel, and a steam train. There are no shopping options atop the hill so you'll need to take care of all your errands before heading up.

Located directly south of the campus and west of the Berkeley hills, **South Berkeley's** population is made up predominantly of students, many of whom live in dormitories, cooperatives, and fraternity and sorority houses. This is the rowdy area of Berkeley, with activity at all times of the day and night. Architecturally, some of the most interesting homes are the large mansions that house the college fraternities and sororities. The Sigmi Phi house on Durant and Piedmont is a classic Arts and Crafts style home, designed by the Greene brothers in 1909. Julia Morgan designed the outdoor Greek Theater, and Bernard Maybeck, architect of San Francisco's Palace of Fine Arts, also made his mark on Berkeley homes.

Much of the 1960s free speech movement and the anti-Vietnam War protests centered around Telegraph Avenue and Sproul Plaza. The plaza still hosts student protests, and when there is little to yell about, musicians, politicians, prophets, and students take center stage. Telegraph Avenue, which begins in downtown Oakland, runs into the southern side of the Cal campus. The Berkeley section of Telegraph is a bustling shopping zone catering to students with clothing, music and bookstores, coffee shops, cheap eats and cafes. Street vendors set up daily, selling handmade jewelry and tie-dyed clothes. Locals have a choice of four well-known independent bookstores on the 2400 block: Cody's, Moe's, Shakespeare & Co., and Shambhala. Every Christmas season the Telegraph Avenue Street Fair hosts an arts and crafts show. UC Berkeley has two of the area's best attended concert sites: the outdoor Greek Theater where the Grateful Dead often played and the indoor Zellerbach Hall which features national and international performers.

The hustle and bustle of university life quiets down once you head south, away from the campus.

Close to College Avenue, the **Claremont** neighborhood, bordering Oakland (east of the Elmwood District and west of the Claremont Resort), is one of Berkeley's grandest and most expensive neighborhoods. The area is named for the huge, 22-acre resort called the Claremont Spa and Hotel, which is so large it can be seen from across the bay. Designed by Charles Dickey, the Claremont has tennis courts and a large outdoor swimming pool. Some of the elegant homes that make up Claremont have bay views. There are two small shopping areas that serve the neighborhood, the Uplands Street area, and along Domingo Avenue where you'll find Berkeley's famous Peet's coffee just across from the Claremont Hotel.

The **Elmwood District**, just down the street and west from the Claremont, is a pleasant area of two- and three-story, brown shingle homes surrounded by tall trees. Houses here are not cheap. To supplement income many families find tenants for their backyard cottages, basements, or attic rooms. According to Ira Serkes, an East Bay realtor, in June 1999, the median price for a 3-bedroom home in the Claremont and Elmwood District was $757,000.

Construction, brought about by the robust US economy, continues unabated in **Downtown Berkeley** with new buildings being raised on almost every block. Berkeley's main post office is downtown at 2000 Allston Way, as well as the main library, 2121 Allston Way, city hall and courthouse, 2171 McKinley Avenue, and a number of commercial buildings. Though not as chic as Fourth Street or College Avenue (see below), Shattuck Avenue in downtown offers a variety of shopping, from furniture, to clothing, to tiny boutiques, to toy stores and movie theaters. For fresh fruits and vegetables, the farmers' market is a local favorite. Held twice a week on Martin Luther King Street, people from all over come to buy straight from the farmers. On Saturdays, the market is at Center Street and Martin Luther King, on Tuesdays head for Derby Street and Martin Luther King.

The theater scene thrives in Berkeley's downtown area, with the Berkeley Repertory Theater, 2025 Addison Street, being most familiar. Though not in downtown proper, Zellerbach Auditorium on the UC Campus, also sponsors live performances, from Marcel Marceau to musician Phillip Glass. Also in downtown, and noteworthy because it is a Bay Area rarity, Iceland, 2727 Milvia Street, is a true ice rink.

Downtown is the central hub for mass transit, including BART (Shattuck and Center) and AC Transit. Just down the street from the Bart Station, people line up early in the morning for a ride into the City. Three passengers to a car constitutes a carpool, plus you do not have to pay the two dollar bridge toll.

Also known as the "Flatlands," **West Berkeley** is considered a transitional area with affordable fixer-upper bungalows, new lofts, and relatively inexpensive rents. This area is neither as safe nor as aesthetically pleasing as other parts of Berkeley, however proximity to the waterfront and to the Fourth Street shopping district is an asset. Berkeley initiatives to improve the area include adding a railway stop, bike routes, and improving the waterfront area. The Berkeley Marina is a mecca for water sports, including sailing, kayaking, and windsurfing. On the Berkeley Pier, fishing is the main vocation. Both California Adventures and the California Sailing Club offer sailing and wind-surfing lessons. Also on the waterfront is Adventure Playground, an outdoor area for children.

Vibrant Fourth Street with its shopping district full of popular restaurants, home and garden shops, boutiques, and outlet stores has revived the surrounding neighborhoods. Perhaps, Berkeley's most upscale shopping area, Fourth Street is an outdoor mall with a welcoming ambiance. Just being there makes you want to reach into your pocketbook. Locals rave about brunch at Bette's Ocean View Diner, 1807 Fourth Street, but there's often a two-hour wait on Sundays. There is also a Crate and Barrel outlet for your home needs, Restoration Hardware, and Cody's bookstore, not to mention the numerous clothing stores.

BERKELEY
Web Sites: www.ci.berkeley.ca.us, www.berkeleychamber.com
Area Codes: 510, 341
Zip Codes: 94701, 94702, 94703, 94704, 94705, 94707, 94708, 94709
Main Post Office: 2000 Allston Way, Berkeley, 800-275-8777
Police: Berkeley Police Department, 2171 McKinley Avenue, 510-644-6743
Libraries: Berkeley Public Library, Central Branch, 2121 Allston Way, Berkeley, 510-644-6100; Claremont Branch, 2940 Benvenue Avenue, 510-644-6880; South Branch, 1901 Russell Street, 510-644-6860; North Branch, 1170 The Alameda, 510-644-6850; West Branch, 1125 University Avenue, 510-644-6870, www.infopeople.org/bpl
Public Schools: Berkeley Unified School District, 2134 Martin Luther King, Jr. Way, Berkeley, 510-644-6147 or www.berkeley.k12.ca.us; college: www.berkeley.edu
Community Publications: *East Bay Express*, 510-540-7400; Hills Newspapers, Incorporated, 510-339-8777, publications include: *The Berkeley Voice*, 510-644-8208, *El Cerrito Journal*, *The Montclarion*, *The Piedmonter*, and *Alameda Journal*; *The (East Bay) Monthly*, 510-658-9811; *The Berkeley Daily Planet*, 510-841-5600; *The Daily Californian*, 510-548-8300
Community Resources: City of Berkeley Parks and Recreation, 201 University Avenue, 510-644-6943; Tilden Park, 510-525-2233; University of California, Berkeley Art Museum, 2626 Bancroft Way, Berkeley, 510-642-0808; Pacific Film Archive Theater, 2575 Bancroft at Bowditch, Berkeley, 510-642-1412; Lawrence Hall of Science, Centennial Drive below Grizzly Peak, 510-642-5132; University of California Botanical Gardens, 200 Centennial Drive, 510-643-2755; Judah L. Magnes Memorial Museum, 510-549-6950; Berkeley Chamber of Commerce, 1834 University Avenue, Berkeley, 510-549-1789; Berkeley Tenants Union, 2022 Blake Street, 510-548-1867; La Pena Cultural Center, 3105 Shattuck Avenue, 510-849-2508

CONTRA COSTA COUNTY

CONCORD, MARTINEZ, WALNUT CREEK
RICHMOND

Contra Costa County, with just under one-million people, is on the eastern side of the East Bay Hills, out where the weather is warm, warmer, and warmest. The population is diverse and all economic levels are represented. Housing options are also varied, ranging from old farmhouses, massive, gated apartment complexes, to duplexes, condominiums, and sprawling, newly landscaped housing developments. Many apartment complexes offer swimming pools and recreation centers. According to the California Association of Realtors, the October 2000 median home price for Contra Costa County was $265,000, an increase of 20.5% from the previous year.

CONTRA COSTA COUNTY
Web Site: www.co.contra-costa.ca.us
Area Codes: 510, 925
Sheriff: 651 Pine Street, Martinez, 510-228-8282
Libraries: Contra Costa County Library, Concord Branch, 2900 Salvio Street, 925-646-5455; Walnut Creek Branch, 1644 North Broadway, 925-646-6773
Public Schools: West Contra Costa Unified School District, 1108 Bissell Avenue, Richmond, 94801, 510-234-3825, www.wccusd.k12.ca.us; Contra Costa Unified School District, 77 Santa Barbara Road, Pleasant Hill, 925-942-3388, www.cccoe.k12.ca.us
Community Publications: *Contra Costa Times*, 2640 Shadelands Drive, Walnut Creek, 925-935-2525; *El Cerrito Journal*, 5707 Redwood Road, Oakland, 510-339-8777; *Family Fair*, 5707 Redwood Road, 510-339-4040; *Oakland Tribune*, 66 Jack London Square, 510-208-6300
Community Resources: Richmond Art Center, Civic Center Plaza, 2540 Barrett Avenue, 510-620-6772; Richmond Museum of History, 400 Nevin Avenue, 510-235-7387; Alvarado Adobe/Blume House, San Pablo, 510-215-3046; John Muir National Historic Site, 4202 Alhambra Avenue, Martinez, 925-228-8860; Blake Garden, 70 Rincon Road, Kensington, 510-524-2449; Martinez Marina, 925-313-0942; Martinez Community Services Department, 925-372-3551; AIDS Program Information and Services, 925-313-6770; Leisure Services, City Hall, 525 Henrietta Street, Martinez, 925-372-3510; Concord Neighborhood Watch Program, 925-671-3237
Public Transportation: *AC (Alameda-Contra Costa) Transit*, 510-891-4777; *BART*, 510-465-2278; *Benicia Transit*, 707-745-0815, *County Connection*, 925-676-7500; *RIDES*, 800-755-7665; *Tri-Delta Transit* and *Brentwood Dimes-a-Ride*, 925-754-4040, *WestCat*, 510-724-7993; *Amtrak*, 800-872-7245

CONCORD, MARTINEZ, WALNUT CREEK

The City of **Martinez**, www.cityofmartinez.org, is the site of naturalist John Muir's historic home, a well-maintained hillside Victorian mansion that is open to the public. **Walnut Creek**, www.ci.walnut-creek.ca.us, is home to more than 65,000 people. With its fine arts programs, including the Dean Lesher Regional Center for the Arts and Bedford Gallery, 1601 Civic Drive, 925-295-1400, its open space projects, public gardens, equestrian center, and the Boundary Oak Golf Course, 3800 Valley Vista Road, 925-934-4775, it is considered by many to be one of the most desirable cities in Contra Costa County. **Concord**, www.ci.concord.ca.us, has the most people, with a population of about 115,000. Houses along the corridor of Highway 680 are going up rapidly because it is possible to live here and drive to Silicon Valley in under an hour. June through September finds the homes on the other side Highway 24's Caldecott Tunnel basking in heat. Opened in 1937, the Tunnel connects Oakland to Orinda. During the summer it's not unusual to be 60° in San Francisco and over 100° here in Concord, Martinez or Walnut Creek.

RICHMOND

POINT RICHMOND

Richmond, the northernmost city in Contra Costa County, was established as a shipyard town with the onset of WW II. Many ships destined for the Pacific front left port from Richmond. Today, many of the residents of Richmond are descendants of people who arrived here for work in the mid-1930s and '40s. Richmond has since fallen upon hard times, suffering from lack of employment. However, with the Bay Area economy continuing to rise and stretch out, Richmond is slowly improving. Compared to the rest of the East Bay, rents and property here are much cheaper.

One lovely enclave in Richmond is **Point Richmond** where, because it is situated close to the bay, the air is fresh and tends to be cleaner than the rest of Richmond. Here, you'll find a bayside artist/sailing community with a quaint, old-fashioned downtown, chock full of cafes and restaurants, as well as a flower shop and grocery store. The community atmosphere is cozy, with neighbors looking out for one another, and shopkeepers remembering everyone's name. The Richmond Yacht Club, 351 Brickyard Cove, is a popular socializing spot. Many of the homes near the yacht club have their own private docks. Public swimming is available in the Richmond Plunge, the Bay Area's largest heated indoor pool, 1 East Richmond Avenue. Some consider this small community to be safer than the rest of Richmond.

RICHMOND
Web Site: www.ci.richmond.ca.us
Area Code: 510
Zip Codes: 94801, 94802, 94804, 94805, 94807, 94808
Post Offices: 104 Washington Avenue; 1025 Nevin Avenue; 3200 Regatta Boulevard; 2100 Chanslor Avenue; 200 Broadway; 12651 San Pablo Avenue, 800-275-8777
Police: Richmond Police Department, 401 27th Street, 510-620-6648
Library: Main Library, 325 Civic Center Plaza, 510-620-6561
Public Schools: West Contra Costa Unified School District, 1108 Bissell Avenue, 510-234-3825, www.wccusd.k12.ca.us
Community Resources: Point Richmond Neighborhood Council, 510-232-5059; Recreation and Parks, 3230 MacDonald Avenue, 510-620-6972; East Bay Regional Park District, 2950 Peralta Oaks Court, P.O. Box 5381, Oakland, 94605, 510-562-PARK; Richmond Yacht Club, 351 Brickyard Cove, 510-237-2821; Richmond Plunge, 1 East Richmond Avenue, 510-620-6820; Masquers Playhouse, 105 Park Place, 510-232-4031

ADDITIONAL CITY WEB SITES—CONTRA COSTA COUNTY

Antioch: www.ci.antioch.ca.us
Danville: www.ci.danville.ca.us
El Cerrito: www.el-cerrito.ca.us
Lafayette: www.ci.lafayette.ca.us
Livermore: www.ci.livermore.ca.us
Orinda: www.ci.orinda.ca.us
Pinole: www.ci.pinole.ca.us
Pittsburg: www.ci.pittsburg.ca.us
Pleasanton: www.ci.pleasanton.ca.us
San Leandro: www.ci.san-leandro.ca.us

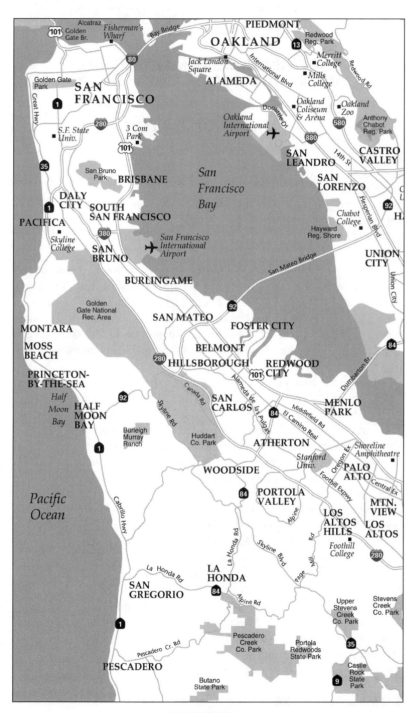

PENINSULA

THE PENINSULA (SAN MATEO COUNTY AND NORTHERN SANTA CLARA COUNTY)

SAN MATEO COUNTY

DALY CITY
PACIFICA
HALF MOON BAY
SAN MATEO, BURLINGAME, BELMONT
HILLSBOROUGH, ATHERTON, WOODSIDE
MENLO PARK

Known as "The Peninsula," San Mateo County is directly south of San Francisco, with Santa Clara County a little farther south and east. It's hard to imagine what this area was like 100 years ago when only a few small towns dotted the road between San Francisco and San Jose. Belmont, Hillsborough, Woodside, Atherton and Palo Alto were not cities or towns, but rather garden spots with estates where wealthy San Franciscans relaxed in tranquil surroundings and glorious weather.

Today San Mateo County, which became independent of San Francisco in 1856, consists of 21 cities, many of which are booming with industry and commerce. The eastern half of San Mateo County, with easy access to Interstate 280 and Highway 101 is heavily populated and busy. Fortunately, the folks who live here have plenty of options to escape civilization since about three-quarters of the county is open space, most of which is located in the western portion where wooded mountains are laced with superb hiking and biking trails, campgrounds, lakes, and beaches.

The most populous city of the county, Daly City, borders San Francisco and marks the beginning of the suburbs. For the longest time, San Mateo, the county (not to be confused with San Mateo, the city), was predominantly middle-class suburbia, especially the communities of San Bruno, Millbrae, Brisbane, Daly City, Redwood City, South San Francisco, and Redwood City. However, with the Bay Area's continued economic boom and relentlessly rising real estate values, folks from all walks of life are choosing this area to call home. San Mateo, Burlingame, and Belmont used to be considered bedroom communities for San Francisco, but now the commute is flowing (sometimes grinding and sometimes not moving at all) south to Silicon Valley as well. The California Association of Realtors reported that the median price for a home in San Mateo County increased 25%, from $394,000 in October 1999 to $22,500 in October 2000.

The Peninsula contains a number of universities and colleges, most famous being Stanford University in Palo Alto. Other universities include Santa

Clara University, San Jose State University, and the College of Notre Dame in Belmont. And, if you live in the center or northern portion of the Peninsula, you will not be far from San Francisco State University.

San Francisco International Airport is located on the bayside of the Peninsula, in the Millbrae/San Bruno area. The airport is a madhouse practically everyday, but especially on holidays. The Peninsula is also served by the CalTrain commuter service and a number of bus lines including Sam Trans (the San Mateo County bus service) which runs into San Francisco. The San Mateo County Board of Supervisors rejected BART service when the system was built more than 25 years ago. Today, most county residents would tell you that was a big mistake, and are now reconsidering this option. People living in the East Bay commute to San Mateo and Silicon Valley via the San Mateo Bridge (to Hayward) or the Dunbarton Bridge (to Fremont). During the past few years, traffic has increased considerably.

Along the western portion, you'll find the ocean-side edge of San Mateo County. This area is trimmed with Highway 1, one of the most beautiful roadways in the world, tracing the pacific coastline from the beach city of Pacifica to the pumpkins of Half Moon Bay to the boardwalk of Santa Cruz. Be on the lookout for gray whales. The coastline is often blanketed with fog, giving the beaches a chilly, romantic feeling.

SAN MATEO COUNTY

Web Site: www.co.sanmateo.ca.us

Area Code: 650

Sheriff: San Mateo County Sheriff's Office, 400 County Center, Redwood City, 650-599-1664

Emergency Hospitals: San Mateo County General Hospital, 222 West 39th Avenue, San Mateo, 650-573-2222; Sequoia Hospital, 170 Alameda de las Pulgas, Redwood City, 650-369-5811; Seton Medical Center, 1900 Sullivan Avenue, Daly City, 650-992-4000; Stanford University Hospital, 300 Pasteur Drive, Stanford, 650-723-4000

Library: Peninsula Library System, 25 Tower Road, San Mateo, 650-780-7018, www.plsinfo.org

Public Schools: San Mateo County Office of Education, 101 Twin Dolphin Drive, Redwood City, 650-802-5300

Community Publication: *San Mateo County Times*, 650-348-4321

Community Resources: San Mateo United Homeowners' Association, 708 Rand Street, San Mateo, 94401; San Mateo Newcomers, 650-344-7512; San Mateo County Park and Recreation Department, 455 County Center, 4th Floor, Redwood City, 650-363-4020; San Mateo County Convention and Visitors Bureau, 111 Anza Boulevard, Suite 410, Burlingame, 650-348-7600

Public Transportation: *RIDES*, 800-755-7665; *CalTrain*, 800-660-4287; *SamTrans*, 800-660-4287; TDD/TTY 650-508-6448

DALY CITY

Calling itself the "The Gateway to the Peninsula," Daly City is directly south of San Francisco. Just after the 1906 earthquake and fire, many San Franciscans sought refuge in the open space of Daly City. Today, the countryside of Daly City no longer exists; instead this 7.5 square mile city is the most populous city of the county, with more than 104,000 residents.

Daly City has its own BART station, providing easy access to downtown San Francisco. For those driving to the station, BART provides 1,400 parking spaces, even so, these spaces fill up quickly, so arrive early or look for parking on a nearby street. San Francisco Airport is less than ten minutes away, which is a plus if you need to fly, though many locals complain about the noise. If you are commuting to Silicon Valley, it could take you anywhere from 40 minutes to two hours, depending on traffic.

Henry Doelger, designer of much of the bland housing that is found in parts of San Francisco's Sunset District, continued in his blah though practical style—a one-car garage at the base which supports the living rooms, which overlook the street and are finished off with two bedrooms, one bath, and a (now) huge tree in the front yard. These "cliffs of Doelger" inspired Malvina Reynolds to write a song about Daly City homes, calling them "...the little boxes made of ticky tacky..." Indeed, though many of the homes here are painted different colors, they are very similar.

Daly City is considered one of the most affordable cities of San Mateo County. Apartments, duplexes, townhouses, condominiums, and single-family homes can be found throughout the city. Many of the homes on the hill have Bay and Ocean views. Though still relatively affordable, property prices in Daly City increased 18.7% between October 1999 and October 2000, going from a median price of $310,000 to $368,000.

In addition to the ticky tacky homes, Daly City is known for having one of the area's major shopping centers, the Serramonte Shopping Center. Home Depot and Nordstrom Rack are south on Highway 101 at the Metro Shopping Center. Locals enjoy their three golf courses, including Lake Merced Country Club, which also has tennis courts.

DALY CITY
Web Site: www.ci.daly-city.ca.us
Area Codes: 415, 650
Zip Codes: 94014, 94015
Post Office: 1100 Sullivan Avenue, 800-275-8777
Police Station: Daly City Police Department, 333 90th Street, 650-991-8119
Emergency Hospital: Seton Hospital, 1900 Sullivan Avenue, 650-992-4000
Library: Serramonte Main Library, 40 Wembley Drive, 650-991-8023

Public Schools: Jefferson Elementary School District, 101 Lincoln Avenue, 650-991-1000; Jefferson Union High School District, 699 Serramonte Boulevard, 650-756-0300

Community Resources: Daly City-Colma Chamber of Commerce, 355 Gellert Boulevard, Suite 231 650-991-5001; Doelger Senior Center, 101 Lake Merced Boulevard, 650-991-8012

PACIFICA

Pacifica (40,719) is no longer a small beach town without sidewalks. The word is out and people are moving in. Populated by middle- to upper-income families and singles, who love living in fog, Pacifica (which means "peace" in Spanish) is just 15 miles south of San Francisco, and only five miles from the San Francisco Airport. Don't look for the town center, because it does not exist. Instead, there are a string of small shopping enclaves. You can also find lovely apartments and homes, many of them overlooking the ocean. Architecturally, the homes are mostly California ranch style, but you can also find Queen Anne Victorians and Cape Cods. Pacifica is relatively affordable, quiet, cool, foggy, and friendly. From October 1999 to October 2000 property prices in Pacifica increased 21.2%, going from a median price of $330,000 to $400,000. There is an abundance of outdoor activities, including surfing, scuba diving, fishing, paragliding, hiking, birding, golf, tennis, and horseback riding. Surfers from all over ride the waves at Rockaway Beach. Most of the beaches here are not crowded, same goes with the local parks and golf courses, except at the end of September when the city hosts thousands of visitors at its annual Fog Festival. Activities include music, food, and artists' booths.

PACIFICA
Web Site: www.ci.pacifica.ca.us
Area Code: 650
Zip Code: 94044
Post Office: 50 West Manor Drive, 800-275-8777
Police Station: 1850 Francisco Boulevard, 650-355-1172
Libraries: Pacifica Library, 104 Hilton Way, Pacifica, 650-355-5196; Sanchez Library, 1111 Terra Nova, 650-359-3397

HALF MOON BAY

A beach-front community about 25 miles south of San Francisco, Half Moon Bay, (11,179) spans some of the most beautiful coastline in California. The smell of salt air is prevalent in this coastal town. As little as a decade ago, the farming of flowers and specialty vegetables was one of the main occupations here. More recently the area has become a bedroom community for Silicon Valley, with housing prices to match. According to the California Association of Realtors the median price for a home increased 17.3% from its October 1999 price of $468,250 to $549,000 in October 2000.

During October, locals enjoy the annual Great Pumpkin Contest, where gourd growers from around the country bring their pumpkins and weigh-off against global competitors, hoping to enter the record books. Recent winners have been in the 900 to 1,000 pound range. The historic downtown area is a hodgepodge of antique shops, clothing boutiques, arts and crafts shops, tiny restaurants and cafes, and cozy bed and breakfasts. During the summer, the monthly flower mart is colorful and fragrant. There are two golf courses to take a swing at, and plenty of access to beaches for surfing, horseback riding, hiking, and biking. Tres Amigos, 200 North Cabrillo Highway, is a local favorite for inexpensive yet delicious Mexican food.

The harbor sports a life of its own, attracting a number of surfers, sailors, and fishermen. Locals venture down to the docks to buy fresh fish straight from the boat. A little farther south on Highway 1 is Ano Nuevo State Reserve, home to thousands of elephant seals, and Mavericks and Waddell Creek, two prime spots for surfers and windsurfers.

Half Moon Bay is a delightful and tranquil community, which feels worlds away from the hectic pace of San Francisco or Silicon Valley. Commuting to the City via Highway 1 may be delayed, especially during winter because of mudslides around the so-called "Devil's Slide." Those commuting south on Route 92 marvel at the change of weather, especially in the summer, when it can be downright hot and sticky in the South Bay, but once they reach the ridge near Half Moon Bay, the fog brings instant cooling relief.

HALF MOON BAY
Web Site: www.half-moon-bay.ca.us
Area Code: 650
Zip Codes: 94018, 94019, 94038
Post Office: 500 Stone Pine Road, 800-275-8777
Police Station: 537 Kelly Avenue, 650-726-8286
Library: Half Moon Bay Library, 620 Correas Street, 650-726-2316

SAN MATEO, BURLINGAME, BELMONT

San Mateo, the city (94,084), has a varied population living in a variety of homes, from traditional ranch styles to English Mediterranean styles, with some condominiums, modest starter homes, and huge mansions mixed in. Once the banking capital of the Peninsula, San Mateo is now a bedroom community for Silicon Valley. According to the California Association of Realtors housing costs here are rising steadily, with the median price of a home up 31% from October 1999 to October 2000—from $404,000 to $528,000. In **Belmont**, the median home priced increased from $525,000 to $575,000 in that same time frame. Belmont's name comes from nineteenth century banker William Ralston who built an eighty-room mansion, which he called Belmont. Homes in **Burlingame** are a bit more upscale, and the median price also has increased, though only about nine percent: from $662,500 to $725,000. Also in Burlingame is the Pez Museum, 214 California Drive, 650-347-2301, featuring hundreds of Pez dispensers. For those in the know, Edward Huss from Austria invented the Pez to help people quit smoking. Burlingame is also known for having one of the last drive-in movie theaters, the Burlingame Drive-in Theater, 650-343-2213, located on Burlingame Avenue off of the Old Bayshore Highway. In all three cities, you'll find young and old families, good schools, and tree-lined streets, a symbol of the Peninsula.

SAN MATEO
Web Site: www.ci.sanmateo.ca.us
Area Code: 650
Zip Codes: 94401, 94402
Post Office: 1630 South Delaware Street, San Mateo, 800-275-8777
Police Station: San Mateo Police Department, 650-522-7620
Library: San Mateo Public Library, 55 West Third Avenue, 650-522-7800

BURLINGAME
Web Site: www.burlingame.org
Area Code: 650
Zip Code: 94010
Post Office: 220 Park Road, 800-275-8777
Police Station: 1111 Trousdale Drive, 650-692-8440
Library: Burlingame Library, 480 Primrose Road, 650-342-1037

BELMONT
Web Site: www.ci.belmont.ca.us
Area Code: 650
Zip Code: 94002
Post Office: 640 Masonic Way, 800-275-8777
Police Station: Belmont Police Department, 1215 Ralston Avenue, 650-595-7400
Library: Belmont Library, 1110 Alameda de las Pulgas, 650-591-8286

HILLSBOROUGH, ATHERTON, WOODSIDE

Much of the rest of the Peninsula is suburbia, including the upscale towns of Hillsborough, Atherton, Woodside, and parts of Menlo Park. If you're looking for rental property the latter is certainly your best bet. The other three communities are heavily mansioned, with homes priced in the millions of dollars. Except for a police department and a town hall, **Hillsborough** does not have much in terms of an infrastructure and is considered to be a bedroom community. According to an FBI report tracking safety in cities with populations over 10,000, Hillsborough is one of the safest towns in the Bay Area. **Atherton**, current home to billionaire Lawrence J. Ellison of Oracle Systems, and previous home of football player Joe Montana, has lovely old estates that were once used by wealthy San Franciscans as summer residences. It is also where you will find the elite Menlo school, a prep school for grades 6-12. **Woodside**, named for its wooded hillsides, has a country feel with its narrow roads, natural streams, and fields of wildflowers.

HILLSBOROUGH
Web Site: www.hillsborough.net
Area Code: 650
Zip Code: 94010
Post Office: 220 Park Road, Burlingame
Police Station: Police Department, 1600 Florabunda Avenue, 650-375-7470
Libraries: Burlingame Library, 480 Primrose Road, 650-342-1037; San Mateo
    Library, 55 West 3rd Avenue, 650-373-4800

ATHERTON
Web Site: www.ci.atherton.ca.us
Area Code: 650
Zip Code: 94027
Post Office: 3875 Bohannon Drive, Menlo Park, 800-275-8777
Police Station: Atherton Police Department, 83 Ashfield Road, 650-688-6500
Library: Atherton Public Library, 2 Dinkelspiel Station Lane, 650-328-2422

WOODSIDE
Web Site: www.ci.woodside.ca.us
Area Code: 650
Zip Code: 94062
Post Office: 1100 Broadway Street, Redwood City, 800-275-8777
Sheriff: San Mateo County Sheriff's Office, 400 County Center, Redwood
    City, 650-599-1664
Library: Woodside Library, 3140 Woodside Road, Woodside, 650-851-0147

MENLO PARK

SHARON HEIGHTS

Halfway between San Francisco and San Jose, Menlo Park (34,600) is like old town USA where you think Kevin Arnold from "The Wonder Years" just may be cruising the street on his bicycle. A quaint, all-American city, Menlo Park's downtown Santa Cruz Avenue is lined with restaurants, coffee shops, retail stores, and ice cream shops. The quiet, tree-lined streets, public swimming pools, and tennis courts mark the 19-square miles of Menlo Park as the quintessential suburb. That's not to say nothing is going on here. Menlo Park is known for having a high number of venture capitalist companies, many of which are located along Sand Hill Road. Other noteworthy ventures include Stanford's Linear Accelerator (SLAC), which literally smashes atoms in its Menlo Park laboratory, Sun Microsystems, which is the biggest high-tech company in the area, and *Sunset Magazine* is headquartered here.

Menlo Park received its official name in 1854 when two Irishmen, Dennis J. Oliver and D.C. McGlynn, purchased about 640 acres and built an estate, including two houses with a common entrance. On a gate, they named the estate, "Menlo Park," with the date, August 1854, under it. In 1863, when the railroad came through, a railroad official looked at the gate and decided to name the station Menlo Park. The rest is history. During WW I, Menlo Park changed almost overnight from an unpopulated agricultural community into a bustling military camp where 43,000 soldiers trained at nearby Camp Fremont. During WW II, Menlo Park's Dibble General Hospital was built to treat thousands of soldiers injured in the South Pacific. For more about the history of Menlo Park contact the Menlo Park Historical Society at 650-858-3368.

Architecturally, you'll find a range of housing options, from 1950s-style apartments to Eichler homes to ranch style homes. You can also find a number of newer apartments. The neighborhoods west of Highway 101 are more desirable. **Sharon Heights**, near the golf course, is Menlo Park's upscale neighborhood, and has views of the mountains. With Stanford University right next door, Menlo Park is home to a number of Stanford faculty, employees, and some students. Residents also include blue- and white-collar workers, some here for generations, others recently arrived. Across San Francisquito Creek and past the stately 1,000-year-old redwood, called "El Palo Alto," is the northernmost reach of Santa Clara County, and the beginning of the much-fabled Silicon Valley. Housing prices in Menlo Park are about the same as what you'll find in San Francisco, but here you tend to get more house for your money.

The city blocks off Santa Cruz Avenue during its annual Fine Arts Festival and its Fourth of July Parade. Both events are downright fun, attracting people from all over the area. Locals rave about Draeger's Bistro, 1010 University

Drive, for its brunch and delicatessen. Draeger's Supermarket, at the same location, is also legendary, offering only the best, from saffron to fresh brie to vine-ripe tomatoes.

Parking is easy in Menlo Park, especially since most of the homes have garages. With Highway 280 on the west side of the city and Highway 101 near the waterfront, access to San Francisco and Silicon Valley is quick. Access to the East Bay is possible via the Dunbarton Bridge. CalTrain and Sam Trans buses are also available.

MENLO PARK
Web Site: www.ci.menlo-park.ca.us
Area Code: 650
Zip Code: 94025
Post Office: 3875 Bohannon Drive, 800-275-8777
Police Station: 701 Laurel Street, 650-858-3300
Library: 800 Alma Street, 650-858-3460

ADDITIONAL CITY WEB SITES—SAN MATEO COUNTY

Brisbane, www.ci.brisbane.ca.us
Foster City, www.fostercity.org
Millbrae, www.ci.millbrae.ca.us
Redwood City, www.ci.redwood-city.ca.us
South San Francisco, www.ci.ssf.ca.us
San Carlos, www.ci.san-carlos.ca.us
San Bruno, www.ci.sanbruno.ca.us

NORTHERN SANTA CLARA COUNTY

PALO ALTO
MOUNTAIN VIEW

Santa Clara County is one of the fastest growing counties in the Bay Area. People are moving here faster than homes can be built, making traffic and housing critical issues. Anyone will tell you that finding a job here is not a problem, the challenge lies in finding a place to live. Both Palo Alto and Mountain View are a part of Santa Clara County. They are also included as part of the amorphous Silicon Valley, a term coined by Don Hoefler, a writer for the weekly *Electronic News*. He used the name in 1971 to describe the electronic firms that were mushrooming out of Santa Clara County. A September 2000 *New York Times* article on "High-Density Rentals for Silicon Valley" reported that the job creation here will likely continue, with an estimated 183,000 jobs expected to be created between 2000 and 2010. However, housing will not likely keep up. It's expected that only an additional 70,000 housing units will be added. Of course these are all estimations, but at the rate things are going, the projections seem plausible. Between October 1999 and October 2000 home prices in Santa Clara County increased 28.6%, from a median price of $350,000 to $450,000.

For Santa Clara County resources, see the **South Bay** section.

PALO ALTO

OLD PALO ALTO
CRESCENT PARK
PROFESSORVILLE DISTRICT
FOREST AVENUE
BARRON PARK

While Menlo Park has street fairs, Palo Alto has evening balls. Indeed, Palo Alto, named after the 1,000 year-old redwood growing at the border with Menlo Park, sports a refined, cosmopolitan attitude. Located 35 miles south of San Francisco, Palo Alto is a town of cafes, bookstores, theaters, and Stanford Shopping Center, the oldest outdoor mall in the country. The city's star is the elite Stanford University, founded in 1891 by US Senator and railroad magnate Leland Stanford, when the local population was only 400. Today, more than 60,000 folks from every corner of the globe call Palo Alto home. Thousands more commute into Palo Alto, often bringing the morning rush hour to a standstill.

Despite its small size relative to San Francisco and San Jose, Palo Alto boasts more than thirty parks, two community centers, seven libraries, including a children's library, a private airport, an upscale shopping center, and a first-rate hospital. Along University Avenue, the downtown is quaint and busy, and a short walk to the Stanford campus. For more of a hometown atmosphere, locals shop and dine on California Avenue. Three of the parks in Palo Alto are particularly magnificent due the natural settings and preserves within them: Arastradero Preserve, Foothills Park, and Palo Alto Baylands Nature Preserve.

In 1939, Hewlett-Packard began in a one-car garage located at 367 Addison Avenue. This garage is now a historical landmark with a plaque describing it as "the birthplace of Silicon Valley." With its headquarters still in Palo Alto, today Hewlett-Packard has more than 86,000 employees and 600 offices in more than 120 countries. Stanford Research Park has more than 60 high-tech and bio-tech companies, including XeroxParc where GUI (Graphics User Interface), the computer mouse, and *Pong* were developed.

Palo Alto has more than 15 different neighborhoods, each with their own charm. Oregon Expressway divides the city and generally speaking, the neighborhoods north of the Oregon Expressway are more established, while those south of the Expressway exemplify the expansion that's occurring to accommodate a growing Silicon Valley. On the north side, you'll find **Old Palo Alto** and **Crescent Park**, with their magnificent mansions, including one owned by Steve Jobs, co-founder of Apple Computer. Also on the north side is **Professorville District**, with its wood-shingled homes (some designed by Julia Morgan and Bernard Maybeck). Here, just south of downtown, you'll find Stanford professors busy working and thinking. Another established neighborhood is College Terrace, nestled between Stanford University and Stanford Research Park, which is home to a mix of students, engineers, musicians and retired people.

Slightly north of Professorville is the **Forest Avenue** neighborhood, which has newer apartments and many condominiums. This neighborhood attracts a younger crowd, many of whom frequent the nearby Whole Foods and St. Michael's Alley, a club where Joan Baez used to sing. South of Oregon Expressway, where the apricot orchards used to grow, is the largest community of Eichler homes, built from 1949 to 1970. Joseph Eichler crafted these homes which are known for their open design (minimal interior walls in their living space), shallow pitched roofs and glass walls. Another interesting neighborhood is **Barron Park**, just west of El Camino and south of Stanford. This area has a rural feel as there are no sidewalks, plenty of grand trees, and mailboxes detached from the homes.

With California's booming economy, rents are high and vacancies rare. Finding housing in the late summer months is difficult, as you will be competing with Stanford students. Property prices are just as high, if not higher, than San Francisco. The median price for a home here was $790,000 in October 2000, up 22.2% from October 1999. Prospective homebuyers are looking cautiously at East Palo Alto, an area which has suffered higher crime rates and poverty since the early 1960s, but which seems to be turning around. A 129-unit apartment complex is being built here to ensure that some residents are not priced out of their neighborhood.

PALO ALTO
Web Site: www.city.palo-alto.ca.us
Area Code: 650
Zip Codes: 94301, 94302, 94303, 94304, 94306, Stanford University 94309
Post Office: 380 Hamilton Avenue, Palo Alto, 800-275-8777
Police Station: 250 Hamilton Avenue, 650-329-2555
Libraries: Palo Alto Children's Library, 1276 Harriet Street, 650-329-2134;
    Main Library, 1213 Newell Road, 650-329-2436

MOUNTAIN VIEW

Located 40 miles south of San Francisco and only eight miles north of San Jose, Mountain View (75,200) is considered the heart of Silicon Valley. For a town that originated as a stagecoach stop in 1850, a lot has happened to this 7-square-mile city. Today it is the fourth most populated city in Silicon Valley (following San Jose, Sunnyvale, and Santa Clara, respectively), and it is home to a number of high-tech companies, including AOL-Netscape Communications, Silicon Graphics, Sun Microsystems, Synopsis, and Intuit. Intel started in Mountain View before it moved to Santa Clara. NASA Ames Research Center is also based in Mountain View.

Locals boast that their town is well organized and clean, and the city sponsors a number of festivals, including the September Art and Wine Festival, and the Affribean Festival. In addition to the festivals locals also enjoy a weekly farmers' market, held every Sunday on Hope Street, between Villa and Evelyn, and easy access to the popular Shoreline Park. This 660-acre park includes a golf course, bicycling and jogging trails, and a man-made lake, which is often jumping with sailors, windsurfers, paddle-boaters and shore-side picnickers. The Outdoor Shoreline Amphitheatre hosts popular musicians; recent bookings include Santana, Pearl Jam, and the Red Hot Chile Peppers.

Many single, high-tech professionals, young families, and students call Mountain View home. Architecturally, you'll find a majority of apartments here; in fact, Mountain View has more apartments than single family homes. Homes that are here include Craftsman-style bungalows and some Eichler homes. Recently, a number of small, single-family unit condominiums and townhouses were added to the housing pool. Neighborhoods are changing all over the city, especially around Castro Street, with the development of both residential and commercial sites. Dramatic changes also can be found in the Whisman area, the southerly portion of the city, home to AOL-Netscape's offices. According to Palo Alto based Marcus & Millichap Real Estate Investment Brokerage, the average rent for a two-bedroom, one bath apartment in Mountain View was $2,150 in September 2000, up almost 25% from 1999. In September 2000, the *New York Times* reported the vacancy rate here at four-tenths of one percent! To help combat the housing crunch, the city recently allowed for the construction a high-density (more than 50% higher than what is normally allowed due to zoning restrictions), mixed-use unit in Mountain View's tiny downtown. Called the Park Place South Apartments, 650-961-6500, the complex is located at 851 Church Street, and offers retail, office, and living spaces in its four stories. Nearby, the Mountain View Center for the Performing Arts, 500 Castro Street, 650-903-6000, is located in a newly rebuilt downtown area centered around Castro and Church streets. The former center for anti-submarine warfare on the Pacific coast, Moffett Field Naval Air

Station, now decommissioned, is in Mountain View with a large hanger for dirigibles still in existence. Some of the complex continues to be used by NASA and federal agencies. When the President flies in, he usually lands at Moffett Airfield. Lockheed was once the major employer in the area, but after its troubles in the 1970s, high-tech firms and support industries in Mountain View, Sunnyvale, San Jose, Palo Alto, and environs are now the major employers.

MOUNTAIN VIEW
Web Site: www.ci.mtnview.ca.us
Area Code: 650
Zip Codes: 94040, 94041, 94043, 94035, 95002
Post Office: 1768 Miramonte Avenue, Mountain View, 800-275-8777
Police Station: 1000 Villa, 650-903-6707
Library: 585 Franklin Street, 650-903-6337

SOUTH BAY (SOUTHERN SANTA CLARA COUNTY)

SAN JOSE
SUNNYVALE
LOS GATOS, MONTE SERENO
CAMPBELL, CUPERTINO
SARATOGA
SANTA CLARA

Here, in Santa Clara County, silicon (atomic #14 in the periodic table) is the main ingredient for electronic chips, essentially the brains in the computers—thus the name, Silicon Valley. Located on the southern tip of San Francisco Bay and extending south all the way to Gilroy, Santa Clara County, with over 1.7 million people, is the center of the high-tech world, from the internet to computers, software, communications devices, and other technological wizardry. It is home to more than 6,000 high-tech companies including Cisco Systems, Hewlett-Packard, Apple Computer, Intel, Sun Microsystems, and many, many more.

Away from the cooling effects of Pacific fog, you'll find Santa Clara County to be much warmer than San Francisco, especially during the summer. The sky is blue and the air warm at least 300 days a year. The Mediterranean-like climate is ideal for agriculture, which was capitalized upon by early settlers here, beginning with the Ohlone Indians. The Spanish settlers came to Santa Clara County in 1777 and established El Pueblo de San Jose de Guadalupe, now known as San Jose. This community raised crops and cattle for the Spanish presidios (army bases) located in San Francisco and Monterey. In 1821, after Mexico declared its independence from Spain, San Jose became a Mexican town. Seven years later with the signing of the Treaty of Guadalupe Hidalgo, all of California joined the United States. In 1849, during the height of the Gold Rush, San Jose was declared the first state capital. In 1851 the state capital was moved to Vallejo and then eventually to Sacramento. Through the late 1800s and into much of the 1900s, agriculture was the primary industry in the area.

It was not until the later half of the 20th century when folks started moving to the area in earnest. With high-tech inventors like David Packard, William Hewlett, and the Varian brothers (inventors of an electron tube which helped develop radar and microwave technology), electronic and biotech industries began to move into areas previously occupied by farmland and orchards. According to state estimates, the city of San Jose grew from 95,000 in 1950 to over 909,000 by 1999—almost a ten-fold increase. Population continues to expand here, and is one of the fastest growing areas of the state. Matching population growth is the cost of housing. Because unemployment in Santa Clara County has been so low, finding a job may be less of a problem than finding a place to live. San Jose and its environs offer some of the highest

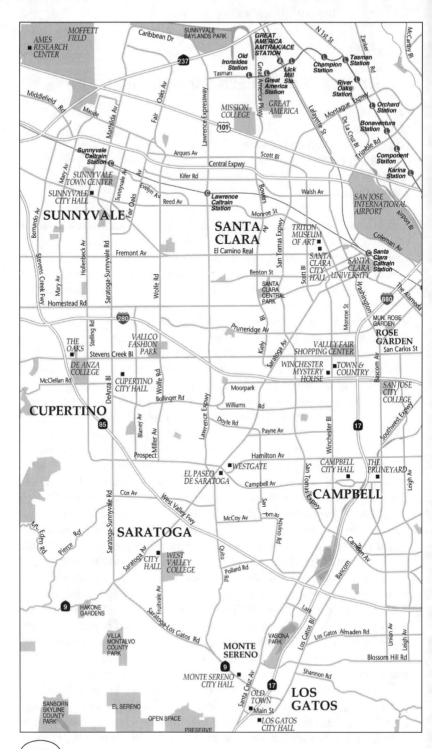

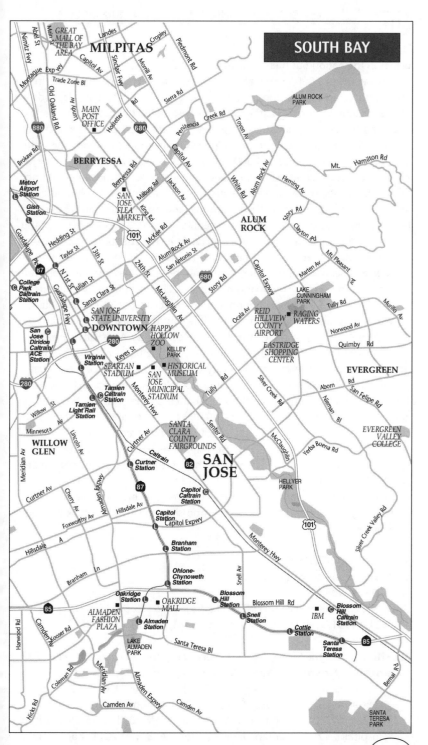

wages in the nation but there's nowhere to live!

In the fall of 2000, a look at the *San Jose Mercury News* listed a no-frills, one-bedroom apartment from about $1,100 to as high as $3,000, depending on the location. According to the California Association of Realtors, the median price of a home in Santa Clara County was reported at $359,000 in October 2000, an increase of 30.6% from the previous year. In this region where the average salary in 2000 was $83,300, a salary of $37,000 (which is the salary for a first-year public schoolteacher) makes one eligible for low-income housing. To combat costs, many people are bunking up, sharing not only houses or apartments, but also rooms. It is not unusual, for instance, for a four-bedroom family home to be rented to ten single people who share bedrooms or use the living and dining rooms as personal spaces. As is the case for most of the Bay Area, the housing crunch is pushing low- to middle-income people—service workers and schoolteachers—out of the area because they cannot afford the high rents. Some people working in Silicon Valley commute by plane from Arizona or Utah. Take a look around and it may seem that South Bay housing developments are springing up all the time, but the pace is not keeping up with demand. According to the Association of Bay Area Governments, between 1994 and 1999, 220,000 new jobs were offered while only 28,000 new living spaces were created. Industry experts and local officials have been decrying the affordable housing shortage. To help first-time home buyers, the County established a specialized home finance program where the County and California Federal provide up to $40,000 (not to exceed 20% of the purchase price) for shared appreciation mortgages. A shared appreciation mortgage assumes that over time a house will appreciate, a percentage of that appreciation amount is then tacked onto the mortgage. For more information, call the CASA Hotline at 888-403-2272.

Don't be discouraged if you want to move here, just bring your creative juices and your scouting hat—it is not impossible to find a place, but it does take diligence.

SANTA CLARA COUNTY

Web Site: www.co.santa-clara.ca.us

Area Code: 408

Zip Codes: 95109, 95110, 95111, 95112, 95113, 95116, 95119, 95125, 95126, 95128, 95129, 95133, 95134, 95136, 95141, 95148, 95150, 95151, 95192, and more

Sheriff: Office of the Sheriff, 55 West Younger Avenue, San Jose, 800-211-2220

Emergency Hospitals: Santa Clara Valley Medical Center, 751 South Bascom, San Jose, 408-885-5000; San Jose Medical Center, 225 North Jackson Avenue, San Jose, 408-259-5000; Columbia San Jose Medical Center, 675 East Santa Clara Street, 408-559-2011; Good Samaritan Hospital, 2425 Samaritan Drive, San Jose, 408-559-2011; Kaiser Santa

Teresa Community Medical Hospital, 250 Hospital Parkway, San Jose, 408-972-7000

Library: Santa Clara County Library System, 1095 North 7th Street, San Jose, 408-293-2326, www.lib.co-santa-clara.ca.us

Public Schools: Santa Clara County Office of Education, 1290 Ridder Road, San Jose, www.sccoe.k12.ca.us

Community Publications: *San Jose Mercury News*, 408-920-5000; *San Jose City Times*, 408-298-8000; *San Jose Post Record*, 408-287-4866; *Metro*, *408-298-8000*; *Business Journal*, 408-295-3800

Community Resources: San Jose Symphony Orchestra, 495 Almaden Boulevard, 408-288-2828, www.sanjosesymphony.org; Opera San Jose, 2149 Paragon Drive, 408-437-4450, www.operasj.org; San Jose Cleveland Ballet, 40 North First, 408-288-2800; Lick Observatory, Mount Hamilton, 408-274-5061; Minolta Planetarium, 12150 Stevens Creek Boulevard, 408-864-8814; Tech Museum of Innovation, 201 South Market Street, 408-795-6100; American Musical Theater of San Jose, Center for the Performing Arts, 408-453-7108

Public Transportation: *Santa Clara Valley Transportation Authority* (*SCVTA*), 408-321-2300, www.vta.org; *RIDES*, 800-755-7665; *CalTrain*, 800-660-4287

SAN JOSE

DOWNTOWN SAN JOSE
ROSE GARDEN
NAGLEE PARK
WILLOW GLEN
EVERGREEN
SANTA TERESA
ALMADEN VALLEY
FRUITDALE

San Jose, the self-proclaimed capital of Silicon Valley, is large (about 176 square miles and over 900,000 residents), and growing larger. Architecturally, housing runs the gamut, from studio apartments, to small 1950s and '60s bungalows, to multi-million dollar, gated estates. Most of the housing stock is fairly new, built since 1960 to meet population demands; however, there are neighborhoods with historic Victorians or old ranch homes built at the turn of the century. Median home prices here increased 30% from October 1999 to October 2000—from $323,000 to $420,000.

Due to its vast size, there are dozens of neighborhoods in San Jose, some officially recognized as such by city leaders, others existing only in the hearts and minds of those residing there. Among the best known in the former category are the Downtown Museum district, Rose Garden Neighborhood, Naglee Park, Willow Glen, Evergreen, Santa Teresa, Almaden Valley, and Fruitdale neighborhoods.

Downtown San Jose has undergone a striking transformation in recent years. Just fifteen years ago many would say the city was suffering from an identity crisis. People drove north to San Francisco for entertainment, and walking in downtown San Jose after hours was almost like being in a ghost town. But today, the city's place as the leader in technology is clear. Since 1984, more than two billion dollars have been pumped into the downtown area, creating museums, convention centers, theaters, a light rail system, fountains, offices, restaurants, and shopping areas. The Plaza de Cesar Chavez, smack in the center of the museums and just across from the newly renovated Fairmont Hotel, has an incredible fountain with nozzles spraying water right out of the sidewalk. It's a perfect place to cool off on a hot summer day. Another addition is the $140 million, 20,000 seat San Jose Arena opened in 1993. Not only is the Arena home to the San Jose Sharks Hockey team, but it also hosts big name entertainers from around the world. Major League Soccer's San Jose Earthquakes play at San Jose State's Spartan Stadium on 7th Street, just south of downtown San Jose.

One of the highlights of the downtown revitalization project is the Tech Museum of Innovation, considered to be the Bay Area's premier science museum. Opened in the early 1990s, the Tech quickly outgrew its original quarters, and in 1998 the ribbon was cut at its new 132,000-square-foot, mango colored facility at the corner of Market Street and Park Avenue. The museum boasts nearly 300 hands-on exhibits that allow visitors to do such things as design their own bicycle and ride a roller coaster. You can also get a 3-D map of your head made by a rotating laser scanner, and catch a film at the state of the art IMAX Dome Theater. The famous Winchester Mystery House, 525 South Winchester Boulevard, 408-247-2000, is a popular outing, and the Overfelt Botanical Gardens, 2145 McKee Road, 408-251-3323, is a perfect place to contemplate life and play in the gardens. On the third Thursday of every month the downtown art galleries stay open late, fostering a cultural nightlife. Also on Thursday evenings in the summer, you can enjoy live concerts in the Plaza de Cesar Chavez. On Friday afternoons, locals frequent the farmers' market on San Pedro Street between Santa Clara and St. John streets.

San Jose International Airport is three miles from downtown and, like Oakland International Airport, is easier and friendlier to use than San Francisco International (SFO). Although recently, with the tremendous growth, there are reports that the airport has been having some problems with respect to parking and crowds.

While there are a few homes in the downtown area, ranging from bungalows to mansions, most people looking for city living head toward one of San Jose's residential areas. The **Rose Garden** neighborhood is centrally located in

San Jose, west of downtown, and bordered by the Alameda Roadway on the east, Interstate 880 on the northwest, and Naglee Avenue on the north. The area is named for the city's magnificent public rose garden located at Dana and Naglee avenues—a lovely place for an early morning stroll. Also in the neighborhood is the Rosicrucian Egyptian Museum and Planetarium, 1342 Naglee Avenue. With the pyramids and sphinxes, you feel like you just might be in Egypt.

Housing choices in the Rose Garden neighborhood include exquisite Queen Anne Victorians, some Tudor-style homes, contemporary apartments, and many new condominiums. With San Jose State University located nearby, you'll find a lot of students here, as well as plenty of professionals and their families. Those interested in architectural preservation may want to get involved in the Rose Garden Neighborhood Preservation Association, www.rgnpa.org. This neighborhood's proximity to the airport and CalTrain tracks may be a noise problem for some.

The oldest neighborhood in San Jose, **Naglee Park**, is in the center core of the city, just east of San Jose State University bordered by Highway 280 on the south, Coyote Creek on the east, 10th Street to the west, and Santa Clara Street to the north. The neighborhood is named for General Henry Naglee who owned a 140-acre estate and lived on 14th and East San Fernando streets. In addition to General Naglee's still-standing house, there are classic Victorian and Craftsman-style homes, and stately mansions dating from the early 1900s, some of which have been divided into apartments and duplexes. You'll also find a number of newer apartment complexes dating from the 1970s and '80s.

Naglee Park locals enjoy the playground at William Street Park, as well as the annual Bark in the Park Festival for dogs, hosted here each July. Then there's the Fourth of July parade, BBQs, and a play-group for moms and tots each morning. The neighborhood is made up of plenty of young families and young, dot.com entrepreneurs; it's also the home of San Jose Mayor Ron Gonzales.

Santa Clara Street which runs east-west through the center of Naglee Park is in the midst of a drastic facelift as a new City Hall, elementary school and symphony are all in various stages of construction. Expected completion for the entire project is slated for 2005. Newcomers looking at housing along Coyote Creek should be aware that the creek sometimes overflows in the winter months. Another family preferred area is the **Willow Glen** neighborhood, just three miles southwest of downtown San Jose, and easily accessible to the light rail system. Named after the willow trees that grow along the creeks and Guadalupe River, the neighborhood is composed of what used to be the town of Willow Glen. Founded in 1927, it was annexed by San Jose just nine years later (this is an oft-repeated story of San Jose's growth). Newcomers to Willow Glen wanting to get involved in the community should consider joining the active Willow Glen Neighborhood Association, www.wgna.net, "a grassroots community organization dedicated to improving life in Willow Glen." Among other neighborhood improvement projects, this organization looks for ways to preserve the history of this area. Architecturally you have the usual Victorians mixed in with Eichlers, Tudors, some ranch-style homes, and Mediterranean-style stuccos. A number of older houses are being torn down and replaced with larger abodes. Young families find this neighborhood attractive because it is safe, comfortable, and more affordable than nearby Los Gatos and Saratoga. Many residents have lived here for a long time, and it seems few have plans to leave any time soon. During the winter holidays many of the houses here are adorned with twinkling lights, reindeer, and elaborate manger scenes, drawing people from all over the Bay Area for a neighborhood tour.

Willow Glen's commercial area, along Lincoln Avenue, is quaint, with restaurants, coffee shops, boutiques, and antique shops. No chain stores here, as locals fight hard to keep this area a one-of-a-kind place. There is a farmers' market every Saturday at the corner of Willow and Lincoln.

Southeast of downtown San Jose, on the eastern side of Highway 101, is the **Evergreen** area, one of the most recently developed areas of the South Bay. Housing here is relatively new. Much of it was built starting about 20 years ago, and is made up largely of modern apartments and large homes with three-, four-, and even five-bedrooms. The Police Academy is located on Evergreen Community College campus at 3095 Yerba Buena Road. South is the golf course, Silver Creek Valley Country Club, 5460 Country Club Parkway, and a gated community with about 1,500 Mediterranean-style homes. One of the main drawbacks of Evergreen is its lack of immediate freeway access; the main road to get to the freeway is the often-gridlocked Yerba Buena Road.

The **Santa Teresa** neighborhood is located at the end of the light rail system, south of Evergreen, and bordered by Blossom Hill Road on the north, Santa Teresa Boulevard on the west, and Monterey Road on the east. Here is where you'll find the sprawling IBM campus, with many of its workforce living in the housing tracts nearby. Most homes here were built in the 1960s, though new developments are being added. A lovely expanse of green space is located nearby at the 1,688-acre Santa Teresa County Park, along Santa Teresa's southern border. For a view of the sprawling city and the mountains, climb Coyote Peak.

Just west of Blossom Valley is **Almaden Valley**, named for the quicksilver mines and also known as Silver Creek Valley. With the Santa Teresa Hills on the east and the foothills of the Santa Cruz Mountains on the west, this area feels more rural than San Jose's other neighborhoods. There is a mixture of housing here—some old, some built in the 1960s—and in the past five years the area has exploded with new, custom-built million dollar plus homes. Many San Jose old timers are in shock that this neighborhood has become so valuable. The often-gridlocked 101 Freeway, and lack of convenient shopping may be problematic for some. Almaden Lake Park, located at the intersection of Almaden Expressway and Coleman Avenue, has a sandy beach and swim area, which comes in handy during hot summer days. Also on the lake are kayaks, pedal boats, and windsurfers.

The **Fruitdale** area, east of San Jose, is named for the fruit orchards, especially prunes, which used to grow here. Today, middle-class homes, shopping malls, and apartments have replaced the orchards. San Jose City College, 2100 Moorpark Avenue, is also located here.

SAN JOSE
Web Site: www.ci.san-jose.ca.us
Area Codes: 408, 699
Zip Codes: 95109, 95110, 95111, 95112, 95113, 95116, 95119, 95125, 95126, 95128, 95129, 95133, 95134, 95136, 95141, 95148, 95150, 95151, 95192
Post Office: 1750 Lundy Avenue, San Jose, 800-275-8777
Police: 201 West Mission, 408-277-8900
Library: 180 West San Carlos, San Jose, 408-277-5700, www.sjpl.lib.ca.us
Public Schools: Santa Clara County Office of Education, 1290 Ridder Road, San Jose, www.sccoe.k12.ca.us
Community Publications: *San Jose Mercury News*, 408-920-5000; *San Jose City Times*, 408-298-8000; *San Jose Post Record*, 408-287-4866; *Metro*, *408-298-8000*; *Business Journal*, 408-295-3800
Cultural Resources: San Jose Silicon Valley Chamber of Commerce, 408-291-5250; Peralta Adobe, 154 West Street John Street, 408-993-8182; San Jose Historical Museum, 1600 Senter Road, 408-287-2290; Santa Clara de Asis Mission, Franklin and Market, 408-554-4023, American Museum of Quilts and Textiles, 766 South Second Street, 408-971-0323; San Jose Museum of Art, 110 South Market Street, 408-294-2787; San Jose Institute of Contemporary Art, 451 South First Street, 408-283-8155; San Jose Symphony Orchestra, 495 Almaden Boulevard, 408-288-2828, www.sanjosesymphony.org; Opera San Jose, 2149 Paragon Drive, 408-437-4450, www.operasj.org; San Jose Cleveland Ballet, 40 North First, 408-288-2800; Lick Observatory, Mount Hamilton, 408-274-5061; Minolta Planetarium, 12150 Stevens Creek Boulevard, 408-864-8814; Tech Museum of Innovation, 201 South Market Street, 408-795-6100; American Musical Theater of San Jose, Center for the Performing Arts, 408-453-7108; Happy Hollow Park and Zoo, 1300 Senter Road, 408-292-8188; Emma Prusch Farm Park, 647 South King Road, 408-926-5555
Community Resources: San Jose Convention and Visitors' Bureau, in the McEnery Convention Center, 150 West San Carlos Street, 408-291-5250; City of San Jose Park, Recreation and Neighborhood Services, 4 North 2nd Street, Suite 600, 408-277-4661; Almaden Community Center, 6445 Camden Avenue, 408-268-1133; Evergreen Community Center, 4860 San Felipe Road, 408-270-2220; Sherman Oaks Community Center, 1800A Fruitdale Avenue, 408-292-2935; Rose Garden Neighborhood Preservation Association, P.O. Box 28761, 408-236-2130; Willow Glen Neighborhood Association, 408-294-9462, www.wgna.net

SUNNYVALE

Considered the heart of Silicon Valley, Sunnyvale (131,000) is reputed to be one of the best-managed municipalities in the nation. Civic leaders have a reputation for listening to local residents, often incorporating their suggestions into civic plans. In fact, government officials from around the country have come to Sunnyvale to study how this city is run, in the hopes of taking back good ideas for their own communities. Sunnyvale is home to a large corporate tax base and therefore has ample funds to run its city. Amenities include 17 parks, 68 tennis courts, two theater groups, two golf courses, a sports complex, a dance company, and much more. Residents also enjoy the Baylands Nature Preserve, 408-730-7709, located at the end of Lawrence Expressway off Highway 237, at Caribbean Drive. This 70-acre park is a bird watcher's paradise. The 10-acre Orchard Heritage Park, 550 East Remington Avenue, 408-739-5004, is one of the area's newest recreation additions.

Houses vary from multi-story condominium townhouses with the requisite pool, to red-tiled Mediterranean-style homes, to multi-mansions. The average price for a home in October 2000 was $565,000, up over 46% from the previous year. Downtown Sunnyvale is undergoing serious construction with a new City Plaza, new office buildings, and a 20-screen movie theater. The historic Murphy Avenue has a number of new restaurants and shops, and a Saturday farmers' market on South Murphy Avenue, between Evelyn and Washington streets. Two shopping malls serve the area, the Silicon Valley WAVE (Walk and Village Entertainment) at 2502 Town Center Lane, and the Town & Country Village at 304 Town and Country.

The 23.8-square-miles of Sunnyvale is said to be home to more high-tech companies than any other city in the world. Advanced Micro Devices, Amdahl, Hewlett-Packard, Applied Signal Technologies, Mercury Interactive, and Lockheed Martin Missiles and Space are only a few of the hundreds of high-tech businesses that operate here. Lockheed alone employs more than 12,000 people. Back in the turn of the century Walter Crossman, the city's first developer, was on to something when he dubbed the scarcely populated agricultural town, "the City of Destiny." If only he could see how prophetic his words were.

SUNNYVALE
Web Site: www.ci.sunnyvale.ca.us
Area Codes: 408, 669
Zip Codes: 94086, 94087, 94088, 94089
Post Office: 580 North Mary Avenue, Sunnyvale, 800-275-8777
Police: 700 All America, 408-730-7110
Library: Main Library, 665 West Olive Avenue, Sunnyvale, 408-730-7309

Public Schools: Santa Clara County Office of Education, 1290 Ridder Road, San Jose 95131, www.sccoe.k12.ca.us

Community Publication: *Sunnyvale Sun*, 408-481-0176, www.sunnyvale-sun.com

Community Resources: Sunnyvale Chamber of Commerce, 499 South Murphy, 408-736-4971; Sunnyvale Community Center Theater, 550 East Remington Drive, 408-733-6611; Sunnyvale Volunteer Services Program, 408-730-7533

LOS GATOS, MONTE SERENO

Considered by many to be one of the loveliest towns in the South Bay, **Los Gatos** is tucked away in the hills just east of the Santa Cruz Mountains, off of Highway 17. This community of about 29,000 is upscale, picture-perfect, woodsy, politically progressive, and prides itself on its strong sense of community. The average household income is considerably more than the rest of the county. According to the Association of Bay Area Governments, the 2000 mean household income for Los Gatos was $128,800, compared to the rest of the county's average of $83,300. With such money it's no wonder the hills are peppered with newly built mansions, especially in the Blossom Hill Manor area. More modest, early 1900s Victorians are still in existence as well. In October 2000, the median price for a home in Los Gatos was $790,000, up 51% from the previous year. For an even more upscale area, visit the city of **Monte Sereno** (population 3,600), right next to Los Gatos. An old, established community, it's known for its multi-million dollar homes sitting on expansive lots. See www.montesereno.org for more information about this quaint town.

With 15 parks, and eight playgrounds, people in Los Gatos have every opportunity to enjoy the outdoors. Year round, the Los Gatos Creek Trail, just outside the downtown on Main Street, abounds with thrill-seeking cyclists, runners, and walkers. The five-mile path winds up into the hills and around the Lexington Reservoir, providing spectacular views guaranteed to please. For an outdoor experience more suited to the family, try Vasona Park where you can picnic, roller blade, jog, bike, or just go for a stroll. For a leisurely afternoon in the lake, rent a paddleboat. Next to Vasona Park is Oak Meadow Park where you can ride a carousel or a miniature train, or just settle down for a picnic.

If shopping is more your thing you'll want visit North Santa Cruz Avenue. This upscale shopping district is full of trendy boutiques, art galleries, restaurants, and cafes that lure people from all over the country. Warm evenings bring locals in to browse the sales, window shop, and stop for cappuccinos or a bite to eat. Singles frequent the Los Gatos Brewing Company at 130-G North Santa Cruz Avenue, and Steamers, 50 University Avenue. In the summer, on Sunday evenings there is music in the plaza, at the corner of Main and North Santa Cruz.

In the fall, Los Gatos High School, 20 High School Court, located just a short walk from downtown, brings in local fans to watch the Friday night football games. During the Christmas season horse drawn carriages prance around the town. All in all life here is pretty good, and the weather hasn't even been mentioned yet. There is, on average, 330 sunny days per year here. Nor is it too cold or too hot; average temperatures in January are 46° Fahrenheit, in July, 71°.

Los Gatos is centrally located for anyone having to commute to Silicon Valley. Better yet, a trip to the beach and boardwalk in Santa Cruz is about 40 minutes south, via Highway 17.

LOS GATOS
Web Site: www.los-gatos.ca.us
Area Code: 408
Zip Codes: 95030, 95031, 95032
Post Office: 101 South Santa Cruz Avenue, 408-354-5801
Police: 110 East Main Street, 408-354-5257
Library: 110 East Main Street, 408-354-6891

CAMPBELL, CUPERTINO

Other cities to consider if you are looking in the South Bay are Campbell (40,000), and Cupertino (55,000). Both are located in the foothills of the Santa Cruz Mountains and both communities are very suburban, with shopping malls, parks with tennis courts and play lots, and many families. In addition, there are some major high-tech companies here, including E-Bay and Apple.

Campbell, home to online auction house E-Bay, borders Willow Glen and Los Gatos. The portion of Cambell between Bascom and Meridian avenues features wide, tree-lined streets with ranch-style and Eichler homes. Named after the prune yard drying days, the Pruneyard Shopping Center on Bascom and Campbell avenues offers a choice of restaurants and stores, including Starbucks, Barnes and Noble, and Trader Joes. The Rock Bottom Brewery, 1875 South Bascom Avenue, is a nice place to have a burger and catch a televised sports game. For family-style Italian fare try Buca di Beppo, 1875 South Bascom Avenue.

The old commercial heart of Campbell is along Campbell Avenue. Here you'll find cafes with internet access, antique shops, dry cleaners, and a hodge-podge of ethnic restaurants and mom and pop stores. The choice for Italian here is Mio Vicino at 384 East Campbell Avenue. Nearby at 1690 South Bascom Avenue is the popular Whole Foods, a gourmet grocery store featuring health food, organic fruits and vegetables, and freshly prepared meals. Many come here during their lunch hour or to pick up dinner on their way home from work. Fresh Choice, 1654 South Bascom, is down the street where, for about $9, you can choose the "all-you-can-eat" salad, soup, pasta, bread, potato, pizza, and dessert bar. On Campbell Avenue, between First Street and Central Avenue there is a year round farmers' market, which is held every Sunday morning, rain or shine.

Property prices in Campbell have increased considerably recently. According to the California Association of Realtors, the October 2000 median home price was $449,000, up 34% from October 1999. To assist first-time homebuyers, Campbell offers a CASA Home Loan Program with a small down payment and low monthly payments. As of December 2000, the maximum household income to qualify for the program was $69,700. For more information, contact the Home Loan Program at 888-403-2272.

The 13-square-mile city of **Cupertino** grew prodigiously after WW II, first as a weekend destination for wealthy San Franciscans, and today as a thriving residential and business community. In 1950, there were only 500 homes in Cupertino; today there are more than 17,000. Cupertino, which borders Saratoga and Sunnyvale, does not have an established downtown center; strip malls are common. High-tech offices include Apple Computer, Hewlett-Packard, and Compaq. The schools here are good, said to be among the best around, with Monte Vista High School gaining worldwide recognition for its computer program.

Travel north on Highway 9 from Saratoga, which becomes Saratoga-Sunnyvale Road, and you'll know you've arrived in Cupertino when you begin to see the many Asian restaurants and grocery stores. To the west of Saratoga-Sunnyvale Road sit the Cupertino Foothills, home to million dollar mansions with acres of open space behind them. Outdoor enthusiasts come here for mountain biking and hiking. There is a Whole Foods in Cupertino at 20830 Stevens Creek Boulevard, and next door, Fontana's, 20840 Stevens Creek Boulevard, is a romantic Italian restaurant. Locals frequent The Oaks Shopping Center at 21275 Stevens Creek Boulevard for its movie-theater, cafe, fitness center (for women only), and the popular, A Clean, Well-Lighted Place For Books. Across the street is De Anza College, and the Flint Center, which features concerts, Broadway plays, and comedians.

If you are looking for a home in Cupertino, you'll find dozens of new condominiums mixed in with single family homes and a few older homes, located along wide boulevards. The median home price in October 2000 was $762,000, up 41% from October 1999.

CAMPBELL
Web Site: www.ci.campbell.ca.us
Area Codes: 408, 669
Zip Code: 95008
Post Office: 500 West Hamilton Avenue, 800-275-8777
Police: 70 North First Street, 408-866-2121

Library: Library of Santa Clara County, 77 Harrison Avenue, Campbell, 408-866-1991

Public Schools: Santa Clara County Office of Education, 1290 Ridder Road, San Jose, www.sccoe.k12.ca.us

Community Publications: *Campbell Express*, 408-374-9700; *Campbell Times*, 408-494-7000

Community Resources: Campbell Community Center, 408-866-2138; Campbell Chamber of Commerce, 408-378-1666

CUPERTINO

Web Site: www.cupertino.org

Zip Codes: 95014, 95015

Area Codes: 408, 669

Post Office: 21701 Stevens Creek Boulevard, Cupertino, 800-275-8777

Police: 408-299-3233

Library: Cupertino Public Library, 10400 Torre Avenue, Cupertino, 408-446-1677

Public Schools: Santa Clara County Office of Education, 1290 Ridder Road, San Jose, www.sccoe.k12.ca.us

Community Publication: *Cupertino Courier*, 408-255-7500

Community Resources: Cupertino Chamber of Commerce, 20455 Silverado Avenue, 408-252-7054; Quinlan Community Center, 10185 North Stelling Road, 408-777-3120; De Anza College Flint Center for the Performing Arts, P.O. Box 1897, 408-864-8816; Cupertino Historical Museum, 10185 North Stelling Road, 408-973-1495; Asian-Americans for Community Involvement, 408-975-2730; Daughters of Norway, 408-255-9828; Language Bank Cupertino Historical Society, 408-973-1495

SARATOGA

Saratoga (31,000) is located 10 miles west of San Jose in the golden foothills of the Santa Cruz Mountains. The city's 12 square miles include numerous creeks, wooded trails, and streets lined with mature oak trees. The city is decidedly upscale with a mean household income in 2000 of about $132,400. According to the *San Jose Mercury News*, Saratoga had the most million dollar home sales in the state in 2000. The median home price in August 2000 confirmed this, at $1.3 million, up 59% from the previous year. Like Los Gatos, the community has easy access to the outdoors. The downtown area, on Big Basin Avenue, is where you'll find upscale restaurants and boutique shopping.

Proximity to the Santa Cruz redwood trees is what put Saratoga on the map; by the mid-1800s it was a thriving lumber town. After lumber, agriculture in the form of fruit orchards, especially prunes, became the economy's mainstay. Around the turn of the 20th century wealthy San Franciscans started building summer cottages here for weekend and summer getaways, which added tourism to the economy. Today the orchards are gone and the area is considered a bedroom community for Silicon Valley. Architecturally, you'll find many grand ranch style estates and two-story Victorians. Famous architect Julia Morgan (best known for the Hearst Castle) designed the Saratoga Foothill Club in 1915. Of note, Steven Spielberg graduated from Saratoga High School and actresses Olivia de Havilland and her sister Joan Fontaine began their careers in Saratoga.

One of the highlights of Saratoga is Hakone Gardens, 21000 Big Basin Way, 408-741-4994, a replica of a 17th century Japanese Zen garden. These gardens were created in 1918 by the former gardener to the Emperor of Japan. It is considered to be the only authentic Japanese garden in Northern California, the Japanese Tea Garden in San Francisco notwithstanding. For summer concerts, locals frequent the Paul Masson Mountain Winery located at 14831 Pierce Road, 408-741-0763. Another getaway is The Villa Montalvo Cultural Center, 15400 Montalvo Road, 408-961-5800, a 175-acre estate with beautiful gardens, a bird sanctuary, and nature trails. The center hosts concerts and plays at its outdoor amphitheater. It received its initial funding from US Senator James Phelan who, upon his death in 1930, left the estate with a mission to support the arts. Today artists live and work at the center. Rock climbers come from all over the Bay Area to Castle Rock State Park at the intersection of Route 35 and Highway 9, which offers challenging belays. Hikers, horseback riders, and mountain bikers also enjoy the 32 miles of trails at the park.

SARATOGA
Web Site: www.saratoga.ca.us
Area Code: 408
Zip Code: 95070
Post Office: 13650 Saratoga Avenue, 408-867-6126
Sheriff: Office of the Sheriff, West Side Substation 408-867-9715
Library: Saratoga Community Library, 13650 Saratoga Avenue, 408-867-6126

SANTA CLARA

The City of Santa Clara, (101,900) started out in 1777 as a Spanish mission, and later evolved into a prime agricultural region with expansive orchards as well as a lumber community. Like many of the other surrounding towns, Santa Clara reaped the immediate benefits of the old growth redwood trees. In 1874, the Pacific Manufacturing Company set up shop, cutting down thousands of redwood trees and becoming one of the largest suppliers of wood. By 1906 Santa Clara's population increased to a whopping 5,000. By 1950, when the semiconductor chip was developed and most of the redwoods had been cut down, many of the orchards were ploughed under, making way for the industrial expansion for which Santa Clara is known today. About 150,000 people work in Santa Clara for companies such as Intel, 3COM, Applied Materials, Yahoo!, and Hewlett Packard.

In addition to high-tech, Santa Clara University, 500 El Camino Real, 408-554-4000, and Mission Community College, 3000 Mission College Boulevard, 408-988-2200, are located in Santa Clara. Founded in 1851 on mission grounds, Santa Clara University is one of the West Coast's oldest universities. Another attraction is Paramount's Great America amusement park on Highway 101 in Santa Clara, 408-988-1776. Also noteworthy is the International Swim Club, 2625 Patricia Drive, which is a training place for swimmers. Since it opened in 1951 more than 50 Olympians have trained here, bringing home 33 gold, 12 silver, and 10 bronze medals.

Because Santa Clara developed earlier than many surrounding areas, you'll find its residential neighborhoods are older. Housing is somewhat more affordable than Sunnyvale or Mountain View, and therefore more appealing to young families and those just getting started. According to the California Association of Realtors, the median home price in October 2000 was $475,000, an increase of 35.7% from the previous year. Santa Clara is home to a substantial number of Italian, Asian and Indian immigrant populations and has the restaurants to prove it.

To learn more about the A, B, Cs of the computer industry that is so entrenched here, visit the Intel Museum, 2200 Mission College Boulevard, 408-765-0503.

SANTA CLARA
Web Sites: www.santaclara.org, www.ci.santa-clara-ca.us
Area Codes: 408, 669
Zip Codes: 95050, 95051
Post Office: 1200 Franklin Mall on Jackson Street, Santa Clara, 800-275-8777
Police: 408-261-5300
Library: Central Library, 2635 Homestead Road, Santa Clara, 408-615-2900
Public Schools: Santa Clara County Office of Education, 1290 Ridder Road, San Jose, www.sccoe.k12.ca.us
Community Publications: *Santa Clara Weekly*, 408-243-3000; *Santa Clara Silicon Valley Visitors' Guide*, 408-244-8244
Community Resources: Santa Clara Convention and Visitor's Bureau, 408-244-8244; Santa Clara Chamber of Commerce, 1850 Warburton Avenue, 408-244-8244; Triton Museum of Art, 1505 Warburton Avenue, 408-247-3754; Intel Museum, 2200 Mission College Boulevard, 408-765-0503; Santa Clara Players, Santa Clara Community Center, 408-248-7993; Louis B. Mayer Theatre, Santa Clara University, 408-554-4989; Santa Clara Historical Museum, 1509 Warburton Avenue, 408-248-2787; Paramount's Great America Amusement Park, Highway 101, 408-988-1776

S AN FRANCISCO'S 43 HILLS PREVENTED CITY PLANNERS FROM IMPLE-
menting a grand, area-wide roadway grid system, so finding the desired
street address here can be a challenge. A good map or atlas is highly recommended. Avoid the small tourist maps; they often distort proportions and
exclude big chunks of geography that will prove important to a resident. Transit
maps are useful if you're not relying on your car to get around but they don't
offer enough detailed information to serve as your primary guidance tool.

City maps are available at stores across the Bay Area, but cartography
buffs will want to check out the **Thomas Bros. Maps** store at 550 Jackson
Street in San Francisco. The company's *Thomas Guide* is the most detailed rep-
resentation of the city you can buy. Call 800-899-6277 or check online at
www.thomas.com for more information. You can also get maps free from the
American Automobile Association (AAA) if you're a member.

With map in hand you may want to spend a few moments locating the
major streets and highways listed below:

- First there's **Market Street**. It's San Francisco's main downtown street, and
  it starts across from the Ferry Building. As with all east-west running streets
  that begin at the downtown's eastern edge, address numbers begin there
  and increase as you head towards the ocean. Market serves as the border
  between the Financial District, Union Square and Tenderloin areas to the
  north, and the South of Market (SOMA) district to the south. For north-
  south running streets, address numbering begins at Market, with the lowest
  numbers at Market. On streets north of Market, the numbers increase as you
  go north. On the other side, the street numbers increase as you travel south.
- Another main street is **Van Ness Avenue**, which runs north-south and
  begins one block west of 10th Street, crossing Market. It serves as part of
  the Highway 101 connection to the Golden Gate Bridge, along with
  Lombard Street, Marina Boulevard, and **Doyle Drive**. Street numbers
  increase as you travel north on Van Ness.
- **Geary Street** splits off from Market in the downtown area, runs east-west,

and goes all the way out to the Pacific Ocean, although once it crosses into "the Avenues" its name changes to **Geary Boulevard**. Numbering begins downtown and increases as you go west.

- **"The Avenues"** is the locally accepted name for the area served by the numbered roadways in the Richmond District, **3rd Avenue** through **46th Avenue**, and it's important to know because the City also has numbered "streets," **1st Street** through **30th Street**. Don't confuse the streets and the avenues as they are entirely different neighborhoods. The avenues also extend down into the Sunset and Parkside districts. The numbered streets begin in the SOMA and run north-south until the Mission District where they run east-west into the Potrero Hill, Bernal Heights, Castro, Noe Valley districts after 14th Street. Thus when someone tells you that the store you want is on "24th" you'll need to clarify, "24th Street or 24th Avenue?"

- **Nineteenth Avenue** is a good roadway to become familiar with since it serves as another connector road, along with **Park Presidio Boulevard**, to the Golden Gate Bridge from **Interstate 280** and **Highway 1**. Both run into the city from San Mateo County to the south. Nineteenth Avenue splits off from 280/1 just inside the San Francisco city limits, runs right in front of San Francisco State University, out through the Sunset District and into Golden Gate Park. Its name changes to Park Presidio Boulevard on the northern side of the park. If traffic is really bad on 19th Avenue, and it often is, **Sunset Boulevard** is just a few blocks to the west and is usually a good route through the Sunset.

- **Highway 101** also enters San Francisco from the south, however it splits off to head for the Oakland-San Francisco Bay Bridge where **I-80** begins. Interstate 80 will take you through the northern half of the East Bay, out to Sacramento, the Sierra Nevada, all the way to New York City.

BEYOND SAN FRANCISCO

Two major highways, running north and south, connect San Francisco with the Peninsula and the South Bay, Highway 101 and Interstate 280. **Highway 101** is notoriously crowded and weaves through the heavily populated cities of the Peninsula and South Bay. Highway 101 goes all the way from Los Angeles to the state of Washington. A more scenic drive and often less crowded is **I-280** (known as Junipero Serra Freeway), which starts near the Bay Bridge on the San Francisco side and goes south past Daly City, continues down the west side of the Bay, and culminates at the I-680 junction. Close to the San Francisco Airport, **I-380** links Highway 101 with I-280. **Highway 85**, also known as **Stevens Creek Freeway**, connects 101 with 280 from Mountain View to Cupertino. **Interstate 880** is another connector for 101 and 280, slicing through the city of San Jose. Father north, **Highway 92** runs through the Peninsula, around San Mateo, and traverses west all the way to the coast ending in Half Moon Bay. Another coastal connector is **Highway 84**, which links Redwood City with Woodside and then, like Highway 92, goes all the way to the coast, ending at Highway 1. Certainly the most scenic highway in the Bay Area, and arguably in the country, **Highway 1** twists and turns itself along the western edge of the US, going south to LA and north to Washington.

Both the San Mateo Bridge and the Dumbarton Bridge connect the South Bay with the East Bay. The longest bridge in the Bay Area, the 6.8 mile **San Mateo Bridge**, links Foster City with Hayward via Highway 92. The **Dumbarton Bridge** connects Fremont and Newark in the East Bay with Palo Alto and Menlo Park. The southernmost bridge crossing the Bay, the Dumbarton Bridge is part of Highway 84, which can be accessed via the Willow Road off ramp from Highway 101.

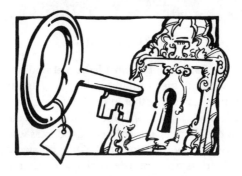

L OOKING FOR A PLACE TO LIVE IN THE BAY AREA CAN BE A DISCOURAG-
ing experience. As you probably are aware, the San Francisco Bay Area is
regularly ranked among the nation's most expensive places to live, and
since 1997 the apartment vacancy rate in San Francisco has been calculated at
less than one percent. In such a tight housing market chances are you won't be
the only applicant for whatever apartment or home you set your sights on.
What's more, don't be surprised if you don't get the apartment or home you
want because someone else offers more for the place. It is not uncommon for
a house or apartment to be listed at one price, only to have interested tenants
or buyers raise the ante and offer more than the listing price! As grim as the
apartment and house hunting process might sound, keep in mind that salaries
are higher here than in most other areas of the country, and there *are* places
available. Persistence is the key to finding what you want here, along with the
willingness to settle for something less while still pursuing your dream apartment or home. Preparation and creativity are also helpful when looking for a
place to live in the Bay Area. During your apartment hunt, be prepared with
checkbook, resume, and letters of reference in hand, and if you like a neighborhood, start talking to the neighbors. They just might know of a place for
rent that has not yet been put on the market.

Housing options in the Bay Area are varied. San Francisco's most distinctive dwellings are its wood-framed Victorian homes, many of which have been
remodeled and turned into flats with two to four units per building. You will
also find a large number of Edwardian apartment buildings each containing
dozens of units. Here in quake country, wood-framed buildings, especially if
they are built on rock, are safest because they give a little when the earth
moves beneath them. Un-reinforced brick buildings are not safe in an earthquake, so if you find a nice apartment in one of these you should be aware of
the added risk. Also, if you're especially worried about earthquakes, steer clear
of homes built on landfill (like in the Marina district), which tends to act like
gelatin during a shaker. See the **Earthquakes** chapter for more on this topic.

APARTMENT HUNTING

DIRECT ACTION

Many arriving to the Bay Area from other large metropolitan areas in the US are comfortable with the idea of finding their own apartment. Methods include reading the classifieds, either in printed form or online, looking for posted rental notices on coffee shop, grocery store, and laundromat bulletin boards, as well as on vacant apartments. Energetic souls will call a building's manager, ask everyone they know for word-of-mouth referrals, and, when all else fails, pound the pavement and talk to people on streets or in neighborhoods they want to live. If this seems like too much work for you or if you haven't the time, check below under **Rental Agents**, **Relocation Services**, **Roommate Services**.

NEWSPAPER CLASSIFIED ADS

Perusing the newspaper classifieds, either online or in print, is the most popular place to begin searching for an apartment. The listings will also give you a good sense of what you can expect to pay for rent each month. You'll see that rates vary significantly by location. When scanning the ads keep in mind that because demand is so great, many landlords don't always list vacancies, and often, by the time a vacancy does appear, the unit has already been rented. Most rental ads are placed in the Sunday newspapers, which are available on Saturday at convenience stores and newsstands.

- **The Berkeley Voice**, a weekly newspaper that focuses on the community of Berkeley; has some rental and roommate listings; comes out Fridays, 510-243-3575.
- **Contra Costa County Times**, published daily, focuses on the East Bay, particularly Concord, Walnut Creek, Pleasant Hill, Martinez, Richmond, Hercules, Benicia, Antioch, Pittsburg and Bay Point areas, 935-935-2525, www.contracostatimes.com.
- **The Daily Californian**, daily, UC Berkeley's student newspaper, good for rental and roommate listings, 510-548-8300, www.dailycal.org.
- **East Bay Express**, a weekly, free alternative newspaper that focuses on the East Bay. Good for rental and roommate listings, 510-540-7400. Found in newsstands and at cafes on Thursdays, www.eastbayexpress.com.
- **Marin Independent Journal**, published daily with listings for Marin, Sonoma and Napa counties, 415-883-8600, www.marinij.com.
- **Oakland Tribune**, published daily, focuses on East Bay listings, especially Oakland, Berkeley, and Alameda areas, 510-208-6300, www.newschoice.com.
- **Pacific Sun**, weekly free, alternative newspaper with listings for Marin

County. Good for rentals and roommate listings; found on Wednesdays at newsstands and cafes, 415-383-4500, www.pacificsun.com.

- **San Francisco Bay Guardian**, a free, weekly, alternative newspaper with extensive listings for San Francisco and the East Bay. Good for rental and roommate listings. 415-255-3100. Published Wednesdays, found at every cafe and newsstands all over city, www.sfbg.com.
- **San Francisco Chronicle** is the most widely read newspaper in the area; includes listings for San Francisco, North Bay, East Bay, and Peninsula counties, and some outlying areas, 415-777-1111, www.sfgate.com.
- **San Francisco Examiner**, published daily, this afternoon newspaper has listings similar to the SF Chronicle, 415-777-2424, www.examiner.com or www.sfgate.com.
- **San Francisco Chronicle/Examiner Sunday Paper**, includes the Bay Area's most extensive listings of the week (available at stores on Saturdays), 415-777-1111, www.sfgate.com.
- **San Francisco Weekly**, a free, weekly, alternative newspaper with San Francisco listings; comes out Wednesdays. Good for rental and roommate listings. Found all over city at newsstands and cafes, 415-541-0700, www.sfweekly.com.
- **San Jose Mercury News**, published daily with the most extensive listings for the South Bay, much of the Peninsula, and areas southeast of the Bay, 408-920-5000, www.mercurycenter.com.
- **San Mateo County Times**, published daily except Sunday, with listings for much of the Peninsula, 650-348-4321, www.sanmateotimes.com.
- **Santa Rosa Press Democrat**, published daily with listings for Sonoma, Marin and Napa counties, 707-546-2020, www.pressdemo.com.

OTHER RENTAL PUBLICATIONS

Many property owners pay to list their units in glossy guides that are free to prospective renters. These guides, available in racks at supermarkets, bus and BART stations, and on many street corners, are designed to make the property look like the Taj Mahal. Keep in mind that while many of them are as nice as they look in the ads . . . others may not be.

Here are just a few of these publications:

- **Apartment Guide**, covers San Francisco and the greater Silicon Valley, 650-364-4900, www.apartmentguide.com
- **A Bay Area Rental Guide Magazine**, 415-929-7777, www.rentalguide.com
- **For Rent Magazine**, general number, 800-452-0845; South Bay, 408-988-5811; East Bay, 510-429-7368, www.aptsforrent.com

RENTAL AGENTS, RELOCATION SERVICES, ROOMMATE SERVICES

Many arriving to the Bay Area realize quickly that paying a rental agent is a worthwhile investment, if for no other reason than to save time. Usually rental agencies charge a prospective tenant a fee for their service, either a flat fee, which is typical of a listing service, or a percentage of the first month's rent, common with agencies who do the necessary footwork to find a place for you and/or create customized lists. Sometimes a property owner will pay the fee, though this would certainly be an exception. If you have friends or coworkers in the area, ask if they can recommend a good agent. Remember to ask the agent who pays the finding fees before entering into any binding agreements.

Below is a partial list of Bay Area rental agencies, check the Yellow Pages under "Apartment Finding and Rental Services" for more listings:

SAN FRANCISCO

- **American Marketing Systems Inc.**, 2800 Van Ness Avenue, 800-747-7784, 415-447-2000, www.amsires.com
- **Bay Area Rentals**, 3027 Fillmore, 415-929-1100, www.bayarearentals.com, is a fee service that boasts a 95% placement rate. Service contracts are for 90 days and include detailed listings and daily updates; also serves the East and North Bay.
- **Craig's List**, www.craigslist.com; housing is just one of the many listings found here. Check for fee and no-fee apartment listings, sublets, and parking spaces. Listings placed by property owners or current occupants looking to sublet their units.
- **Metro-Rent**, 2021 Fillmore Street, 415-563-7368, www.metrorent.com; listing service and roommate matching
- **North Beach Roommate Unite**, 815 Greenwich Street, 415-292-5170
- **Rental Solutions**, 4054 18th Street, 415-863-7368, www.rentalsolutions.com; an agent is assigned to hunt for a unit that matches your criteria. Units found usually within two business days; $30 screening fee and an additional fee based on the value of chosen apartment.
- **RentNet**, www.rentnet.com; web site includes listings for apartment rentals all around the Bay Area
- **RentTech**, 4054 18th Street, 415-863-7368, www.renttech.com, rental and roommate finding service; lists pet-friendly units
- **Roommate Link** 610A Cole Street, 415-626-0606, www.roommatelink.com
- **San Francisco for Rent**, www.SF4rent.com, free listing service, includes pet-friendly Pacific Investment Properties

- **SF Real Estate Services**, 150 Lombard Street, 415-788-4488, www.SFReal
  EstateServices.com; has a rental department
- **Saxe Real Estate**, 1188 Franklin Street, 415-474-2435; 1551 Noriega
  Street, 415-661-8110
- **Spring Street**, 2285 Jackson Street, 415-771-0447; 3129 Fillmore Street, 415-
  441- 2309, www.springstreet.com; nation-wide listing service/relocation site.
- **Trinity Properties**, 333 Bay Street, 415-433-3333; specializes in short-
  term furnished rentals for corporate clients; does have some unfurnished
  units for long-term lease.
- **UCSF Campus Housing Office**, Milberry Union 500 Parnassus, 415-476-
  2231, www.stu-housing-mac17.ucsf.edu

EAST BAY/NORTH BAY

- **Craig's List**, www.craigslist.com; see above for description.
- **E-Housing**, 2161 Shattuck Avenue, Berkeley, 510-549-2000, www.ehous-
  ing.com; continuously updated databases; web, e-mail, and walk-in service
  provided. Open seven days.
- **Homefinders**, 2158 University Avenue, Berkeley, 510-549-6450,
  www.homefindersbulletin.com; oldest rental listing service in the East Bay;
  additional services provided, including credit reports and cell phone rentals.
- **Marin Rentals**, 305 Miller Avenue, Mill Valley, 415-383-1161
- **Metro-Rent**, 2840 College Avenue, Berkeley, 510-845-7821,
  www.metrorent.com; listing service and roommate matching
- **Rental Solutions**, 2213 Dwight Way, Berkeley, 510-649-3880, www.rental–
  solutions.com; see above for a description.
- **Roommate Express**, 2340 Broadway, Oakland, 510-893-4220,
  www.roommateexpress.com, www.e-roommate.com
- **Roommates**, 1924 Grant Street, Concord, 925-676-3426
- **Share Rentals Unlimited**, 400 West 3rd Street, Santa Rosa, 707-576-0904
- **Tenant Finders**, 2110 Oak Street, Concord, 510-939-2200, www.tenant-
  finders.com; free registration and rental lists; custom lists for 30 days cost $39.

PENINSULA

- **Craig's List**, www.craigslist.com; see above for description.
- **M&M Relocation Center**, 4906 El Camino Real, Los Altos, 650-988-
  0100; www.rentnet.com, click on "corporate housing." Long term and
  short term lease units available.
- **Corporate Living Network**, Redwood City, 650-366-0123
- **Roommate Express**, www.e-roommate.com, www.roommateexpress.com,
  2706 Harbor Boulevard, Suite 212, Costa Mesa, 650-948-4300, 800-487-8050

- **HIP-Homesharing**, 364 South Railroad Avenue, San Mateo, 650-348-6660, www.hiphousing.org; specializes in shared housing in San Mateo County. Call to set up an interview.

SOUTH BAY

- **Bay Area Rentals**, 3396 Stevens Creek Boulevard, San Jose, 408-244-4901, www.bayarearentals.com, is a fee service that boasts a 95% placement rate. Service contracts are for 90 days and include detailed listings and daily updates.
- **CAL Rentals**, 3911 Stevens Creek Boulevard, Santa Clara, 408-244-2300 www1.calrentals.com; open seven days, 8 a.m. to 8 p.m.; provides tailored information about available units, based on your needs; continuously updated lists.
- **Craig's List**, www.craigslist.com; see above for description.
- **M&M Corporate Housing/Relocation**, 4906 El Camino, Los Altos, 650-988-0100; see above for description.
- **Metro-Rent**, 2050 South Bascom Avenue, Campbell, 408-369-9700, www.metrorent.com; listing service and roommate matching.
- **Rental Experts**, 249 South Mathilda Avenue, Sunnyvale, 408-732-8777, www.rentalexperts.net; a fee-listing service, offers 90 days worth of unlimited listings; will e-mail or fax apartment listings that match your criteria.
- **Roommate Express**, 1556 Halford Avenue, Santa Clara, 408-727-2077 www.roommateexpress.com
- **Santa Clara University Student Resource Center**, 500 El Camino Real, Benson Center, Room 203, Santa Clara, 408-554-4109 (available to students and non-students).

SUBLETS

If you're unsure how long you are going to stay in the Bay Area, or if you are having trouble finding a long-term place to lease, consider subletting an apartment or a house. A sublet allows you to rent a unit on a short-term basis while the original tenant is temporarily away. In San Francisco, while subletting is common, most leases prohibit a tenant from subletting to another tenant without the landlord's approval. Be sure to speak to the landlord before signing with a tenant. If you find a room, apartment, or a house to sublet for a limited time, you must vacate when the original tenant returns. If the original tenant decides not to return, you are not considered to be the legal tenant until you enter into a separate agreement with the landlord. For those wishing to stay, the landlord can require you to sign a lease at a higher rent than what you had been paying.

Subletting from a "master tenant" who is the sole lease signer, and who already lives on the premises and will continue to do so while you also live there, is common, but again must usually be approved by the landlord. While it is illegal for the master tenant to charge you more than the rent he/she pays to the landlord, he/she can charge you up to the full amount in rent that he/she is paying. The master tenant must disclose this amount in writing. The master tenant always has the right to evict you with thirty days written notice, for any reason.

SHARING

Considering the dozens of schools and universities, the high cost of rent, and the preponderance of rambling Victorian flats—with odd-shaped little rooms and formal dining rooms that do new duty as bedrooms—house sharing is ubiquitous in the Bay Area. For a thousand dollars a month, a studio with an efficiency kitchen may seem paltry and cramped when compared to renting a room in a house with a big kitchen, pantry, a shared dining and living room, and a backyard, all for the same amount of rent or less. Of course roommate situations are not for everybody. There are households, a better term might be co-ops, comprised solely of non-smoking, cat loving, vegetarian, political activists who go to the farmers' market together and share cooking duties each evening. And that's just one scenario. The options are endless.

There are two ways to enter into lease agreements with roommates. Some or all of you can be "co-tenants," which means that whoever signs the lease with the landlord has equal rights and equal responsibilities. The worst case scenario here is if living together does not go as well as anticipated. Because everyone has signed the lease, everyone has the right to remain in the house and no one can force anyone else to go. The other lease option is to have a master tenant who signs the lease, pays the rent in one check, and deals with the landlord. The other roommate or roommates are then considered sub-tenants. Should you, as a sub-tenant, be unable to pay your rent the landlord cannot go after you, but your roommate can. In fact, the master tenant can evict you with thirty days written notice, regardless of cause.

Roommate situations can bring lifelong friends or a few months of living hell. While not legally binding, it's wise to get together with your prospective roomies to compose and sign a so-called "pre-nup," which may help to ensure promises made today won't go ignored tomorrow. For more on what should be included in a roommate contract check www.springstreet.com/apartments/fyp/reading_room/roommates/prenup.

If you don't mind paying a fee to find a roommate, hire a roommate service (see above under **Rental Agents, Relocation Services, Roommate Services**). The cost to match you with a roommate generally is reasonable, ranging from $35.00 to $110.00. If you'd rather not pay the roommate referral service fee there are free alternatives, chief among them **bulletin boards** at universities, colleges, local grocery stores (generally not the chains), and coffeehouses. The Rainbow Grocery in the Mission District at Folsom and 12th

ı large roommate board. In the East Bay, the bulletin board at the
vvı̈uı̈ . ⸺ ds Supermarket at Ashby and Telegraph avenues is a popular post-
ing place. Housing offices at universities and colleges also may be of some use.

CHECKING IT OUT

The rental market is so tight in the Bay Area that you shouldn't be overly fussy
when applying for your first place. Chances are good that when you view an
apartment or house there will be swarms of other prospective tenants already
there, so if you pull out a white glove and measuring tape, or produce a list of
items that must be fixed before moving in, the landlord may not view you as
favorably as some other interested soul. You'll find quickly that it is you who
has to cater to the landlord, not vice versa. But, while the market precludes you
from being picky, you shouldn't be miserable either. Maintain a sense of what
you want/need and what you are willing to do without before you view a
place. Here are some things to consider during your search:

- Are the kitchen appliances clean and in working order? Do the stove's
  burners work? How about the oven? How's the kitchen sink? Is there suffi-
  cient counter and shelf space?
- Check the windows—do they open, close and lock? Do the bedroom win-
  dows open onto a noisy or potentially dangerous area?
- How are the closets? Are they big enough to accommodate your belongings? Is there any private storage space?
- How's the water pressure? Try turning on the shower and the sink. Does
  the toilet flush adequately?
- Are there enough electrical outlets for your needs? Do the outlets work?
- Are there any signs of insects or other pests?
- What about laundry facilities? Are they in the building or is there a laundromat nearby?
- Outside, do you feel comfortable? Will you feel safe here at night? Is there
  secured parking? How many spaces? If two, are they tandem (so that one
  car blocks the other) or side by side? Is there an extra fee for parking? What
  about public transportation and shopping?
- Are you responsible for paying gas, water, and/or electricity? This policy
  varies from place to place and paying any combination or none at all are
  possible.
- Watch for discrimination. In San Francisco, it's illegal to deny housing
  based on race, religion, age or any other personal basis.

   Ed Sacks' *Savvy Renter's Kit* contains a thorough renter's checklist for those
interested in augmenting theirs.

   If it all passes muster be prepared to stake your claim without delay!

STAKING A CLAIM

When you view a unit, come *prepared*. Bring your checkbook so that if the place looks good you can hold it with a deposit. Also bring a copy of your credit report for the building manager (see **Money Matters**). Prepare a renter's resume with addresses of your last three residences, including the names, phone numbers, fax numbers, and e-mail addresses of your previous landlords, building managers, and roommates. Better yet, before you come to the Bay Area, bring letters of recommendation from the aforementioned that vouch for your sterling qualities. Employment information may also be helpful.

It wouldn't hurt to mention casually that you don't have a dog, cat or monkey, and that you don't smoke or play the drums. Feel free to rave about the unit and how great it feels (after all, a landlord is human too). If there's a garden, mention that you love gardening and have a very green thumb.

Keep in mind that when applying for a place, landlords can require that the amount of money you earn monthly be equivalent to three times the amount of rent you are expected to pay. Also, they can request only non-smokers, they can prohibit pets other than a working dog, and they can bar you from having overnight guests for more than a certain number of nights per year. (If you think you'll have lots of visitors, watch out for a lease containing such a clause, as this may not bode well for your tenant/landlord relationship.)

LEASES/RENTAL AGREEMENTS AND SECURITY DEPOSITS

If you want a preview of what a typical Bay Area lease or rental agreement looks like, take a trip to any well-stocked office supply store. Standard lease/rental agreements are sold in tear-off pads. Of course, the numbers will not have been entered, but you'll at least get a glimpse at how most landlords handle deposits, rent due dates and grace periods, appliances, pets and the like.

The law requires that a lease of one year or more be in writing. Every lease must also specify a termination date. If the termination date is not included, the tenant and landlord are considered to have entered into a month to month rental agreement. An oral agreement to rent for more than one year is considered a month to month rental agreement, *not* a lease. Also, unless it is a fixed term lease, it will convert to a month-to-month rental agreement at the conclusion of the first tenancy period. While rare, some landlords will ask you to sign another yearlong lease.

It is customary and acceptable for California landlords to demand various combinations of up-front charges before entering into a lease or rental agreement with you. Those charges will likely include a fee for running a credit check (not refundable), the first month's rent, possibly last month rent (which differs from a security deposit), a key deposit, sometimes a cleaning deposit, and, perhaps, a pet deposit. If the property manager asks for last month's rent, keep in mind it ed for just that. That way, when you give your customary 30-days notice of intent to vacate, you're paid up. No lease or rental agreement may include non-refundable deposits. In California all deposits are returnable if all agreed-to conditions are met. Landlords are also required to pay five-percent interest on security deposits at the termination of the lease, if the unit was held for longer than a year. If your security deposit is not returned within three weeks of your vacancy date you can talk to a tenants rights organization or seek recourse in small claims court. If you are a co-tenant or a sub-tenant, the landlord does not have to return your portion of the security deposit directly to you. The deposit on the unit is returned only when the entire unit is vacated which means you will have to get your part of the deposit money from the co-tenants or master tenant.

Should you find yourself in the uncomfortable position of having to break a lease, you have a number of ways to mitigate the situation, making it less contentious, less costly to yourself, and more palatable to your landlord. If you need to move out before the lease is up, the landlord must make an effort to rent your unit and he/she may not double-dip, that is he/she may not accept rent from you (who has moved out) and a new tenant at the same time. When breaking a lease, try to do it with as much care and savvy as possible. Give the landlord written notice of intent as far in advance as possible, and if you can, try to find a new tenant for your unit, making sure he or she is financially capable of taking on the responsibility. If you know that your old unit has been rented and you are still being held responsible for the lease, take action. Speak to the new tenant, photograph a new name on your old mailbox, and seek help from a tenant's organization. (See below.)

RENT AND EVICTION CONTROL

Before you've secured a place of your own, be aware that San Francisco has a Rent Stabilization and Arbitration Ordinance that offers protection against some rent increases. The ordinance does not apply to post-1979 apartment units, government regulated housing, and short-term residential hotels. For those units covered by the ordinance, landlords are allowed to raise the rent once a year, beginning on the anniversary of your move-in date, as long as a thirty-day written notice is given. The amount by which the rent may be raised is determined by the San Francisco Rent Board and is announced each March. By law it will always be between zero and seven percent.

East Palo Alto also has rent control (see listing below). In San Jose only mobile homes and apartments built before September 1979 are protected by rent control. An eight percent rent increase is allowable yearly for these kinds of units. Berkeley is the only other rent-controlled city in the region. The rent increase allowance is variable, check with the Berkeley Rent Stabilization Program for more information (see below).

In the remaining Bay Area, you can expect a rent increase at the end of your lease (with 30 days notice). Also, you can be evicted without "just cause" when your lease expires, again with 30 days notice.

Berkeley and San Francisco have stringent eviction protection for tenants. In San Francisco there are fourteen "just cause" reasons for eviction, and in Berkeley there are twelve. These include: failure to pay rent, failure to sign a new lease that is the same as the old lease, illegal activity on the premises, breaking the terms of the lease, willful damage to property or allowing others to damage the property (Berkeley), disturbing other tenants, refusing the landlord legal access to the premises when the landlord needs entry in order to bring the unit up to code or to make substantial repairs, an owner-move-in eviction, the landlord has received a permit to demolish the unit, a subletting tenant refuses to vacate the temporary housing offered by the landlord after the landlord has repaired the tenant's prior unit (Berkeley). In addition, one of the newest quirks in San Francisco is landlords' use of the Ellis Act, a state law permitting owners to evict tenants on the grounds that they are permanently removing the rental units from the market.

The sale of property, the expiration of a rental agreement, or a change in the Federal Section 8 status of a unit do *not* constitute "good cause" for eviction.

The laws of every other locality are generally state tenancy laws. A comprehensive source of information on the legal aspects of tenancy, *Tenant's Rights*, is published by Berkeley-based Nolo Press, 510-549-1976, www.nolo.com. Nolo also publishes the *Landlord's Law Book*, for those on the other side of the rental property wall. Knowing the rights and responsibilities of both sides may prove valuable when it comes time to sign on the dotted line, and again when you're ready to move out, as security deposits, apartment cleaning, and repairs become potential issues of concern. Also, you can view the California Civil Code on the web, www.leginfo.ca.gov/calaw.

If you're in need of help, you can also get information on tenant's rights from a number of offices:

- **Berkeley Rent Stabilization Program**, 2125 Milvia Street, 510-644-6128, www.ci.berkeley.ca.us/rent
- **California State Fair Employment and Housing Department**, www.dfeh.ca.gov, 455 Golden Gate Avenue, Suite 7600, San Francisco, 415-703-4175, 800-884-1684; 1515 Clay Street, Suite 701, Oakland, 510-622-2941; 111 North Market Street, Suite 810, San Jose, 408-277-1277
- **East Palo Alto Rent Stabilization Program**, 650-853-3109
- **Eviction Defense Center**, 1611 Telegraph Avenue, #726, Oakland, 510-452-4541
- **Eviction Defense Collaborative**, 433 South Van Ness Avenue, San Francisco, 415-986-9586
- **Housing Rights Committee**, 427 South Van Ness Avenue, San Francisco, 415-398-6200
- **Housing Rights, Inc.**, 2718 Telegraph #100, Berkeley, 510-548-8776, www.housingrights.com

- **Project Sentinel**, specializes in landlord/tenant disputes in Sunnyvale, 408-720-9888
- **St. Peter's Housing Committee**, 474 Valencia Street, San Francisco, 415-487-9203
- **San Francisco Rent Board**, 25 Van Ness Avenue, #320, San Francisco, 415-252-4600
- **San Francisco Tenants Union**, 558 Capp Street, San Francisco, 415-282-5525, www.sftu.org
- **San Jose Community Legal Services**, 2 West Santa Clara Street, 8th floor, San Jose, 408-283-3700; call for a pre-screening.
- **San Jose Housing Counselor Program**, 408-283-1540
- **San Jose Rental Dispute Program**, 4 North 2nd Street, #600, San Jose, 408-277-5431

LANDLORD/TENANT RIGHTS AND RESPONSIBILITIES

In the state of California, landlords must rent premises (grounds, buildings, and units) that are free of rubbish and vermin. There must be adequate containers for garbage and recycling. The floors, hallways, and railings must be in good repair. Electrical wiring must be in good working order and up to the safety standards at the time of installation. There must be adequate and safe heating facilities. There must be hot and cold running water and a sewage disposal system. There must be plumbing, electricity and gas, all in good working order. There must be effective waterproofing on the walls and roofs. Windows and doors must be unbroken, and locks must be in working order.

Landlords are not allowed to enter your premises without giving 24 hours notice and receiving your permission, unless there is an emergency that threatens damage to the unit. You must permit the landlord to enter to make repairs, to show the apartment to prospective buyers, tenants, contractors, appraisers, and the like. The landlord is not allowed to harass you verbally or physically or make threats. A landlord cannot lock you out of the premises until you have been legally evicted nor turn off your utilities in an attempt to get you to vacate without due process. Tenants are responsible for maintaining the premises in working and sanitary condition, for paying the rent on time, and for following the rules written in the lease.

Renting situations in the Bay Area vary widely, from renting a typical apartment in a complex to renting an attic room in someone's home. To learn more about local ordinances order the book *California Tenants: A Guide to Residential Tenants and Landlords Rights and Responsibilities*, available from the Department of Consumer Affairs. Send a request with $2, to: California Tenants c/o Department of Consumer Affairs P.O. Box 989004, Sacramento, CA 95798, or visit www.dca.ca.gov.

RENTER'S INSURANCE

Renter's insurance provides relatively inexpensive coverage against theft, water damage, fire, and in many cases personal liability. In this earthquake prone area, try to find a policy that covers earthquake damage to personal possessions. Be sure to shop around as insurance rates vary considerably, and when deciding on a policy, consider replacement cost coverage rather than a cash value policy. It's usually worth the extra premium. Those with several housemates may not be eligible for coverage.

Web sites worth investigating as you search for renter's insurance are Quotesmith, www.quotesmith.com, which offers instant quotes from over 300 insurance companies; QuickenInsurance, www.insuremarket.com, the number one pick of *Smart Money's* 2000 Internet Guide for finding inexpensive insurance rates online; and for answers about general insurance questions check www.insure.com. This last site is geared toward both professionals in the insurance business and consumers, and offers details about what a policy should cover, tips on making a claim, and has a listing of complaints filed against insurance companies.

Finally, probably the most helpful resource for finding renter's insurance is the Winter/Spring 1998 edition of the *Bay Area Consumers' Checkbook*. Their comprehensive article on homeowner's/renter's insurance offers advice and money saving tips for finding coverage in the Bay Area. Go to www.checkbook.org, and ask for article #4-030 (there is a $10 fee for downloading this article from their site). Call 510-763-7979 to order this article by mail. See **Helpful Services** for more information on *Bay Area Consumers' Checkbook*.

BUYING

Many people come to the Bay Area with the intention of buying a house, but the sticker price often scares them into renting and longing for life back in Kansas. Like the rental market, the housing market is very tight. With more buyers than sellers, it is not unusual for buyers to bid against each other—often in increments of thousands of dollars. As a buyer, you need patience, persistence and stamina. Be prepared to bid on a number of houses before your bid is accepted.

While it's good to have a clear idea of what you want, you'll need to be willing to make concessions—both in terms of price and neighborhood. To figure out what you can afford to pay for a house, the general rule of thumb is to multiply your monthly salary by three or four. For example, if you make $100,000 a year, you should plan on spending no more than $400,000 on your new home. The bad news is that you will be hard pressed to find a home for $400,000 in much of the Bay Area. Another important point to remember is that you will be required to place about 20% of the purchase price as a down payment, and don't forget about closing costs, which are generally one to three percent of the purchase price, depending on your loan.

It's true that in such a tight housing market you may not be able to get all the amenities a house can have, and so it is a good idea to compose a personal list of what you need to be happy in your new home. Think about the neighborhood, the commute, parking, schools, the number of bedrooms and bathrooms, etc. Consider your lifestyle. If you are a gourmet cook, is the kitchen spacious enough? Do you want to live in a gated community? How about a historic property? If you are looking for a fixer-upper you'll need to consider how much time, money, and effort you will be willing to put into a place. Drafting such a list will let a real estate agent focus on what's truly important to you and your family. In addition, before meeting with a real estate agent, it's a good idea to do a little footwork on your own. Investigate the cost of properties in the neighborhood where you would like to live, and compare that to your financial situation.

CONDOMINIUMS, CO-OPS, TENANCIES-IN-COMMON

In the Bay Area, detached single-family homes are plentiful, but usually expensive. Alternative housing options include condominiums, co-ops, and tenancies-in-common. **Condominiums** or "condos" are communal associations or cooperative developments where the co-owners share interest and responsibility for the common areas (elevator, garden, laundry room, and hallways), but hold sole ownership of their unit. Condos are common in the Bay Area and new ones are being built all the time. A **co-op** is a corporation; owners hold shares in the property and have voting rights. An owner has the right to sell those shares, but the board members or fellow co-op members reserve the right to refuse to sell to someone whom they consider undesirable. Co-op residences are generally in larger, older buildings. With **tenancies-in-common**, known as TICs, co-owners usually buy an existing building of two to six units. By law the co-owners all must live on the premises as their primary residences. The co-owners own a percentage of the entire building, but while they enjoy exclusive use of their unit they do not own that unit outright. The finances of TIC co-owners, with regard to the building, are entwined, perhaps making it riskier to buy into than a condo. Due to the tight housing market, TICs have become a viable option for those who want out of the rental market but cannot afford to purchase a traditional, single-family home. San Franciscans concerned about the dwindling supply of affordable rental units in the Bay Area have opposed the recent rise in condo and TIC conversions, and legislation has been proposed to curb this trend.

REHABBING

High housing costs in the Bay Area tempt many would-be-homeowners into considering purchasing a fixer-upper. Be aware, fixer-uppers here usually need a lot of work. No one in this real estate market is going to sell a home for under market value when all that is needed is a fresh coat of paint, some new counter tops, and a couple of light fixtures. For those seriously in the market for a fixer-upper, and if this is where your talent lies, or what you consider a fun hobby, hunt long enough and hard enough and you can get a good price on a home that needs work. Keep in mind that materials and labor are more expensive in California. If you give up and need help, you can contact the Handyman Connection at 800-466-5530 for contractor referrals in your neck of the woods.

FINDING A REALTOR

Certainly, buying a pad is not something you do every day and, while it is possible to find a house or condo on your own, in this fast paced sellers' market you'll probably be better off with the help of an expert. According to the *San Francisco Chronicle*, less than five percent of homes here are bought and sold without an agent. Even if you find a home that appeals to you, say in cyberspace, you will most likely need an agent to show you the place and complete the transaction. What's more, homes in the Bay Area are often sold before they make it to the MLS (Multiple Listing Service); in fact, the average shelf life of a property in the Bay Area is only 10 days!

One of the best ways to find a real estate agent is through word of mouth. Ask your friends, colleagues or your employer's relocation administrator. Open houses held in the neighborhood of your choice are another good way to meet agents. It's important to meet with and talk to a few agents before choosing one. Be sure to look for someone who will represent you as a buyer—a buyer's broker—and make sure that whomever you choose, he/she is someone who seems trustworthy and has a good reputation. Check a realtor's credentials, and call his/her references to find out if his/her previous clients were satisfied.

Once you find a home you want, your realtor will help make sure that your offer is accepted, which can include pitching your "story" to the seller. When making an offer, it is also important to structure it with minimal contingencies. In today's market some buyers are willing to accept a house on an as is basis; some offer to pay a portion of the seller's closing costs. A real estate agent who is familiar with these and other tactics, as well as the going prices for properties, can be a great help in this market.

REAL ESTATE AGENTS

Below is a list of real estate agents to help you get started. This list is far from comprehensive.

SAN FRANCISCO

- **BJ Droubie Real Estate**, 4128 24th Street, 415-550-1300
- **Coldwell Banker**, 2633 Ocean Avenue, 415-564-6600; 1823 Union Street, 415-922-7100, www.coldwellbanker.com
- **Hill &Company**, 2107 Union Street, 415-921-6000, www.hill-co.com
- **Herth Real Estate**, 555 Castro Street, 415-861-5200, www.herth.com
- **Get Real Estate, Inc.**, 2455 Union Street, 415-931-4700
- **Lofts Unlimited**, 461 Second Street, 415-546-3100, www.loftsunlimited.com
- **McGuire Real Estate**, 2001 Lombard Street; 560 Davis Street, 800-4-RESULTS, www.mcguire.com
- **Pacific Union**, 6001 Van Ness Avenue, www.pacunion.com, 415-474-6600; 1700 California Street, 415-447-6200
- **Prudential California Realty**, 677 Portola Drive, 415-664-9400, 2200 Union Street, 415-921-0113, www.pruweb.com
- **Zephyr Real Estate**, 4200 17th Street, 415-552-9500; 4040 24th Street, 415-695-7707; 318 Brannon Street, 415-905-0250

NORTH BAY

- **Frank Howard Allen Realtors**, 915 Diablo Avenue, Novato, 415-897-3000; 902 Irwin Street, San Rafael, 415-456-3000; 215 Second Street, Sausalito, 415-331-9000; 905 East Washington Boulevard, Petaluma, 707-762-7766; 2245 Montgomery Drive, Santa Rosa, 707-537-3000, www.fhallen.com
- **Coldwell Banker**, 901 Reichert Avenue, Novato, 415-899-8400, www.cbnorcal.com
- **McGuire Real Estate**, 1040 Redwood Highway, Mill Valley, 415-383-8500, www.mcguire.com
- **Prudential California Realty**, 1604 Sir Francis Drake Boulevard, San Anselmo, 415-457-7340, www.prucalmarin.com
- **RE/MAX Realty**, 523 4th Street, San Rafael, 415-258-1500, www.central-marinrealestate.com

EAST BAY

- **Berkeley Hills Realty**, 1714 Solano Avenue, Berkeley, 510-524-9888, 800-523-2460

- **Better Homes Realty**, 5942 MacArthur Boulevard, Oakland, 510-562-8600; 5353 College Avenue, Oakland, 510-339-8400, www.ebrd.com
- **Coldwell Banker**, 1495 Shattuck Avenue Berkeley, 510-486-1494
- **East Bay Realtor**, www.ebayrealtor.com
- **Marvin Gardens**, 1577 Solano Avenue, Berkeley, 510-527-2700, www.marvingardens.com
- **Miller & Co.**, 702 Gilman Street, Berkeley 510-558-3464
- **Prudential California Realty**, 660A Central Avenue, Alameda, 510-337-8670; 1539 Shattuck Avenue, Berkeley, 510-849-3711; 2077 Mountain Boulevard, Oakland, 510-339-9290
- **Red Oak Realty**, 1891 Solano Avenue, Berkeley, 510-527-3387; 2983 College Avenue, Berkeley, 510-849-9990, www.redoakrealty.com
- **RE/MAX Realtors**, 1758 Solano Avenue, Berkeley, 510-526-1200; 2070 Mountain Boulevard, Oakland, 510-339-4100, www.home-buy-sell.com

PENINSULA

- **Alain Pinel Realtors**, 620 Santa Cruz Avenue, Menlo Park, 650-462-1111; 578 University Avenue, Palo Alto, 650-323-1111, www.alainpinel.com
- **Alhouse King Realty**, 2600 El Camino Real, Palo Alto, 650-857-0116
- **Century 21**, 871 Hamilton Avenue, Menlo Park, 650-328-6100; 385 Foster City Boulevard, Foster City, 650-341-2121; 1503 Grant Road, Mountain View, 650-966-1100; 450 Dondee Way, Pacifica, 650-355-2121; 123 South San Mateo Drive, San Mateo, 650-347-3888, www.century21alliance.com
- **Coldwell Banker**, 496 First Avenue, Los Altos, 650-947-2200; 930 Santa Cruz Avenue, Menlo Park, 650-323-7751; 1745 El Camino Real, Redwood City, 650-369-8050; 2969 Woodside Road, Woodside, 650-851-1940
- **McGuire Real Estate**, 360 Primrose Road, Burlingame, 650-348-0222, www.mcguire.com
- **Peninsula Homes Realty**, 605 Cambridge Avenue, Menlo Park, 650-324-2200, www.penhomes.com
- **Prudential California**, 1116 South El Camino Real, San Mateo, 650-578-0200, www.1prudential.com; 100 El Camino Real, Burlingame, 650-696-7020, www.pruweb1.com
- **RE/MAX Realtors**, 670 Woodside Road, Redwood City, 650-364-2660

SOUTH BAY

- **Better Homes Realty**, 1725 South Bascom Avenue, Ste. 216 Campbell, 408-559-5000; 1185 Branham Lane, San Jose 408-448-5600
- **Coldwell Banker**, 1550 South Bascom Avenue, Campbell, 408-559-0303; 761 First Street, Gilroy 408-847-3000; 480 South Mathilda Avenue, Sunnyvale, 408-616-2600

- **ERA Real Estate**, 10062 Miller Avenue, Cupertino, 408-366-2800; 2021 The Alameda, San Jose, 408-236-6650
- **Prudential California Realty**, 408-281-7800; 841 Blossom Hill Road, Suite 112, San Jose, 408-281-7800; 17500 Monterey Road, Suite A, San Jose, 408-779-7066, www.prudential.com
- **Silicon Valley Association of Realtors**, 650-949-9115, www.siliconva-lley-realtors.org
- **www.somaliving.com** is a specific site geared toward San Francisco's South of Market District, Potrero Hill, South Beach and Mission Bay areas offers profiles, on these areas and agent listings, home listings, and financing information.

FOR SALE BY OWNER

Intrepid souls who want to buy or sell a house without an agent can check online sites specializing in home listings by owners:

- **www.4SaleByOwner.com**
- **www.econorealty.com**
- **www.fisbos.com**
- **www.FSBOnenetwork.com**
- **www.HomesByOwner.com**
- **www.owners.com**
- **www.econobroker.com**, 888-989-4MLS; this service will list your home (for a fee) on the Multiple Listing Service, which is a list used by real estate agents nationwide.

GET YOUR FINANCES IN ORDER

Many buyers consult with a mortgage broker or direct lender and get pre-qualified even pre-approved for a loan prior to finding a house. This is a good idea, particularly in the Bay Area where speed is of the essence. Once you have determined your budget, contact a mortgage broker who can help you sort through your credit report and find a lender. To find a good mortgage broker, ask your real estate broker, your bank, colleagues or friends. You can even find one in the yellow pages or online through various web sites. See below.

ONLINE RESOURCES—HOUSE HUNTING

These days you can start your search for a home on the internet, before you even arrive in the Bay Area. While searching the web probably won't get you a house, since many are sold as quickly as they are listed, it will give you a good idea about what's on the market, where you should look once you get here, and about how much you can expect to pay. Not every site lists every home in the Bay Area but every home in the Bay Area for sale is probably now listed on at least one site.

Some useful sites to help your search include:

- **www.ziprealty.com** claims to be the first online real estate brokerage to host online transactions.
- **www.cyberhomes.com** lists homes for sale across the nation and lists other pertinent real estate information
- **www.homeadvisor.com** is a popular home-buying site with information on homes for sale, moving and relocating, home improvement and more.
- **www.homefair.com**, realty listings, moving tips, and more
- **www.homestore.com**, lists homes for sale, apartments, and roommates, includes moving tips, and a section on home improvement
- **www.realtylocator.com** has thousands of home listings nationwide; neighborhood data; discussions about real estate
- **www.homeseekers.com** is a database system of the Multiple Listing Services.
- **http://realestate.yahoo.com** this site list homes for sale, mortgage loans, community profiles, listing for home inspectors, real estate agents, title companies and more

ONLINE RESOURCES—MORTGAGES

Everyone likes to complicate mortgages, but think of them simply as an agreement between the buyer and the lender about the amount of money being borrowed. There are a few other elements of mortgages like points, interest rates and terms, but don't get overwhelmed by the language. Remember everything is negotiable so shop around for the best mortgage. You may want to find a mortgage broker to assist you with the process. The web and the bookstore are good places to begin figuring out mortgages. **Www.mtgprofessor.com**, a web site written by Professor Jack Guttentap of the Wharton School of the University of Pennsylvania, contains helpful information about mortgages.

Today, there are hundreds of web sites offering mortgage loans. If this avenue appeals to you, be aware that some online companies cannot process mortgage applications fast enough for the Bay Area's short escrow period, typically 30 days or less. Below is a list of web sites to help you get started with the process.

- **www.countrywide.com** offers moving services, branch locators, locked rates, mortgage rates, credit evaluations, mortgage tools, and relocation services just to name a few.
- **www.iown.com** the site claims to have the best loans online and helps find loans, and gives information about buying and selling a home and relocating to a new city.
- **www.homeadvisor.com** can help you find loans, and find homes, and

neighborhood profiles, and can help you with credit cards, auto financing, and refinancing your home.

- **www.freddiemac**.com provides information on lower cost loans and homes for renter and buyers.
- **www.lendingtree**.com helps you find any type of loan, from a mortgage to a student loan
- **www.owners**.com offers loan status, mortgage rates, credit evaluations, mortgage tools, and virtual tours of homes for sale
- **www.realtor**.com offers property listings, virtual tours, and lender and realtor listings.

HOMEOWNER'S INSURANCE

For most everyone, dealing with a bank or mortgage lender is necessary when buying a new home, and getting homeowner's insurance is a required part of the process. Replacement value insurance is recommended but recently some of the largest insurance companies stopped offering replacement value policies. Instead they are offering coverage for 120% to 125% of the face value of your house and belongings. In the event of a catastrophic loss, this percentage would not provide the necessary coverage to replace your home and its contents, so you should look for an insurer who can offer a replacement value policy. Factors that insurance companies consider when determining the rate of your policy include the fire resistance of your house—wood frames cost more to insure than masonry structures—and your location. Being in a high theft neighborhood or far from a fire hydrant or fire station will add to the cost of your policy.

There are ways to get lower homeowner's insurance rates: requesting a higher deductible can lower your premium by as much as 25%; coupling homeowner's insurance with an automobile policy may result in a discount on both; and most insurance companies offer lower premiums for homes with safety devices such as dead-bolt locks, security alarm systems, and fire extinguishers.

Earthquake insurance in the Bay Area is a good idea, although it's expensive and for a while was difficult to obtain. In 1994, as a result of the costs associated with the Northridge Earthquake, many insurance companies stopped writing new homeowner's and renter's insurance policies and some pulled out of California altogether. In response, the State of California established the **California Earthquake Authority (CEA)**, which provides basic earthquake-damage coverage. Insurance companies operating in California are required to either supply their own earthquake coverage to their policyholders or to offer the CEA's policy. According to the 1998 Winter/Spring edition of the *Bay Area Consumers' Checkbook*, 70% of California's earthquake policies were written by the CEA. For more information about the CEA call 916-323-8161. For answers to any other insurance-related questions, contact the **California Department of Insurance** in Los Angeles at 213-897-8921 or look at the California

Insurance web site at www.insurance.ca.gov. For a comprehensive article on homeowner's insurance policies in the Bay Area, go to www.checkbook.org, and ask for article #4-030 (there is a $10 fee for downloading this article from their site). Call 510-763-7979 to order this article by mail. See **Helpful Services** for more information on *Bay Area Consumers' Checkbook*. For online resources, see above under **Renter's Insurance**.

ADDITIONAL RESOURCES—HOUSE HUNTING

Following are resources that may be of interest for those in the market for a new home:

*   *100 Questions Every First Time Homebuyer Should Ask* by Ilyce R. Glink
*   *Opening the Door to a Home of Your Own* is a pamphlet published by the Fannie Mae Foundation for first-time homebuyers; it can be obtained by calling 800-834-3377.
*   *How to Buy a House in California* by Ralph E. Warner, Ira Serkes, and George Devine; published by Nolo Press
*   *Your New House: the Alert Consumer's Guide to Buying and Building a Quality New Home* by Alan and Denise Fields; now in its third edition and picked by the *San Francisco Chronicle* as one of its top ten "Best Real Estate Books."
*   **www.scorecard.org**, check this site if you are nervous about toxic waste issues in or near your prospective neighborhood; sponsored by the Environmental Defense fund.

BEFORE YOU CAN START YOUR NEW LIFE IN THE BAY AREA, YOU AND your worldly possessions have to get here. How difficult that will be depends on how much stuff you've accumulated, how much money you're willing or able to spend on the move, and where you're coming from.

TRUCK RENTALS

The first question you need to answer: am I going to move myself or will I have someone else do it for me? If you're used to doing everything yourself, you can rent a vehicle and head for the open road. Look in the Yellow Pages under "Truck Rental" and call around and compare. Below we list four national truck rental firms and their toll-free numbers and web sites. For the best information you should call a local office. Note: most truck rental companies now offer "one-way" rentals (don't forget to ask whether they have a drop-off/return location in or near your destination) as well as packing accessories and storage facilities. Of course, these extras are not free and if you're cost conscious you may want to scavenge boxes in advance of your move and make sure you have a place to store your belongings upon arrival. Also, if you're planning on moving during the peak moving months (May through September) call well in advance of when you think you'll need the vehicle. A month at least.

Once you're on the road, keep in mind that your rental truck may be a tempting target for thieves. If you must park it overnight or for an extended period (more than a couple of hours), try to find a safe place, preferably somewhere well-lit and easily observable by you, and do your best not leave anything of particular value in the cab.

- **Budget**, 800-428-7825, www.budget.com
- **Penske**, 800-222-0277, www.penske.com
- **Ryder**, 800-467-9337, www.ryder.com
- **Uhaul**, 800-468-4285, www.uhaul.com

Not sure if you want to drive the truck yourself? Commercial freight carriers, such as **Consolidated Freightways** and **ABF** offer an in-between service: they deliver a 28-foot trailer to your home, you pack and load as much of it as you need, and they drive the vehicle to your destination (usually with some commercial freight filling up the empty space). Available through their web sites at www.cfmovesu.com and www.upack.com.

MOVERS

Surveys show that most people find movers through the **Yellow Pages**. If that's too random for you, probably the best way to find a mover is through a personal recommendation. Absent a friend or relative who can point you to a trusted moving company, you can try the **internet**; just type in "movers" on a search engine and you'll be directed to dozens of more or less helpful moving-related sites. For long distance or interstate moves, the **American Moving and Storage Association's** site, www.moving.org, is useful for identifying member movers both in California and across the county. In the past, *Consumer Reports* (www.consumerreports.org) has published useful information on moving, as has *Bay Area Consumers' Checkbook*. (Go to www.checkbook.org or call 510-763-7979 and request article #4-035. See the **Consumer Protection** section in **Helpful Services** chapter for more on this organization.) Members of the **AAA** can call their local office and receive discounted rates and service through AAA's Consumer Relocation Service.

Disagreeable moving experiences, while common, aren't obligatory. To aid you in your search for a hassle free mover, we offer a few general recommendations. First and foremost, make sure any moving company you are considering hiring is **licensed by the appropriate authority**:

- **Intrastate moves** (moves within the state of California) are regulated by the **California Public Utilities Commission (CPUC)**. All movers operating within the state of California are required to have an active CPUC permit, called a "Cal-T-number." Among other things, to receive a permit, the carrier must have public liability and cargo insurance. Once you have the Cal-T-number, and the name, address, and phone number of the mover, be sure to verify that the permit is current by calling the CPUC at 800-877-8867. California movers are required to give out a consumer pamphlet to their prospective customers. Entitled "Important Information for Persons Moving Household Goods," the information provided is useful and answers many frequently asked questions. Be sure to ask for a copy and review it before moving day.

- **Interstate moves** are regulated by the Department of Transportation's **Federal Motor Carrier Safety Administration (FMCSA)**. When reviewing prospective carriers, make sure the carrier has a Department of Transportation MC ("Motor Carrier") or ICC MC number that should be displayed on all advertising and promotional material as well as on the truck. With the MC number in hand, you can contact FMCSA at 202-358-7028, 916-498-5050 or check www.fmcsa.dot.gov to see if the carrier is licensed and to check if they are insured. Before a move takes place, federal regulations require interstate movers to furnish customers with a copy of "Your Rights and Responsibilities When You Move," prepared by the old Interstate Commerce Commission. If they don't give you a copy, ask for one. FMCSA's role in the regulation of interstate carriers has to do with safety issues, not consumer issues. To find out if any complaints have been filed against a prospective mover check with the Better Business Bureau (www.bbb.org) in the state where the moving company is licensed, as well as with that state's Attorney General or Consumer Protection Office.

Additional recommendations:

- If someone recommends a mover to you, get names (the salesperson or estimator, the drivers, the loaders). To paraphrase the NRA, moving companies don't move people, people do.

- Once you've narrowed it down to two or three companies, ask a mover for references, particularly from customers who did moves similar to yours. If a moving company is unable or unwilling to provide such information or tells you that they can't give out names because their customers are all in the federal Witness Protection Program...perhaps you should consider another company.

- Even though movers will put numbered labels on your possessions, you should make a numbered list of every box and item that is going in the truck. Detail box contents and photograph anything of particular value. Once the truck arrives on the other end, you can check off every piece and know for sure what did (or did not) make it. In case of claims, this list can be invaluable. Even after the move, keep the list; it can be surprisingly useful.

- Be aware that during the busy season (May through September), demand can exceed supply and moving may be more difficult and more expensive than during the rest of the year. If you must relocate during the peak moving months, call and book service well in advance of when you plan on moving. A month at least. If you can reserve service way in advance, say four to six months early, you may be able to lock in a lower winter rate for your summer move.

- Whatever you do, *do not* mislead a salesperson about how much and what you are moving. And make sure you tell a prospective mover about how far they'll have to transport your stuff to and from the truck as well as any stairs, driveways, obstacles or difficult vegetation, long paths or sidewalks, etc. The clearer you are with your mover, the better he or she will be able to serve you.

- You should never have to pay for an estimate. For an intrastate move in California generally you will be given a "not to exceed" price, which means that you will not be charged more than the guaranteed price, and if your shipment is lighter than the salesperson estimated, you will be charged less. In rare cases you will be given a written "fixed price charge," which will be the amount due, regardless of shipment weight or hours worked. Interstate movers offer a binding or fixed price charge, which is based on the distance of the move, the estimated weight, and necessary manpower, or a non-binding estimate. A caveat to fixed price charges: if your shipment is much heavier or much more difficult than the salesperson estimated, the driver may cry foul and require an adjustment to the quote at the point of origin. If a potential problem is not taken care of at the point of origin, the delivering driver may protest the shipment and require a "backweigh" and an adjustment to the quote on the other end. To avoid such a hassle, see the preceding recommendation. For more information on hiring a moving company for inter or intrastate moves see "How to Move Your Household" in the Winter/Spring 1998 edition of the *Bay Area Consumers' Checkbook* (article #4-035); www.checkbook.org, 510-763-7979. Another publication, *Steiners Complete How to Move Handbook* by Clyde and Shari Steiner, offers a comprehensive overview of the moving process.

- Remember that price, while important, isn't everything, especially when you're entrusting all of your worldly possessions to strangers. Choose a mover you feel comfortable with.

- Think about packing. Depending on the size of your move and whether or not you are packing yourself, you may need a lot of boxes, tape and packing material. Mover boxes, while not cheap, are usually sturdy and the right size. Sometimes a mover will give a customer free used boxes. It doesn't hurt to ask. Also, *don't* wait to pack until the last minute. If you're doing the packing, give yourself at least a week to do the job, two or more is better.

- Above all, ask questions and if you're concerned about something, ask for an explanation in writing.

- Listen to what the movers say; they are professionals and can give you expert advice about packing and preparing. Also, be ready for the truck on both ends—don't make them wait. Not only will it irritate your movers, but it may cost you. Understand, too, that things can happen on the road that are beyond a carrier's control (weather, accidents, etc.) and your belongings may not get to you at the time or on the day promised.

- Treat your movers well, especially the ones loading your stuff on and off the truck. Offer to buy them lunch, and tip them if they do a good job.

- Ask about insurance, the "basic" 60 cents per pound industry standard coverage is not enough. If you have homeowner or renter's insurance, check to see if it will cover your belongings during transit. If not, consider purchasing "full replacement" or "full value" coverage from the carrier for the estimated value of your shipment. Though it's the most expensive type of coverage offered, it's probably worth it. Trucks get into accidents, they catch fire, they get stolen—if such insurance seems pricey to you, ask about a $250 or $500 deductible. This can reduce your cost substantially while still giving you much better protection in the event of a catastrophic loss. Irreplaceable items such as jewelry, photographs or key work documents should be transported by yourself.

- Be prepared to pay the full moving bill upon delivery. Cash or bank/cashier's check may be required. Some carriers will take VISA and MasterCard but it is a good idea to get it in writing that you will be permitted to pay with a credit card since the delivering driver may not be aware of this and may demand cash. Unless you routinely keep thousands of dollars of greenbacks on you, you could have a problem getting your stuff off the truck.

- Finally, before moving pets, attach a tag to your pet's collar with your new address and phone number in case your pet accidentally wanders off in the confusion of moving.

Those **moving within the Bay Area** with minimal belongings (renters, singles, etc.) probably won't need a huge truck to complete the task. If you (and all of your friends) are not interested in loading and unloading a rented truck, you may want to consider hiring one of the following local movers:

- **All Star Moving & Storage**, 1468 14th Street, Oakland, 510-839-4862; rated highly for quality and price by the 1998 Winter/Spring edition of the *Bay Area Consumers' Checkbook.*

- **Charles Moving & Storage**, 705 Walsh Avenue, Santa Clara, 408-986-0186

- **Delancey Street Movers**, 600 Embarcadero Street, San Francisco, 415-512-5110, rated highly for quality and price by the 1998 Winter/Spring edition of the *Bay Area Consumers' Checkbook*, specializes in moves throughout the Bay Area, has over 35 trucks in operation.

- **Emerald Moving and Storage**, 974 Valencia Street, San Francisco, 415-584-5578

- **One Big Man and One Big Truck**, 1407 Baker Street, San Francisco, 415-931-0193; has more than one big man and more than one big truck, specializes in small, quick moves—one-bedroom apartments in two to four hours.

- **Shmoover Movers**, 3751 Bay Road, Menlo Park, 650-327-5493, covers Santa Rosa to Monterey.

- **Starving Students Inc.**, 1360 Van Dyke Avenue, San Francisco, 415-863-4500; 864 Barron Avenue, Redwood City, 650-369-1113; 800-441-6683

- **Stu Miller's Movers**, 1709 Shattuck Avenue #1101, Berkeley, 510-848-9395

Local movers generally charge by the hour, not by the size and weight of your shipment. When shopping around for a local mover you will be given a "not to exceed price" for you move, which is based on how much stuff you have and the arrangement of the place you are moving out of, as well as the place you are moving into (how many stairs, how far to the truck, etc.). This "not to exceed" price is given in written form, covers all services and means that you will not be charged more than that amount, and if your move goes quicker than the salesperson estimated, you will be charged less. Other contributing cost factors include how many men will be needed to move your belongings, the size of the van, the distance traveled to your new place, etc.

CONSUMER COMPLAINTS—MOVERS

If you have a problem with your mover that you haven't been able to resolve directly, you can file a complaint about an intrastate move with the CPUC's Consumer Services Division, 800-FON-4-PUC, or go to their web site at www.cpuc.ca.gov. If yours was an interstate move, your options are limited in terms of government help. Once upon a time, the now-defunct Interstate Commerce Commission (ICC) would log complaints against interstate movers. Today, you're pretty much on your own. The Federal Motor Carrier Safety Administration recommends that you contact the Better Business Bureau in the state where the moving company is licensed as well as that state's consumer protection office to register a complaint. If satisfaction still eludes you, begin a letter writing campaign: to the state Attorney General, to your congressional representative, to the newspaper, the sky's the limit. Of course, if the dispute is worth it, you can hire a lawyer and seek redress the all-American way.

STORAGE

If your new pad is too small for all of your belongings or if you need a temporary place to store your stuff while you find a new home, self-storage is the answer. Most units are clean, secure, insured, and relatively inexpensive, and you can rent anything from a locker to your own mini-warehouse. You'll need to bring your own padlock and be prepared to pay first and last month's rent up front. Many places offer special deals to entice you, such as second month free. Probably the easiest way to find storage is to look in the Yellow Pages under "Storage—Self Service" or "Movers & Full Service Storage;" online go to Pacific Bell's www.smartpages.com, or check www.storagelocator.com.

Keep in mind that demand for storage surges in the prime moving months (May through September)...so try not to wait till the last minute to rent storage. Also, if you don't care about convenience, your cheapest storage options may be out in the boonies. You just have to figure out how to get your stuff there and back.

A word of warning: unless you no longer want your stored belongings, pay your storage bill and pay it on time. Storage companies may auction the contents of delinquent customers' lockers.

CHILDREN

Studies show that moving, especially frequent moving, can be hard on children. According to an American Medical Association study, children who move often are more likely to suffer from such problems as depression, worthlessness and aggression. Often their academic performance suffers as well. Aside from not moving more than is necessary, there are a few things you can do to help your children through this stressful time:

- Talk about the move with your kids. Be honest but positive. Listen to their concerns. To the extent possible, involve them in the process.
- Make sure the child has his or her favorite possessions with them on the trip; *don't* pack "blankey" in the moving van.
- Make sure you have some social life planned on the other end. Your child may feel lonely in your new home and such activities can ease the transition.
- Keep in touch with family and loved ones as much as possible. Photos and phone calls are important ways of maintaining links to the important people you have left behind.
- If your child is of school age, take the time to involve yourself in their new school and in their academic life. Don't let them fall through the cracks.

For younger children, there are dozens of good books on the topic. Just a few include, *Alexander, Who's Not (Do You Hear Me? I Mean It!) Going to Move* by Judith Viorst; *The Moving Book: A Kid's Survival Guide* by Gabriel Davis; *Goodbye/Hello* by Barbara Hazen, *The Leaving Morning* by Angela Johnson; and the *Little Monster's Moving Day* by Mercer Mayer.

For older children, try: *Amber Brown is Not a Crayon* by Paula Danziger; the *Kid in the Red Jacket* by Barbara Park; *Hold Fast to Dreams* by Andrea Davis Pinkney; *Flip Flop Girl* by Katherine Paterson and *My Fabulous New Life* by Sheila Greenwald.

A moving kit recommended by the Parents Choice Foundation in 1998, "Goodbye-Hello: Everything You Need to Help Your Child When Your Family Moves" might be particularly useful for those with children in the 4-12 age group. In addition to a booklet for parents, the kit includes a child's wall calendar, change of address post cards, a moving journal, markers and more.

For general guidance, read *Smart Moves: Your Guide through the Emotional Maze of Relocation* by Nadia Jensen, Audrey McCollum and Stuart Copans (Smith & Krauss).

Visit firstbooks.com to order any of the above resources.

TAXES

If your move is work-related, some or all of your moving expenses may be tax-deductible—so you may want to keep those receipts. Though eligibility varies, depending for example, on whether you have a job or are self-employed, generally, the cost of moving yourself, your family and your belongings is tax deductible, even if you don't itemize. The criteria: in order to take the deduction your move must be employment-related, your new job must be more than 50 miles away from your current residence, and you must be here for at least 39 weeks during the first 12 months after your arrival. If you take the deduction and then fail to meet the requirements, you will have to pay the IRS back, unless you were laid off through no fault of your own or transferred again by your employer. It's probably a good idea to consult a tax expert regarding IRS rules related to moving. However, if you're a confident soul, get a copy of IRS Form 3903 (www.irs.gov) and do it yourself!

ONLINE RESOURCES—RELOCATION

- *Bay Area Consumers' Checkbook*, Winter/Spring 1998 edition, "*How to Move Your Household* (article #4-035), www.checkbook.org, 510-763-7979; for more details about this organization see **Helpful Services** chapter under **Consumer Protection**.
- **www.erc.org**, the Employee Relocation Council, a professional organization, offers members specialized reports on the relocation and moving industries
- **www.firstbooks.com**, relocation resources and information on moving to Atlanta, Boston, Chicago, Los Angeles, Minneapolis-St. Paul, New Jersey, New York City, Philadelphia, Seattle, Washington, DC, as well as London, England
- **www.moverquotes.com**, comparison shop for mover quotes
- **www.moving.com**, a moving services site: packing tips, mover estimates, etc.
- **www.moving-guide.com**, movers and moving services
- **www.moving.org**, American Moving and Storage Association site
- **www.rent.net**, apartment rentals, movers, relocation advice and more
- **www.movedoc.com**, visit this site to order a copy of *Steiners Complete How to Move Handbook* by Clyde and Shari Steiner; $14.95.
- **www.usps.com**, relocation information from the United States Postal Service

ONE OF THE FIRST THINGS YOU'LL WANT TO DO WHEN YOU ARRIVE IN the Bay Area is set up a checking and perhaps a savings account. Opening one is usually painless. Since San Francisco is a regional financial center, there is no shortage of banks, savings and loans, and credit unions.

Most financial institutions offer a variety of account options, from no-fee checking and savings with a sizable minimum balance to inexpensive service if you do all your banking by ATM. If you have time, shop around for the best deal or if you are in a rush during the move, sign up with one of the big boys, then research other banks and change later if/when you find a better deal. Keep in mind that smaller banks may be less expensive, in terms of fees, than their colossal nationwide counterparts, while offering you a more navigable bureaucracy to deal with when you need help from your bank.

CHECKING ACCOUNTS

Setting up a checking account should be no problem, as long as you have picture identification with signature, an address, and some money. Most banks prefer to see that you've had an account at another financial institution, and they'd love to have your previous account numbers, if you still have them. You're likely to be issued temporary checks on the spot for use until your printed ones arrive, usually within a week to ten days. However, most merchants don't like those non-printed ones, so keep some cash on hand just in case. Once the printed ones arrive you'll have no trouble writing checks at most places, as long as you have a driver's license or similar picture identification. Chances are you'll also get a debit/ATM card when you open your account, but if bank personnel don't mention it, go ahead and ask for one. The card usually arrives in the mail in just a few days, ready to use. Most of your accounts can be linked to each other and to the card, making it easy to do your basic banking without ever going into a branch. For those unfamiliar with a debit card, think of it as an electronic check. It looks very much like a credit card and can be used to purchase goods and services. The difference is that a debit card draws money directly out of your checking account—you will not receive a statement apart from your monthly bank statement.

SAVINGS ACCOUNTS

Just as easy to set up as a checking account, individual characteristics of savings accounts differ from bank to bank in fees, interest, and required minimum balances. Often your savings account can be linked to your checking account to provide overdraft protection, usually for a fee. Again, your savings account can easily be accessed with your debit/ATM card, although you may have to ask that it be set up that way.

AREA BANKS

Here's a list of some of the biggest banks in the area and their downtown main offices. Call them for the address and phone number of neighborhood branches if you'd rather bank closer to home or work.

SAN FRANCISCO
- **Bank of America**, 345 Montgomery Street, 650-615-4700
- **Bank of the West**, 295 Bush Street, 415-765-4886
- **Bayview Bank**, 201 Montgomery Street, 415-421-6364
- **California Bank and Trust Bank**, 465 California Street, 800-254-2265
- **California Federal**, 4 Montgomery Street, 800-843-2265
- **Union Bank of California**, 370 California Street, 415-705-7000, 800-238-4486, (24-hr. Customer Service)
- **Washington Mutual**, 401 California Street, 800-788-7000
- **Wells Fargo Bank**, 464 California Street, 800-869-3557

NORTH BAY
- **Bank of America**, 1000-4th Street, San Rafael, 415-499-5151
- **Bank of Marin**, 50 Madera Boulevard, Corte Madera, 415-927-2265
- **Bank of the West**, 1313 Grant Avenue, Novato, 415-897-1131
- **Glendale Federal**, 101 Tiburon Boulevard, Mill Valley, 415-381-6545
- **Wells Fargo**, 715 Bridgeway, Sausalito, 415-332-3355

EAST BAY
- **Bank of America**: 1500 Park Street, Alameda, 510-649-6600; 2129 Shattuck Avenue, Berkeley, 510-649-6600; 300 Lakeside Drive, Oakland, 510-649-6600; 1400 East 14th Street, San Leandro, 510-649-6600
- **Bank of the West**: 1969 Diamond Boulevard, Concord, 925-689-4410; 11100 San Pablo Avenue, El Cerrito, 510-235-2980; 3305 Broadway, Oakland, 510-834-1780

- **Bayview Bank**: 5870 Stoneridge Mall, Pleasanton, 925-463-0600; 1250 Fairmont Drive, San Leandro, 510-352-1500
- **Mechanics Bank**: 1 Kaiser Plaza #750 Oakland, 510-452-5114; 1350 North Main, Walnut Creek, 925-210-8170
- **Union Bank**: 2333 Shattuck Avenue, Berkeley, 510-843-6353; 3223 Crow Canyon Road #100, San Ramon, 925-866-0422; 1970 Franklin Street, Oakland, 510-891-9505
- **Wells Fargo**, 1221 Broadway, Oakland, 510-891-2011

PENINSULA
- **Bank of America**, 530 Lytton Avenue, Palo Alto, 650-615-4700
- **Bayview Bank**, 414 California Avenue, Palo Alto, 650-327-6000
- **Union Bank**, 400 University, Palo Alto, 650-859-1200
- **Washington Mutual**, 300 Hamilton Avenue, Palo Alto, 650-853-2602
- **Wells Fargo**, 400 Hamilton Avenue, Palo Alto, 650-855-7677

SOUTH BAY
- **Bank of America**: 777 North 1st Street San Jose, 408-983-0588; 2905 Stevens Creek Boulevard, Santa Clara, 408-983-0588; 921 East Arques Avenue, Sunnyvale, 408-983-0588
- **Bank of the West**: 2395 Winchester Boulevard, Campbell, 408-998-6769; 890 North First Street, San Jose, 408-998-6800; 1705 El Camino Real, Santa Clara, 408-998-6964
- **Bayview Bank**: 10050 North Wolfe Road, Cupertino, 408-253-5200; 127 North Santa Cruz Avenue, Los Gatos, 408-354-6676
- **Union Bank**, 990 North 1st Street, San Jose, 408-279-7400
- **Washington Mutual**, 55 West Santa Clara Street, San Jose, 408-291-3331
- **Wells Fargo**, 7076 Santa Teresa Boulevard, San Jose, 800-869-3557

ONLINE BANKING

Many banks now offer online banking. Most of these systems use software provided by the banks utilizing programs such as Intuit's Quicken or Microsoft Money. As with checking and savings accounts, fees and services differ from bank to bank, so shop around to find one that best suits your needs. Many banks also offer touch-tone telephone access to your accounts, allowing you to check your balances, make transfers, and even pay some of your bills without having to write a check or spend money on postage. Banks love it when you set up the direct deposit of your paycheck into your account, and may even give you a break on account fees. If you like that idea, ask your employer if direct deposit is available.

INTERNET BANKING

While online banking has been provided by traditional brick and mortar banks for years, there is a new breed, the so-called "stand-alone online banks" rippling through the system, such as **TeleBank**, www.telebank.com, **NetBank**, www.netbank.com, and **CompuBank**, www.compubank.com. Although word is still out as to whether online banks really can stand alone (several have recently partnered up with other banks or businesses to diversify offerings), or whether consumers will give up the comfort and personal service provided by traditional banks, some believe that online banking will be commonplace in the not too distant future. Even if you choose to do most of your banking at a traditional bank up the street, it might be worth your while to investigate an online bank for high interest rate products like CDs.

According to a survey done by **Bankrate.com** (an industry-tracking site which provides information about auto loan rates, credit cards, CDs, home-equity loans, etc.), online banks that offer completely free checking and no minimum balance (some even offer interest on your account) include:

- **BankCaroLine**, www.bankcaroline, 877-692-2765
- **BankDirect**, www.bankdirect.com, 877-839-2737
- **First Interstate Bank of Indiana**, www.firstib.com, 888-873-3424
- **Security First Network Bank**, www.sfnb.com, 800-736-2321
- **USABancShares**, www.usabancshares.com, 877-482-2650
- **USAccess Bank**, www.usaccessbank.com, 877-369-2265
- **WingspanBank**, www.wingspanbank.com, 888-736-8611

CREDIT UNIONS

Some of the best financial service deals are offered by credit unions. The goal of a credit union is to offer affordable, bank-like services, including checking and savings accounts, and low interest loans, and to do it in a way that makes fiscal sense for the organization. On the downside, usually credit unions offer fewer locations than banks and often do not have easily accessible teller machines. You'll have to pay a fee when using a non-credit union ATM. Generally, membership to a credit union is available through some kind of group affiliation, often your place of work or residence. Find out if your company sponsors one, check online at www.ccul.org for a list of dozens of Bay Area credit unions, or try:

- **Pacific Service Federal Credit Union**, P.O. Box 8191, Walnut Creek, 94596, 925-296-6200; open to employees, and families of employees of PG&E.
- **Marin County Federal**, 30 North San Pedro Road, #115, San Rafael 94903, 415-499-6295; Marin County employees and family members.
- **Municipal Employees Credit Union of San Jose**, 140 Asbury Street, San Jose, 95110, 408-294-8800

- **Silicon Valley Federal Credit Union**, P.O. Box 50870, Palo Alto, 94303
  650-424-6115; open to employees of more than 100 Silicon Valley companies.

CREDIT CARDS

If you're not bringing a wallet full of credit cards with you, and you'd like to apply for one or more, you'll be happy to know issuers of those cards have simplified the process in recent years. Application forms have become shorter, and many card companies will take your application over the telephone.

Here are the major ones:

- **American Express** offers a number of different cards, each of which requires a minimum annual income and an annual fee. In most cases your Amex balance must be paid in full each month. Call 800-528-4800.
- **Diner's Club/Carte Blanche**: this card costs $80 per year just for the privilege of having it in your wallet. You'll also need to show a minimum annual income of $24,000. Call 800-234-6377.
- **Discover Card**: Dean Witter issues this card that pays cash back at the end of the each anniversary year, depending on how much you use the card over the period. Call 800-347-2683.
- **VISA/MasterCard**: banks, S&Ls, and various financial institutions, as well as nearly every other organization imaginable now offer VISA and/or MasterCard, at widely varying interest rates. Some cards are free, some offer lower interest rates, some offer frequent flyer miles … shop around for the best deal for you (see below).
- **Others**: oil companies, department stores, home improvement outlets, electronics stores, clothing retailers and many others offer their own credit cards, usually with high interest rates. San Francisco has Macy's, Nordstrom, JC Penney, Mervyns, Brooks Brothers, and Eddie Bauer to name just a few that offer credit accounts, many of them instantly with proper identification. One benefit of these types of accounts: the issuer notifies cardholders in advance of upcoming sales and specials.

A list of low-rate card issuers can be found on the internet at **CardWeb**, www.cardweb.com, 800-344-7714, the **Consumer Action** site, www.consumer-action.org, **BankRate.com**, www.bankrate.com, and **iMoneynet.com**, www.imoneynet.com.

Those interested in seeing their personal credit report can go to www.icreditreport.com. At this site you can receive a copy (for $8) of your credit report from the three main credit bureaus. Just don't do it more than once a year, otherwise it could adversely affect your credit rating. Or contact each credit bureau directly:

- **Equifax**, 800-685-1111, www.equifax.com

- **Experian**, 888-397-3742, www.experian.com
- **Trans Union Corporation**, 800-916-8800, www.transunion.com

TAXES

FEDERAL INCOME TAX

The Internal Revenue Service has offices in the Bay Area where you can pick up the forms you need to file your income tax return and get the answers to your tax questions. However, be advised that recent studies have found that the answer you get from an IRS representative often depends upon the person giving it rather than any clearly defined rule or regulation. The IRS says it is working on standardizing responses.

Many Bay Area post offices stay open until midnight on April 15th to give procrastinators extra time to fill out their return and get it in the mail with the proper postmark. The largest IRS office in the Bay Area is in the Twin Tower high-rise building at 1301 Clay Street in Oakland. There is also an IRS facility in San Francisco at 450 Golden Gate Avenue. The phone numbers for both are the same. For answers to your tax questions call 800-829-4477. To request tax forms call 800-829-3676. Tax forms are also available at most post offices and libraries during filing season (January-April), or check online, www.irs.ustres.gov.

ELECTRONIC INCOME TAX FILING

If you have the time and the inclination, you can file your federal tax return online via your computer. Online filing promises a faster process and swifter receipt of a refund. Totally paperless electronic tax filing, which generally is limited to those individuals or couples filing a 1040, 1040A, or 1040EZ with no required attachments other than forms W-2, W-2G, or 1099-R, is now available through a self-select PIN option. To find out more about this and other online filing options, visit the official Internal Revenue Service web site at www.irs.ustreas.gov. Here you will be directed to IRS accepted software brands and other tax related internet sites. To simply download forms you can visit www.etaxforms.com. Small business owners might find www.toolkit.cch.com helpful. If you want to install tax filing software try: www.taxcut.com, www.taxact.com, www.securetax.com, or www.turbotax.com.

For some qualified individuals (singles or couples below a certain income level), the IRS accepts electronic filing over the telephone, call 800-829-5166 for more details.

STATE INCOME TAX

State income tax forms and answers to your state income tax questions can be found at the State Franchise Tax Board offices at 345 Larkin Street in San

Francisco or at 1970 Broadway in Oakland. Telephone numbers for both are the same. Hours are Monday-Friday, 8 a.m. to 5 p.m., call 800-338-0505, TDD, 800-822-6268, www.ftb.ca.gov. State tax filing deadline is the same as for federal taxes, April 15. Tax forms are available at most post offices and libraries during tax season (January-April).

SALES TAX

The local sales tax is 8.25% throughout the Bay Area. It has risen over the years to its current level to help fund the BART transit system and to pay for earth-quake damage repairs.

STARTING OR MOVING A BUSINESS

With a well-educated pool of workers and a booming economy, the Bay Area is a great place to start a business or move your existing business.

To protect your efforts and investment you should probably hire a local attorney to help you through the maze of state rules and regulations, especially if you are moving your business from another state. Resources include:

- **California State Franchise Tax Board** at 415-929-5700, 800-338-0505, www.ftb.ca.gov, is the agency to check with regarding payroll, unemployment insurance, and disability insurance taxes.
- **Chambers of Commerce**: Berkeley, 1834 University Avenue, 510-549-7003, www.berkeleychamber.com; Oakland, 475 14th Street, 510-874-4800, www.oaklandchamber.com; San Francisco, 235 Montgomery Street, 12th floor, 415-392-4520, www.sfchamber.com; San Jose, 310 South First Street, 408-291-5250, www.sjchamber.com
- **Internal Revenue Service**, 800-829-1040, www.irs.gov, call them for information about an employer tax ID number.
- **Referral Service of the San Mateo County Bar Association**, which also serves Santa Clara County, 650-369-4149.
- **San Francisco Bar Association Lawyer Referral Service**, 415-989-1616
- **Service Corps of Retired Executives** (**SCORE**) 415-744-6827; call them for one-on-one counseling when starting a new business, free of charge.
- **State Bar of California**, 415-538-2000
- **State of California's Department of Finance**, www.dof.ca.gov
- **US Small Business Administration** (**SBA**), www.sbaonline.sba.gov; go online for information about starting up and financing a business, as well as learning about the SBA's services and local offices.

CONGRATULATIONS! YOU'VE FOUND A PLACE TO LIVE, WHICH IS NEVER easy here. Now it's time to set up your utilities and basic services and settle in. You may want to subscribe to the local paper, find a doctor, get a library card, and register to vote while you're at it. Details follow.

UTILITIES

GAS AND ELECTRICITY

To have existing service transferred to your name or to initiate gas and electric service call **Pacific Gas & Electric Company** (**PG&E**), www.pge.com. The 24-hour number is 800-743-5000 and covers San Francisco, the North Bay, East Bay, and parts of the South Bay and the Peninsula. If you're speech or hearing impaired, the TDD/TTY number is 800-652-4712, also 24 hours. Santa Clara County has its own utility service, the **Santa Clara County Municipal Utilities**, 408-984-5111, 8 a.m. to 5 p.m., and the **City of Palo Alto Utilities** (**CPAU**), 650-329-2161, is the only municipal utility in California that operates city-owned utility services that include electric, gas, water, and waste-water collection.

If you have questions about utilities, the **Public Utilities Commission** has a general information line, 800-253-0500, or check www.cpuc.ca.gov. When you are settling into a new place, turn on the hot water tap to make sure the water heater is on. If you don't have hot water, you need to find out why. If the water heater is in your unit, check to see if the pilot light is on. If it's not, follow directions on the heater for lighting the flame, or, if you're nervous about doing it yourself, call your landlord or PG&E and have them do it. While you're looking at the water heater, check to see if it is strapped to the wall. Many post-quake fires are started by ruptured gas lines to water heaters, and attaching the heater to the wall is an important safety precaution here in earth-quake country. (See **Earthquakes** for more details.)

Most people pay their PG&E bills by mail or online. There are also numerous drug stores and other neighborhood businesses set up to collect money for PG&E. Customer service representatives should be able to tell you where one is in your area. You may also drop off your payments at any PG&E office. There are two customer service offices in San Francisco: 863 Clay Street in the Chinatown area, and at 2435 Mission Street in the Mission district. For other locations, call 800-743-5000.

A number of new companies are getting people to use renewable energy, such as power generated from hydro, geothermal, and wind sources. The best known of these is **Green Mountain Energy Sources**, 888-461-9929, www.greenmountain.com, which buys earth-friendly energy from a wide variety of sources and then re-sells it to residential customers. The company also contributes a portion of its profits to environmental causes.

TELEPHONE

At one time, you had only one choice when it came to local telephone service throughout the Bay Area, and that was Pacific Bell. With ongoing industry deregulation, dozens of companies are now offering services. To search for a provider other than Pacific Bell check the Yellow Pages under "Telecommunications." **Pacific Bell** (**PacBell**), owned by Texas-based Southwestern Bell Company (SBC), is still the major operator in the Bay Area. Phone hook-up is easy, just call 800-310-2355, Monday-Friday, 8 a.m. to 5:30 p.m. and Saturday 8:30 a.m. to 5 p.m. for the entire Bay Area. A deposit is not required, but PacBell does charge about $35 to turn on the line to your unit. That fee will be added to your bill, and may be paid in three monthly payments. Basic phone service runs about $12 a month. Pacific Bell offers other telephone services, at additional cost, including the message center, which acts as your personal answering machine, call waiting, and caller ID. Hearing-impaired persons may establish TDD and TTY service by calling 800-772-3140.

PacBell customers dial "611" for repair service.

LONG DISTANCE SERVICE

When it comes to long distance service, there are a dizzying number of companies in this business, and they are not bashful about going after you. Below are just a few of the long-distance service providers available in the Bay Area. For help comparing long distance and wireless calling plans, visit the **Telecommunications and Research and Action Center** (**TRAC**) (not affiliated with the communications industry), www.trac.org or call them at 202-263-2950. The TRAC site also provides directory assistance via the internet.

- **AT&T**, 800-222-0300, www.att.com
- **GTC Telecom**, 800-486-4030, www.gtctelecom.com

- **IDT**, 877-535-2368, www.idt.com
- **MCI-WorldCom**, 800-444-3333, www.mci.com
- **Qwest**, 800-899-7780, www.qwest.com
- **Sprint**, 800-877-7746, www.sprint.com
- **Utility.com**, www.utility.com
- **Verizon**, 800-343-2092, www.verizon.com
- **Working Assets**, 877-255-9253, www.workingforchange.com

CELLULAR PHONES AND PAGING SERVICES

These days it seems everyone in California carries a cell-phone or wears a pager, and there are as many cellular pricing plans as there are makes and models of pagers and cell phones. Sprint's Free and Clear and AT&T's Digital One-Rate are flat-rate cell-phone plans which sell you a set number of minutes per month. These minutes can be used for any call, anytime, anywhere, however you do have to pay for unused minutes. Many people who have flat-rate plans use their cell phones for long distance calling. The market is changing rapidly, so your best bet is to call around and determine for yourself which service and pricing structures best meet your needs. The web can make it easier: www.point.com allows you to compare service plans in your area; the **Cellular Telecommunications Industry Association's** consumer resource page, www.wow-com.com/consumer, offers helpful consumer tips; and the **Telecommunications Research and Action Center (TRAC)**, out of Washington DC, is a consumer organization that publishes charts, comparing plans and prices: www.trac.org, 202-263-2950. Following are the Bay Area's largest cellular, **Personal Communication Service (PCS) providers**:

- **CellularONE**, 800-424-1999, www.cellone-sf.com
- **Nextel Communications**, 800-639-8359, www.nextel.com
- **Pacific Bell Wireless**, 800-393-7267, www.pbwireless.com
- **Verizon Wireless**, 800-551-4483, www.verizonwireless.com

Most businesses that sell cellular phones can also activate them for you on the spot, saving you the trouble of having to call the service provider yourself. Some even give you the phone for free, if you sign up and pay for a service contract with the company they represent.

Setting up **pager service** is even easier, and the equipment is available to rent or buy. Here are a few of the companies standing by ready to help you get "beeped."

- **Arch Wireless** (formerly Mobilecom), 800-879-7585
- **PageNet**, 800-322-7243
- **Skytel**, 800-858-4338

ONLINE SERVICE PROVIDERS

There are hundreds of internet service companies offering basic internet access via existing phone lines. A number of such companies provide service free of charge, though often such free services bombard you with advertisements. For a complete list of internet service providers located near you, go to www.cnet.com. You can also find a list of providers in the Yellow Pages under "Internet Access."

For high speed internet access, consider signing up for service on a Digital Subscriber Line (known as DSL), or via Cable Modem Access. DSL runs over the type of copper wires used for telephone calls, but on a separate line. Unlike a dial-up option, a DSL connection is always on, making logging on to the internet nearly instantaneous. Cable Internet access is available from cable TV providers. Like DSL, the cable modem is always on. One possible disadvantage to cable modem is your access speed may decrease if your neighbors also use cable. Before you sign up for cable modem, ask the provider what speed they guarantee.

Whatever type of internet connection you select, here are a few questions you may want to ask:

- Is the service easy to set up and use?
- What will the provider need to do to your home when physically installing the system?
- Does the provider offer technical support?
- What are the hours of the technical support?
- What is the average wait on the telephone for technical support?
- Does the provider offer e-mail accounts?
- Will the provider host your web site?
- What are the costs for all the services?

Here are a few of the companies that offer Dial-Up Access, DSL and/or Cable Modem:

- **AT&T World Net**, www.att.com/worldnet, 800-967-5363; high-speed access, www.home.att.com
- **America Online**, www.aol.com, 888-265-8003
- **Broadwing**, www.broadwing.net, 888-714-1565
- **Earthlink/Sprint**, www.earthlink.com, 800-511-2041
- **Excite-@home**, www.home.net, 877-959-MORE
- **First World**, www.firstworld.com, 888-423-3477
- **Juno**, www.juno.com, 800-879-5866
- **Pacific Bell**, www.pacbell.com, 800-708-4638
- **Rhythms**, www.rhythms.net, 877-557-0142
- **Speakeasy**, www.speakeasy.net, 800-556-5829

ONLINE DIRECTORY ASSISTANCE

In today's web-oriented world, directory assistance does not have to cost a lot of money. An online Yellow Pages is available from **Pacific Bell**, www.smart-pages.com, and numerous sites are dedicated to providing telephone listings and web sites, including the following:

- **www.555-1212.com**
- **www.altavista.com**
- **www.anywho.com**
- **www.bigbook.com**
- **www.people.yahoo.com**
- **www.switchboard.com**
- **www.whowhere.lycos.com**
- **www.worldpages.com**
- **www.zip2.com**

CONSUMER PROTECTION—UTILITY COMPLAINTS

In the state of California, utility rates and practices relating to telephone, electric, and gas are governed by the state **Public Utilities Commission** (**PUC**). The San Francisco Public Utilities Commission handles water issues. Officials at both organizations strongly suggest you take your complaints first to the utility involved. If you don't get satisfaction there, then the PUCs will listen to you.

- **California PUC**, 505 Van Ness Avenue, San Francisco, 415-703-2782, 800-848-5580, www.cpuc.ca.gov
- **San Francisco PUC**, 1155 Market Street, San Francisco, 415-554-3155, www.ci.sf.ca.us/puc

Interestingly, if you have problems with the PUC, there is a public watchdog organization that keeps tabs on the effectiveness of each of the PUCs. It's called **Toward Utility Rate Normalization** (**TURN**). If you don't get what you need from either PUC you may want to turn to TURN, 711 Van Ness Avenue, San Francisco, 415-929-8876, 800-355-8876, www.turn.org.

With the break-up of Ma Bell and the proliferation of long distance telephone service providers have come the inevitable scamsters. If you look at your phone bill and think you've been "slammed" (your long distance provider or established services were changed without your approval) or "crammed" (calls you didn't make were added to your bill), and your local service provider and state attorney general's office cannot assist you, contact the **Federal Communications Commission's Consumer Center**, 888-225-5322, www.fcc.gov, or the **Federal Trade Commission**, 202-382-4357, www.ftc.gov, to file a complaint.

See the **Helpful Services** chapter for more on consumer protection.

WATER

Water in the Bay Area is provided by several water districts (see list below). Accounts and billing are handled either directly through the water district or by your city's municipal services. Unlike many parts of the US, here in the Bay Area renters generally are responsible for paying for water.

In 1974, the United States Congress enacted a program to ensure safe drinking water for US residents. Amended in 1986, the Safe Drinking Water Act set up a comprehensive program for monitoring drinking water. Among many things, the Act banned all future use of lead pipe and lead solder in public drinking water systems, set up a monitoring system, mandated greater protection of ground water sources of drinking water, and streamlined enforcement procedures to ensure that suppliers comply with the Safe Drinking Water provisions. About 85% of San Francisco's water supply comes from Hetch Hetchy, a remote area of Yosemite National Park in the Sierra Nevada Mountains. Because of its pristine source, the quality of San Francisco's water is higher than most cities, however it's not entirely sterile or free of all organisms. The other 15% of San Francisco's water comes from watersheds in San Mateo, Santa Clara and Alameda counties.

Outside of San Francisco, about two-thirds of the state, or 22 million people, obtain water from the San Francisco Bay and the Sacramento Delta (located northeast of Contra Costa County) through a series of pumps and canals. Recently, especially in the Los Angeles area, there has been concern over water contamination caused by the gasoline additive methyl tertiary butyl ether (MTBE), which is mixed in with gasoline to make it burn cleaner. However, scientists have discovered that MTBE, can contaminate groundwater, and is not as readily removable as other contaminates. In 1999, Governor Davis ordered a phase-out of MTBE use in the state by December 31, 2002. The likelihood of having MTBE in the groundwater may depend on how close you live to a gas station. If you are within 1,000 feet, check with the station to find out if they have had any leaks or spills. The Santa Clara Valley Water District found MTBE in some of their water. If you are moving to the South Bay in Santa Clara County contact the Santa Clara Water District, 408-265-2600, www.scvwd.dst.ca.us for more information about the MTBE issue.

If you are living in the City and are concerned about the quality of your tap water, contact the **San Francisco Water Quality Division** at 650-872-5950. Those outside the San Francisco can contact the **Water Quality Control Board, San Francisco Bay Region**, 1515 Clay Street, Oakland, 510-622-2300 and ask them to send you a copy of their annual report on water quality. If you feel the need to take extra precaution, contact a private laboratory to perform water quality tests. Check the Yellow Pages under "Laboratories-Analytical" or get a referral from your county health department.

For further questions on tap water quality, contact the **California Department of Health Services**, 916-323-4344; the **US Environmental Protection Agency Safe Drinking Water Hotline**, 800-426-4791; or the **Water Quality Association**, 800-749-0234, www.wqa.org. Information regarding home water filtration systems is covered in an Environmental Protection Agency pamphlet, "Home Water Treatment Units: Filtering Fact from Fiction" www.epa.gov/ogwdw.

To **set up water service** you will need to contact one of the following water districts or municipal services. Most of the web sites included here provide detailed information about setting up your account, as well as the county's annual water quality report:

- **Alameda County Water District**, 43885 South Grimmer Boulevard, Fremont, 510-659-1970, www.acwd.org
- **Contra Costa Water District**, 1331 Concord Avenue, Concord, 925-688-8044, www.ccwater.com
- **East Bay Municipal Utility District**, 375 11th Street, 510-287-1380, www.ebmud.com
- **Marin Municipal Water District**, 220 Nellon Avenue, Corte Madera, 415-945-1455, www.marinwater.org
- **City of Palo Alto Utilities** (**CPAU**), 650-329-2161
- **San Francisco Water Department**, 1155 Market Street, San Francisco, 415-923-2400, www.ci.sf.ca.us/puc
- **Santa Clara Valley Water District**, 5750 Almaden Expressway, San Jose, 408-265-2600, www.scvwd.dst.ca.us; to set up service contact one of the following:
- **San Jose Water Co.**, 408-279-7900, serves Campbell, Los Gatos, and Saratoga, and parts of the cities of San Jose and Cupertino
- **San Jose Municipal**, 408-277-4036, and **Great Oaks Water**, 408-227-9540, serve San Jose
- **California Water Service**, 650-917-0152, serves Cupertino
- **Sonoma County Water Agency**, 2150 West College Avenue, Santa Rosa, 707-526-5370, to set up service in Sonoma County contact one of the following:
- **Santa Rosa Water District**, 707-543-3150, serves Santa Rosa
- **City of Sonoma City Hall**, #1 the Plaza, Sonoma, 707-938-3681, serves Sonoma
- **North Marin Water District**, 415-897-4133, serves Novato and parts of West Marin

GARBAGE/RECYCLING

In San Francisco landlords pay for garbage collection for apartments, and some duplexes and single-family homes. Homeowners must order and pay for disposal service; the collection fee is based on how many trashcans you fill up each week. To set up garbage collection in San Francisco call: **Sunset Scavenger**, 415-330-1300, www.sunsetscavenger.com or **Golden Gate Disposal**, 415-626-4000, www.goldengatedisposal.com. Outside San Francisco call one of the following:

- **Marin Sanitary Services**, Marin County, 415-456-2601
- **BFI**, San Mateo County, 650-592-2411
- **BFI**, Santa Clara County, 408-432-1234
- **Pleasanthill Bayshore Disposal**, serves most of Contra Costa County, 925-685-4711
- **Waste Management**, Alameda County (north), 510-430-8509, www.stopwaste.org
- **BFI**, Alameda County (south), 510-657-3500
- **Tri-Cities Waste Management**, East Bay, 510-797-0440

Curbside recycling collection is available throughout the Bay Area and generally is included in the cost of your other garbage pickup. In San Francisco residents of apartment buildings with fewer than five units are responsible for picking up the approved plastic containers themselves. Landlords are responsible for setting up recycling programs if the building has five or more units. Landfill space is scarce in the Bay Area, making recycling all the more important. To find out more about recycling in the Bay Area call:
- **Bay Area Action**, based in Palo Alto, www.baaction.org
- **Household Hazardous Waste**, 415-554-4333
- **Marin Recycling Center**, 415-485-6806
- **Recycle America of Northern California**, 510-638-4327, ext. 308
- **Recycle Palo Alto Program**, 650-496-5910
- **SF Recycling Program**, 415-554-3400
- **South Bay, USA Waste Management**, 408-451-0520, Recycle@green-team.com

If you'd like to deliver recyclables to collection centers that will pay you for them, the **California Integrated Waste Management Board** has set up a hotline that provides the addresses and hours of operation of the centers throughout the area. That number is 800-CLEAN-UP. For information specifically dealing with beverage container collection centers, call the **California Department of Conservation** at 800-732-9253.

If you've got a green thumb and you'd like to compost, the ultimate recycle, contact the **San Francisco League of Urban Gardeners** (**SLUG**) at 415-285-7585. They call it the ROT-line, as opposed to a HOT-line. In the East Bay call the **Alameda County Waste Management Authority's Home Composting Education Program** at 510-635-6275.

DEPARTMENT OF MOTOR VEHICLES (DMV)

DRIVERS' LICENSES

If you've moved here from out-of-state and you want to drive in California, you have ten days from your arrival to apply for a new driver's license from the Department of Motor Vehicles. While there is no penalty for filing late, if you are pulled over for a traffic violation after the 10-day grace period, the officer can give you a citation. You will need to bring your current driver's license and a birth certificate or passport for proof of age. Provided your out-of-state license has not yet expired, you will not be asked to take any written or driving tests, but your eyesight will be checked. A driver's license costs $12 and it is good for up to four years, expiring on your birth date. If you are moving to the Bay Area from within California, you have ten days to notify the DMV of your address change, call 415-557-1179 or go to www.dmv.ca.gov.

The DMV also handles the issuance of **state identification** cards. In order to get one you'll need to bring a birth certificate, your Social Security card, and $6.

AUTOMOBILE REGISTRATION & INSURANCE

If you bring a car into the state of California you are supposed to register it within 20 days of your arrival. The DMV requires that emission control devices on your car operate correctly; any non-diesel vehicle that is four years old or older must pass an emissions test. Most service stations will do the test for less than $50. When you've received emission certification, bring it, along with your current automobile registration and your checkbook, to the nearest DMV. Registration is good for one year; subsequent registrations are less expensive.

All California drivers are required by law to carry liability insurance on their vehicles. Although efforts are underway to require automobile owners to supply proof of coverage when registering at the DMV, at this point it is not required. Insurers estimate that 30% to 40% of the drivers on California roads do not carry proper coverage. All the more reason to cover yourself.

DMV OFFICES

The DMV in San Francisco is notorious for its long lines. If you can, spare this frustration and instead go to the DMV in Marin County or San Mateo County. Or you can make an appointment; choose the office where you would like to be seen, call and they'll set you up. Make sure to show up early—not late— they won't wait for you! Hours vary slightly from office to office, but in general Bay Area DMVs are open from 8 a.m. to 5 p.m., Monday-Friday. Daly City, El Cerrito and Fremont offices are open Saturdays from 8 a.m. to 5 p.m. The internet inclined should go online before calling or arriving at a DMV as many services can be handled on the web at www.dmv.ca.gov.

SAN FRANCISCO/NORTH BAY
- San Francisco, 1377 Fell Street, 415-557-1179
- Corte Madera, 75 Tamal Vista Boulevard, 415-924-5560

EAST BAY
- Concord, 2075 Meridian Park Boulevard, 925-671-2876
- El Cerrito, 6400 Manila Avenue, 510-235-9171
- Fremont, 4287 Central Avenue, 510-797-0515
- Hayward, 150 Jackson Street, 510-537-6723
- Oakland, 501 85th Avenue; 5300 Claremont Avenue, 510-450-3670
- Walnut Creek, 1910 North Broadway, 925-935-4464

PENINSULA/SOUTH BAY
- Daly City, 1500 Sullivan Avenue, 650-994-5700
- Redwood City, 300 Brewster Street, 650-368-2837
- San Mateo, 425 North Amphlett, 650-342-5332
- San Jose, 111 West Alma Street, 408-277-1301

PARKING—SAN FRANCISCO

In the City of San Francisco vacant parking spaces are some of the most sought-after real estate. Many residential areas require parking permits, which allow neighborhood residents or temporary guests to park without time limits in the neighborhood. Those without a permit are required to move their cars frequently, usually after two hours. If you're not sure if your neighborhood or the neighborhood you are visiting requires a residential parking permit, check for signs posted along the street. Also check to see when the street sweeper is coming—illegally parked vehicles on street-sweeping days will be towed.

Residential Parking Permits are available at 27 Van Ness Avenue in the City's Civic Center area. The office is open 8 a.m. to 5 p.m. Monday-Wednesday and Friday. On Thursday it's open until 6 p.m. In order to get your permit you'll need to bring valid car registration that shows your new address, which means you'll first need to visit the nearby DMV. Also bring proof of address: your lease, a utility-bill with your address on it, a bank statement or a personalized check. Your driver's license is *not* an acceptable proof of residency. The full-fledged parking permit is good for a year and will set you back $27. For more information on the program call 415-554-5000.

When it comes to **parking** in San Francisco's downtown core your choices are limited to streetside meters or parking garages. There are more than ten thousand garage spaces in the downtown area, and they are certainly the most costly option. Fees vary somewhat; in general, depositing your car in one of these spots will cost $20-$30 a day. Some outdoor lots in the South of Market area will sell you a monthly spot for as little as $100, but more often than not those lots are sold out. For general information on parking in San Francisco call the **Department of Parking and Traffic** at 415-554-7275 or check online at www.ci.sf.ca.us/dpt. Here are just a few of San Francisco's downtown parking garages:

- **Portsmouth Square Garage**: 733 Kearny Street, 415-982-6353, 500+ spaces
- **St. Mary's Square Garage**, 433 Kearny Street, 415-956-8106, 800+ spaces
- **Sutter-Stockton Garage**: 330 Sutter Street, 415-982-7275, 1800+ spaces
- **Union Square Garage**: 333 Post Street, 415-397-0631, 1100+ spaces
- **Ellis-O'Farrell Garage**: 123 O'Farrell Street, 415-986-4800, 1200+ spaces
- **Fifth and Mission Yerba Buena Garage**: 5th and Mission Street, 415-982-8522, 2600+ spaces

There are many more lots in the City, so if the one you want to patronize is full or closed you'll only need to drive a couple of blocks and you'll probably find one with space. While driving around watch for the much less expensive metered parking spaces, but make certain you read and understand all the postings. The only people faster at their jobs than the meter-readers are the tow truck operators they call out. Fortunately parking is easier in outlying areas and there is plenty of street parking in most cities; in fact there have been cases of people moving out of San Francisco just for the parking. To **pay a traffic citation by phone**, have your VISA or MasterCard ready and dial 415-255-3999 or 800-532-2357.

PARKING—SURROUNDING AREAS

For information on parking tickets, towing, and other unpleasantness in the North Bay, contact the **Marin County Traffic Authority**, 800-281-7275. Some cities require a residential permit allowing you to park in your neighborhood for an extended period of time. To obtain a residential parking sticker in Sausalito call the **Sausalito Parking Services**, 415-289-4100, ext. 144. Most of the other cities in Marin do not require parking stickers.

In the East Bay, Oakland residents should call the **Oakland Parking Bureau**, 510-238-3099 or the **Traffic Division of the Superior Court**, 510-268-7673, located in Oakland. In Berkeley, contact the **City of Berkeley Transportation, Customer Relations**, 510-644-6470. For UC Berkeley call the **UC Berkeley Parking and Transportation Office**, 510-642-4283.

In the South Bay/Peninsula, call: **Palo Alto Parking Permits**, 650-329-2317; **San Mateo Parking Permits, Residential & City Parking Facilities**, 650-522-7326; and in San Jose, contact the **Residential Parking Permits** at 408-277-4304.

GETTING YOUR TOWED CAR BACK

If your car is towed in San Francisco, chances are it will be waiting for you at **City Tow**, 850 Bryant Street, at the Hall of Justice, 415-621-8605. To obtain your vehicle's release you must appear in person with picture identification and be prepared to pay not only the towing cost and ticket, but also any outstanding parking tickets written against the vehicle, and storage costs. Ouch!

In surrounding Bay Area counties, if your car is missing, call the local police station first and they will provide you with the name of the towing company contracted out by that city. Police department numbers are listed at the end of the neighborhood profiles.

SAN FRANCISCO PARKING FINES

Failure to curb your wheels on a hill $25
Meter violation $25
Parking in a red or yellow zone $25
Parking in white or green zone $23
Parking on a sidewalk $25
Removing a chalk mark from tire (first time) $77
Removing a chalk mark from tire (second time) $103
Removing a chalk mark from tire (third time) $103
Failure to move car for street sweeper $30
Parking too long in a residential zone w/out permit $33
Blocking a driveway. $50
Double parking $50
Abandoned vehicle $53
Parking in a bus zone $250
Parking in a blue (handicapped) zone $275

COLORED CURBS

Red . . . . Fire Zone—don't even think of parking here
Yellow. . . . . . Commercial loading zone only, for times posted
White . . . . . . Passenger pick-up or drop-off only
Green . . . . . . Temporary (usually 20-30 minutes) parking only—as posted
Blue . . . . Handicapped parking only, special placard required

VOTER REGISTRATION

Registering to vote in the Bay Area is easy. Frequent voter registration drives literally bring the process to you, along downtown sidewalks, in malls, and in public transit facilities. You can also register by visiting the **Registrar of Voters** or **Elections Department** in the county where you live. The deadline to register is 29 days before an election.

You can register with any political party in California, sign up as an independent, or decline to state a party affiliation. Voters may cast their ballots in person or vote via absentee ballot. If you want to vote absentee, you must call your local registrar's office and request the forms. Be sure to allow ample time, usually about a month, for them to receive your forms in the mail. Your registrar's office will be able to tell you what the cut-off date is for sending in an absentee ballot.

Here are the locations and phone numbers for voter registration officials in each of the nine Bay Area counties:

- **San Francisco**, City Hall, Room 48, San Francisco, 415-554-4375
- **Alameda**, 1225 Fallon Street, Oakland, 510-272-6973
- **Contra Costa**, 524 Main Street, Martinez, 925-646-4166
- **Marin**, 3501 Civic Center Drive, San Rafael, 415-499-6456
- **Napa**, 900 Coombs Street, Napa, 707-253-4321
- **San Mateo**, 40 Tower Road, San Mateo, 650-312-5222
- **Santa Clara**, 1553 Berger Drive, San Jose, 408-299-8302
- **Solano**, 510 Clay Street, Fairfield, 707-421-6675
- **Sonoma**, 435 Fiscal Drive, Santa Rosa, 707-565-1800

LIBRARIES

San Francisco is home to one of the finest city libraries in the world. Opened in early 1996, the shiny new facility called **New Main**, 415-557-4400, www.sfpl.org, across the Civic Center plaza from City Hall, holds more than one million books, magazines and research tomes. It also provides internet access and multi-media presentations via dozens of computers. The entire library system's card catalog is on computer and accessible at terminals on every floor. However, despite its gleaming new surroundings, the library is in the process of raising more money to implement renovations needed to accommodate more shelving and ease egress, which now is confusing and sometimes silly (one needs to go up a set of stairs in order to go down). Library cards are free, and you don't have to be a San Francisco resident to get one. Just bring proper ID, such as a driver's license, and something else with your current address on it, such as a utility bill. The card is valid at all San Francisco library branches; addresses and phone numbers are listed in the **Neighborhoods** section of this book. New Main is easy to get to; it's just a short walk from the Civic Center BART/MUNI station.

PASSPORTS

Those needing to leave the country quickly will find passport services available through the **San Francisco Passport Agency** at 95 Hawthorne Street, 5th

Floor. For detailed passport information, pour yourself a cup of tea, put your feet up, and call the Passport Agency's extensive recording at 415-538-2700. The services at this office are reserved for those in need of expedited service. It is open Monday-Friday from 9 a.m. to 4 p.m. If you're crunched for time, get there when the office opens, as waits of one to two hours are not uncommon.

For those who do not need expedited service it is possible to have your passport processed at your local post office, city hall or the department of public health. The Bureau of Consular Affairs' web site, www.travel.state.gov, lists the public agencies that process passports. Passports generally take six to seven weeks to arrive by mail, but can take longer. If you've been called out of town on an emergency, it is possible to get a passport the same day, but it will cost extra for speedy service. In San Francisco, the San Francisco Passport Agency is the only agency that can expedite the passport application. However, if you are outside of the City, check with your city hall and they may be able to expedite the process. In San Jose, the **Santa Clara County Recorders Office** at the County Government Center, East Wing, 70 West Hedding Street, 408-299-2481, can process your passport application within 10 to 14 days. The current fee for a new adult passport is $60; $40 to renew. You can pay with *exact* cash (they won't make change), check or money order. You will also need to bring a previous passport, if you have one, two identical 2" x 2" photographs, proof of identification (driver's license, state ID card, military ID), and you'll have to fill out the application available at the passport office, the post office or city hall. Passports are good for ten years (for adults). You may download the passport application form (DSP-11) by visiting the **Bureau of Consular Affair's** web site, www.travel.state.gov.

TELEVISION STATIONS

Broadcast television reception in the Bay Area is fairly good, unless you live in a particularly hilly area, in which case hooking up to the cable is the way to go. If you're not interested in cable, a standard roof antenna will probably suffice to pull in most of the stations listed below. Apartment dwellers may want to consider getting a pair of "rabbit ears," a small indoor antenna that sits on top of the television set.

CHANNEL	CALL LETTERS	NETWORK	LOCATION
2	KTVU	Fox	Oakland
4	KRON	NBC	San Francisco
5	KPIX	CBS	San Francisco
7	KGO	ABC	San Francisco
9	KQED	PBS	San Francisco
14	KDTV	Univision	San Francisco
20	KBWB	WBN	San Francisco

```
26. . . . . . . . KTSF. . . . . . . . . . Independent. . . . San Francisco
36. . . . . . . . KICU . . . . . . . . . Independent. . . . San Jose
44. . . . . . . . KHBK . . . . . . . . . Independent. . . . San Francisco
50. . . . . . . . KFTY . . . . . . . . . Independent. . . . Santa Rosa
54. . . . . . . . KTEH . . . . . . . . . PBS. . . . . . . . . . San Jose
60. . . . . . . . KCSM. . . . . . . . . PBS. . . . . . . . . . San Mateo
66. . . . . . . . KPST . . . . . . . . . Chinese. . . . . . . San Francisco
```

CABLE TELEVISION

If broadcast television (those listed above) doesn't provide you with adequate entertainment options, you'll probably need to get cabled. Cable television is available throughout the nine Bay Area counties, with service levels governed by agreements reached with municipalities. Each cable provider offers various packages based on how many channels you wish to receive. Naturally, the more channels you receive, the more you pay.

Here are some of the largest local cable providers:

- **AT&T Cable and Broadband Services**: San Francisco, 800-945-2288; San Jose, 408-991-1501; Peninsula, 800-945-2288; Marin, 800-436-1999; Contra Costa County, 925-432-0364, www.att.com
- **Direct TV**, 800-675-8668

RADIO STATIONS

There are 80 radio stations located within the nine county Bay Area, 30 AMs and 50 FMs. AM reception is fairly consistent throughout the area, with no special equipment needed. FM reception can be spotty, especially if you live in a hilly area of San Francisco (which is most of the City), the East Bay or North Bay. You may need an FM antenna in those areas. Here are some of the most listened to stations in the Bay Area and their formats.

AM

SAN FRANCISCO
```
KABL 960. . . . . Oldies
KCBS 740 . . . . All News
KBZS 1220 . . . Business Network
KFRC 610 . . . . Oldies
KGO 810. . . . . News/Talk
KIQI 1010 . . . . Hispanic
KJOI 1510 . . . . Adult standards
KNBR 680 . . . . Sports/Talk
KYCY 1550 . . . Country
```

```
KSFO 560 . . . . Conservative Talk
KSRO 1350 . . . News/Talk
KOIT 1260. . . . Adult Contemporary
```

NORTH BAY

```
KXBT 1190 . . . Asian
KRRS 1460. . . . Hispanic
KDIA 1640. . . . Talk/Catholic
```

SOUTH BAY/PENINSULA

```
KTCT 1050 . . . Sports
KAZA 1300 . . . Hispanic
KSJX 1500 . . . . Vietnamese
CNN 1590. . . . News
```

FM

SAN FRANCISCO

```
KALW 91.7 . . . News and Information (NPR)
KBRG 100.3. . . Romantic/Hispanic
KISQ 98.1 . . . . Classic soul
KBLX 102.9 . . . Adult Contemporary
KCSM 91.1 . . . Jazz, News (NPR)
KDFC 102.1. . . Classical
KFOG 104.5 . . Rock
KFRC 99.7 . . . . Oldies
K101 101.3 . . . Adult Contemporary
KJOY 100.7 . . . Oldies/Nostalgia
KITS 105.3. . . . Modern Rock
KKSF 103.7 . . . Jazz/New Age
KMEL 106.1 . . Urban
KOIT 96.5 . . . . Light Rock
KUFX 98.5. . . . Modern Rock
KPFA 94.1 . . . . News/Information/Variety
KPOO 89.5 . . . Music/Talk/Variety-Listener Sponsor
KQED 88.5 . . . News/Information (NPR)
ALICE 97.3. . . . Modern Adult Contemporary
KUIC 95.3 . . . . Adult Contemporary
KWLD 94.9 . . . Urban top 40
KSJO 92.3 . . . . Rock
KUSF 90.3 . . . . Alternative rock, Ethnic, Religious
KYCY 93.3 . . . . Country
KEAR 106.9 . . . Religious
```

KFOG 104.5 . . Adult alternative
KZQZ 95.7 . . . Top 40

EAST BAY
KALX 90.7 . . . . Alternative rock
KFJO 92.1 . . . . Rock

NORTH BAY
KJZY 93.7. . . . . Jazz
KMGG 97.7. . . Oldies
KRSH 98.7 . . . . Rock

SOUTH BAY/PENINSULA
KBAY 94.5 . . . . Soft rock
KFFG97.7 . . . . Adult alternative
KEZR106.5 . . . Adult contemporary
KFJC 89.7 . . . . Alternative rock
KZSU 90.1 . . . . Eclectic music

FINDING A PHYSICIAN

Much like finding a place to live in the Bay Area, finding a physician is never easy. You must first consider your needs—are you looking for a pediatrician, family physician, OB/Gyn, or all of the above? Do you want someone who staffs the hospital nearest you? Are you interested in an MD or an Osteopath? And perhaps most importantly, does your health plan limit who you can see? Here in the Bay Area you will find cutting-edge, top-notch care at the University of California San Francisco Medical Center located at 505 Parnassus, 415-476-1000, famous for its pioneering work in areas such as pediatrics, high-risk obstetrics, organ transplantation, cancer care, cardiac care, neurosurgery and orthopedics. However, because it is an educational facility, you may have observing students following you about. Probably the most popular way to find a good doctor is through word of mouth, talking to friends, neighbors, colleagues or other doctors. To assist in your research, consider ordering a back issue of the *Bay Area Consumers' Checkbook* Fall 1998/Winter 1999 edition, which listed the Bay Area's outstanding physician specialists. Go to www.checkbook.org, or call 510-763-7979 and ask for article #4-052; you can order the entire edition or only the article, there is a charge for the service. See the **Helpful Services** chapter for information about *Consumers' Checkbook*. To determine if a physician you are considering is board certified, check with the American Board of Medical Specialties Board Certification Verification at 800-776-2378, between 9 a.m. and 6 p.m. (EST) or go online to www.certifieddoctor.org.

If you are strapped for cash while in transition, the **Haight-Ashbury Free**

Medical Clinic, 558 Clayton Street, 415-487-5632, offers free, primary health care, and specialty care, including podiatry, chiropractic care, pediatrics, HIV testing, comprehensive HIV treatment services, and community information and referral services. The Medical Clinic welcomes everyone who walks through the door. However, the clinic is unable to treat emergency medical problems, such as broken bones, severe bleeding, trauma, abdominal pains, etc. For emergency medical problems go immediately to the nearest hospital emergency room.

If you've only recently arrived to the Bay Area and find yourself in sudden need of a physician, the Traveler's Medical Group, 490 Post Street, Suite #225, 415-981-1102, can send a doctor who speaks your language, 24 hours a day, seven days a week.

Hopefully you'll never need the following. The **Medical Board of California**, 1426 Howe Avenue, Suite 54, Sacramento, CA 95825, 800-633-2322, www.medbd.ca.gov, and the **Osteopathic Medical Board of California**, 2720 Gateway Oaks Drive, Suite 350, Sacramento, CA 95833, 916-263-3100, are the two state organizations that handle complaints against medical professionals in California. Write or call for more information.

PET LAWS & SERVICES

If you're bringing Fido, Fluffy or Spot with you to the Bay Area, you're no doubt wondering what local ordinances may apply to your dog or cat. Area agencies can answer your specific questions about leash laws, immunizations, and the like, or, at least, refer you to the right organization. SF DOG (San Francisco Dog Owners Group), www.sfdog.org, has a comprehensive web site that lists dog-friendly areas, events and important contact numbers. Your courthouse should be able to provide details about licensing your pets and local leash laws. Contact the Golden Gate National Recreation Area at 415-556-0560 for a "pet trail map." Additional pet services found in the Bay Area include pet sitters and boarding and grooming establishments. Look in the Yellow Pages under "Pet Services."

You and Fido can take MUNI together, but your dog must pay her own way and wear a muzzle. Call 415-673-MUNI for more information. Also noteworthy is PAWS which stands for "Pets are Wonderful Support," an organization dedicated to preserving the relationship of people with AIDs and their pets, call 415-241-1460 to volunteer.

Bay Area Dog Lovers' Companion, by Maria Goodvage provides valuable information for the best places to explore, sleep and eat with your dog in the nine Bay Area counties. On the web, www.pets.com, is a good resource for finding veterinarian, pet-friendly lodgings, dog walkers and more. You can also try: www.dogfriendly.com, www.petswelcome.com, and www.travel-dog.com. There is even a glossy quarterly magazine devoted to dogs called *The Bark,* www.thebark.com, 2810 Eighth Street, Berkeley, 877-227-5639.

What follows is a list of for-profit and non-profit services for animals:

SAN FRANCISCO
- **Claws and Paws Pet Sitting**, 415-921-1577
- **Department of Animal Care & Control**, 1200 15th Street, 415-554-6364
- **Ladies and the Tramp**, 415-923-1943
- **PAWS (Pets Are Wonderful Support)**, 415-241-1460
- **Prime Time Pet Care**, 415-648-6855
- **SF Society for the Prevention of Cruelty to Animals (SPCA)**, 2500 16th Street, 415-554-3000
- **SF DOG (Dog Owners Group)**, 415-339-7461, www.sfdog.org

EAST BAY
- **Berkeley-East Bay Humane Society**, 2700 9th Street, Berkeley, 510-845-7735
- **East Bay SPCA**, 8323 Baldwin Street, Oakland, 510-569-0702
- **Benicia-Vallejo Humane Society**, 1121 Sonoma Boulevard, Vallejo, 707-645-7905
- **Abbie's Animal Care**, 510-382-1214
- **Home Alone**, 510-531-1211
- **Tender Loving Care**, 510-758-4616

SOUTH BAY/PENINSULA
- **Affordable Pet Sitting**, 650-591-4473
- **Animal House Dog & Cat Grooming**, 408-462-3235
- **Bayshore Dog & Cat Care**, 650-342-0941
- **Critter Care**, 408-241-2416
- **Home Alone**, 408-379-2033
- **Humane Society**, 12 Airport Boulevard, San Mateo, 650-340-8200
- **Palo Alto People for Unleashed Pet Space (PUPS)**, 650-562-1777, www.canineworld.com/pups
- **Palo Alto Pet Care**, 650-852-9190
- **Nice Dogs Outside** supports Peninsula access for dogs, www.prusik.com/pads, 650-562-1777
- **Pet Sitters International**, 800-268-PETS
- **Santa Clara Humane Society**, 2530 Lafayette Street, Santa Clara, 408-727-3383
- **Rainbow Plus**, 408-384-4508
- **The Pet Spa**, 408-379-8911
- **West Valley Pet Shelter**, 100b Gilman Avenue, Campbell, 408-374-3700

NORTH BAY
- **Marin County Humane Society**, 171 Bel Marin Keys Road, Novato, 415-883-4621
- **Napa County Humane Society**, 942 Westimola Avenue, 707-255-8118

- **Humane Society of Sonoma County**, 5345 Sebastapol Road, Santa Rosa, 707-526-5312
- **Second Chance Rescue**, 1767 Stonecreek Drive, Petaluma, 707-721-1721
- **Amelia's Pet Care**, 707-226-9477
- **Critter Care**, 415-388-9222
- **Happy Tails Cat**, 415-925-0457
- **Holistic Animal Care**, 707-538-4643
- **We Care Pet Sitters**, 707-795-1230

FINDING A VETERINARIAN/EMERGENCY HOSPITALS

To alleviate the high cost of veterinarian bills, you may want to consider obtaining health coverage for your pet. Contact the national organization **Veterinary Pet Insurance**, 800-872-7387, or the pet HMO **Pet Assure**, 888-789-7387, for more details.

Most neighborhoods have at least one vet. To limit your travel time, try a vet in your area first. Perhaps the best way to get the inside scoop on vets, is to frequent the dog park and talk to neighborhood owners. There's **Nob Hill Cat Clinic**, 415-776-6122, and **Pets Unlimited**, 415-563-6700, in Pacific Heights, which serves many areas of the City and is also an adoption center. Or try the **California Veterinary Medical Associations** site at www.cvma.org. You choose the city in which you are interested, and they will give you in-depth details about selected vets there. The CVMA's parent organization at www.avma.org will also give you information on your critter questions.

If your dog has ingested anything poisonous, contact **ASPCA National Animal Poison Control Center**, 24 hour emergency informational service, there is a $45 charge, 888-426-4435. You can also go straight to an emergency pet hospital at the following locations:

SAN FRANCISCO
- **All Animals Emergency Hospital**, 1333 9th Avenue, 415-566-0531
- **Pets Unlimited Veterinary Hospital**, 2343 Fillmore Street, 415-563-6700
- **Balboa Pet Hospital**, 3329 Balboa Street, 415-752-3300

NORTH BAY
- **Calistoga Pet Clinic**, 1124 Lincoln Avenue, Calistoga, 707-942-0404
- **Madera Pet Hospital**, 5796 Paradise Drive, Corte Madera, 415-927-0525
- **Novato Veterinary Hospital**, 7454 Redwood Boulevard, Novato, 415-897-2173

EAST BAY
- **Albany Veterinary Clinic**, 1550 Solano Avenue, Berkeley, 510-526-2053
- **All Bay Animal Hospital**, 1739 Willow Pass Road, Concord, 925-687-7346

SOUTH BAY/PENINSULA
- **Skyline Pet Hospital**, 70 Skline Plaza, Daly City, 650-756-4877
- **Stanford Pet Clinic**, 4111 El Camino Real, Palo Alto, 650-493-4233
- **Mayfair Veterinary Hospital**, 2810 Alum Rock Avenue, San Jose, 408-258-2735

OFF-LEASH AREAS

Off-leash areas in San Francisco where you and your dog can play and let off some steam include the following:
- **Alta Plaza Park** in Pacific Heights at Jackson, Clay, Steiner, and Scott streets. Most dogs roam with their owners before and after work.
- **Baker Beach**, south of Golden Gate Bridge off-leash along the beach and the new pathway bordering the bay.
- **Bernal Heights Park** on Bernal Hill is off-leash.
- **Buena Vista Park**, the off-leash area is at the intersection of Buena Vista Avenue and Central Street, south of Haight Street.
- **Corona Heights Park/Red Rock Park**, near the Randall Museum at Museum Way and Roosevelt Avenue. There is a fenced off-leash area at the end of the upper field near the base of the hill.
- **Crissy Field** in the Presidio. Dogs are allowed to run free on the beach and the in the bay, east of Fort Point. Make sure that your dog does not enter the fenced off restoration area as the National Park Rangers will cite you.
- **Dolores Park** near the Mission District by Dolores, 18th, 19th, and 20th streets
- **Fort Funston**, south of Ocean Beach with the paragliders and hang-gliders is a popular and scenic place for dogs to roam off-leash, but beware of the cliffs.
- **Golden Gate Park**, is an official off-leash park, except for the areas near Stowe Lake and Strawberry Hill and the panhandle, an 8 block strip of land bounded by Oak and Fell streets.
- **Lafayette Park**, near Sacramento, Octavia and Gough is a popular canine communing park.
- **Lake Merced**, dogs are allowed to run wild at the north end of the lake.
- **McKinley Square** in Potrero Hill where San Bruno Avenue ends at 20th Street. Off-leash dogs are allowed only on the unimproved western slope.
- **McLaren Park** near the intersection of Mansel Street and Shelly Drive is off-leash.
- **Mountain Lake Park**, in the Richmond District. Enter at 8th Avenue and Lake Street
- **Ocean Beach** is mostly on-leash, but dogs are allowed off-leash south of Sloat Boulevard or north of Fulton. Make sure our dog does not stray north of Sloat or south of Fulton. There have been numerous reports of citations by National Park Service rangers.

- **Stern Grove** on Wawona Street between 21and 23rd avenues allows dogs to be off their leash.

NEWSPAPERS AND MAGAZINES

- *Asian Week*, 809 Sacramento Street, San Francisco, 415-397-0221, www.asianweek.com
- *Bay Area Business Woman*, classified listings of local businesses seminars, classes, events, 510-654-7557, 5337 College Avenue, Suite 501, Oakland, www.owm.com.
- *Bay Area Consumers' Checkbook*, evaluates quality and prices of local service firms and stores; 202-347-7283, www.checkbook.org.
- *Bay Area Naturally*, 7282 Sir Francis Drake Boulevard, San Rafael, 800-486-4794; a free directory of community resources for natural living, published by City Spirit Publications and distributed in businesses. Includes holistic health professionals, green products and services, schools and educational centers, a natural food restaurant guide, and a calendar of events.
- *Contra Costa County Times*, published daily with East Bay listings, focusing on Concord, Walnut Creek, Pleasant Hill, Martinez, Richmond, Hercules, Benicia, Antioch, Pittsburg, and Bay Point areas, 925-935-2525, www.hotcoco.com.
- *East Bay Express*, P.O. Box 3198, Berkeley, 510-540-7400, www.eastbayexpress.com, a free weekly alternative paper; focuses on the East Bay. Good for rental and roommate listings; found in newsstands and at cafes.
- *East Bay Monthly*, distributed free throughout the East Bay, 1301 59th Street, Emeryville, 510-658-9811.
- **Hills Newspapers, Inc.**, publications include: *The Berkeley Voice, El Cerrito Journal, The Montclarion, The Piedmonter*, and *Alameda Journal*, 510-339-8777
- *Marin Independent Journal*, published daily with listings for Marin, Sonoma and Napa counties, 415-883-8600, www.marinij.com.
- *Metropolitan*, 1717 17th Street, San Francisco; for the cocktail set, 415-487-9090.
- *Metro*, 550 South 1st Street, San Jose, 408-298-8000
- *Oakland Tribune*, published daily with a focus on the East Bay, especially Oakland, Berkeley, and Alameda, 510-208-6300, www.newschoice.com.
- *Pacific Sun*, a free, weekly alternative; listings for Marin County. Found in newsstands and cafes. Good for rentals and roommate listings, 415-383-4500, www.pacificsun.com.
- *San Francisco Arts Monthly*, thorough arts listing calendar, 653 Bryant Street, San Francisco, 415-543-6110
- *San Francisco Bay Guardian*, weekly free alternative paper with extensive listings for San Francisco and the East Bay. Published Wednesdays. Found at

every cafe, corner store and, newsstands all over city. Good for rental and roommate listings, 415-255-3100, www.sfbg.com.

- *San Francisco Business Times*, 275 Battery, San Francisco, 415-989-2522
- *San Francisco Chronicle*, the most-read newspaper in the area; includes listings for San Francisco, North Bay, East Bay, Peninsula counties, and some outlying areas, 415-777-1111, www.sfgate.com.
- *San Francisco Examiner*, daily afternoon newspaper that publishes listings similar to the Chronicle, 415-777-2424, www.sfgate.com and www.examiner.com.
- *San Francisco Chronicle/Examiner*, the Sunday paper for both of the above, with the most extensive listings of the week for the Bay Area, www.sfgate.com.
- *San Francisco Magazine*, 243 Vallejo Street, San Francisco, 415-398-2800
- *San Francisco Weekly*, a free weekly alternative paper with San Francisco listings. Good for rental and roommate listings; published Wednesdays; found all over city at newsstands and cafes, 415-541-0700.
- *San Jose Mercury News*, published daily; most extensive listings for the South Bay as well as much of the Peninsula and southern East Bay, 408-920-5000, www.mercurycenter.com.
- *San Mateo Times*, published daily except Sunday with listings for much of the Peninsula, 650-348-4321, www.newschoice.com.
- *Santa Rosa Press Democrat*, published daily; listings for Sonoma, Marin and Napa counties, 707-546-2020, www.pressdemocrat.com.

A WORD ABOUT SAFETY

San Francisco, and indeed the Bay Area, suffers from the same problems with crime as does most every other large metropolitan area. What's unusual here is that San Francisco suffers from an inordinate number of pedestrian fatalities, in fact, according to *NBC Nightly News*, in 2000, 54% of all traffic fatalities in San Francisco were pedestrians! Please be careful when you walk, bike or drive. Because police can't be everywhere all the time, you need to beware for our own safety. Fortunately, common sense can reduce your chances of being victimized. Below are a few simple urban safety tips:

- Walk with determination, and remain aware of your surroundings at all times.
- If you're carrying a handbag or backpack do so with the strap across your chest. However, if someone demands what you are carrying, give it up! Your life is much more valuable than anything you're carrying
- On the street, you do not owe a response to anyone who asks for one. This may seem callous but it is better to err on the side of bad manners than bad judgment.
- At all costs, avoid getting into a car with a stranger.
- On the bus, ride in the front next to the driver

- Keep clear of abandoned/deserted areas; If you must go into an area that you feel may be unsafe, do it in the daytime and, if possible, with someone else
- Lock your house, both when you leave and when you are at home
- If you like to jog, try to find a running partner, particularly if you run in at night.
- Know where the local police and fire stations are located
- If something does happen to you or if you witness a crime, notify the police immediately.

Neighborhood Watch programs are on the increase throughout the Bay Area, but they're not in every community yet. These programs encourage neighbors to get to know each other and watch out for each other, and to notify authorities of anything suspicious. Check with the police department in your neighborhood to find out if a watch program is up and running, and if not you may want to take the lead and set one up yourself. You can also visit the neighborhood watch web site at www.ncpc.org, which gives you general safety information and instructs you on how to set up a neighborhood watch in your neighborhood. In addition, the District Attorney's office set up a community DA program where district attorneys in San Francisco volunteer in their own neighborhood and share their expertise.

The San Francisco Police Department is looking for volunteers to assist in crime prevention, neighborhood policing, and other areas. For more information, contact the Volunteer Coordinator, 850 Bryant Street Room 570, San Francisco, 415-553-9152.

In San Francisco, neighborhood crime statistics are available online at www.ci.sf.ca.us/police/crimes/districts.

Finally, if you are a victim of a crime contact the police immediately, by dialing 911. For family violence, the crisis hotline is 415-552-7550. For more listings, see **Crisis Lines** in the **Useful Phone Numbers and Web Sites** chapter.

NOW THAT YOU'VE FOUND A PLACE TO HANG YOUR HAT, AND YOU'VE taken care of some of the basics like turning on electricity and making sure your stove works, it's time to make your place feel like home. This chapter covers furniture and computer rentals, domestic services, finding an automobile repair shop, receiving and sending packages, as well as services for people with disabilities, a resource section for gays and lesbians, and more.

RENTAL SERVICES

In keeping with the business adage, "find a need and fill it," just about anything you can imagine can be rented in the Bay Area, from silverware to pagers to televisions and stereos to furniture to wedding wear to steamrollers. If you don't own everything and you need to set up house here, have no fear—someone has it and they're ready to rent. Generally speaking, you'll probably save money by opting to buy instead of renting, even buying on credit is financially better, but you just may need to rent something, like a bed for visitors or even a computer.

FURNITURE

There are numerous furniture rental outfits here that will rent anything from a single ottoman to enough furniture and appliances to fill an entire house. Many of them offer "rent-to-own" options, but such options are often costly. It will always be less expensive to purchase your furniture outright than to go the rent-to-own route.

Before visiting a furniture rental place, measure your living space, and get an idea about where you want to put certain furniture. Go into the store with those measurements in hand and a detailed idea of how many pieces you need. Delivery and setup is usually free and accomplished within 48 hours. Here are just a few of the rental companies in the Bay Area.

SAN FRANCISCO/NORTH BAY
- **Brook Furniture Rental**, 500 Washington Street, 415-776-0666
- **Cort Furniture Rental**, 1480 Van Ness Avenue, 415-771-6115
- **Globe Furniture Rental**, 700 Larkspur Landing Cir, 415-673-6700
- **Rent-A-Center**, 3030 Mission Street, 415-282-2277
- **Rent-A-Center**, 1375 Fillmore Street, 415-567-3313

EAST BAY
- **Brook Furniture Rental**, 1531 Locust Street, Walnut Creek, 925-947-1005
- **Cort Furniture Rental**, 1900 Mount Diablo Boulevard, Concord, 925-645-1853
- **Cort Furniture Clearance Center**, 1240 Willow Pass Road, Concord 925-609-9127
- **Rent-A-Center**, 2701 Telegraph Avenue, Oakland, 510-271-8077

PENINSULA
- **Brook Furniture Rental**, 4916 Camino Real, Los Altos, 650-961-9152
- **Brook Furniture Rental**, 999 Edgewater Boulevard, Foster City, 650-573-5120
- **Cort Furniture Rental**, 626 San Antonio Road, Mountain View, 650-966-1758
- **Cort Furniture Rental**, 2001 Windward Way, San Mateo, 650-650-341-3488
- **Lullaby Lane**, 570 San Mateo Avenue, San Bruno, 415-588-4878 (specializes in children's furniture)
- **Rent-A-Center**, 1401 El Camino Real, Redwood City, 650-368-9180

SOUTH BAY
- **Brook Furniture Rental**, 4949 Stevens Creek Boulevard, Santa Clara, 408-247-4860
- **Central Rents**, 1789 East Capitol Expressway, San Jose, 408-532-9274
- **Cort Furniture Rental**, 2925 Mead Avenue, Santa Clara, 408-727-1022
- **Cort Furniture Clearance Center**, 1830 Hillsdale Avenue, San Jose, 408-264-9600
- **Rent-A-Center**, 1605 West San Carlos Street, San Jose, 408-287-2183

TELEVISION & VCR RENTAL

SAN FRANCISCO
- **Laser City Home Entertainment**, 1390 Market Street 415-241-9644
- **Rent-A-Center**, 3030 Mission Street, 415-282-2277; 1375 Fillmore Street, 415-567-3313; 6298 Mission Street, Daly City, 415-757-9034
- **Sunset Richmond TV**, 1885 11th Avenue, 415-564-3890

EAST BAY
- **Central Rents**, 20848 Mission Boulevard, Hayward, 510-276-5000
- **Granada TV & Video**, 4001 1st Street, Livermore, 925-443-2200
- **Lafayette Television Center**, 3574 Mount Diablo Boulevard, Lafayette 925-283-6223
- **Rent-A-Center**, 2701 Telegraph Avenue, Oakland, 510-271-8077

PENINSULA
- **A-Alliance Muni TV**, 3624 Florence Street, Redwood City, 650-366-4953
- **Rent-A-Center**, 1401 El Camino Real, Redwood City, 650-368-9180
- **San Mateo TV & VCR**, 633 South B Street, San Mateo, 650-344-8119

SOUTH BAY
- **Central Rents**, 1789 East Capitol Expressway, San Jose, 408-532-0274
- **Laserland Home Theater**, 1080 South De Anza Boulevard, San Jose, 408-253-3733
- **Rent-A-Center**, 1605 West San Carlos Street, San Jose, 408-287-2183

MAJOR APPLIANCE RENTAL

SAN FRANCISCO/NORTH BAY
- **Rent-A-Center**, 3030 Mission Street, 415-282-2277
- **Rent-A-Center**, 2050 Florida Street, Vallejo, 707-643-7368
- **Rent-A-Center**, 1902 North Texas Street, Fairfield, 707-643-7368
- **Rent-A-Center**, 711 Stony Point Road, Santa Rosa, 707-542-6522
- **Renter's Choice**, 3475 Sonoma Boulevard, Vallejo, 707-643-1733
- **Renter's Choice**, 3181 Cleveland Avenue, Santa Rosa, 707-567-1022

EAST BAY
- **Central Rental**, 3351 East 14th Street, Oakland, 510-535-1500
- **Central Rents**, 20848 Mission Boulevard, Hayward, 510-276-5000
- **Rent-Center**, 3400 International Boulevard, Oakland, 510-532-0210
- **Renter's Choice**, 690 Bailey Road, Bay Point, 925-778-3811

PENINSULA/SOUTH BAY
- **Central Rents**, 1789 East Capitol Expressway, San Jose, 408-532-0274
- **Mike's Appliance Rental**, 1224 Lynhurst Way, San Jose, 408-266-5640.
- **Rent-A-Center**, 1605 West San Carlos Street, San Jose, 408-287-2183

COMPUTER RENTAL AND LEASE

This being the information age, and the Bay Area being high-tech ground zero, it is understandable that the Yellow Page entries for computer rental companies goes on and on and on. Many companies offer rent-to-own options or lease agreements that come with free or low-cost setup and maintenance packages. Because prices vary depending upon rental agency and computer model, it pays to shop around. Here are a few rental companies and phone numbers to get you going. Most have multiple offices so ask for the location that's most convenient for you.

- **Computertime**, 800-459-8080
- **AAA Frog's Rent-a-Computer**, 800-840-3764
- **Computer-rental.com**, 800-799-2112
- **Bit by Bit**, 800-248-2924
- **DCR**, 800-736-8327
- **MicroRent**, 800-444-8780
- **PCR**, 800-473-6872
- **Rent-A-Computer**, 415-398-7800

DOMESTIC SERVICES

As many of us work more than we care to, you may find there just isn't enough time to keep up with domestic details, particularly house cleaning. Rest assured, the Bay Area has a whole bunch of people who'd be more than happy to clean your abode, for a fee. Many housekeepers advertise on coffeehouse, grocery store and university/college bulletin boards, as well as in newspaper classifieds. In San Francisco, Parent's Place, 3272 California Street, 415-563-0335, has a bulletin board full of ads posted by people looking for housecleaning and child-care jobs. **Professional housecleaning services** are listed in the Yellow Pages under "House Cleaning." Here are a few numbers to get you started.

SAN FRANCISCO
- **Cinderella's Housekeeping**, 415-864-8900
- **Here's Help**, 415-931-4357
- **Marvel Maids**, 415-392-3222
- **New Dimensions**, 415-731-4900
- **Self-Help for the Elderly**, 415-982-9171

NORTH BAY
- **Merry Maids**, 415-897-9420
- **Marry Maids**, 707-257-8788
- **Molly Maids**, 415-257-8788

EAST BAY
- **Merry Maids**, 510-595-7545; 925-932-6313

PENINSULA

- **Bay Area Maid Service**, 650-364-6243
- **Made For You**, 650-324-2915
- **Merry Maids**, 650-961-8288
- **Molly Maids**, 650-969-9599

SOUTH BAY

- **Complete Cleaning**, 408-248-4162
- **European Touch**, 408-269-5210
- **Housekeepers**, 408-993-1715
- **Maids**, 408-245-9341
- **Merry Maids**, 408-971-6243
- **Molly Maids**, 408-445-0448

DIAPER SERVICES

- **ABC Linen and Diaper**, 510-549-1133
- **Dy-Dee Wash Cotton Diaper Service**, 650-761-4445
- **Tiny Tots Diaper Service**, 800-794-5437

PEST CONTROL

As with the rest of the US, the Bay Area has some cockroaches, ants, and termites, but in general there are far fewer pests here than in many parts of the country. Some older buildings, especially those with restaurants on the premises, are prone to cockroaches. In winter months ants can be a problem. Fleas may bug you in the late fall, particularly if you live near the beach, at ground level, or have pets. Pigeons can become bothersome if they decide to roost on the ledges of your building, especially near the entryway – protect your head! In warmer, damper regions mosquitoes can be a nuisance. Alameda, San Mateo, Santa Clara, Marin and Sonoma, Napa, Solano and Contra Costa counties have mosquito abatement programs. The telephone numbers of the abatement programs are listed below and may be helpful regarding other pest issues. Some homes also suffer from termites; if you are in the market to buy a house consider having it inspected for termites. In more rural areas ticks, raccoons, opossums and skunks can be a problem.

If you are renting your place it is the landlord's responsibility to keep your premises free from vermin, although keeping your home or apartment clean always helps. Non-toxic and humane means of controlling pests are available. Following are a few pest control companies. Check the Yellow Pages under "pest control services" for more listings.

SAN FRANCISCO
- **A Waterworks Bird Moving Company**, 415-488-1143
- **Arnest Termite Control**, 415-239-6977
- **Biological Works Pest Control**, 415-552-1502
- **Fleabusters of S F RX for Fleas, Incorporated**, 415-982-3532
- **Golden Gate Termite Control**, 415-334-6751
- **Dewey Pest Control**, 415-468-6660, for birds and rodents
- **Terminex**, 415-648-8933

NORTH BAY
- **Marin-Sonoma Mosquito Abatement District**, Petaluma, 707-782-2236
- **Napa County Mosquito Abatement District**, Napa, 707-258-6044
- **Orkin Exterminating Co., Inc.**, Mill Valley, 4000000015-381-1725
- **Rodex of California Pest Control Service Inc.**, Mill Valley, 415-388-3442

EAST BAY
- **Alameda County Mosquito Abatement District**, Hayward, 510-78? 7744
- **( )ntra-Costa County Mosquito Vermin Control District**, Concord, 925-685-9301
- **Hydrex Pest Control**, Oakland, 510-839-9292
- **Hydrex Pest Control**, Hayward, 510-886-1515 (for other areas, 800-284-7985)
- **Webbs Pest Control**, 610 16th Street, Oakland, 510-601-1118
- **Orkin Exterminating Co., Inc.**, Oakland, 510-261-1830; Richmond, 510-799-0152

PENINSULA
- **A & R Termite Control**, Palo Alto, 650-494-3655
- **Alert Pest Control Co., Inc.**, 182 School Street, Daly City, 650-756-2225
- **Orkin Exterminating Co., Inc.**, San Mateo, 650-348-3404; Menlo Park, 650-321-5281
- **San Mateo County Mosquito Abatement District**, Burlingame, 650-344-8592

SOUTH BAY
- **AAA Animal Removal**, San Jose, 408-363-8722
- **Homeguard Exterminators Incorporated**, 510 Madera Avenue, San Jose, 408-993-1900
- **O'Halloran Pest Control**, Sunnyvale, 408-245-1243
- **Santa Clara County Vermin Control District**, San Jose, 408-299-2050
- **Terminix International**, 1271 Alma Court, San Jose, 408-283-0492
- **Terminix International**, San Jose, 408-725-0690

MAIL SERVICES

If you're in between addresses but still need a place to get your mail, there are dozens of businesses that will rent you a mailbox. The following mail service companies are in San Francisco. Check your Yellow Pages under "Mailing Services" for a location near you.

- **Ames Mailboxes**, Noe Valley, 415-282-5008
- **Jet Mail**, Pacific Heights, 415-922-9402
- **Mail Access**, Upper Market/Castro, 415-626-2575
- **Mail Boxes Etc**. **(MBE)**, Downtown, 415-495-6963; Marina District, 415-922-4500; Nob Hill, 415-441-4954; Noe Valley, 415-824-1070; Pacific Heights District, 415-922-6245; Richmond district, 415-751-6644; Sunset district, 415-566-2660
- **NetUSA**, South of Market, 415-543-5100
- **Postal Annex**, Lakeside, 415-587-7661; Richmond District, 415-752-1515; downtown, 415-882-1515; North Beach, 415-772-9022
- **Potrero Mail**, Potrero District, 415-826-8757
- **Safe & Lock**, North Beach, 415-441-7472
- **Union Street Eagle**, Marina/Pacific Heights, 415-921-1850

MAIN POST OFFICES

Neighborhood post offices are listed at the end of each neighborhood profile. Check there for the one nearest you. For postal rates, post office locations, zip codes and more, you can also contact the post office at 800-ASK-USPS, www.usps.com or try any of the post offices listed below.

A tip for those needing to claim already sent mail (say wedding invitations that went out the day before the wedding was called off)—go to your local Post Office and fill out form 1509. Be sure to ask questions about the retrieval process, as incurred expenses will be charged to the applicant.

SAN FRANCISCO/NORTH BAY
- Napa, 1625 Trancas Street (Monday-Friday, 8:30 a.m. to 5 p.m.; closed Saturday)
- San Francisco, 1300 Evans Avenue (Monday-Friday, 7 a.m. to 8:30 p.m.; Saturday, 8 a.m. to 2 p.m.)
- San Rafael, 40 Bellam Boulevard (Monday-Friday 8:30 a.m. to 5 p.m.; Saturday, 10 a.m. to 1 p.m.)
- Santa Rosa, 730 2nd Street (Monday-Friday, 9 a.m. to 4:30 p.m.; Saturday, 9 a.m. to 12 p.m.)

EAST BAY
- Berkeley, 2000 Allston Way (Monday-Friday, 8:30 a.m. to 6 p.m.; Saturday, 10 a.m. to 2 p.m.)

- Concord, 2121 Meridian Park Boulevard (Monday-Friday, 9 a.m. to 6 p.m.; Saturday, 9 a.m. to 2 p.m.)
- Oakland, 1675 -7th Street (Monday-Friday, 12 a.m. to 12 p.m.; closed Saturday)
- Walnut Creek, 2070 North Broadway (Monday-Friday, 7 a.m. to 6 p.m.; Saturday, 9 a.m. to 4 p.m.)

PENINSULA/SOUTH BAY
- Palo Alto, 2085 East Bayshore Road (Monday-Friday, 8:30 a.m. to 5 p.m.; closed Saturday)
- San Mateo, 1630 South Delaware Street (Monday-Friday, 8:30 a.m. to 5 p.m.; Saturday, 8:30 a.m. to 12:30 p.m.)
- San Jose, 1750 Lundy Avenue (Monday-Friday, 8 a.m. to 8 p.m.; Saturday, 9 to 3 p.m.)

JUNK MAIL

Everyone gets it, and most hate it – junk mail. There are a number of strategies for curtailing the onslaught. Try writing a note, including your name and address, asking to be purged from the Direct Marketing Association's list (Direct Marketing Association's Mail Preference Service, P.O. Box 9008, Farmingdale, NY 11735). This may work, although some catalogue companies need to be contacted directly with a purge request. Another option is to call the "Opt-out" line at 888-567-8688 and request that the main credit bureaus not release your name and address to interested marketing companies. Perhaps the most foolproof method: don't give out your name and address unless you think it's worth it to do so.

SHIPPING SERVICES

- **Airborne Express**, 800-247-2676, www.airborne.com
- **DHL Worldwide Express**, 800-225-5345, www.dhl.co.id
- **Federal Express**, 800-238-5355, www.fedex.com
- **Roadway Package Systems**, 800-762-3725, www.roadway.com
- **United Parcel Service** (UPS), 800-742-5877, www.ups.com
- **US Postal Service Express Mail**, 800-222-1811, www.usps.com

AUTOMOBILE REPAIR

Everything in your world is going great: you have a place to live, a good job, the sun is shining ... and then your car breaks down. If this happens on the freeway, hopefully you already have some kind of service plan that will get your car towed to a service station. American Automobile Association, known as AAA, is a popular plan (see below). Insurance companies that offer auto insurance, as well as some fuel companies offer auto emergency plans similar to AAA. Your next dilemma—how do you find a reputable auto repair place? This is not an easy process, no matter where you live. Probably the most popular way to find a repair place is to ask around—friends, co-workers, neighbors, etc. Going to your auto dealer, while generally a reliable option, can be expensive. Value Star, a leading rating organization of local service businesses and professionals, is headquartered in Oakland. To use their rating service go to www.valuestar.com or call 800-310-6661. At *Bay Area Consumers' Checkbook* (see below) you can order article #3-055, which deals specifically with auto repair shops in the Bay Area. Remember, it's always a good idea to check with the Better Business Bureau (see below under **Consumer Protection**) to find out if any complaints have been filed against a service station you are considering using. And finally, on the lighter side, try calling *Car Talk* on National Public Radio, 415-553-2129, or just tune in to KQED 88.5-FM, at 10 a.m. on Sundays as Click and Clack, the Tappet brothers, discuss, in a most humorous fashion, cars and the problems of their owners.

AAA (AMERICAN AUTOMOBILE ASSOCIATION)

Founded at the turn of the century by Jim Wilkins, proprietor of the Cliff House, the American Automobile Association (AAA) began as an automobile club when there were only a dozen self-propelled vehicles navigating the hills of San Francisco. Today, more than 3.8 million people belong to AAA. Membership costs $46 a year plus a one time $17 enrollment fee. As a member, you receive 24-hour emergency road service, free maps, travel services, discounts at numerous hotels, DMV services and more. If you are caught out of gas, have a flat tire, or worse yet, a blown transmission, AAA can come rescue you. Just call their **Emergency Road Service Number** at 800-222-4357. Here's a list of number of the AAA offices, you can also call, 800-922-8228 to find an office near you:

SAN FRANCISCO/NORTH BAY
- San Francisco, 150 Van Ness Avenue, 415-565-2012
- Greenbrae, 100 Drakes Landing Road, 415-925-1200
- Napa, 800 Trancas Street, 707-226-9961
- San Rafael, 99 Smith Ranch Road, 415-472-6700
- Sonoma, 650 2nd Street West, 707-996-1083

EAST BAY
- Berkeley, 1775 University Avenue, 510-845-8890
- Concord, 2055 Meridian Park Boulevard, 925-671-2708
- Lafayette, 3390 Mount Diablo Boulevard, 925-283-9450

- Oakland, 380 West MacArthur Boulevard, 510-652-1812
- Richmond, 3060 Hilltop Mall Road, 510-223-8080

PENINSULA/SOUTH BAY
- Cupertino, 1601 South de Anza Boulevard, Suite 148, 408-996-3553
- Los Gatos, 101 Blossom Hill Road, 408-395-6411
- Mountain View, 900 Miramonte Avenue, 650-965-7000
- Palo Alto, 430 Forest Avenue, 650-321-0470
- Santa Clara, 80 Saratoga Avenue, 408-985-9300
- San Jose, 5340 Thornwood Drive, 408-629-1911

CONSUMER PROTECTION

Got a beef with a merchant or a company? There are a number of agencies that monitor consumer related businesses and will take action when necessary. It goes without saying that the best defense against fraud and consumer victimization is to avoid it—read contracts before you sign them, save all receipts and canceled checks, get the name of telephone sales and service people, check a contractor's license number with the Department of Consumer Affairs for complaints. But sometimes you still get stung. A dry cleaner returns your blue suit, but now it's purple and he shrugs. A shop refuses to refund as promised on the expensive gift, which didn't suit your mother. Your landlord fails to return your security deposit when you move. After $898 in repairs to your automobile's engine, the car now vibrates wildly, and the mechanic claims innocence. Negotiations, documents in hand, fail. You're angry, and embarrassed because you've been had. There *is* something you can do.

- **Better Business Bureau**: San Francisco: 415-243-9999; San Mateo County, 650-552-9222; Santa Clara and Santa Cruz counties, 408-278-7400; all other Bay Area counties: 510-238-1000, maintains consumer complaint files about businesses in the counties of San Francisco, Alameda, Contra Costa, Marin, Napa and more. You can also research businesses on their website at www.bbb.goldengate.org.
- **Better Business Bureau Automotive Line**, 800-955-5100
- **Bureau of Automotive Repair**, 800-952-5210
- **California Attorney General**, 800-952-5225, http://caag.state.ca.us, maintains a public inquiry unit that reviews consumer complaints.
- **California State Agencies Directory of Information**, 916-657-9900
- **California Department of Consumer Affairs**, 510-785-7554, 800-952-5210, www.dca.ca.gov, is a state agency that investigates consumer complaints.
- **Contractors State License Board**, 800-321-2752
- **SF District Attorney**, 415-551-9595, maintains a consumer protection unit that investigates and mediates consumer/business disputes.

MEDIA SPONSORED CALL FOR ACTION PROGRAMS

The following are consumer advocacy programs operated by Bay Area television/radio stations:
- **KGO Seven On Your Side**, 900 Front Street, San Francisco, CA 94111, 415-954-8151
- **KRON-TV Contact 4**, 1001 Van Ness Avenue, San Francisco, 415-441-4444
- **San Jose Mercury News Action Line**, 750 Riddler Park Drive, San Jose, CA 95190, 888-688-6400

LEGAL MEDIATION/REFERRAL PROGRAMS

- **Berkeley Dispute Resolution Service**, 1769 Alcatraz Avenue, Berkeley, 510-428-1811
- **California Community Dispute Service**, 502 7th Street, San Francisco, 415-865-2520
- **Community Boards of San Francisco**, 1540 Market Street, Suite 490, 415-552-1250
- **Conciliation Forums of Oakland**, 663 13th Street, 510-763-2117
- **San Francisco State University Legal Referral Center**, 1600 Holloway Avenue, #M-113, San Francisco, 415-338-1140

LEGAL ASSISTANCE FOR THE ELDERLY

- **Legal Assistance for Seniors**, 614 Grand Avenue, Suite 400, Oakland, 510-832-3040
- **Legal Assistance to the Elderly**, 1453 Mission Street, Suite 500, San Francisco, 415-861-4444

SMALL CLAIMS COURTS

SAN FRANCISCO/NORTH BAY
- 575 Polk Street, 415-551-4000; serves San Francisco
- Hall of Justice, Room 113, San Rafael, 415-499-6218; serves Marin County
- 825 Brown Street, Napa, 707-253-4574; serves Napa County
- 321 Tuolumne Street, Vallejo, 707-553-5346; serves Solano County
- 600 Administration Drive, Room 107J, Santa Rosa, 707-565-1100; serves Sonoma County

EAST BAY
- 2233 Shoreline Drive, Alameda, 510-268-7479; serves Alameda
- 2000 Center Street, Berkeley, 510-644-6303; serves Berkeley, Albany

- 39439 Paseo Padre Parkway, Fremont, 510-795-2345; serves Fremont, Newark, Union City
- 600 Washington Street, 3rd floor, Oakland, 510-268-7737; serves Oakland, Piedmont, Emeryville
- 24405 Amador Street, Hayward, 510-670-5650; serves San Leandro, Hayward
- 100 37th Street, Richmond, 510-374-3137; serves Contra Costa County Bay District

PENINSULA
- 1050 Mission Road, South San Francisco, 650-877-5775; serves Colma, Daly City, Pacifica, San Bruno, South San Francisco
- 800 North Humbolt Street, San Mateo, 650-573-2605; serves San Mateo, Belmont, Burlingame, Foster City, Half Moon Bay, Hillsborough, Millbrae
- 750 Middlefield Road, Redwood City, 650-363-4303; serves Atherton, Menlo Park, Portola Valley, San Carlos, East Palo Alto, Woodside, Redwood City

SOUTH BAY
- 14205 Capri Drive, Los Gatos, 408-792-2881; serves Los Gatos, San Jose, Santa Clara, Milpitas, Campbell, Saratoga, Monte Sereno
- 207 Grant Avenue, Palo Alto, 650-324-0391; serves, Palo Alto, Mountain View, Los Altos, Sunnyvale
- 12425 Monterey Road, San Martin, 408-686-3522; serves San Martin, Gilroy, Morgan Hill

The *Bay Area Consumers' Checkbook* is a pro-consumer guide published by the Center for the Study of Services. It is a "non-profit magazine, free of advertising, free of outside influence, dedicated to helping Bay Area consumers find high-quality, reasonably priced services." The quality of information is excellent. Articles can be ordered online at www.checkbook.org or through the mail, call 510-763-7979, Monday-Friday, 8:30 a.m. to 2:30 p.m. There is a fee for ordering articles. A subscription to the magazine is $30 for two years; call the same number used for ordering articles.

For consumer protection information regarding utilities see **Consumer Protection—Utility Complaints** in the **Getting Settled** chapter.

SERVICES FOR PEOPLE WITH DISABILITIES

Long before there was an *Americans with Disabilities Act*, the Bay Area's sensitivity to the needs of the disabled was raised by a group of handicapped college applicants who fought for admission to the Berkeley campus of the University of California. Their efforts, in the early 1970s, not only achieved the group's goal but also spawned the **Independent Living Center**, which now boasts offices across the country. Its representatives work hard to protect the rights of the disabled, and the centers offer training and rehabilitation services to those with disabilities, as well as referrals to support groups and organizations.

Rose Resnick's Lighthouse for the Blind and Visually Disabled provides assistance, equipment, support and referrals to the visually impaired. Fully trained guide dogs are available through **Guide Dogs for the Blind**, which is based in Marin County. **The Hearing Society for the Bay Area** provides testing, education, support and referrals to the hearing impaired.

Another great resource for information on disability access in the City is *San Francisco Access*, a guide with information on hotels, dining, shopping and local attractions. To order a copy, contact the Convention and Visitors Bureau, 900 Market Street, 415-391-2000, TDD 415-392-0328, www.AccessNCA.com.

Here's how to get in touch with several helpful organizations:

- **Access Northern California**, 436 14th Street, Oakland, 510-419-0527
- **APRIA Healthcare**, 390 9th Street, San Francisco, 415-864-6999; 4095 Pike Lane, Concord, 925-827-8800; 480 Carlton Court, South San Francisco, 650-864-6999; 2040 Corporate Court, San Jose, 408-432-0950; 3636 North Laughlin Road, Santa Rosa, 707-586-1199
- **California Deaf-Blind Services**, 415-405-3567
- **City of San Jose Deaf Services**, 80 North First Street, San Jose, 408-998-5299
- **Deaf and Disabled Telecommunications Program**, 510-302-1100, TTY 510-302-1101
- **Deaf Disability Project**, 1844 Addison Street, Berkeley, 510-644-2000
- **Deaf Services of Palo Alto**, P.O. Box 60651, Palo Alto, 650-856-2558
- **Environmental Traveling Companion**, Fort Mason, Building C, 474-7662
- **Independent Living Center**, 649 Mission, 3rd Floor, San Francisco, 415-543-6222, TTY 415-543-6698
- **Center for Independent Living**, 2539 Telegraph Avenue, Berkeley, 510-841-4776, TTY 510-841-3101
- **Guide Dogs for the Blind**, 350 Los Ranchitos Road, San Rafael, 415-499-4000
- **Hearing Society**, 870 Market Street, 3rd Floor, 415-693-5870, TTY 415-834-1005
- **National Association for the Visually Handicapped**, 3201 Balboa Street, 415-221-3201
- **Recreation Center for the Handicapped**, 207 Skyline Boulevard, 415-665-4100; TTY 415-665-4107
- **Rose Resnick Lighthouse for the Blind**, 214 Van Ness Avenue, 415-431-1481; TTY 415-431-4572
- **Support for Families of Children with Disabilities**, 2601 Mission Street, 415-282-7494

GETTING AROUND

All BART stations are wheelchair accessible with elevators at every station and available discount tickets. Most public transit buses throughout the Bay Area are also equipped to handle wheelchairs by use of ramps and lifts. Fares are significantly lower for the disabled. For more information on public transit options for the disabled call the appropriate transit agency (BART, MUNI, AC Transit, SamTrans, and CalTrain are listed in the **Transportation** chapter). Wheelchair rentals are available at a number of medical equipment and supply businesses. You can also purchase new and used wheelchairs at various stores. Check under "wheelchairs" in the Yellow Pages. Here are a few businesses that rent and sell wheelchairs:

- **ITC Medical**, 415-661-4900
- **Wheelchairs of Berkeley**, 415-284-9424
- **Mobility Equipment Inc**. 415-564-2098
- **Wheelchairs of San Mateo**, 650-342-4864

Applications for handicapped parking permits are available at any local **Department of Motor Vehicles**. You can also request an application by writing to DMV, 2415 1st Street, Sacramento, CA 95818. They will send you an application that must be signed by your doctor. You can submit the application along with $6 to any local DMV office to receive your placard.

COMMUNICATION

California has a telephone relay service, which provides a communication system for the hearing- and speech-impaired. This system allows people who are deaf or hard of hearing to phone people who do not have a TTY (Tele-Tex Yok—communication device for the deaf). The operator will contact your party and relay your conversation. This service is free except for any toll charges.

- TTY: 800-735-2929
- Speech to speech communication, 800-854-7784
- Voice users, call 800-735-2922

If you need help with sign language, contact the following organizations. They usually require one week's notice. **Bay Area Communication Access**, 415-356-0405, TTY 415-356-0376; **Hands On**, 800-900-9478, TDD 800-900-9479

HOUSING

Some of the organizations listed above can help you with finding accessible housing, including the **Independent Living Center** in San Francisco at 415-543-6222 and the **Center for Independent Living** in Berkeley, 510-841-7776.

GAY AND LESBIAN LIFE

For gay and lesbian nightlife, dance clubs, comedy, and theater, the Castro and the Mission districts are the places to go. Check *Gay USA: Where the Babes Go*, by Lori Hobkirk, for information about lesbian life in San Francisco. Or try www.gaysf.com.

The biggest gay oriented events are the **Gay Pride Parade** in June. Festivities are held all over the City, especially in SOMA and The Castro. See **A Bay Area Year** for more detail. In June check out **The International Lesbian & Gay Film Festival**, 415-703-8650.

PUBLICATIONS

- *Bay Area Reporter*, 395 9th Street, San Francisco, 415-861-5019, has been around for almost 30 years and offers entertainment listings, hard news, sports, classifieds, personals and more. It is distributed citywide every Tuesday; free.
- *San Francisco Bay Times: The Gay, Lesbian, Bi, Trans Newspaper*, 3410 19th Street, San Francisco, 415-626-0260, offers news, reviews, employment listings, therapy and support groups, etc. Distributed citywide every other Thursday; free.

If you happen to be a gay Republican you needn't feel alone. You can join the **Log Cabin Club**, call 415-522-2944.

BOOKSTORES

- **A Different Light Bookstore**, 489 Castro Street, 415-431-0891, is arguably the premier gay and lesbian bookstore.
- **Modern Times**, 888 Valencia, 415-282-9246, is a progressive women's bookstore with a good selection of lesbian, bi, and gay literature.
- **West Berkeley Women's Books**, 2514 San Pablo Avenue, Berkeley, 510-204-9399, right next door to the famous Lesbian cafe and breakfast joint, the Brick Hit Cafe.

WORSHIP AND FELLOWSHIP

Unless otherwise noted the following are in San Francisco:
- **Congregation Sh'ar Z'hav**, 290 Dolores Street, 415-861-6932, is a reform synagogue that offers classes and children's programs

- **Dignity San Francisco**, 415-681-2491, is for Catholic gay, lesbian, bisexual, and transgendered people and their friends. Weekly services are at the Seventh Avenue Presbyterian Church, 1329 7th Avenue, on Sunday evenings.
- **Metropolitan Community Church**, 150 Eureka Street, 415-863-4434, www.mccsf.org, offers social activities, recovery groups, counseling. The Parishioners also serve meals to the homeless, provide showers for homeless, and tutor children at Harvey Milk Civil Rights Academy.
- **Most Holy Redeemer Church**, (Catholic) 100 Diamond, 415-863-6259, offers services, reconciliation and confession, and AIDS support groups.
- **Saint Francis Lutheran**, 152 Church Street, 415-621-2635; this entire church has been excommunicated from the mainstream Lutheran Church. They offer over 30 self-help groups, senior meetings, and bingo.
- **The Pacific Center For Human Identity**, 2712 Telegraph Avenue, Berkeley, 510-548-8283, offers counseling and a range of daily support groups.

W HEN MOVING TO A NEW AREA, ONE OF THE MOST CHALLENGING and overwhelming prospects parents face is finding good childcare and/or schools. While the process is not an easy one, with time and effort it is possible to find what you are looking for, be it in-home or on-site daycare, an after-school program, or a good public or private school. The keys, of course, are research and persistence.

PARENTING PUBLICATIONS

If you have childcare concerns upon arriving here, it's a good idea to get a copy of the *Bay Area Parent*, a monthly publication with a circulation of about 67,000 that includes a calendar of events and articles on parenting resources in San Francisco and the Bay Area. The same company also publishes several related publications including *Bay Area Baby* and *Parenting Bay Area Teens*. To subscribe, call their office at 408-399-4842, or visit them online at www.parenthood.com. *Parent's Press*, 1454 Sixth Street, Berkeley, CA 94710, 510-524-1602, offers online magazines for parents: www.parents-press.com and www.parent-teen.com (for families with teens).

DAYCARE

Probably the best way to find a good daycare provider is by referral from someone you know and trust. That said, being new to the Bay Area might not create such an option for you. The **California Childcare Resource & Referral Network**, 111 New Montgomery Street, 7th floor, San Francisco, CA 94105, 415-882-0234, www.rrnetwork.org, a state-wide information service that provides referrals to childcare agencies throughout California, should be able to assist you with your search. The **National Association for the Education of Young Children** (**NAEYC**) may be helpful as well. Call or write for a list of daycare centers in your area, accredited by them: 202-232-8777, NAEYC,

1509 16th Street NW, Washington, DC, 20036.

Those affiliated with a major university in the Bay Area may have access to a university operated referral agency and/or a university run childcare center. Inquire at the student services desk of your university. Sometimes university graduate student divisions provide such referrals and services.

For a childcare referral agency in your area check with the following:

SAN FRANCISCO/NORTH BAY

For those living in San Francisco contact **Children's Council of San Francisco**, 575 Sutter Street, 2nd Floor, San Francisco, CA 94102, 415-243-0111, www.childrenscouncil.org, or **Wu-Yee**, 888 Clay Street, Lower Level, San Francisco, CA 94108, 415-391-4956, www.wuyee.org (an agency devoted to servicing the needs of San Francisco's large Cantonese-speaking community). Both agencies provide a variety of services in English, Spanish, and Cantonese, including training for childcare providers, health and safety training, needs assessment and food programs, resource library, parent support information about employing in-home workers, referral service for licensed childcare, and listings of nanny services.

In Marin County, contact **Marin Childcare Council**, 555 Northgate Drive, San Rafael, CA 94903, 415-479-CARE, www.marinchildcarecouncil.org.

EAST BAY

For childcare referrals in Alameda County contact **Bananas**, 5232 Claremont Avenue, Oakland, CA 94618, 510-658-0381, www.bananasinc.org, or **Child Care Links**, 1020 Serpentine Lane, Suite 102, Pleasanton, CA 94566, 925-417-8733, www.childcarelink.org. For referrals in Hayward, San Leandro and the Tri-Cities Area, call **4Cs of Alameda County**, 22351 City Venter Drive, Suite 200, Hayward, CA 94541, 510-582-2182 (Hayward and San Leandro), and 510-790-0655 (Tri-Cities Area). In Contra Costa County, call **Contra Costa Child Care Council**, 2280 Diamond Boulevard, Suite 500, Concord, CA 94520, 925-676-KIDS, www.contracostachildcare.org.

PENINSULA/SOUTH BAY

For the San Mateo area, consult with **Childcare Coordinating Council of San Mateo County**, 700 South Claremont Boulevard, Suite 107, San Mateo, CA 94402, 650-696-8787, www.thecouncil.net. The **Community Childcare Council Santa Clara**, 111 East Gish Road, San Jose, CA 95112, 408-487-0749, www.4c.org, provides information and referrals in Santa Clara County.

WHAT TO LOOK FOR IN DAYCARE

When searching for the best place for your child, be sure to visit prospective daycare providers—preferably unannounced. In general, look for safety, cleanliness and caring attitudes on the part of the daycare workers. Check that the kitchen, toys, and furniture are clean and safe. Observe the other kids at the center. Do they seem happy? Are they well behaved? Ask for the telephone numbers of other parents who use the service and talk to them before committing. It's a good idea to request a daily schedule—look for both active and quiet time, and age appropriate activities. Since the weather in California allows for year-round outdoor activities, such as sports, games, and field trips, make sure the childcare curriculum includes such things.

Keep in mind that being licensed does not necessarily guarantee service of the quality you may be seeking. If you think a provider might be acceptable, be sure to call your county's daycare licensing bureau and check to see if they're licensed and not in trouble for anything. In San Francisco and the Peninsula, call the **San Francisco and Bay Area Day Care Licensing Bureau**, also known as the **State Department of Social Services Community Care Licensing**: 415-266-8843; in the South Bay call 408-277-1286; in the East Bay call 510-450-3984. If you find an unlicensed childcare provider and want to ascertain their reliability, contact **Trust Line**, 800-822-8490, an organization that conducts background checks on childcare providers exempt from licensing.

For drop-in childcare while you go shopping or to a movie, try **Kids' Park Centers**. They have four locations close to the major shopping malls in Silicon Valley and accept children age two to twelve years. In the East Bay, call 510-792-9997; in San Jose call 408-281-8880. In 2000 rates were $5.50 per hour for one child with discounted rates for siblings. They limit the number of hours that you can use their service (five hours per day and up to 15 hours per week) to ensure that the center provides drop-in rather than regular childcare. While reservations are not necessary, it's a good idea to call first to be sure they have room on a particular day.

ONLINE RESOURCES—DAYCARE

In addition to the information above, which is Bay Area specific, there are several helpful online agencies and organizations that can assist with the details of finding quality childcare, a good school, etc. **Care Guide**, www.careguide.com, offers assistance to those needing childcare or eldercare. This free service provides pertinent care-related news articles and advice. The **National Child Care Information Center's** internet site, www.nccic.org, provides links to other childcare sites on the web. **Child Care Aware**, 800-424-2246, provides free referrals to childcare agencies in your community. A program funded by the **US Maternal and Child Health Bureau**, www.nrc.uchsc.edu, 800-598-KIDS, is the National Resource Center for Health and Safety in Child Care. Check their site for a section on health and safety tips, state childcare licensure regulations, a list of national health and safety performance standards and helpful links to other programs and agencies. And finally, the **National Parent Information Network** offers information on parenting, child development, family life, and parent-education partnerships. Call them at 800-583-4135 or log onto their web site at www.npin.org.

NANNIES

If you are looking for a nanny, in San Francisco or Silicon Valley you can expect to pay $500 to $700 per week for a live-in nanny, depending on the nanny's experience, education, the number of kids in your family, and whether housekeeping and driving is expected. There are many agencies that can assist you in finding a qualified nanny. Online, try **The Nanny Network** at www.nannynet.net or call them at 925-256-8575. This organization provides reliable nanny referral services within Alameda and Contra Costa counties. The **National Nanny Registry**, www.nannyregistry.com, affiliated with **I Love My Nanny**, 408-99-NANNY, offers help with screening and recruiting nannies and baby-sitters. The registry assists in matching you with a nanny, whether it is a young student or a grandmother figure, and provides answers to other questions about hiring and working with a nanny. Other useful resources for employing a nanny include **Mom's Away**, 510-559-9195, **Nannies Limited**, 925-803-1040, and the popular **Town and Country Resources**, www.tandcr.com, 415-461-7755 (North Bay), 415-567-0956 (San Francisco), 650-326-8570 (Palo Alto). The latter places childcare and household professionals in homes, including nannies, baby nurses, personal assistants, housekeepers and cooks. You can also log onto **Bay Area Sitters**, www.bay-area-sitters.com, a free message board that connects parents looking for childcare with baby-sitters and nannies.

Be sure to check all references prior to hiring someone. If you decide to hire a nanny without using an agency, you will need to take care of taxes, disability, unemployment insurance, and social security. For information, call 800-NANNI-TAX or check www.4nannytaxes.com. Many parents choose to run background checks on prospective nannies. **California Trustline**, an agency of the state of California, conducts fingerprint searches through the FBI for high misdemeanors and felonies in all states. This service is available to prospective childcare employers who live in any state, but keep in mind that searches can require three or four months to complete. Call 800-822-8490 or check www.trustline.org.

AU PAIRS

The US Information Agency oversees and approves the organizations which offer this service where young adults between the ages of 18 and 26 provide a year of in-home childcare and light housekeeping in exchange for airfare, room and board, and a small stipend per week. The program offers a valuable cultural exchange between the host family and the (usually European) *au pair*, as well as a flexible childcare schedule for parents. Unfortunately, the program only lasts one year and the *au pairs* don't have the life or work experience of a career nanny. Nevertheless, in California *au pairs* are a popular way to satisfy families' childcare needs. In the Bay Area, most *au pairs* come from Poland, Germany, France, and Scandinavia. The agencies that bring over the *au pairs* run background checks before making placements, and orientation and training sessions once the placements have been made. Here are some of the agencies you can contact if you'd like to find an *au pair*:

- **EF Au Pair**, 800-333-6056
- **Interexchange, Au Pair USA**, 800-479-0907 or 800-287-2477
- **Au Pair International**, 800-654-2051
- **Au Pair in America**, 800-928-7247
- **Au Pair Care**, 800-4AU-PAIR, www.aupaircare.com

SCHOOLS

Choosing the right school for your child(ren) was probably a difficult task in your old community, factor in moving to a new city and, for many, it becomes a stressful proposition. Add to that the reputation of California's public schools—overcrowded, staffed by underpaid and inexperienced teachers, etc.—and the search for the right school can be downright intimidating. Many parents who are new to the area rush to the conclusion that the only way to offer their child a good education here is to shell out a lot of money for an expensive private school. In fact, the Bay Area offers a great multitude of schooling possibilities, including an excellent public charter program, year round schooling programs—both private and public—as well as myriad private options.

CHOOSING A SCHOOL

Quantitative measures, such as graduation rates and test scores are important, but just as important are the subjective impressions and feelings you and your child will gain from visiting a prospective school. That's why the crucial ingredients for finding the right school are: visit, visit, visit, and talk, talk, talk.

When visiting a school, your gut reactions will tell you a lot. Ask yourself these questions:

- Am I comfortable here? Will my child be comfortable here?
- Does the school feel safe? Are the bathrooms clean and free of graffiti?
- Does this school meet her/his learning style? Are elementary-age students moving around naturally, but staying on task?
- What are the halls like in junior-high and high schools when classes change—how are students interacting with one another and with their teachers as their class changes?

- Are students actively engaged in discussions or projects? Is student work displayed?
- Ask elementary teachers about reading and math groups and if children move up as they build skills.
- Find out if there are any special programs offered to assist new students with their transition to their new school.
- Check for after-school or enrichment activities that your child will enjoy.
- Ask if parents are encouraged to volunteer in the classroom.
- Look at the faculty and curriculum as well as facilities and equipment. Are adults a presence in all parts of the building and grounds? Are the computer labs up to date with enough computers? Are instructional materials plentiful and new? Do textbooks cover things you think are important? Does the school have a clearly articulated mission statement? Do the teachers that you observe seem to teach with that mission in mind? Can teachers speak articulately about the mission of the school and the educational philosophy? Do you see opportunities for your child to do things he/she likes to do—art, music, science, etc.?
- Finally, if the school that you are visiting is located near one of the Bay Area's many colleges and universities, ask whether there are programs that bring college students to schools for presentations and talks. Inquire about field trips to Bay Area's museums and other attractions.

Satisfying answers to all these questions might be a somewhat unrealistic and time-consuming dream yet, with research and visits, you will be able to find a good match for your child's needs and interests. The time put in at the front end of the decision-making process is definitely worth the effort.

To find out about California Public Schools' performance indicators, accountability procedures, and reform efforts, log on to the **California Department of Education's** *Public Schools Accountability Act* home page, www.cde.ca.gov/psaa.

Another excellent site for gathering specific information about Bay Area schools is called **Great Schools**, www.greatschools.net. This non-profit organization is dedicated to providing clear and objective information about local schools. Visit their web site to learn about schools' test scores, programs, facilities, student body size, and teacher qualifications.

To orient yourself to the public schools in the Bay Area you might want to consult several helpful publications in your local bookstore and/or online. *Choosing a Public School,* by School Wise Press, offers a three volume edition (one each for elementary, middle, and high schools), that includes details about San Francisco schools' locations, programs, staff, and class sizes, as well as statistical profiles and ratings. This information as well as many other resources can be found at their web site, www.schoolwisepress.com. *Getting the Public School You Want* may also be useful. Call 415-487-8190 to order a copy. Or try Mark Matrucci's *The San Francisco Bay Area School Ratings Guidebook*, which rates 1,100 Bay Area public schools on the basis of test scores, safety, diversity, graduation rates, and teacher/student turnover.

To become better acquainted with schools in your district consider contacting the for-profit organization **SchoolMatch Inc.**, this firm maintains a database on public and private schools, and offers student-teacher ratios, test scores and per-pupil spending. Call 800-992-5323 for more information or check www.schoolmatch.com. The cost for a basic "snapshot" of a school district's national ranking is $19; $49 will get you a more comprehensive "report card" and for $97.50, School Match's "full search service" will give you a statistical analysis of up to ten school systems in your requested area.

BAY AREA PUBLIC SCHOOLS

Thirty years ago California spent more money on its public schools than most other US states. However, due to property tax cuts implemented a couple of decades ago, California's spending on schools dropped dramatically and its overall school performance recently ranked a dismal 41st in the nation. Concerned about its school record, the state government has taken several measures to improve public education in California including, in 1998, an increase of funds to elementary education, and minimizing class sizes in elementary schools—from 30 to 20 students per class. In July 2000, the California governor approved a new education measure, known as *Smaller Classes, Safer Schools, and Financial Accountability Act*, which allotted more funds to the K-12 division. This money will be used to facilitate class-size reduction, provide classroom access to computer and internet technologies, repair and rebuild dilapidated schools, and to ensure accountability in spending. Another recent measure, Proposition 98 guarantees that California per pupil spending is no less than the national average.

In 1994 Bay Area public schools adopted an **open enrollment** policy, which offers a student the option to enroll in any public school in his/her district, if parents believe that the school within a students' immediate vicinity is not right for their child. In addition, throughout the Bay Area, the length of the academic year is becoming more flexible. Now you can decide whether a traditional ten-month or the newly adopted and increasingly popular **yearlong academic program** is the best for your child. For instance, educators at Allendale Elementary in Oakland, one of the largest year-round elementary schools in the Bay Area, believe that year-round education offers advantages to children who, during long summer breaks, would otherwise not be exposed to educational activities.

One of the biggest recent changes in California public education has been the growth of the charter school movement. Unlike most public schools, **charter schools**, which are bound by their own charter agreements, are free from some of the traditional school regulations. A charter school is a public program created by a group of individuals, usually teachers, parents, and community leaders, and must have approval of the local school district governing board. First and foremost, the purpose of a charter school is to improve student learning. To do this, many charter schools promote the use of innovative teaching methods, expand the learning base outside the classroom, and encourage parent/community involvement in the school. In California, students in charter schools are required to take part in the Standardized Testing and Reporting Program. If students in a given charter school do not perform at a certain level or meet certain goals listed in their charter agreement with the local school district governing board, the school may be closed. Charter school enrollment is voluntary and not determined by geographic location, which means parents can select any school, as long as space allows. While most charter schools do not focus on specific subjects (as do magnet schools, which often specialize in language arts or the sciences), their charters propose certain programmatic guidelines for the general educational process. For example, Aurora High School in Redwood City guarantees its students personalized learning plans, which are created to help students realize their full potential. There are several charter schools in San Francisco, including Gateway and Leadership high schools, which have been quite successful. For more information about charter programs and charter school policies in the Bay Area visit www.uscharterschools.org.

Although individual class years in public schools tend to be fairly large, sometimes above one thousand students, there is always an opportunity for your child to get individualized attention. Inquire about programs for children with special needs, including those with learning disabilities or programs for gifted and talented children (GATE). Again, the importance of visiting schools and asking lots of questions before enrolling your child cannot be underestimated.

BAY AREA SCHOOL DISTRICTS

The following school organizations will provide you with information concerning schools in your area, as well as details about referrals, enrollment testing, and any available special programs.

- For official information on public schools in **San Francisco**, contact the **San Francisco Unified School District**, 135 Van Ness Avenue, San Francisco, CA 94102, 415-241-6000, www.sfusd.k12.ca.us. This district oversees 76 elementary, 17 middle, and 21 high schools, as well as many specialized educational programs in the City.
- If you plan to reside in the **North Bay**, consult the **Marin County Office of Education**, 1111 Las Gallinas Avenue, San Rafael, CA 94903, 415-472-4110, http://marin.k12.ca.us.
- For information on the **East Bay**, go to the **Alameda County Unified School District**, 313 West Winton Avenue, Hayward, CA 94544, 510-

887-0152, www.alameda-coe.k12.ca.us. The largest school districts that this office includes are:

- **Fremont Unified School District** with student enrollments of around 30,000. Contact them at 4210 Technology Drive, Fremont, CA 94538, 510-657-2350, www.fremont.k12.ca.us.
- **Hayward Unified School District** enrolls 22,000 students, 24411 Amador Street, Hayward, CA 94540, www.husd.k12.ca.us.
- **Newark Unified School District**, with enrollments of 15,000 students, 5715 Musick Avenue, Newark, CA 94560, 510-794-2141, www.nusd.k12. ca.us.
- **Oakland Unified School District**, with enrollments of around 55,000 students in its 60 elementary, 15 middle and 10 high schools can be contacted at 1025 Second Avenue, Oakland, CA 94606, 510-879-8100, www.oakland.k12.ca.us.
- **Pleasanton Unified School District**, 12,000 enrolled students, 4665 Bernal Avenue, Pleasanton, CA 94566, 925-462-5500, www.pleasanton.k12.ca.us.
- For information on **Contra Costa County**, visit the **Contra Costa County Office of Education**, 77 Santa Barbara Road, Pleasant Hill, CA 94523, 925-942-3388, www.cccoe.k12.ca.us.
- Those on the **Peninsula** should contact the **San Mateo County Office of Education**, 101 Twin Dolphin Drive, Redwood City, CA 94065, 650-802-5300, www.smcoe.k12.ca.
- For information on **Silicon Valley schools**, visit the **Santa Clara County Office of Education**, 1290 Ridder Road, San Jose, CA 95131, 408-453-6500, www.sccoe.k12.ca.us, which incorporates 33 elementary, high, and unified school districts. This office's publications department can also mail you a hard copy of demographic profiles of school districts in the county if you call 408-453-6879. If you would like to purchase the *Santa Clara County Public Schools Directory* ($12.50 plus tax), call 408-453-6959.

PRIVATE AND PAROCHIAL SCHOOLS

If you are ready to finance your child's studies, there are many different private programs in the Bay Area. You'll find private schools, which offer educational programs based on particular learning philosophies, including Montessori and Waldorf programs, as well as parochial schools, which often provide more traditional settings and curriculum. The diverse educational offerings of private schools and their smaller classroom sizes often better accommodate children's individual talents and interests. To find a private school that suits your needs, two web sites may be useful: **www.baprivateschools.com**, offers a guide to private schools in the Bay Area and includes information, locations, and links to private and parochial schools; and **www.privateschoolsearch.com**, a private school search engine. In addition, the **California Department of Education**, P.O. Box 271, Sacramento, CA 95812, 800-995-4099, www.cde.ca.gov, publishes the *California Private School Directory* which you can order for about $25. Other helpful publications on finding a good private school include: *Peterson's Private Secondary Schools*, www.petersons.com, and Susan Vogel's *Private High Schools in the San Francisco Bay Area*, and *San Francisco Private Schools K-8*.

PRIVATE SCHOOLS

- For information on area Montessori schools, contact **Montessori Schools of California**, 16492 Foothill Boulevard, San Leandro, CA 94578, 510-278-1115, www.montessorica.com.
- For **Waldorf schools** check the following: San Francisco Waldorf School, K-11, 2938 Washington Street, San Francisco, CA 94115, 415-931-2750, www.sfwaldorf.org; Marin County, 755 Idylberry Road, San Rafael, CA 94903, 415-479-8190, www.marinwaldorf.org; East Bay, 3800 Clark Road, El Sobrante, CA 94803, 510-223-3570; Silicon Valley, Waldorf School of the Peninsula K-8, 11311 Mora Drive, Los Altos, CA 94024, 650-948-8433.
- **Challenger Schools** are famous for their engaging approach to elementary and middle school education. Their mission, "to prepare children to become self-reliant, productive individuals; to teach them to think, speak, and write with clarity, precision, and independence; and to inspire them to embrace, challenge, and find joy and self-worth through achievement." Call 888-748-1135, 408-377-2300, or visit www.challengerschool.com for more information.

PAROCHIAL SCHOOLS

- Information regarding Catholic schools in San Francisco, San Mateo and Marin counties is provided by the **Archdiocese of San Francisco Office of Catholic Schools**, 443 Church Street, San Francisco, CA 94114, 415-565-3660. The **Archdiocese of Oakland, Office of Catholic Schools**, 2900 Lakeshore Avenue, Oakland, CA 94610, 510-893-4711, can give you information for Alameda and Contra Costa counties. In the South Bay, call the **Parochial School Office**, 1100 5th Street, San Jose, CA, 408-454-4455 or the **Office of Religious Education**, 408-296-3484.
- For information on **Jewish education** in the Bay Area, consult *The Resource: A Guide to Jewish Life in the Bay Area*, which provides listings and brief information on all the Jewish schools in the Bay Area. Online, go to www.jewishsf.com/resource.

Since admission to private schools can be competitive, the sooner you call a school to find out about admission deadlines and open houses the better. The registration process begins as early as October, the year prior to the desired academic start date. Be sure to visit schools to learn about their unique philosophies and teaching methodologies. As private schools are not required to follow state standards (though most do), a visit can be an extremely important aspect of the admissions process. Many parents and children have a visceral reaction when walking into a school, and can often sense whether a school is "right" for them. Since private schooling is expensive and signing up for a private program is an often-arduous task, finding a good match between child and school is important.

HOME SCHOOLING

Home schooling is becoming increasingly popular in the state of California at large, and in the Bay Area specifically. Many believe that they, with their in-depth knowledge of their child's psychological and intellectual needs, are better suited to design an educational program that will engage and challenge their youngsters to the utmost. If you have the time and energy to plan and execute a comprehensive study program for your children there are many organizations that can assist you. For information and support for your home schooling project, visit the **HomeSchool Association of California** at www.hsc.org. The mission of this organization is to provide information, monitor legislation, and cultivate connections among home schoolers and the society at large. Another organization that might be helpful is **California Homeschool Network**, www.cahomeschoolnet.org; it too provides information on home schooling and works to protect the rights of the family to educate children at home.

CALIFORNIA IS WORLD RENOWNED FOR ITS QUALITY INSTITUTIONS OF higher learning, the Bay Area in particular. Whether you are looking to enroll in a Bachelor's, Master's, continuing education, or night degree program, or perhaps you are interested in attending a lecture series or evening theatrical performance, the list of possibilities is endless.

SAN FRANCISCO

- **Golden Gate University** is a private, non-profit, and accredited program, located in the downtown area. It offers a wide variety of graduate and undergraduate programs in business, law, and public administration; located at 536 Mission Street, 415-442-7000.
- **San Francisco State University**, part of the California State University system, SFSU offers a wide range of undergraduate and graduate degrees. Serving more than thirty thousand students a year, SFSU is one of the largest schools in the CSU system. Located at 1600 Holloway Avenue, 415-338-1111.
- **University of San Francisco**, founded in 1855 by Jesuit fathers, USF was San Francisco's first institution of higher learning. It is fully accredited and beautifully situated on a 50-acre hilltop. USF offers undergraduate and graduate degrees in nursing, business, education, law, and many other disciplines. Located at Parker and Fulton streets, 415-422-5555.

NORTH BAY

- **Dominican College**, affiliated with the Catholic Church, is known for its counseling psychology, education and music programs; Bachelor's and Master's degrees offered. Located at 1520 Grand Avenue, San Rafael, 415-457-4440.
- **Sonoma State University** was founded in 1960 and is one of the youngest

universities in the California State University system. Located 50 miles north of San Francisco, the 220-acre campus east of Rohnert Park reminds many of a park. Degrees and certificates offered in a wide variety of disciplines. Located at 1801 East Cotati Avenue, Rohnert Park, 707-664-2880.

EAST BAY

- **California State University, Hayward** is situated on a hilltop overlooking the city of Hayward to the west. CSU Hayward is a small but respected operation, known locally for its math and education departments. The school offers a variety of undergraduate and graduate degree programs. Located at 25800 Carlos Bee Boulevard, Hayward, 510-885-3000.
- **John F. Kennedy University**, founded in 1964, offers courses geared toward the adult student looking for a BA and/or MA degree, in fields such as counseling, library or museum arts, management, law and liberal arts. Located at 12 Altarinda Road, Orinda, 925-254-0200.
- **Mills College**, founded in 1852, is the oldest women's college in the western United States. Mills has a long history of excellence in the fields of liberal arts and science. The college offers women undergraduate and graduate degrees, and admits men to some graduate programs. Located at 5000 MacArthur Boulevard, Oakland, 510-430-2255.
- **Saint Mary's College**, founded in 1863 by the Christian Brothers, is located in the hilly, wooded, secluded community of Moraga. Classes are small, instruction excellent. Undergraduate and graduate degrees offered. You can find Saint Mary's at 1928 St. Mary's Road, Moraga, 925-631-4000.
- **University of California, Berkeley** is considered by many to be the finest school in the UC system. Founded in 1868 and located on a 1,500 acre wooded urban campus, UC Berkeley has top-notch facilities, faculty, and course offerings in hundreds of disciplines, undergraduate and graduate. Entrance competition is stiff, to say the least. Call 510-642-6000. You can visit UC Berkeley's web site at www.berkeley.edu.

PENINSULA/SOUTH BAY

- **San Jose State University** is located in the heart of Silicon Valley in downtown San Jose. SJSU offers some unique opportunities including the use of the nation's only undergraduate nuclear science lab, its own deep-sea research ship, and centers for the study of Beethoven and John Steinbeck. Graduate programs also offered. You can find SJSU at One Washington Square, San Jose, 408-924-2000.
- **Santa Clara University** is considered by many to be one of the finest universities in the country. Santa Clara was founded in 1851 by the Jesuits and is recognized as California's oldest institution of higher learning. Today it is

known for its law, business and engineering schools. Located at 500 El Camino Real, Santa Clara, 408-554-4000.

- **Stanford University** is certainly one of the nation's premier universities. Stanford is located in comfortable Palo Alto, at the northern end of Silicon Valley. Established in 1885 by former California Governor and Senator Leland Stanford and his wife Jane, Stanford is known for its excellence in the arts and sciences, and its highly-regarded faculty and facilities, including its medical center. Call 650-723-2300 for more information.

SURROUNDING AREAS

- **University of California, Davis** is located about 70 miles northeast of San Francisco and 15 miles west of Sacramento. UCD is a top-notch research university offering undergraduate and graduate degrees in a wide range of fields. The city of Davis is a beautiful college town, and is known for being one of the most bicycle-friendly communities in the nation. Undergraduate admission information is available at 175 Mrack Hall, UCD, Davis. Graduate admission information is available at 252 Mrack Hall, UCD, Davis, 916-752-1011.

WITHOUT EXAGGERATION, IT IS FAIR TO SAY THAT THE BAY AREA IS a shopper's paradise. Whether you like to shop in familiar chain stores or if you enjoy finding unique boutiques, they're all here. If you don't want to spend a lot, used clothing, furniture and appliances are available at second-hand stores, such as the Salvation Army or Goodwill, which run their own department stores. There are numerous flea markets and because of the mild climate, garage and yard sales occur year round. Discount shopping is also available from one end of the Bay to the other. If money is of no concern, you can be sure you'll have plenty of opportunities to hand it over to a delighted sales associate at an upscale emporium.

MALLS/SHOPPING CENTERS

No matter what you're looking for or how much or little you're willing to spend, you can probably find it at one of the following Bay Area malls. Check their web sites for mall specials, directions, and for store directories.

SAN FRANCISCO
- **Crocker Galleria**, 50 Post Street, 415-393-1505, www.shopatgalleria.com
- **Embarcadero Center**, One Embarcadero Center, 415-772-0500, www.embarcaderocenter.com
- **Ghirdelli Square**, 900 North Point, 415-775-5500, www.ghirardellisq.com
- **San Francisco Shopping Centre**, 865 Market Street, 415-495-5656, www.sanfranciscocentre.com
- **Stonestown Galleria**, 3251 20th Avenue, 415-759-2623, www.stonestowngalleria.com

NORTH BAY
- **Northgate Mall**, San Rafael, 415-479-5955, www.themallatnorthgate.com
- **Larkspur Landing**, Larkspur, 415-277-6800

- **Strawberry Shopping Center**, Mill Valley, 415-389-8586
- **The Village**, Corte Madera, 415-924-8557, www.villageatcortemadera.com
- **Town & Country**, Corte Madera, 415-924-2961

EAST BAY
- **Hilltop Mall**, Richmond, 510-223-1933
- **The Willows**, Concord, 925-825-4000, www.willosshoppingcenter.com
- **Sun Valley**, Concord, 925-825-2042, www.shopsunvalley.com
- **New Park Mall**, Newark, 510-794-5522, www.hometownmall.com/malls/ca/newpark
- **South Shore Center**, Alameda, 510-521-1515, www.southshorecenter.com
- **Bayfair Mall**, San Leandro, 510-357-6000, www.bayfair-mall.com
- **Great Mall of the Bay Area**, Milpitas 800-625-5229, www.greatmallbayarea.com

PENINSULA
- **Hillsdale Mall**, San Mateo, 650-345-8222, www.hillsdale.com
- **Serramonte Center**, Daly City, 650-992-8686, www.serramontecenter.com
- **Stanford Shopping Center**, Palo Alto, 650-617-8230, www.stanfordshop.com
- **Tanforan Park**, San Bruno, 650-873-2000, www.tanforanpark.com
- **Westlake Shopping Center**, Daly City, 650-756-2161

SOUTH BAY
- **Oakridge Mall**, San Jose, 408-578-2910
- **The PruneYard**, Campbell, 408-371-4700, www.thepruneyard.com
- **Silicon Valley WAVE** (Walk and Village Entertainment), Sunnyvale, 408-245-6585
- **Town and Country Village**, Sunnyvale, 408-736-6654
- **Vallco Fashion Park**, Cupertino, 408-255-5660, www.shopyourmall.com
- **Valley Fair Shopping Center**, San Jose, 408-248-4450

OUTLET MALLS

Whether these places actually offer more affordable merchandise than elsewhere is debatable but what is certain is their nationwide popularity and rapid growth. Check the web at www.outletsonline.com for more information. Below are a few of the outlet malls located in the Bay Area:
- **Marina Square**, San Leandro, no main number, 1259 Marina Boulevard
- **Pacific Outlet Mall**, Gilroy, 408-847-4155, Highway 101 at Leavesley exit
- **Vacaville Commons**, Vacaville, 707-447-0267, 2098 Harbison Drive

DEPARTMENT STORES

- **Gumps**: the upscale Grand Dame of San Francisco department stores. Gumps stocks furniture and other home accessories with special attention paid to *objets d'art*, impeccably displayed. The service is top-notch; 135 Post Street, 415-982-1616.
- **JC Penney**: national department store chain that sells just about everything you'd need for your home, including major appliances, televisions, stereos, VCRs, linens, bedding and furniture as well as clothing, shoes, jewelry and cosmetics. Numerous Bay Area locations, but none in San Francisco, including Tanforan Shopping Center, San Bruno, 650-873-4100; Southland Mall, Hayward, 510-783-0300; Richmond Hilltop Mall, Richmond, 510-222-4411.
- **Macy's**: the Union Square store is reportedly the largest in the nation, outside of the flagship store in Manhattan. You could fully stock your closets and furnish your entire home here if you were so inclined, as Macy's carries clothing, shoes, linens, bedding, appliances, cookware, gourmet items, luggage, and more. Service, once notoriously bad, has improved of late. Bay Area locations include: San Francisco, Union Square, Stockton & O'Farrell streets 415-397-3333; Peninsula, Daly City, 1 Serramonte Center, 650-994-3333; East Bay, San Leandro, Bayfair Mall, 510-357-3333; North Bay, San Rafael, Northgate Mall, 415-499-5200
- **Mervyns**: medium priced department store specializing in clothing, shoes, linens, bedding, home accessories, known for big and frequent sales. Numerous locations across the Bay Area: San Francisco, 2675 Geary Boulevard, 415-921-0888; Peninsula, 63 Serramonte Center, 650-756-9022; East Bay, South Shore Center, Alameda, 510-769-8800; Southland Mall, Hayward, 510-782-8000; North Bay, Northgate Mall, San Rafael, 415-499-9330
- **Neiman-Marcus**, Post at Stockton, San Francisco, 415-362-3900; 400 Stanford Shopping Center, Palo Alto, 650-329-3300. The opulent Texan retailer carries expensive non-necessities, has nice restaurants, a fairly good gourmet department, and is known for the Christmas tree in the rotunda.
- **Nordstrom**: employees at this Seattle-based retailer have a reputation for being helpful, courteous and knowledgeable about the products they sell. Merchandise ranges from shoes and clothing for the entire family to jewelry and cosmetics, though no home furnishings. Perhaps most popular here are the women's shoe sales. Their online service also is top-notch, voted "favorite cyber clothier" in *Smart Money's* 2000 Internet Guide, www.nordstrom.com. Bay Area locations include: San Francisco, SF Shopping Centre, 865 Market Street, 415-243-8500; Stonestown Galleria, 285 Winston Drive, 415-753-1344; Peninsula, Hillsdale Mall, San Mateo, 650-570-5111; North Bay Village Corte Madera, 1870 Redwood Highway, Corte Madera, 415-927-1690; East Bay, 1200 Broadway Plaza, Walnut Creek, 925-930-7959.

- **Saks Fifth Avenue**: upscale. Clothing, jewelry, cosmetics, *objets d'art*. Located in San Francisco at 384 Post Street on Union Square, 415-986-4300.
- **Wilkes Bashford**, 375 Sutter Street, 415-986-4380; Wilkes Bashford isn't strictly speaking a department store since it sells only clothing and decorative items, but most department stores don't sell much else these days either. It is the only San Francisco-based department store remaining and there's only one. It's still run by Wilkes Bashford himself. What you'll find here is high-end, high-style gear in a low-key, service oriented environment, without the cookie cutter feel of many chain stores.

DISCOUNT DEPARTMENT STORES AND OUTLETS

Discount chains, such as **K-mart**, **Target**, and **WalMart** all do business throughout the Bay Area. Check the Yellow Pages for the nearest location of your favorite. Below are a few of the discount outlet stores in the area.

- **Any Mountain Outlet Store**, 2990 Seventh Street, Berkeley, 510-704-9440
- **California Big & Tall**, 625 Howard Street, 415-495-4484, for men; the exclusive outlet for Rochester Big & Tall
- **Cut Loose Factory Outlet**, 690 Third Street, 415-495-4581, outlet store for local women's clothes manufacturer
- **Georgiou Outlet**, 925 Bryant Street, 415-554-0150
- **Gunny Saxe Discount Outlet**, 35 Stanford, 415-495-3326
- **Loehmann's Inc.**, 222 Sutter Street, 415-982-3215, is a local favorite for discount designer clothes and shoes for both men and women.
- **Marjorie Baer Outlet Store**, 2660 Harrison Street, 415-821-9971, contains samples and discontinued items of costume jewelry
- **Nordstrom Rack**, Metro Shopping Center, 81 Colma Boulevard, Colma, 650-755-1444. This is the discount rack for all the Nordstrom stores.
- **North Face Outlet**, 1325 Howard Street, San Francisco, 415-626-6444; 1238 Fifth Street, Berkeley, 510-526-3530; 4952 Almaden Expressway, San Jose, 408-269-9300
- **Sierra Designs Outlet**, 1255 Powell Street, Emeryville, 510-450-9555
- **Specialtees Outlet**, Rheem Shopping Center, 572 Center Street, Moraga, 925-376-8337

ELECTRONICS/APPLIANCES

There are dozens of individually owned and operated electronics and appliance stores throughout the Bay Area as well as all the familiar national chains. To find what you're looking for close to your home, check the Pacific Bell Yellow Pages. Here are a few of these businesses:

- **Best Buy**, 180 Donahue Street, Marin City, 415-332-6529; 1490 Fitzgerald

Road, Pinole, 510-758-0112; 1133 Industrial Road, San Carlos, 650-622-0050
- **Circuit City**, 1200 Van Ness Avenue, San Francisco, 415-441-1300; 1880 South Grant, San Mateo, 650-578-1400; 4080 Stevens Creek Boulevard, San Jose, 408-296-5522
- **Fry's**, 340 Portage Avenue, Palo Alto, 650-496-1177; 600 Hamilton Avenue, Campbell, 408-364-3700; 1177 Kern Avenue, Sunnyvale, 408-733-1770
- **Good Guys**, 1400 Van Ness Avenue, 415-775-9323; Serramonte Shopping Center, Daly City, 650-301-8855; 1247 West El Camino Real, Sunnyvale, 408-962-0101; 3149 Stevens Creek Boulevard, San Jose, 408-978-6664
- **Montgomery Wards**, Serramonte Center, Daly City, 650-991-6268
- **Dale Sanford's**, 1509 Shattuck Avenue, Berkeley, 510-845-0400

COMPUTERS

In the Bay Area there are plenty of options when it comes to buying anything computer related. This is, afterall, headquarters of the global digital revolution. Below is a short list of some well-known computer retailers. Check the Yellow Pages for additional options. Locations are in San Francisco unless otherwise noted.

Another good place to look for computer information is *Computer Currents* magazine. It comes out bi-weekly and is free. Look for it on streetside racks throughout the Bay Area or contact them at 510-527-0333 or on the Internet at www.currents.net.
- **Best Buy**, 180 Donahue Street, Marin City, 415-332-6529; 1490 Fitzgerald Road, Pinole, 510-758-0112; 1133 Industrial Road, San Carlos, 650-622-0050
- **Circuit City**, 1200 Van Ness Avenue, 415-441-1300
- **CompUSA**, 1250 El Camino Real, San Bruno, 650-244-9980; 3839 Emery, Emeryville, 510-450-9500; 3561 El Camino Real, Santa Clara, 408-554-1733
- **Good Guys**, 1400 Van Ness Avenue, 415-775-9323; 2727 El Camino Real, San Mateo 650-574-5100; 3149 Stevens Creek Boulevard, San Jose, 408-554-9700.
- **Fry's**, 340 Portage Avenue, Palo Alto, 650-496-1177; 600 Hamilton Avenue, Campbell, 408-364-3700; 1177 Kern Avenue, Sunnyvale, 408-733-1770

BEDS, BEDDING, & BATH

Some area department stores sell bedding as well as beds. For their names, locations and phone numbers see the previous entries under **Department Stores**. Here's a list of just some of the San Francisco stores that deal exclusively in these items.

- **Beds and Bedding**, 9th and Harrison Streets, 415-621-0746
- **Bed Bath and Beyond**, 555-9th Street, 415-252-0490; call 800-GO-BEYOND (800-462-3966) to find numerous other Bay Area locations
- **Dreams Inc.**, 921 Howard Street, 415-543-1800
- **Discount Depot**, 520 Haight Street, 415-552-9279; 2020 San Pablo, Berkeley, 510-549-1478
- **Duxiana**, 1803 Fillmore Street, 415-673-7134
- **Earthsake**, 2076 Chestnut Street, 415-441-2896; One Embarcadero Center, 415-956-4555
- **Futon Shop**, 3545 Geary, 415-56-FUTON
- **Futon Gallery**, 2951 El Camino Real, Palo Alto 650-322-9193; 998 El Camino Real, Sunnyvale, 408-720-8036
- **The Linen Factory Outlet**, 475 Ninth Street, 415-861-1511
- **Mattress Factory Outlet**, 1970 West El Camino Real, Mountain View, 650-969-7580
- **McRoskey Airflex Mattresses**, 1687 Market Street, 415-861-4532
- **Oysterbeds**, 17th & DeHaro Street, 415-626-4343
- **Scheuer Linens**, 340 Sutter Street, 415-392-2813
- **Stroud's**, 731 Market Street, 415-979-0460; Corte Madera, 415-924-450; 1330 South California Boulevard, Walnut Creek, 925-933-1113; 1236 West El Camino Real, Sunnyvale, 408-733-0910; 700 El Camino Real, Menlo Park, 650-327-7680
- **Warm Things**, 3063 Fillmore Street, 415-931-1660

CARPETS & RUGS

- **Armstrong Carpets**, 626 Clement Street, 415-751-2827
- **Carpet Center**, 1065 Ashby Avenue, Berkeley, 510-549-1100
- **Carpet Connection**, 390 Bayshore Boulevard, 415-550-7125
- **Conklin Brothers**, 1100 Shelby, 415-282-1822
- **Cost Plus Imports**, 2552 Taylor Street, 415-928-6200; 785 Serramonte Boulevard, Daly City, 415-994-7090; 201 Clay Street, Oakland, 510-893-7300
- **Claremont Rug Company**, 6087 Claremont Avenue, Oakland, 510-654-0816, fine antique carpets
- **The Floor Store**, 5327 Jacuzzi Street, El Cerrito, 510-527-3203
- **MMM Carpets**, 375 Gellert Boulevard, Daly City, 415-994-4000
- **Omid Carpets**, 590-10th Street, 415-626-3466, a full range of Oriental carpets
- **Pier One Imports**, 3535 Geary Boulevard, 415-387-6642; 101 Gellert Boulevard, Colma, 415-755-6600; 2501 El Camino Real, Redwood City, 650-364-6608; 1255 West El Camino Real, Sunnyvale, 650-969-8307; 20610 Stevens Creek Boulevard, Cupertino 408-253-4512; 1807 Saratoga Avenue, San Jose, 408-255-3533

FURNITURE

There are too many furniture stores in the Bay Area to list them all, but here are a few well-known names to get you started in your search for perfect and affordable home furnishings.

- **Berkeley Mills**, 2830 Seventh Street, Berkeley, 510-549-2845
- **Berkeley Bungalow**, 2508 San Pablo Avenue, Berkeley, 510-981-9520
- **Busvans for Bargains**, 244 Clement Street, San Francisco, 415-752-5353; 900 Battery Street, 415-981-1405
- **Cort Furniture Clearance Center**, 2925 Meade Avenue Santa Clara, 408-727-1470
- **Flegel's Home Furnishings**, 1654 2nd Street, San Rafael, 415-454-0502
- **Ethan Allen**, 1060 Redwood Highway, Mill Valley, 415-383-3600
- **Evolution Home Furnishings**, 271 Ninth Street, San Francisco, 415-861-6665; 805 University Avenue, Berkeley, 510-665-0200; 511 East Francisco Boulevard, San Rafael, 415-482-1600
- **Hoot Judkins**, offers a wide selection of finished and unfinished furniture at reasonable prices; 1142 Sutter Street, San Francisco, 415-673-5454; 1269 Veterans Boulevard, Redwood City, 650-367-8181; 1400 El Camino Real, San Bruno, 650-952-5600; 5101 Mowry Avenue, Fremont, 510-795-4890
- **IKEA**, 4400 Shellmound Street, Emeryville, 510-420-4522
- **Limn**, high-end cutting edge design furniture and housewares; 290 Townsend at Fourth, San Francisco, 415-543-5466
- **Macy's Furniture Clearance Center**, 1556 El Camino Real, South San Francisco, 415-397-3333
- **Max Furniture**, 1633 Fillmore Street, 415-440-9002 residential commercial design furniture
- **Mike**, 2142 Fillmore, San Francisco, 415-567-2700
- **Noriega Furniture**, 1455 Taraval Street, San Francisco, 415-564-4110
- **Roche Bobois**, 1 Henry Adams Street, 425-626-8613; Westgate Mall, San Jose, 408-871-2600
- **San Francisco Furniture Mart**, 1355 Market Street, 415-552-2311, is open to the public twice a year, once in May and once in November, and offers wholesale prices.
- **Scandinavian Designs**, 317-South B Street, San Mateo, 650-340-0555; 2101 Shattuck Avenue, Berkeley, 510-848-8250; 1212 4th Street, San Rafael, 415-457-5500
- **Slater/Marinoff**, 1823 4th Berkeley, 510-548-2001
- **The Wooden Duck**, 2919 Seventh Street, Berkeley, 510-848-3575
- **Z Gallerie**, 2154 Union Street, San Francisco, 415-567-4891, call for other city locations; 1731 Fourth Street, Berkeley, 510-525-7591; 320 Corte Madera Town Center, 415-924-3088; 340 University Avenue, Palo Alto, 650-324-0693

- **Zonal**, distressed and "found" furniture, San Francisco: 568 Hayes Street, 415-255-9307; 1942 Fillmore Street, 415-359-9111; 2139 Polk Street, 415-563-2220

USED FURNITURE

Shopping for second hand furnishings can be just as much fun as shopping for new. The chance of finding a lost heirloom adds to the excitement of saving a bit of cash. Here are a few places to begin your bargain-hunting adventure. See **Second Hand Shopping** below for additional possibilities.

- **Berkeley Outlet**, 711 Heinz Avenue, Berkeley 510-549-2896
- **Busvan Bonded Dealers & Appraisers**, two locations in San Francisco: 900 Battery Street, 415-981-1405; 244 Clement Street, 415-752-5353
- **Cottrell's Moving and Storage**, 150 Valencia Street, San Francisco, 415-431-1000
- **Harrington Brothers**, 599 Valencia Street, San Francisco, 415-861-7300
- **People's Bazaar**, 3258 Adeline, Berkeley, 510-655-8008
- **Second Act**, 12882 S Saratoga Road, Saratoga, 408-741-4995
- **Thrift Center**, 1060 El Camino Real, San Carlos, 650-593-1082

HOUSEWARES

Most department stores carry dishes, glassware, and other items needed for the home, so if you have a favorite that may be the place to start. There are also numerous specialty outlets from which to choose, including the following:

- **Bed Bath and Beyond**, 555-9th Street, 415-252-0490; call 800-GO-BEYOND to find other Bay Area locations.
- **Crate & Barrel**, 125 Grant Avenue, San Francisco, 415-986-4000; The Village at Corte Madera, Corte Madera, 415-924-5412; Stanford Shopping Center, Palo Alto, 650-321-7800; Hillsdale Shopping Center, San Mateo, 650-341-9000; Valley Fair Shopping Center, Santa Clara, 408-243-7500; Broadway Plaza, Walnut Creek, 925-947-3500; Crate & Barrel Outlet Store, 1785 4th Street, Berkeley, 510-528-5500
- **Dansk**, 1760 Fourth Street, Berkeley, 510-528-9226
- **Home Chef**, 3527 California Stret, 15-668-3191; 329 Town Center, Corte Madera, 415-927-3191; 1600 Saratoga Avenue, San Jose, 408-374-3191
- **IKEA**, 4400 Shellmound Street, Emeryville, 510-420-4522
- **Lechter's**, Stonestown Galleria, 415-759-0528; 24 Serramonte Center, Daly City, 415-992-5047; 119 Eastridge Center, San Jose, 408-238-5688; 137 Oakridge Mall, San Jose, 408-365-1703
- **Vallco Fashion Park**, Cupertino, 408-466-5785
- **Pier One Imports**, 3535 Geary Boulevard, 415-387-6642; 101 Colma Boulevard, Colma, 650-755-6600; 2501 El Camino Real, Redwood City,

650-364-6608; 1255 West El Camino Real, Sunnyvale, 650-969-8307; 20610 Stevens Creek Boulevard, Cupertino, 408-253-4512; 1807 Saratoga Avenue, San Jose, 408-255-3533; 1009 Blossom Hill Road, San Jose, 408-978-9555

- **Pottery Barn**, 1 Embarcadero Center, 415-788-6810; 2100 Chestnut Street, 415-441-1787
- **Sur La Table Cookware**, kitchenware, linens, small appliances, and tableware: 77 Maiden Lane, 415-732-7900; 1806 Fourth Street, Berkeley, 510-849-2252; 23 University Avenue, Los Gatos, 408-395-6946
- **Williams Sonoma**, San Francisco Center, 415-546-0171; 150 Post Street, San Francisco, 415-362-6904; 2 Embarcadero Center, San Francisco, 415-421-2033; Stonestown Galleria, San Francisco, 415-681-5525; Hillsdale Mall, San Mateo, 650-345-8222; 180 El Camino Real, Palo Alto, 650-321-3486; The Village, Corte Madera, 415-924-2940; 1009 Blossom Hill Road, San Jose, 408-978-9555

HARDWARE/PAINTS/WALLPAPER/GARDEN CENTERS

Nearly everything you might need to fix up your new place is readily available at a local hardware store, but if the local store doesn't have that special color of paint you want for the sun porch you can head for one of many cavernous home improvement centers (see below). Unless otherwise indicated, the following hardware stores and garden centers are in San Francisco.

- **Bauerware Cabinet Hardware**, 3886 17th Street, 415-864-3886, www. Bauerware.com, offers knobs, pulls, and handles the array and design of which you may never have seen. You can't not find something you like here.
- **Restoration Hardware**, 1733 Fourth Street, Berkeley, 510-526-6424; Hillsdale Mall, San Mateo, 650-577-9807; 281 University Avenue, Palo Alto, 650-328-4004
- **Urban Ore General Store**, 6th and Gilman, Berkeley, 510-559-4450; this place has corner sinks, clawed tubs, chain toilets and all the delights of the not-so-modern world.
- **Victorian Interiors**, 575 Hayes Street, San Francisco, 415-431-7191/7144; if you move into a Victorian and you don't like the 1970s wood paneling or 1980s track lighting that has been installed, go here to find original wall papers, ceiling fixtures, carpets, wainscoting and much more.
- **Victoriana SF Moulding**, 2070 Newcomb Avenue, San Francisco, 415-648-0313, specializes in Victorian moldings, wallpapers, draperies, tiles, fabrics, carpets and more.

ACE HARDWARE STORES

- **Brownie's Hardware**, 1552 Polk Street, 415-673-8900
- **Cole Hardware**, 956 Cole Street, 415-753-2653
- **Discount Builders**, 1695 Mission Street, 415-621-8511
- **Cliff's Variety**, 479 Castro, 415-431-5365
- **Fredericksen's Hardware**, 3029 Fillmore Street, 415-292-2950
- **Golden Gate Building**, 1333 Pacific Avenue, 415-441-0945
- **Standard 5-10-25**, 3545 California Street, 415-751-5767
- **Standard Hardware**, 1019 Clement Street, 415-221-1888

TRUE VALUE HARDWARE STORES

- **Creative Paint**, 5435 Geary Boulevard, 415-666-3380
- **Pacific Heights Hardware**, 2828 California Street, 415-346-9262
- **Progress Hardware**, 724 Irving Street, 415-731-2038
- **Sunset Hardware**, 3126 Noriega Street, 415-661-0607
- **True Value Hardware**, 2244 Irving Street, 415-753-6862

GARDENING STORES

- **Broadway Terrace Nursery**, 4340 Clarewood Drive, Oakland, 510-658-3729
- **Plant'It Earth**, 2215 Market Street, 415-626-5082
- **Smith and Hawken**, 2040 Fillmore Street, San Francisco, 415-776-3424; 35 Corte Madera Avenue, Mill Valley, 415-381-1800; 1330 10th Street, Berkeley, 510-527-1076; 26 Santa Cruz Avenue, Los Gatos, 408-354-6500; 705 Stanford Shopping Center, Palo Alto, 650-321-0403
- **Sloat Garden Centers**, A full range of garden supplies, plants and trees, classes, and friendly and helpful advice; 3rd Avenue between Geary and Clement, San Francisco, 415-752-1614; 2700 Sloat Boulevard, San Francisco, 415-566-4415; 2000 Novato Boulevard, Novato, 415-897-2169; 1580 Lincoln Avenue, San Rafael, 415- 453-3977; 828 Diablo Boulevard, Walnut Creek, 925-743-0288
- **Woolworth Nursery**, 4606 Almaden Expressway, San Jose, 408-266-4400; 725 San Antonio Road, Palo Alto, 650-493-5136

HOME IMPROVEMENT CENTERS

The big do-it-yourself centers are located outside of San Francisco, but the ones listed below are all within a 15 to 30 minute drive of the City.
- **Orchard Supply Hardware (OSH)**, 2245 Gellert Boulevard, South San

Francisco, 650-878-3322; 900 El Camino Real, Millbrae, 415-873-5536; 1151 Anderson Drive, San Rafael, 415-453-7288; 1025 Ashby Avenue, Berkeley, 510-540-6638
- **Home Depot**, 1125 Old County Road, San Carlos, 650-592-9200; 1781 East Bayshore, East Palo Alto, 650-462-6800; 1933 Davis Street, San Leandro, 510-636-9600; 11955 San Pablo Avenue, El Cerrito, 510-235-0800
- **Yardbirds**, 13901 San Pablo Avenue, San Pablo, 510-236-4630; 1801 4th Street, San Rafael, 415-457-5880

SPORTING GOODS

Californians are an outdoorsy bunch, thanks to the fact that the Golden State has deserts, beaches, mountains, hiking, biking and running trails, downhill and cross-country skiing, camping and backpacking opportunities galore, and much, much more. As you might expect, there is no shortage of merchants ready to cater to your every sporting whim. Those listed below are in San Francisco unless otherwise noted.
- **Big 5**, 314 Gellert Boulevard, Daly City, 415-994-3688
- **Copeland Sports**, Stonestown Galleria, 415-566-5521
- **Don Sherwood Golf and Tennis**, 320 Grant Avenue, 415-989-5000
- **Kaplan's Surplus and Sporting Goods**, 1055 Market Street, 415-863-3486
- **Lombardi Sports**, 1600 Jackson Street, 415-456-0600
- **Marmot Mountain Works**, 901 Sir Francis Drake Boulevard, Kentfield, 415-454-8543; 3049 Adeline Street, Berkeley, 510-849-0735
- **North Face**, 1325 Howard Street, 415-626-6444; 180 Post Street, 415-433-3223; 1238 5th Street, Berkeley, 510-526-3530
- **Oshman's**, Tanforan Mall, San Bruno, 415-588-0741; 1119 Industrial Road, San Carlos, 415-508-2330
- **Patagonia**, 770 North Point, 415-771-2050
- **Play It Again**, 45 West Portal Avenue, 415-753-3049
- **REI**, 1338 San Pablo Avenue, Berkeley, 510-527-4140, www.rei.com
- **SportMart**, 3839 Emery, Emeryville, 510-450-9400
- **Sunset Soccer Supply**, 3214 Irving Street, 415-753-2666
- **Tennis Shack**, 3375 Sacramento, 415-928-2255

FOOD

The Bay Area is blessed with a wide selection of supermarket chains that range from inexpensive to downright exorbitant. The budget grocery stores offer bulk quantities of your regular fare while the more expensive stores emphasize fresh produce, organics and imported goods. The big grocery chains fall in between those two extremes. For budget shopping head for **Foods Co.**, **Food 4-Less**, **Grocery Outlet**, **Smart and Final** or **Pak-N-Save**. **Bell Markets**,

Lucky, Safeway, and SaveMart are the next rung up the ladder. Trader Joe's is somewhere in between. Andronico's reigns supreme at the high end. Real Foods and Whole Foods are the chain health food stores.

Home delivery in the Bay Area is available from www.peapod.com and www.webvan.com.

SPECIALTY GROCERS

SAN FRANCISCO
- **Bombay Bazar**, 548 Valencia, 415-621-1717
- **Cost Plus Imports**, 2552 Taylor Street, 415-928-6200
- **Chinese** food markets are sprinkled throughout Chinatown, Irving Street in the Sunset and Clement Street in the Richmond District
- **Rainbow Grocery and General Store**, 1745 Folsom Street, San Francisco, 415-863-0620
- **Whole Foods**: 1765 California Street, 415-674-0500; 501 Haight Street, 415-552-6077; 1550 Bryant Street, 415-431-6777; 1970 Innes Avenue, 415-206-9380

NORTH BAY
- **Mill Valley Market**, 12 Corte Madera, Mill Valley, 415-388-3222
- **Mollie Stones**, 100 Harbor Drive, Sausalito, 415-331-6900
- **Whole Foods**, 414 Miller Avenue, Mill Valley, 415-381-1200; 340 3rd Street, San Rafael, 415-451-6333

EAST BAY
- **Berkeley Bowl**, 2777 Shattuck, Berkeley, 510-841-6346; bulk seafood, wide variety of goods and great prices
- **Cost Plus Imports**, 201 Clay Street, Oakland, 510-893-7300
- **G.B. Ratto and Co.**, 821 Washington Street, Oakland, 510-832-6503, ethnic import sausages great fun
- **Market Hall**, 5655 College, Oakland, 510-652-0390, specialty stores for wine, coffee, tea, pasta, produce, poultry meat and fish
- **Monterey Market**, 1550 Hopkins, Berkeley, 510-526-6042, incredible produce
- **Monterey Fish Market**, 1582 Hopkins, Berkeley, 510-525-5600
- **Pacific East Mall**, 3288 Pierce Street, Richmond, 510-527-3000
- **Whole Foods**, 3000 Telegraph Avenue, Berkeley, 510-649-1333

PENINSULA/SOUTH BAY
- **Beltramos**, 1540 El Camino Real, Menlo Park, 650-325-2806, Wines and beers
- **Cosentino's** vegetable haven, South Bascom and Union avenues, San

Jose, 408-377-6661: vegetables bulk items, ethnic condiments
- **Cost Plus Imports**: 785 Serramonte Boulevard, Daly City, 415-994-7090
- **Draegers**, 1010 University Avenue, Menlo Park, 650-688-0677: imported cheeses, deli, produce and wine
- **Fiesta Latina**, 1424 Cary Avenue, San Mateo, 650- 343-0193
- **Oakville Grocery**, 715 Stanford Shopping Center, Palo Alto, 650-328-9000
- **Takahashi**, 221 South Claremont, San Mateo, 650-343-0394; Southeast Asian, Hawaiian and more

FARMERS' MARKETS

San Francisco is surrounded by some of the most productive farmland in the world (the San Joaquin Valley, and the counties of Sonoma, Salinas and Monterey), and many of the men and women who run these farms take at least one day a week to hawk their fruits and vegetables at **Farmers' Markets** all around the Bay Area. Organic produce is also available and most sellers will offer you a taste before you buy. Here's a list of some of the markets held in or close to San Francisco.
- **San Francisco City & County**, 100 Alemany Boulevard, Saturday, dawn to dusk, year round; Ferry Plaza on the Embarcadero, Saturday, 9 a.m. to 2 p.m., year round; United Nation's Plaza, Market Street (between 7th and 8th streets), Sunday and, Wednesday, 7 a.m. to 5 p.m., year round
- **Marin County**, Corte Madera: Village Shopping Center, Wednesday, 1 p.m. to dusk, May-October; Novato: Downtown (Sherman Avenue between Grant and Delong Avenues), Tuesday, 4 p.m. to 8 p.m., May-October; San Rafael: Downtown (4th at B Street), Thursday, 6 p.m. to 9 p.m., April-October; San Rafael: Marin Civic Center, Sunday and Thursday, 8 a.m. to 1 p.m., year round; Sausalito: Dunphy Park, Napa and Bridgeway, Saturdays, 9:30 a.m. to 1:30 p.m.
- **San Mateo County**, Daly City: Serramonte Center, Thursday, 10 a.m. to 2 p.m., year round; Menlo Park: Downtown Parking Plaza, Sunday, 10 a.m. to 2 p.m., May-November; Millbrae: 200 Broadway, Saturday, 8 a.m. to 1 p.m., year round
- **Alameda County**, Berkeley: Center Street at MLK (Martin Luther King) Way, Saturday, 10 a.m. to 2 p.m., year round; Oakland: Jack London Square, Sunday, 10 a.m. to 2 p.m., year round; El Cerrito: El Cerrito Plaza, Tuesday, 9 a.m. to 1 p.m., year round
- **Santa Clara County**, Palo Alto: Hamilton and Gilman, Saturday, 8:00 a.m. to noon, May-November; San Jose downtown: Jackson between Seventh and Eighth, Thursdays, 10 a.m. to 2 p.m., May-November

To find a farmers' market in another locale call 800-949-FARM.

WINES

- **Beverages and More**, for Bay Area locations call 888-772-3866
- **Calistoga Wine Stop**, 1458 Lincoln Avenue, # 2, Calistoga, 707-942-5556
- **Cost Plus Imports**, 2552 Taylor Street, San Francisco, 415-928-6200; 785 Serramonte Boulevard, Daly City, 415-994-7090; 201 Clay Street, Oakland, 510-893-7300
- **The Jug Shop**, 1567 Pacific Avenue, San Francisco, 415-885-2922
- **Marin Wine Cellar**, 2138 Fourth Street, San Rafael, 415-459-3823
- **North Berkeley Wine Company**, 1505 Shattuck, Berkeley, 510-848-8910
- **The Wine Stop**, 1300 Burlingame Avenue, Burlingame, 650-342-0570; 101 West 25th Avenue, San Mateo, 650-573-1071

Don't forget to visit the hundreds of wineries in Napa and Sonoma.

RESTAURANTS

Depending on your interest in food, dining out here can be a convenience, a diversion, a hobby, a sport, a religion, or a vocation. Offering every cuisine imaginable, the San Francisco Bay Area is one of the food capitals of the world, with more restaurants per person than any other area in the US. In fact, many new arrivals to the Bay Area are part of the food industry, serving as either wait staff, suppliers, growers, chefs, managers, investors, etc. If you are interested in finding out more about dining out in the Bay Area, track down a copy of the *Bay Area Consumers' Checkbook Guide to Bay Area Restaurants*; check your local bookstore or call 510-763-7979, www.checkbook.org. The *Zagat Survey, San Francisco Bay Area Restaurants*, www.zagat.com, is also a popular guide.

WAREHOUSE SHOPPING

Two giants in the club-shopping business have merged creating **Price-Costco**, cavernous warehouse-type facilities stacked from floor to ceiling with restaurant-trade items, such as gallon jars of olives, mayonnaise, six-packs of everything from chopped tomatoes to pet food, tires, cleaning supplies, clothing and pharmaceuticals. Basic membership costs $40 a year, and there are numerous locations around the Bay Area. The San Francisco store is located at 450 10th Street, 415-626-4341.

SECOND-HAND SHOPPING

The Advertiser is a weekly newspaper that lists items sold by individuals or at flea markets. The publication is free and can be found at most supermarkets and many newsstands. Call 415-863-3151 to sell or buy anything from cars to computers, from bedroom sets to budgies.

Your mother might call it second-hand but today that pair of 1970 elephant bottoms in the bottom of a box in the basement may be high fashion "vintage" to an aficionado. In San Francisco, dressing in stylish cast-offs has been all the rage for decades and there are scores of stores specializing in it. There are also plenty of shops that sell second-hand items that don't quite qualify as vintage. Vintage is consistently more expensive than second-hand and usually in excellent condition. Here are some places in San Francisco to start.

- **Attic Shop**, Cathedral School, 1036 Hyde Street, 415-776-6630, second-hand
- **Discovery Shop**, 1827 Union Street, 415-929-8053, second-hand
- **Goodwill**, 1500 Mission Street, 415-550-4500; (main office, numerous locations), second-hand
- **Repeat Performance**, 2223 Fillmore Street, 415-563-3123, vintage
- **Salvation Army**, 1185 Sutter Street, 415-771-3818, second-hand
- **St. Vincent de Paul**, 1745 Folsom Street 415-626-1515; 1519 Haight Street, 415-863-3615; 186 West Portal Avenue, 415-664-7119, second-hand
- **Third Hand Store**, 1839 Divisadero Street, 415-567-7332, second-hand
- **Thrift Town**, 2101 Mission Street, 415-861-1132, second-hand
- **Town School Closet**, 3325 Sacramento Street, 415-929-8019, vintage
- **Victorian House**, 2318 Fillmore Street, 415-923-3237, vintage

FLEA MARKETS

- **Berkeley Flea Market**, 1937 Ashby Avenue, Berkeley, 510-644-0744, a non-profit, community service flea market.
- **Coliseum Swap Meet**, 66th Street off Highway 880, Oakland, 510-534-0325
- **Midgley's Country Flea Market**, 2200 Gravenstein Highway South, Sebastapol, 707-823-7874
- **Norcal Swap Meet**, 1150 Ballena Boulevard, Alameda, 510-769-7266
- **San Francisco Flea Market**, 140 South Van Ness, 415-626-4353
- **San Jose Flea Market**, 1590 Berryessa Road, San Jose, 408-453-1110 or 800-BIG FLEA; this is a huge flea market with everything old for sale, plus live music, fresh produce, dozens of food stands, two playgrounds and more
- **San Pablo Flea Market**, 6100 San Pablo Avenue, Berkeley, 510-420-1468
- **Treasure Island Flea Market**, Avenue C at 4th Street on Treasure Island, an upscale outdoor market held every Sunday and voted the by the *San Francisco Bay Guardian* as the "Best of the Bay 1999."

ANTIQUES

There are pages of antique dealers listed in the San Francisco Yellow Pages; check there first for stores in your neighborhood. The 400 block of Jackson

Street, in San Francisco's Financial District, is known for its high concentration of antique stores. Most of the Jackson Street dealers are members of the Antique Dealers Association of California, and if they don't have what you're looking for they can steer you in the right direction. Market Street at Franklin has several lower priced antique shops. Sacramento Street in Presidio Heights has an array of fine antique shops. In Marin County San Anselmo has a small antique row along Sir Francis Drake Boulevard.

WITH ALL THE DIVERSE AND HIGHLY ACCLAIMED CULTURAL EVENTS in the Bay Area you may have trouble deciding what to do first. San Francisco boasts a world class symphony and chorus, opera, ballet, and a vibrant live theater scene, with everything from the experimental and off-beat to big, brash Broadway musicals. And, the cultural offerings in the surrounding Bay Area are rich and varied as well. It's a rare evening here when one of the current stars of the pop music scene is not appearing locally. For those in the hip-hop, dance, or alternative music scene, check out the South of Market Area, the hub for young hipsters.

Art lovers indulge themselves at major museums in San Francisco's downtown area and in Golden Gate Park as well as in smaller galleries throughout the City. Oakland, Berkeley, and the South Bay have myriad museums and galleries as well. There are also science museums, aquariums, planetariums and top-notch zoos. The South Bay, not surprisingly, has a number of technology oriented museums.

All of the Bay Area's newspapers print entertainment schedules on a regular basis, so you'll have no trouble finding out what's happening. The most comprehensive listing can be found in the *San Francisco Chronicle/Examiner's* Sunday "Datebook." The *Chronicle* also publishes a daily "Datebook" section in the morning newspaper. San Francisco's *Bay Guardian* weekly and the *SF Weekly* also have extensive listings and movie reviews, and they're free. Look for them in street-side racks and cafes.

Tickets for most events and performances may be purchased at the venue box offices or by calling **BASS/Ticketmaster** at 510-762-2277; 408-998-2277 for South Bay and Peninsula; 707-546-2277 for the North Bay. It's always a good idea to get your tickets as far in advance as possible since many shows, concerts, exhibits, and events sell out in advance. When calling ahead, have your credit card ready and be prepared to pay service fees (if your sense of thrift won't allow you to pay the often-steep service fees, buy your tickets in person at the box office). For discount, same-day tickets to San Francisco theater productions and full-price tickets to other selected local events check out the **TIX Bay Area** ticket booth on the east side of Union Square. This is where last minute open seats are sold for half-price, and while your choices are usually limited you can score great bargains. Call TIX at 415-433-7827—cash only for half-price tickets, VISA and MasterCard accepted for full-price purchases. Other ticket agencies are listed in the Yellow Pages under "Tickets."

MUSIC—SYMPHONIC, OPERA, CHORAL

SAN FRANCISCO/NORTH BAY

The **San Francisco Symphony** is one of the country's premier orchestras. The symphony and its **Chorus** have both won Grammy awards and toured much of the world, performing to packed houses and critical acclaim. World-renowned conductor Michael Tilson Thomas, known as MTT, runs the show.

When at home, the San Francisco Symphony and Chorus perform separately and in tandem at their glittering glass, brass and concrete home, the $33 million Louise M. Davies Symphony Hall. Opened in 1980, the structure underwent an acoustic upgrade in 1992. The concert hall and box office are located in the Civic Center area, at 201 Van Ness Avenue. Call the ticket office at 415-864-6000. Ticket prices start around $10, and go up from there. Concert season runs from September through May.

The **San Francisco Opera** performs at the War Memorial Opera House, which is right across Van Ness Avenue from City Hall, north of Davies Symphony Hall. This company attracts many of the opera world's biggest stars and is known for its often-lavish productions. Tickets can be on the expensive side, with decent seats starting around $75. The curtain comes up on the opera season with a gala event in September and continues into the summer. Get your tickets in person at the box office at 199 Grove Street or call 415-864-3330.

San Francisco is also home to the highly acclaimed vocal ensemble, **Chanticleer**. This a cappella group of 12 men works year-round, traveling all over the world, performing live and making new recordings. The ensemble specializes in "early music," but is also adept at classical choral works, jazz, pop, and spirituals. Catch them when they're in town—you'll be amazed by what you hear. To find out more, call the Chanticleer office at 415-896-5866.

San Francisco's own **Kronos Quartet** specializes in modern, experimental music, and they too travel the globe playing to sold-out audiences. Check newspaper entertainment guides for the few times Kronos is in the Bay Area to play for its adoring local followers. If you like modern chamber music you're sure to become one of Kronos' many fans.

If you'd like to hear some of the professional musicians of the future, the place to go locally is the **San Francisco Conservatory of Music**. The school is located in the city's Sunset district, at 201 Ortega Street at 19th Avenue.

Frequent concerts are staged here, featuring classical and contemporary, solo, and ensemble performers. For more information on upcoming events at the conservatory call 415-759-3477.

At **San Francisco Community Music Center**, 544 Capp Street, 415-647-6015, you can take a class or view inexpensive, sometimes free performances by students, instructors, and professionals of worldwide acclaim.

At the striking Frank Lloyd Wright designed Civic Center in San Rafael you can hear the **Marin Symphony**. Call 415-479-8100 for more details.

The areas surrounding San Francisco and the North Bay host an abundance of classical musical offerings. Not all musical groups have permanent homes. Instead some play at a variety of locations which means that people have an opportunity to hear live classical music pretty close to home no matter where they live.

EAST BAY
In Contra Costa County the **Dean Lesher Regional Center for the Arts** houses a number of performance companies such as the **Contra Costa Chamber Orchestra** and the **Diablo Light Opera Company**, 1601 Civic Drive, Walnut Creek, 925-939-6161. Also here:
- **Berkeley Opera**, 2640 College Avenue, Berkeley, 510-841-1903, www.berkeleyopera.com
- **Berkeley Symphony Orchestra**, various locations, 510-841-2800
- **Oakland East Bay Symphony**, 1999 Harrison Street, Oakland, 510-444-0801

PENINSULA
In the groves of academe at Stanford University you can hear the **Stanford Symphony Orchestra**, the **Symphonic Chorus** and **The Chamber Chorale**. Call 650-723-3811 or visit www.leland.stanford.edu//group for more information.
- **Palo Alto Chamber Orchestra**, 723 Matadero Avenue, Palo Alto, 650-856-3848
- **Palo Alto Philharmonic**, various locations, www.paphil.ai.sri.com
- **Peninsula Civic Light Opera**, various locations, 650-579-5568
- **West Bay Opera**, Lucie Stern Theatre, Palo Alto, 650-424-9999

SOUTH BAY
- **American Musical Theater of San Jose**, Center for the Performing Arts, San Jose, 408-453-7108
- **San Jose Symphony Orchestra**, 495 Almaden Boulevard, San Jose, 408-288-2828 or try www.sanjosesymphony.org
- **Cupertino Symphonic Band**, various locations, 408-262-0471, www.netview.com/csb
- **Opera San Jose**, 2149 Paragon Drive, San Jose, 408-437-4450, www.operasj.org

BALLET & DANCE

At any given time dance lovers in the Bay Area can enjoy watching Celtic Step dancing, Native American dancing, Russian or Balkan dancers, and modern dance companies. Look in the newspaper or any of the local weeklies for listings.

SAN FRANCISCO/NORTH BAY

- The **San Francisco Ballet** is a small company with a big reputation. The ballet season follows the opera season starting with the perennially popular "Nutcracker" in November and proceeding throughout the late winter and spring. Performances are at the War Memorial Opera House at Van Ness and Grove. For performance and ticket information call 415-865-2000.
- **Marin Ballet**, Marin Veterans Memorial Auditorium, 3501 Civic Center Drive, 415-453-6705, performs the Nutcracker every Christmas.
- Michael Smuin, formerly a choreographer with the San Francisco Ballet started his own company, **Michael Smuin Ballet**. They perform modern and classical pieces often reworked by Smuin at Yerba Buena Center for the Arts and Cowell Theater at Fort Mason Center. Call 415-665-2222 for information.
- **ODC Theatre** (Oberlin Dance Collective with its roots at Oberlin College), performs modern dance at ODC Theatre, 3153 17th Street, 415-863-9834, www.odc.org, and elsewhere. They also put on the popular "Velveteen Rabbit" for children each Christmas at Yerba Buena Center for the Arts.
- Other modern dance troupes include **Lawrence Pech Dance Company**, 415-626-7176, **Deborah Slater Dance Theatre**, 415-267-7687, **Margaret Jenkins Dance Company**, 415-826-8399, **Nancy Karp and Dancers**, 415-934-8442, **Footloose**, 415-626-2169, **Joe Goode Performance Group**, 415-648-4848. This is only a partial list. New companies form, combine and move in all the time.
- **Theatre Flamenco of San Francisco**, 415-826-1305, and **Rosa Montoya Bailes Flamenco** at 415-824-1960 enliven the Spanish dancing scene.

EAST BAY

- **Cal Performances**, presents dancers of world renown who perform through UC Berkeley at the Greek Theater, Hertz Hall, or Zellerbach Auditorium, 510-642-9988.
- **Oakland Ballet** performs at the beautiful Paramount Theater and other locations. They are known for their innovative approach and the use of ethnic elements in their work. Call 510-452-9288 to find out what they're up to.
- **Diablo Ballet**, Dean Lesher Regional Center for the Arts, Civic Drive, Walnut Creek, 925-939-6161
- **Valley Dance Theatre**, 925-443-6953

PENINSULA/SOUTH BAY
- **Janlyn Dance Company**, 408-255-4055, modern dance, various locations
- **Peninsula Ballet Theatre**, 600 North Delaware Street, San Mateo, 650-343-8485
- **San Jose Cleveland Ballet**, 40 North First San Jose, 408-288-2800
- **San Jose Dance Theater**, 408-293-5665

THEATER

The San Francisco theater scene is an active one offering works that range from experimental to mainstream. The theater district, located two blocks west of Union Square on Geary Street, is where you'll find the Curran and Geary theaters. The Curran stages musicals such as the immensely successful "Phantom of the Opera" and other visiting Broadway productions, as well as shows being prepared for the trip to New York's Great White Way. The Geary Theater plays host to what many would consider more serious productions, such as works by Shakespeare, Chekhov, and Sam Shepard. It is also is home to one of the country's most respected companies, the American Conservatory Theatre. The Golden Gate Theater, in the nearby Tenderloin district, stages big, splashy musicals. The surrounding streets are on the seedy side, and that puts many people off when it comes to attending shows here. However, there is safety in numbers, so if possible, stick with the crowd when traveling through this area.

Once you leave the theater district, productions take on a less commercial, more experimental feel, and there are many to choose from. Of course, local high schools, colleges and universities also put on shows, as do many local theater groups. Look for listings for all of the above in newspaper entertainment guides, or call the theaters. Here are just a few **San Francisco theaters**:
- **Brava**, 2789 24th Street, 415-641-7657, focuses on women's issues
- **Club Fugazi**, 678 Green Street, 421-4222, home of the immensely popular "Beach Blanket Babylon."
- **Curran**, 445 Geary Street, musicals, call BASS for tickets.
- **Eureka Theatre**, 215 Jackson Street, 415-788-7469, music, plays, classes
- **Exit Theatre**, 156 Eddy Street, 415-931-1094
- **Geary**, 415 Geary Street, 415-749-2228, serious drama
- **Golden Gate**, 42 Golden Gate Avenue, 415-551-2000, musicals
- **Intersection for the Arts**, 446 Valencia Street, 415-626-3311, plays, readings, musicals, music, and dance
- **Lorraine Hansberry**, 620 Sutter Street, 415-474-8800, known for top-notch African-American drama
- **Magic**, Fort Mason, Building D, 415-441-8822, experimental
- **Marines Memorial**, 640 Sutter Street, 415-771-6900, varied
- **New Conservatory Theatre Center**, 25 Van Ness, 415-861-8972, traditional, new, musical, gay and lesbian themes

- **Orpheum**, 1192 Market Street, 415-512-7700, opera, musicals, serious drama
- **Shelton Theater**, 533 Sutter Street, 415-441-3687, new and old plays, comedy and drama
- **Theater on the Square**, 450 Post Street, 415-433-9500
- **Theatre Rhinoceros**, 2926 16th Street, 861-5079, gay and lesbian themes

NORTH BAY

- **Marin Community Playhouse**, 27 Kensington Road, San Anselmo, 415-456-5550, films, lectures, dance, drama, music
- **Marin Theatre Company**, 397 Miller Avenue, Mill Valley, 415-388-5208, new plays and classes
- **Marin Shakespeare Theatre**, various locations, 415-499-1108
- **Mountain Play Association**, 177 East Blithedale, Mill Valley, 415-383-1100, yearly outdoor summer musicals

EAST BAY

- **Actors Ensemble of Berkeley**, 1301 Shattuck, 510-525-1620
- **Antioch Regional Theatre**, 213 F. Street, Antioch, 925-757-5036, children's theater, comedy, musicals
- **Aurora Theatre Co.**, 2315 Durant Avenue, Berkeley, 510-843-4822, old standards and new plays
- **Berkeley Repertory Theatre**, 2025 Addison, Berkeley, 510-845-4700, nationally known, new and reworked plays
- **Black Repertory Group**, 3201 Adeline Street, Berkeley, 510-652-2120
- **Contra Costa Civic Theatre**, 951 Pomona Avenue, El Cerrito, 510-524-9132
- **Center Repertory**, 1601 Civic Drive, Walnut Creek, 925-943-SHOW
- **East Bay Center for the Performing Arts**, 339 11th Street, Richmond, 925-234-5624
- **Lamplighter Music Theatre**, Dean Lesher Center for the Performing Arts, 925-943-7469
- **Moraga Playhouse**, 250 Moraga Way, Orinda, 925-376-200
- **Oakland Ensemble Theatre**, 1428 Alice Street, Oakland, 510-763-7774, top-notch Afro-American troupe

PENINSULA

- **Palo Alto Players**, 1305 Middlefield Road, Palo Alto, 650-329-0891, six shows a year at good prices
- **Manhattan Playhouse**, Manhattan Avenue, Palo Alto, 650-322-4589, two shows per season
- **TheatreWorks**, Various locations, 650-903-6000, staged readings to Broadway musicals

SOUTH BAY

- **City Lights Theater Company**, 529 South Second Street, San Jose 408-295-4200, eclectic new plays
- **Louis B. Mayer Theatre**, Santa Clara University, Santa Clara, 408-554-4989
- **San Jose Stage Company**, 490 South First Street, San Jose, 408-283-7142
- **San Jose Repertory Theatre**, 101 Paseo de San Antonio, 408-291-2255, classics and originals
- **Santa Clara Players**, Santa Clara Community Center, Santa Clara, 408-248-7993
- **Stage One**, 408-293-6362, cutting edge contemporary

CONTEMPORARY MUSIC

San Francisco draws star entertainers as well as up-and-comers from all over the world.

If rock and roll, in any one of its current manifestations, is your cup of tea, no doubt the name Bill Graham will be familiar to you. Graham, the prolific concert promoter, died a few years ago when his helicopter hit a transmission tower in the North Bay, but his company, Bill Graham Presents (BGP), presses on. Graham is remembered for, among other things, the local concerts he staged at the Fillmore and the Oakland Coliseum, two of his favorite venues.

The Coliseum is still one of the Bay Area's premier outdoor concert sites, and it also has an indoor stage. There are a number of other outdoor facilities used for concerts, chief among them the Shoreline Amphitheatre in Mountain View and the Concord Pavilion in Concord. Both have covered seating up front close to the stage, and loads of uncovered lawn behind the seats. Bring a blanket, stretch out, and listen to the music.

As previously mentioned, San Francisco's SOMA district is the hub of the Bay Area's alternative, hip-hop and dance music scene. Jazz, blues, and folk are also well represented here. Dozens of nightclubs showcase the talents of the artists you may see at the top of the charts tomorrow, as well as those who do what they do because they love it, with little concern about making it to "the show."

For the latest on who's playing where and when consult the *San Francisco Chronicle's* "Datebook" or the entertainment guides in the *Bay Guardian* or the *SF Weekly* newspapers. You could also phone the establishment. Here are some of their numbers and locations.

BAY AREA CONCERT FACILITIES

- **Concord Pavilion**, 2000 Kirker Pass Road, Concord, 925-676-8742
- **Cow Palace**, Geneva Avenue and Santos Street, Daly City, 415-469-6065
- **Fillmore**, 1805 Geary Boulevard, San Francisco, 415-346-6000

- **Great American Music Hall**, 859 O'Farrell Street, San Francisco, 415-885-0750
- **Greek Theater**, UC Berkeley (near football stadium), Berkeley, 510-642-9988
- **Oakland Coliseum & Arena**, Hegenberger Road and I-880, Oakland, 510-639-7700
- **Shoreline Amphitheatre**, 1 Amphitheater Parkway, Mountain View, 650-962-1000
- **Warfield Theatre**, 982 Market Street, San Francisco, 415-775-7722

NIGHTCLUBS

We offer you a list of places to get you started though this list is by no means comprehensive. Call ahead: here today, gone tomorrow is often the case in this fast-paced scene.

SAN FRANCISCO
- **Annabelle's**, 77 4th Street, 415-777-1200, jazz
- **Bahia Cabana**, 1600 Market Street, 415-861-4202, salsa, Brazilian
- **Biscuits & Blues**, 401 Mason Street 415-292-2583, blues
- **Bottom of the Hill**, 1233 17th Street, 415-621-4455, rock, hip-hop, blues
- **Cafe du Nord**, 2170 Market Street, 415-861-5016, rock, hip-hop, blues, jazz
- **Club Dread**, 401 6th Street, 415-284-6331, world music, reggae
- **Edinburgh Castle**, 950 Geary Street, 415-885-4074, rock, hip-hop, blues
- **Elbo Room**, 647 Valencia Street, 415-552-7788, rock, hip-hop, blues, jazz
- **Fillmore**, 1805 Geary Boulevard, 415-346-6000, rock, hip-hop, blues
- **Gathering Cafe**, 1326 Grant Street, 415-433-4247, world music, reggae
- **Hotel Utah**, 500 4th Street, 415-421-8308, rock, hip-hop, blues
- **Mick's Lounge**, 2513 Van Ness Avenue, 415-928-0404, rock, blues
- **Noe Valley Ministry**, 1021 Sanchez Street, 415-454-5238, rock, blues, jazz
- **Paradise Lounge**, 1501 Folsom Street, 415-861-6906, rock, hip-hop, blues, country
- **Pearl's**, 256 Columbus Avenue, 415-291-8255, jazz
- **Plough & Stars**, 116 Clement Street, 415-751-1122, Irish music
- **Radio Valencia**, 1199 Valencia Street, 415-826-1199, rock, hip-hop, blues jazz
- **Slim's**, 333 11th Street, 415-522-0333, rock, hip-hop, blues
- **330 Ritch**, 330 Ritch Street, 415-541-9574, world music, reggae

NORTH BAY
- **19 Broadway**, 17 Broadway, Fairfax, 415- 459-1091, open seven nights a week, with two shows nightly, rock to raga.
- **Sweetwater**, 153 Throckmorton Drive, Mill Valley, 415-388-2820, a Marin fixture, this place has national and international musical acts.

EAST BAY

- **Ashkenaz**, 1317 San Pablo Avenue, Berkeley, 510-525-5054, rock, hip-hop, blues, world, country
- **Freight & Salvage**, 1111 Addison Street, Berkeley, 510-548-1761, rock, blues
- **Kimball's East**, Emeryville Public Market, Emeryville, 510-658-0606, jazz
- **La Pena Cultural Center**, 3105 Shattuck, Berkeley, 510-849-2568, hip-hop, soul, world
- **Starry Plough**, 3101 Shattuck Avenue, Berkeley, 510-841-2082, country, world
- **Yoshi's**, 6030 Claremont Avenue, Oakland, 510-652-2900, jazz

PENINSULA

- **Fanny and Alexander**, 412 Emerson Street, Palo Alto, 650-326-7183, rock
- **Los Altos Bar and Grill**, 169 Main Street, Los Altos, 650-948-4332, rock, jazz, etc.
- **Pioneer Salon**, 2925 Woodside Road, Woodside, 650-851-8487, country, rock

SOUTH BAY

- **Boswell's**, Pruneyard Shopping Center, 1875 South Bascom, Campbell, 408-371-4404, rock
- **Cactus Club**, 417 South First Street, Santa Clara, 408-491-9300, rock, hip-hop
- **J.J.'s Blues**, 14 2nd Street, San Jose, 408-286-3066, rock/hip-hop/blues

SWING

Swing is the in thing here and has been for the last several years. What was an underground youth movement has caught the imagination of old timers, former hippies, young people, and everyone in between. There are numerous swing bands, swing street fairs, swing clubs, and now the old swank night spots like Bimbos, and Top of the Mark hire young swing bands to keep their patrons hopping. Vintage clothing stores have run out of original 1940s swing attire so smart young designers are making their own replicas of everything from zoot suits to flattering floral print rayons for the gals. Almost every venue hosts pre-event dance classes for the beginner. So there's no excuse not to lindy. Contact www.sonicswing.com for Bay Area wide classes and venues.

COMEDY

There's a lot to laugh about in life, and San Francisco provides ample opportunity to do so at a number of comedy clubs. Some headline the big names in modern comedy, including local-boys-made-good Robin Williams, Will Durst, Bobby Slayton and female-funnies Ellen DeGeneres, Carrie Snow, Margaret

Cho and Marga Gomez. Others offer open-mike opportunities for up-and-coming jokesters. If your funny bone needs tickling here are a few of the places you may want to visit for comic relief:

- **Cobb's**, 2801 Leavenworth Street, San Francisco, 415-928-4320
- **Josie's**, 3583 16th Street, San Francisco, 415-861-7933
- **Punch Line**, 444 Battery Street, San Francisco, 415-397-7573
- **Rooster T. Feathers**, 157 West El Camino Real, Sunnyvale, 408-736-0921
- **Maestro's**, 2323 San Ramon Valley Boulevard, San Ramon, 925-743-1500
- **The Last Laugh**, 150 South First Street, San Jose, 408-287-5255

If comedy is your bag you'll want to plan for the *San Francisco Examiner's* Comedy Celebration Day in Golden Gate Park. It's held every July and features dozens of comedians doing their thing for free. Thousands of people come by car, bus, bike, skateboard, etc. to take in the event. Call the *Examiner* for more information at 415-777-2424.

MUSEUMS

San Francisco is blessed with excellent art museums, most notably: the M.H. de Young Memorial Museum and the Asian Art Museum, both in Golden Gate Park, the new San Francisco Museum of Modern Art at Yerba Buena Gardens, and the newly remodeled California Palace of the Legion of Honor in Lincoln Park. Those are the big ones. Throughout the Bay Area there are also many smaller art museums and galleries, as well as museums related to history, culture, and science, and interesting one-of-a-kind centers. Here's a sampling:

ART MUSEUMS

SAN FRANCISCO/NORTH BAY

- **African-American Museum**, Fort Mason, Building C, 415-441-0640
- **Ansel Adams Center**, a must-see for any serious photographer or amateur photo buff. The center features photographs taken by its namesake and others, and has a well-stocked bookstore. Located at 240 4th Street, San Francisco, 415-495-7000. Open seven days, 11 a.m. to 5 p.m. Admission: $5 for adults, $3 for students, $2 for youths and seniors, free for those under 13.
- **Asian Art Museum**, featuring artwork, ceramics, architectural displays, jade and textiles from China, Korea, India, Tibet, Japan and Southeast Asia. This is the largest museum of its type on the West Coast and is indicative of the Bay Area's large Asian population, 415-379-8801. Open Tuesday-Sunday, 9:30 a.m. to 5 p.m. Admission: $7 adults, $5 seniors, $4 youths.
- **California Palace of the Legion of Honor**, a beautiful building perched

atop a hill in Lincoln Park, it was given to the city in 1924 by the Spreckels family as a monument to the state's war dead. The art collection features European art from the medieval to the 20th century including a cast of Rodin's *The Thinker*, which sits outside the main entrance, 415-863-3330. Open Tuesday-Sunday, 9:30 a.m. to 5 p.m., second Wednesday of the month is free. Admission: $8, $6 for seniors, and $5 for students, under age 12 free.

- **Headlands Center for the Arts**, 944 Fort Barry, Sausalito, 415-331-2787, www.headlands.org

- **M.H. de Young Museum**, named for Michael de Young, a former publisher of the *San Francisco Chronicle*, this museum has been located in Golden Gate Park since construction of the park began in 1917. It features American works from Colonial to Modern, as well as African, British, Egyptian, Greek, Roman, and Asian items. The museum is also the site of many lectures and gala events. The current building is not earthquake retrofitted so exhibits are limited by insurance considerations. A new building is in the works with a scheduled completion date of 2005. Call 415-863-3330 or 415-750-7645 for more information. Open Wednesday-Sunday, $7 adults, $5 for seniors, and $4 for students, under age 12 free. Free admission the first Wednesday of the month.

- **Mexican Museum**, the oldest (at merely 25) and largest (at 10,000 objects) collection of Mexican and Chicano art in the country moves from cramped quarters to new digs at Yerba Buena Gardens sometime in 2001. Until then it will continue to display works by the likes of Diego Rivera and Nahum Zenil in the Fort's Building D. Fort Mason is in the Marina District. Call the museum at 415-441-0404. Hours of operation: 12 p.m. to 5 p.m., Wednesday-Friday; Saturday and Sunday, 11 a.m. to 5 p.m. Closed Monday and Tuesday. Admission: $4, $3 for seniors and students, under age 12 free.

- **Museo Italoamericano**, Fort Mason, Building C, 415-673-2200, admission: $3, $2 for seniors and students, under age 12.

- **Performing Arts Library and Museum**, 399 Grove, 415-255-4800

- **SF Craft and Folk Art Museum**, Fort Mason, 415-775-0990

- **San Francisco Museum of Modern Art (SFMOMA)** at Yerba Buena Gardens is one of the most exciting buildings in the city. Swiss architect Mario Botta designed the building, and its massive cylindrical skylight is a sight to behold. Exhibits include works by Henri Matisse, Pablo Picasso and Jackson Pollock, to name just three. SFMOMA was the West Coast's first museum dedicated solely to 20th century art. Located at 151 3rd Street, 415-357-4000. Hours of operation: Monday, Tuesday, Friday, Saturday, Sunday, 11 a.m. to 6 p.m. Admission: $9 for adults, $6 for seniors, $5 for students, under age 12 free. Free on the first Tuesday of the month.

- **Yerba Buena Center for the Arts**, 701 Mission Street, 415-978-2700, open 11 a.m. to 6 p.m., seven days. Admission: $5 adults, $3 for students and seniors, under age 12 free.

EAST BAY

- **Judah Magnes Museum**, 291 Russell Street, Berkeley, Jewish art and objects, 510-549-6950, open Sunday-Thursday, 10 a.m. to 4 p.m. Admission: $3.
- **Oakland Museum**, 1000 Oak Street, 510-238-2200, California art and history, open Wednesday-Saturday, 10 a.m. to 5 p.m., closed Monday. Admission: $6 for adults, $4 for seniors and students, under age 12 free.
- **University Art Museum and Pacific Film Archive**, 2626 Bancroft Way, Berkeley, 510-642-0808, open Wednesday-Sunday, 11 a.m. to 5 p.m., until 9 p.m. Thursdays. Admission: $6 adults, $4 for youths, students, and seniors.
- **Urban Sculpture Garden**, Harrison and Fifth streets, Oakland

PENINSULA/SOUTH BAY

- **American Museum of Quilts and Textiles**, 766 South Second Street, San Jose, 408-971-0323, features contemporary and traditional quilt making and textile design.
- **De Saisset Museum**, Santa Clara University, 408-554-4528
- **Palo Alto Cultural Center**, 1313 Newell Street, 650-329-2366, features contemporary local artwork
- **San Jose Museum of Art**, 110 South Market Street, San Jose, 408-294-2787, features 20th century traveling exhibits.
- **San Jose Institute of Contemporary Art**, 451 South First Street, San Jose, 408-283-8155
- **Triton Museum of Art**, 1505 Warburton Avenue, Santa Clara, 408-247-3754, features modern art.

HISTORY AND CULTURAL MUSEUMS AND CENTERS

- **California History Center**, 21250 Steven's Creek Boulevard, Cupertino, 408-864-8712
- **Cartoon Art Museum**, 814 Mission Street, San Francisco 415-227-8666
- **Cable Car Museum**, get a close look at the history and inner workings of the nation's only moving landmark, San Francisco's world famous cable cars. Located at Washington and Mason streets in San Francisco, 1201 Mason Street, 415-474-1887, www.cablecarmuseum.com.
- **Chinese Historical Society of America**, San Francisco's Chinatown has long been one of the largest Chinese communities in the country, and this small museum is dedicated to the Chinese-American story. Located at 650 Commercial Street, San Francisco, 415-391-1188.
- **Chinese Cultural Center**, Holiday Inn, Third Floor, 750 Kearny Street, San Francisco, 415-986-1822
- **Cupertino Historical Museum**, 10185 North Stelling Road, Cupertino, 408-973-1495

- **Falkirk Cultural Center**, 1408 Mission, San Rafael, 415-485-3328
- **Jack London Square and Village**, Embarcadero between Alice and Broadway in Oakland, here you'll find shops and restaurants as well as a museum of African Antiquities. The **Jack London Museum** is at 30 Jack London Square.
- **Jewish Museum**, this modest historical museum doubles as an art museum featuring works by Jewish artists. Located at 121 Steuart Street, San Francisco, 415-543-8880.
- **Marin County Historical Society**, 1125 B Street, San Rafael, 415-454-8538
- **Maritime Museum**, Aquatic Park, San Francisco, 415-556-3002
- **Mission San Rafael**, 1104 5th Avenue, San Rafael, 415-456-3016
- **Museum of American Heritage**, 351 Homer Avenue, Palo Alto, 650-321-1004, historical tableaux of day-to-day life
- **Museum of the City of San Francisco**, 2801 Leavenworth Street, San Francisco, 415-928-0289
- **Pacific Bell Museum**, 140 New Montgomery Street, San Francisco, 415-542-0182
- **Paramount Theatre**, 2025 Broadway, Oakland, tours available, call 510-893-2300.
- **Peralta Adobe**, 154 West St. John Street, San Jose, 408-993-8182
- **North Beach Museum**, 1435 Stockton Street, in the Bayview Bank, San Francisco, 415-391-6210
- **San Francisco Fire Department Museum**, 655 Presidio Avenue, San Francisco, 415-558-3546
- **San Jose Historical Museum**, 1600 Senter Road, San Jose, 408-287-2290
- **Santa Clara de Asis Mission**, Franklin and Market, San Jose, 408-554-4023
- **Santa Clara Historical Museum**, 1509 Warburton Avenue, Santa Clara, 408-248-2787
- **Saratoga Historical Museum**, 20450 Saratoga Los Gatos Road, 408-867-4311

SCIENCE MUSEUMS & ZOOS

The Bay Area is a world scientific research center, home to the Lawrence Livermore and Lawrence Berkeley Laboratories, medical research facilities at UCSF, and Stanford University Medical Center. In Silicon Valley, and elsewhere in the Bay Area, the next generation of computer, communications, and medical technologies are being developed. That said you don't have to be a tech guru or rocket scientist to enjoy the abundant science museums in the Bay Area. Below is a partial list:

SAN FRANCISCO
- **California Academy of Sciences**, located in a sprawling building in

Golden Gate Park right across the street from the de Young art museum, was founded in 1853 and is the oldest scientific institution in the western United States. The facility includes the **Morrison Planetarium**, and the **Steinhart Aquarium**. One of the aquarium's most popular attractions is the Fish Roundabout that allows you to watch as all manner of water creatures, including shark, bat rays, and eel glide around you in a one hundred thousand gallon tank. There are astounding displays of reptiles and amphibians, as well as a varied display of underwater plant-life. Call 415-750-7145, for information on the academy and the aquarium. For information on activities at the planetarium call 415-750-7141. Open daily, 10 a.m. to 5 p.m.

- **Exploratorium**, located in the Palace of Fine Arts in the Marina district, this is a true "hands on" scientific experience for everyone. There are nearly 700 exhibits, many of them interactive, and all highly educational. One of the most popular attractions is the Tactile Dome. Reservations are required for the opportunity to tumble around inside this darkened dome, where you rely on nothing but touch and sound. Located at 3601 Lyon Street, 415-563-7337. Open Tuesday-Sunday, 10 a.m. to 5 p.m.
- **San Francisco Zoo**, this 65-acre facility is perhaps best known for its koalas and Gorilla World. The koalas are a real treat to see as they cling, fast asleep, to their habitat's eucalyptus branches. The gorilla display is reportedly one of the world's largest. There's also a Children's Zoo, which allows kids to pet some of the animals, and an Insect Zoo. Located on Sloat Boulevard at 45th Avenue, 415-753-7080. Open daily, 10 a.m. to 5 p.m.
- **Underwater World**, opened in 1996 at the tourist magnet of Pier 39, this attraction takes visitors literally into the aquarium through a long, inches thick, viewing tunnel. All around you the aquarium's residents glide by in an environment that can make you feel as though it is people, rather than fish, that are on display, 415-623-5300. Open Monday-Friday, 10 a.m. to 6 p.m., Saturday and Sunday, 10 a.m. to 7 p.m.

NORTH BAY

- **Bay Area Discovery Museum**, located under the Golden Gate Bridge, 415-289-7296, hands on exhibits for kids.
- **San Francisco Bay Model**, 2100 Bridgeway, Sausalito, 415-332-3870, open Tuesday-Saturday, 9 a.m. to 4 p.m., no charge.

EAST BAY

- **Holt Planetarium-Lawrence Hall of Science**, Centennial Drive, Berkeley, 510-642-5132
- **Oakland Zoo**, 580 East Golf Links Road, Oakland, 510-632-9525
- **UC Berkeley Botanical Gardens Centennial Drive**, 510-642-3343, offers plants and hiking trails

SOUTH BAY

- **Intel Museum**, 2200 Mission College Boulevard, Santa Clara, 408-765-0503
- **Hiller Aviation Museum**, 601 Sky Way, San Carlos, 650-654-0200
- **Lick Observatory**, Mount Hamilton, San Jose, 408-274-5061
- **Los Gatos Museum**, 4 Tait Avenue, Los Gatos, 408-354-2646
- **Minolta Planetarium**, 21250 Stevens Creek Boulevard, Cupertino, 408-864-8814
- **NASA Ames Research Center**, Moffet Field, Mountain View, 650-654-0200
- **Stanford Linear Accelerator**, 2275 Sand Hill Road, Menlo Park, 650-926-2204
- **The Tech Museum of Innovation**, 201 South Market Street, San Jose, 408-795-6100

LITERARY LIFE

BOOKSTORES

The Bay Area has all the national chain bookstores, but also you will find a large number of good independent, specialized, and used bookstores, many of which host author readings and other literary programs. Check their bulletin boards or get on their mailing lists to be notified of upcoming events. Below is a list of just some of these, though once you move here, you'll probably discover many more. The university towns of Palo Alto and Berkeley have many good new and used bookstores encircling their campuses. Here are some of the familiar standards as well as a few interesting local independents worth visiting. Unless otherwise noted, the following establishments are in San Francisco.

- **Black Oak Books**, 1491 Shattuck Avenue, Berkeley, 510-486-0698
- **Builder's Booksource**, architectural, design, and construction books for the amateur and professional; 900 North Point, Ghirardelli Square, 415-440-5773; 1817 Fourth Street, Berkeley, 510-845-6874
- **Citylights Bookstore**, 261 Columbus Avenue, 415-362-8193, www.citylights.com
- **A Clean, Well Lighted Place for Books**, 601 Van Ness, 415-441-6670
- **Cody's Books, Inc.**, 2454 Telegraph Avenue, Berkeley, 510-845-7852
- **Get Lost Books**, 1825 Market Street, 415-437-0529
- **Green Apple Books and Music**, 506 Clement Street, 415-387-2272
- **9th Avenue Books**, 1348 9th Avenue, 415-665-2938
- **Moe's Bookstore**, 2476 Telegraph Avenue, Berkeley, 510-849-2087
- **Nolo Press Outlet Bookstore**, 950 Parker Street, Berkeley, 510-704-2248
- **Rand McNally Map and Travel Store**, 595 Market Street, 415-777-3131

- **Thomas Bros. Maps and Books**, 550 Jackson Street, 415-981-7520, 800-969-3072, www.thomas.com

BOOKSTORE CHAINS

- **B. Dalton Bookseller**, 200 Kearny, San Francisco, 415-956-2850; 20510 Stevens Creek Boulevard, Cupertino, 408-257-5530; Eastridge Shopping Center, San Jose, 408-270-1070; Oakridge Mall, San Jose, 408-226-0387; Hilltop Mall, Richmond, 510-233-7942; Northgate Mall, San Rafael, 415-479-4511
- **Barnes and Noble**, 2550 Taylor Street, San Francisco, 415- 292-6762; 1940 South El Camino Real, San Mateo, 650-312-9066; Hamilton Plaza, Campbell, 408-559-8101; 2352 Shattuck Avenue, Berkeley, 510-644-0861; 2020 Redwood Highway, Greenbrae, 415-924-1016
- **Books Inc.**, www.booksinc.net, specialize in discounted books. They have a good cookbook section. Stanford Shopping Center, Palo Alto, 650-321-0600; 3515 California Street, San Francisco, 415-221-3666
- **Borders Books and Music**, 15 Ranch Drive, Milpitas, 408-934-1180; 400 Post Street, San Francisco, 415-399-1633; 5903 Shellmound, Emeryville, 510-654-1633; 588 West Francisco Boulevard, San Rafael, 415-454-1400
- **Stacey's** are known for their business books: 581 Market Street, San Francisco, 415-421-4687 or 800-926-6511; 19625 Stevens Creek Road, Cupertino, 408-253-7521
- **WaldenBooks**, 1150 El Camino Real, San Bruno, 650-583-7717; Vallco Shopping Center, Cupertino, 408-255-0602

MOVIES—ART, REVIVAL, INTERNATIONAL

Mainstream theaters showing the latest Hollywood blockbusters are located throughout the Bay Area—some of which still offer bargain matinees in the afternoon. Below is a list of harder-to-find "art houses" which specialize in foreign and/or alternative films.

SAN FRANCISCO
- **Bridge**, 3010 Geary Boulevard, 415-352-0810
- **Castro**, Castro Street near Market Street, 415- 621-6120
- **Clay**, Fillmore Street near Clay Street, 415-352-0810
- **Embarcadero**, 1 Embarcadero Center, 415-352-0810
- **Four Star**, Clement Street and 23rd Avenue, 415-666-3488
- **Gateway**, 215 Jackson Street, 415-352-0810
- **Lumiere**, California Street near Polk Street, 415-352-0810
- **Opera Plaza**, Van Ness and Golden Gate avenues, 415-352-0810

- **Red Vic**, 1727 Haight Street, 415-668-3994
- **Roxie**, 3117 16th Street, 415- 863-1087
- **San Francisco Cinematheque**, 701 Mission, 415-558-8129
- **Vogue**, Sacramento Street and Presidio Boulevard, 415-221-8183

SURROUNDING BAY AREA
- **Stanford Theater**, 221 University Avenue, Palo Alto, 650-324-3700
- **Camera One and Camera Three**, 366 South First Street and 288 South Second Street, San Jose, 408-998-3005
- **Los Gatos Cinemas**, 41 Santa Cruz Avenue, Los Gatos, 408-395-0203
- **Towne Theatre**, 1433 The Alameda, San Jose, 408-287-1433
- **Rafael Film Center**, 1118 Fourth Street, San Rafael, 415-454-1222
- **Elmwood Fine Arts Cinema**, 2451 Shattuck Avenue, Berkeley, 510-848-1143
- **New Pacific Film Archive Theater**, 2725 Bancroft Avenue, Berkeley, 510-642-1412
- **UC Theatre**, 2063 University Avenue, Berkeley, 510-843-6267

FILM FESTIVALS

The Bay Area hosts several annual film festivals. If you're a film buff, you'll want to mark your calendar.
- **San Francisco Asian Film Festival** (March), 415-863-0814
- **San Francisco International Film Festival** (April), 415-931-3456
- **International Lesbian & Gay Film Festival** (June), 415-703-8650
- **Jewish Film Festival** (July), 510-548-0556
- **Festival Cine Latino** (September), 415-553-8135
- **Mill Valley Film Festival** (October), 415-383-5256

CULTURE FOR KIDS

There is so much for kids to do culturally in the Bay Area that they'll grow up before they can try it all. Beside numerous technical, history, science, nature, ethnic, and art museums there are dozens of dance, theater, poetry, and musical performances aimed at or comprised of children. Now that schools are less inclined to offer an array of language classes, kids can learn another language at some of the local cultural institutes as well. During the holidays the **San Francisco Ballet** performs their version of "The Nutcracker" and the **ODC** performs a modern version of the "Velveteen Rabbit." This smattering of listings for events and places that children might enjoy represents only a little of what the Bay Area has to offer.

For more ideas on how to entertain the kids see the **Quick Getaways** chapter.

SAN FRANCISCO

- **Exploratorium**, the **San Francisco Zoo**, and **Underwater World**, are made for kids. See descriptions above under **Science/Zoos**.
- **International Children's Art Museum**, Ferry Building, 415-772-1822
- **The Metreon**, 4th and Mission, 415-369-6000, www.metreon.com, offers gardens paths, waterfalls and fountains full of birds, 15 movie theaters, an IMAX theater, restaurants, hot dog stands, shops and theme entertainment, an ice-skating rink, a kid-sized bowling alley, a playground, a merry-go-round. The high-tech museum Zeum, and the Where the Wild Things Are exhibit are interactive attractions with cutaway models showing how things in the world work. Both exhibits are sure to catch the imaginations of young and old alike.
- **Randall Junior Museum**, 199 Museum Way, 415-554-9600, this museum, which features an earthquake exhibit, live animals, art and science programs, films, lectures, concerts, and plays, is a perennial favorite among children. Open 10 a.m. to 5 p.m.

SURROUNDING BAY AREA

- **Marin Dance Theatre**, 1 St. Vincent's Drive, San Rafael, 415-499-8891, children and adult classical ballet classes and performances.
- **Billy Jones, Wildcat Railroad**, Oak Meadow Park, Los Gatos, 408-395-7433
- **Children's Discovery Museum of San Jose**, 180 Woz Way, 408-298-5437, www.cdm.org
- **Emma Prusch Farm Park**, 647 South King Road, San Jose, 408-926-5555
- **Happy Hollow Park and Zoo**, 1300 Senter Road, San Jose 408-295-8383
- **Winchester Mystery House**, 525 South Winchester Boulevard, San Jose, 408-247-2000
- **Barbie Doll Hall of Fame**, 433 Waverly Street, Palo Alto, 650-326-5841
- **Coyote Point Museum for Environmental Education**, Coyote Point Drive, San Mateo, 650-342-7755
- **Palo Alto Junior Museum**, 1451 Middlefield Road, Palo Alto, 650-329-2111
- **Berkeley Youth Orchestra**, 2322 Shattuck Avenue, Berkeley, 510 653-1616
- **Oakland Youth Orchestra**, 1428 Alice Street, Oakland, 510-832-7710
- **Young People's Symphony Orchestra**, Berkeley, 510-849-9776

THE BAY AREA IS ONE OF THE BEST URBAN PLAYGROUNDS IN THE world. With its ocean beaches, wide-open green spaces, nearby mountain ranges, and all the activities that accompany such environs, it may be difficult to decide what to do with your free time. Surfing (with a wet suit) at Ocean Beach is one option, as well as kayaking, windsurfing or rowing—though probably not in the ocean. Biking, hiking and running in either Golden Gate Park, the Presidio, or Mount Tamalpais are popular choices. Bird watching is fabulous at the Palo Alto Baylands; and these are only a few of the opportunities available. However, if all you really want to do on your day off is kick back and be a spectator, you are in luck. The Bay Area has plenty of professional and college teams to cheer on.

PROFESSIONAL

Bay Area sports fans are blessed (although some might say cursed) with professional teams in all of the major leagues: baseball, basketball, football, hockey, and soccer. For the latest, consult the sports section of the *San Francisco Chronicle, Oakland Tribune, Marin Independent Journal* or the *San Jose Mercury News.* In today's electronic world, most professional teams and leagues have web sites filled with up-to-the-minute information about their games and teams.

BASEBALL

One of the Bay Area's most intense sports rivalries exists between the National League **San Francisco Giants** and the American League **Oakland Athletics** (the A's). Each spring the Giants and the A's wind up the preseason by squaring off against each other in the Bay Bridge Series. The last time the A's and Giants met in the World Series was in 1989. That series was disrupted by the October 17th Loma Prieta earthquake that rattled then-Candlestick Park. (The game was canceled, and the A's went on to win the series four games to three.)

- **San Francisco Giants** (National League), Pacific Bell Park, 24 Willie Mays Plaza, San Francisco, CA 94107, 800-5-GIANTS, www.sfgiants.com; the big news for the Giants is their gorgeous new stadium. Completed in March 2000, this 40,800-seat ballpark in China Basin is known as the Pacific Bell Park (PacBell for short). For those wanting to attend a game, there are a number of ways to purchase tickets: online at www.sfgiants.com; at the stadium's Double Play Ticket Window; from Tickets.com/BASS Tickets Outlets, 510-762-BALL; or from any Giants Dugout Store—check the Giants' web site for more details. Individual ticket prices for the 2000 season ranged from $10 for bleacher seats all the way up to $42. Season tickets are difficult, if not impossible, to obtain. For those on a more last-minute schedule, 500 day-of -the-game tickets are available at the stadium, two hours before each scheduled home game. These tickets range in price from $8.50 for adults to $6.00 for seniors (60 and over) and children (14 and under).
- **Oakland Athletics**, (American League), Oakland Coliseum, I-880 and Hegenberger Road, Oakland, 510-638-0500, www.oaklandathletics.com; affectionate and brotherly, rumor has it that members of the A's enjoy playing baseball together so much they are willing to take a pay cut in order to stay on the same team. If this sounds like a fun night out, you can track down tickets several ways: check online at www.tickets.com/BASSOutlets or visit a BASS Ticket Outlet, 510-762-BALL; go to the Oakland Coliseum ticket window or to the A's on Deck Store at the Stoneridge Mall in Pleasanton. Ticket prices for the 2000 season ranged from $5 for bleacher seats to $24 for a Plaza Club seat.

BASKETBALL

The NBA's **Golden State Warriors** play their home games in Oakland's Arena, just off I-880 in Southern Oakland, from November through June. Tickets can be purchased at the Warrior Ticket Office, call 510-986-2222, at any BASS Ticket Outlet or at the Oakland Arena on the day of the game. For more information check the Warriors' web site, www.warriors.com.

FOOTBALL

Similar to the baseball rivalry between the A's and the Giants, competition between the Oakland Raiders and the San Francisco 49ers is fierce. These teams, two of the most successful franchises in the National Football League, rarely play each other because they are in different conferences, but when they do, the air is thick with anticipation and the cheers are passionate and loud.

- The **Raiders** play at the Oakland Coliseum, I-880 and Hegenberger Road, Oakland, 510-638-0500, www.raiders.com. For tickets, call 888-44-

RAIDERS or purchase them at www.Tickets.com/BASS Outlets.

- The **San Francisco 49ers**, www.sf49ers.com, play at 3COM Park (formerly known as Candlestick Park) which is notoriously cold and windy. For tickets call the 49ers' ticket office, 415-468-2249 or write to the Ticket Office, 3COM Park, Room 400, San Francisco, 94124. You can also purchase tickets through Ticketmaster on the web at www.ticketmaster.com, by calling 415-421-8497 or at Ticketmaster outlets such as Tower Records or any Rite Aid location.

HOCKEY

The **San Jose Sharks** of the National Hockey League is the ice-hockey team for the Bay Area. Pre-season starts in September; the season runs until April. They play in the San Jose Arena, affectionately known as the "Shark Tank." Tickets for the Sharks are available at the arena ticket office, 408-999-5757, at Ticketmaster locations: Tower Records and Rite Aids, 415-421-8497 or on the web, www.ticketmaster.com. Consult the Sharks' web site, www.sj-sharks.com, for more information.

HORSE RACING

Pack your mint juleps and don your Kentucky Derby hat—horse racing is not far from San Francisco. You have two choices: just across the bay you can attend **Golden Gate Fields**, located at 1100 Eastshore Highway, in the City of Albany. Entrance fees range from $3 to $15, depending on the location of your viewing stand. Fall season runs from November to January, and spring season from April to June. For more information call 510-559-7300. On the Peninsula, you can bet on the horses at **Bay Meadows**, 2600 South Delaware Street, San Mateo, 650-574-7223. Take CalTrain from the Peninsula, South Bay, or San Francisco right to the tracks.

SOCCER

The year 1996 brought professional soccer to the Bay Area for the first time in years, in the form of Major League Soccer's San Jose Clash. At the inaugural match against DC United, the Clash won, 1-0. Today, the renamed **San Jose Earthquakes**, www.sjearthquakes.com, play at Spartan Stadium on 7th Street, just south of downtown San Jose. The season runs from April through September. For ticket information call the San Jose Earthquakes' ticket sales office at 408-985-4625.

In 2001 the Bay Area welcomed the newly formed professional women's soccer team, the **Cyber Rays**, to compete in the Women's United Soccer Association (WUSA) league. At the time of this writing, the Cyber Rays were expected to play most of their games at Spartan Stadium (see above under San

Jose Earthquakes). For more information, contact the Cyber Rays at www.bayareacyberrays.com.

COLLEGE SPORTS

If you'd like to watch the sports stars of tomorrow, check out one of the Bay Area college or university teams. Probably the most closely followed collegiate sports contest in the Bay Area is football's annual Big Game that pits the **University of California Golden Bears** against the **Stanford Cardinal**. It's usually a spirited event, and a consistent sellout, so get your tickets early.

Another popular attraction is the Stanford women's basketball team. Under Coach Tara VanDerveer, the Stanford women have been one of the best teams in the country, and Cardinal fans are hoping that trend continues. **Stanford University** plays basketball at Maples Pavilion, football at Stanford Stadium, both located on the university campus in Palo Alto. For information call 800-STANFORD or check www.gostanford.com. **University of California at Berkeley** plays basketball in the Harmon Arena, football at Memorial Stadium, both on the Berkeley campus. For more information call 800-462-3277 or check www.berkeley.edu.

The following schools also stage sporting events:
- **San Francisco State University**, 415-338-2218
- **St. Mary's College**, 925-631-4392
- **Santa Clara University**, 408-554-4063
- **San Jose State University**, 877-757-8849

PARTICIPANT SPORTS & ACTIVITIES

The Bay Area is a haven for sports enthusiasts. Popular activities include walking, running, biking, hiking, camping, sailing, tennis, baseball, football, soccer, swimming, lifting weights, and aerobics. Crissy Field in the Golden Gate National Recreation Area is home to some of the world's best windsurfing, and Mount Tamalpais and the Marin Headlands have excellent hiking and biking trails. Area **Parks and Recreation Departments** can assist those interested in specific programs (also see following, under **Baseball/Softball** for city parks departments):
- **California Department of Parks and Recreation**, P.O. Box 942896, Sacramento, California, 94296, 916-653-6995, www.cal-parks.ca.gov
- **East Bay Regional Park District**, 2950 Peralta Oaks Court, P.O. Box 5381, Oakland, 94605, 510-562-PARK, www.ebparks.org
- **Mid-Peninsula Regional Open Space District**, 330 Distel Circle, Los Altos, CA 94022-1404, 650-691-1200, www.openspace.org
- **San Francisco Recreation and Park Department**, 501 Stanyon Street, San Francisco, 94117-1898, 800-990-9777, www.parks.sfgov.org

- **Santa Clara County Park and Recreation**, 298 Garden Hill Drive, Los Gatos, CA 95032-7669; 408-358-3741, www.parkhere.org

BASEBALL/SOFTBALL

Play ball! There are a number of softball and baseball leagues around the Bay Area. The Northern California Amateur Softball Association sponsors slow and fast pitch adult and junior leagues. Visit their web site at www.nor-calstate-asa.org, or contact the individual ASA commissioners in the county nearest your new home: San Francisco, 501 Stanyon, 415-554-9524; Oakland, 1099 East Street; Hayward, 510-881-6723; Santa Clara, 515 Junipero Avenue; Pacific Grove, 831-648-3130.

For Little Leagues contact, www.littleleague.org, and for Pony Leagues contact www.scponybaseball.org, 408-369-8095.

City parks and recreation departments are another good place to look for baseball and softball games. The numbers listed below can help you get started:

SAN FRANCISCO
- **Golden Gate Sport and Social Club**, 1766 Union Street, 415-921-1233 www.sportandsocialclubs.com
- **San Francisco Parks and Recreation**, 415-753-7022, www.softball.com
- **San Francisco, Sausalito and Marin City Little League**, 415-263-0510, www.wenet.net

EAST BAY
- **Berkeley Community Services, Park and Recreation Department**, Berkeley, 510-644-6530
- **Oakland Park and Recreation Department**, Oakland, 510-238-3187
- **Pony League**, Fremont, www.fremontbaseball.org
- **Shockers Girls Fastpitch Inc.**, 3856 Bayview Circle, Concord, 925-687-1828
- **Blue Ice Girls Softball Club**, a non-profit, girls (ages 8 to 16) fast pitch club out of Walnut Creek; P.O. Box 3542, Antioch, 94531, 925-778-1048

PENINSULA/SOUTH BAY
- **Belmont Recreation**, 1225 Ralston Avenue, Belmont, 650-595-7441
- **Brisbane Recreation**, 50 Park Lane, Brisbane, 415-467-6330
- **Cupertino Parks and Recreation Department**, Cupertino, 408-777-3129
- **Daly City Parks and Recreation**, 111 Lake Merced Boulevard, Daly City, 650-991-8003
- **Foster City Parks**, 650 Shell Boulevard, Foster City, 650-286-3392
- **Menlo Park**, 701 Laurel Street, Menlo Park, 650-858-3484
- **Milbrae Recreation**, 477 Lincoln Circle, Millbrae, 650-259-2368
- **Pacifica Recreation**, 170 Santa Maria Avenue, Pacifica, 650-738-0564
- **Pony League of San Jose**, 408-536-0657, www.sjpacificponybaseball.org

- **Redwood City Recreation**, 1120 Roosevelt Avenue, Redwood City, 650-780-7317
- **San Bruno Recreation**, 567 El Camino Real, San Bruno, 650-616-7182
- **San Carlos Recreation**, 1017 Cedar Street, San Carlos, 650-802-4475
- **San Mateo Recreation**, 2001 Pacific Boulevard, San Mateo, 650-377-4733

BASKETBALL

San Francisco has a professional/amateur basketball league, one for men and one for women. Teams play at Kezar Pavillion on Stanyon and Waller. Check www.sanfranciscoproam.com for information about dates and times. For something a little less competitive, check with your local parks and recreation department (see above) or try your community gymnasium or health club, which may have its own league. Among other neighborhood basketball programs are the Eureka Valley's league, 415-554-9528, and the SOMA league, 415-554-9528. The Sunset has a men's over-35 league, 415-753-7098. For more information about basketball games and leagues going on throughout the US, check www.hoopsnation.com.

BICYCLING

There are numerous biking trails and bike lanes throughout the Bay Area offering a wide variety of terrain and views. One of the most exciting developments in recent years is the installation of a biking/walking trail ringing the entire bay. While only portions of this so-called Bay Trail have been built to date, supporters insist it will eventually be completed, and will be a definite boon to cyclists.

According to California law, bike riders younger than 18 must wear a bike helmet. Violators are subject to fines.

If pro-bicycle activism interests you, consider joining the local Critical Mass campaign. Since 1992, this bicyclists' movement (they adamantly call themselves a "movement" and not a "group") have taken to the streets on the last Friday of every month. Literally hundreds (sometimes thousands) gather at Justin Herman Plaza and then bicycle, en masse, through the city streets. Their goal is to make their presence known, in the hope that drivers will be more courteous and city leaders will be inspired to make the streets safer for cyclists. This monthly "movement" usually has a police escort to protect them from irate drivers who resent being held up by the group.

Some of the best biking in **San Francisco** is in Golden Gate Park, along the Embarcadero and the Golden Gate Promenade beneath the south end of the Golden Gate Bridge. The stretch runs from the Marina, all the way to Fort Point. For more information about trails in San Francisco, bicycle groups, and resources call the **San Francisco Bicycle Coalition**, 1095 Market Street, room 215, 94103, 415-431-BIKE, www.sfbike.org.

The South Bay and the Peninsula have more than 440 miles of biking trails. On the **Peninsula**, the Long Ridge Open Space Preserve provides lovely views, great oaks, grassy knolls, and some of the best single track riding in the area. The trail parallels Skyline Boulevard between Page Mill Road and Highway 9. Another great ride is along Montebello Road just off Stevens Canyon Road in **Cupertino**. Here, you'll find creeks, steep hills, and the Ridge Winery. Upper Steven's Creek County Park is another spectacular ride with steep canyons amidst hardwood forests. For more information about biking in the mid-Peninsula, contact the **Silicon Valley Bicycle Coalition** at 408-867-9797, www.svbcbikes.org. Another good resource for maps and hooking up with other bikers is through the Trail Center, 650-968-7065, www.trailcenter.org.

Taking your bike across to the biking trails in the **East Bay** and **Marin County** is a fairly easy task as the BART system accommodates bicycles in the last train car, during non-commute hours. Some bus systems also accommodate bikes, as do the many ferryboats that crisscross the bay. Marin Headlands and Mount Tamalpais are fantastic areas to ride. For more information call the **Bicycle Trails Council of Marin**, 415-456-7512. In the East Bay check with **The Bicycle Trail Council for the East Bay**, 510-933-2942. For some exceptional trails try Tilden Park (see under **Hiking**), Redwood Regional Park, Wildcat Canyon, and Briones Park.

There are many bicycle shops in the Bay Area, and the following list of bike shops is by no means complete. Consult your Yellow Pages for more listings:

SAN FRANCISCO
- **Pacific Bicycle**: 4239 Geary Street, 415-666-3377; 1161 Sutter Street, 415-928-8466
- **Start to Finish Bikes**: 2530 Lombard Street, 415-202-9830; Golden Gate Park, 672 Stanyon Street, 415-221-7211; 599 2nd Street, 415-243-8812
- **Valencia Cyclery**, 1077 Valencia, 415-550-6600

NORTH BAY
- **Bicycle Odyssey**, 1417 Bridgeway, Sausalito, 415-332-3050
- **Mike's Bicycle Shop**, 1601 4th Street, San Rafael, 415-454-3747
- **Pacific Bicycle**, 132 Vintage Way, Novato, 415-892-9319
- **Start to Finish**, 116 Throckmorton Avenue, Mill Valley, 415-388-3500

EAST BAY
- **Alameda Bicycle**, 1522 Park Street, Alameda, 510-522-0070
- **Missing Link**, 1988 Shattuck Avenue, Berkeley, 510-843-7471
- **Start-to-Finish**, 2200 Bancroft Avenue, Berkeley, 510-704-1000
- **REI Inc. Bicycle Department**, 1338 San Pablo Avenue, Berkeley, 510-527-4140

PENINSULA/SOUTH BAY
- **Cupertino Bike Shop**, 19685 Stevens Creek Boulevard, Cupertino, 408-399-9142
- **Pacific Bicycle**, 101 Blossom Hill Road, San Jose, 408-264-3570
- **Summit Bicycles**, 111 East Main Street, Los Gatos, 408-399-9142

BOWLING

Some might argue that it's not quite a sport, but few would argue that it's a lot of fun. While San Francisco is woefully under-bowled (there are two bowling alleys in the whole city), you can find more opportunities in the rest of the Bay Area:
- **Japantown Bowl**, 1790 Post, San Francisco, 415-921-6200; boasts 40 lanes, a coffee shop, lounge, satellite TV, and best of all, three free hours of validated parking at the Japan Center Garage across the street.
- **The Rooftop at Yerba Buena Center Gardens-Ice Skating and Bowling Center**, 750 Folsom Street, San Francisco, Skating Center, 415-777-3727
- **Presidio National Park Bowl**, Building #93 (between the Presidio's Moraga and Montgomery streets), San Francisco, 415-561-2695
- **Albany Bowl**, 540 San Pablo Avenue, Albany, 510-526-8818
- **AMF Bowling Center**, 300 Park Avenue, Alameda, 510-523-6767
- **Moonlight Lanes**, 2780 El Camino Real, Santa Clara, 408-296-7200
- **Saratoga Lanes**, 1585 Saratoga Avenue, San Jose, 408-252-2212
- **AMF Fiesta Lanes**, 1523 West San Carlos, San Jose, 408-294-2810
- **Fourth Street Bowl**, 1441 North Fourth Street, San Jose, 408-453-5555

BUNGEE JUMPING

- **Icarus Bungee**, P.O. Box 801, Alameda 510-521-5867; established in 1990, holds jumps off 14 different bridges throughout Northern California, perfect safety record. In 2000, the charge was $85 per person for two jumps.
- **Mach 1 Bungee Jumping**, P.O. Box 1971, San Leandro, 510-729-1743; holds jumps off 20 bridges throughout Northern California. Sign up online for a discount, www.bungeebrent.com.

GOLFING

The Bay Area is home to a fantastic array of golf courses.

SAN FRANCISCO
- **Presidio Golf Club**, 300 Finley Road (in the Presidio), 415-561-4653
- **Lincoln Park Golf Course**, 34th Avenue and Clement Street, 415-221-9911
- **Harding Park**, 1 Harding Road, 415-664-4690

- **Mission Bay Golf Center**, (driving range, putting green) 1200 6th Street, 415-431-7888
- **Olympic Club**, 599 Skyline Boulevard, 415-587-4800

NORTH BAY
- **Peacock Gap Golf & Country Club**, 333 Biscayne Drive, San Rafael, 415-453-3111
- **Mill Valley Golf Course**, 280 Buena Vista Avenue, Mill Valley, 415-388-9982
- **San Geronimo Golf Course**, 5800 Sir Francis Drake Boulevard, San Geronimo, 415-488-4030
- **Marin Country Club**, 500 Country Club Drive, Novato, 415-382-6707
- **McInnis Park Golf Center**, 350 Smith Range Road, San Rafael, 415-492-1800
- **Indian Valley Golf Club**, 3035 Novato Boulevard, Novato, 415-897-1118
- **Mare Island Golf Course**, 1800 Club Drive, Vallejo, 707-644-3888
- **Sonoma Golf Club**, 17887 Carriger Road, Sonoma, 707-996-7255
- **Napa Municipal Golf Course**, 2295 Streblow Drive, Napa, 707-255-4333

EAST BAY
- **Tilden Park Golf Course**, Grizzly Peak Boulevard and Shasta Road, Berkeley, 510-848-7373
- **Chuck Corica Golf Course**, One Clubhouse Memorial Road, Alameda, 510-522-4321
- **Montclair Golf Course**, 2477 Monterey Boulevard, 510-482-0422

PENINSULA/SOUTH BAY
- **Lake Merced Golf and Country Club**, 2300 Junipero Serra Boulevard, 650-755-2233
- **Cypress Golf Course**, 2001 Hillside Boulevard, Colma, 992-5155
- **Blackberry Farm**, 22100 Stevens Creek Boulevard, Cupertino, 408-253-9200
- **Sharp Park Golf Course**, Pacifica, 650-355-8546
- **Half Moon Bay Golf Links**, Highway 1- 2000 Fairway Drive, Half Moon Bay, 650-726-4438
- **Deep Cliff Golf Course**, 10700 Clubhouse Lane, Cupertino, 408-253-5357
- **Crystal Springs Golf Course**, 6650 Golf Course Drive, Burlingame, 650-342-0603
- **Shoreline Golf Links**, 2600 North Shoreline Boulevard, Mountain View, 650-969-2041
- **Del Monte Golf Course**, 1300 Sylvan Road, Monterey, 831-373-2700
- **Pruneridge Golf Club**, 400 Saratoga Avenue, Santa Clara, 408-248-4424
- **San Jose Municipal Golf Course**, 1560 Oakland Road, San Jose, 408-441-4653
- **Pebble Beach Golf Links**, 77 Asilomar Boulevard, Seventeen Mile Drive, Pacific Grove, 831-622-8733

FISHING

There are a large number of fishing spots across the Bay Area (the following only details a smattering of the fishing opportunities). Check with your local outfitter for more ideas.

In San Francisco, people fish for bass, perch, shark, and even crab right off the pier near Crissy Field in the Presidio. The piers near Fisherman's Wharf are also popular fishing spots. Kaplan's Surplus and Sporting Goods, 1055 Market Street, 415-863-0127, is a good source for more information.

Lake Merced is stocked with trout and catfish, and the Lake Merced Boating and Fishing Company, 415-753-1101, sells lures and can provide more information about fishing here. Lake Anza, north of Berkeley, in Tilden Park is open for fishing throughout the year. Oakland's Lake Temescal, located next to the junction of highways 24 and 13, is stocked periodically with rainbow trout. Other fish in Lake Temescal include largemouth bass, red-eared sunfish, bluegill, and catfish.

For those more interested in fishing on the open ocean, check www.sfs-portfishing.com, where the San Francisco Bay Area commercial fishing fleets have pooled charter information onto one page. This web site lists the fleet of boats leaving from the Fisherman's Wharf, Emeryville Marina, Berkeley Marina, Half Moon Bay, Point San Pablo, Sausalito, and San Rafael. The California Department of Fish and Game, 1416 Ninth Street, Sacramento, requires you to obtain a permit/license to fish. You can contact them at 916-227-2245, www.dfg.ca.gov. Or visit your local bait and tackle store.

ULTIMATE FRISBEE

Contact the local **Ultimate Players Associations**, 800-UPA-4384, for more information.

HANG GLIDING/PARAGLIDING

Originated by French Mountain climbers eager to descend the mountain before sundown, paragliding is a popular sport in the Bay Area. Venture down to Fort Funston to watch the paragliders and hang gliders soar through the air.

SAN FRANCISCO
- **Skytimes Paragliding**, P.O. Box 687, Bolinas 94924, 415-868-1330
- **Merlin Flight School**, 415-456-3670, www.merlinflightschool.com
- **Weather Fort Funston**, Skyline Boulevard, 415-333-0100

NORTH BAY
- **Chandelle San Francisco, Inc.**, 220 Shaver Street, San Rafael, 415-454-3464
- **Skytimes Paragliding**, P.O. Box 687, Bolinas, 415-868-1330

EAST BAY
- **San Francisco Hang gliding Center**, 510-528-2300, www.sfhanggliding.com; specializes in tandem flights
- **Glidell Paragliding**, 1266 1/5 Bowlinger Canyon Road, Moraga, 925-377-8810

PENINSULA/SOUTH BAY
- **Glidell Paragliding**, 555 Bryant Street #256, Palo Alto, 650-424-9704
- **Mission Soaring Center**, 1116 Wrigley Way, Milpitas, 408-262-1055
- **Natural Flying**, 17506 Hoot Owl Way, Morgan Hill, 408-779-7976
- **Wings of Rogallo Weather**, Monument Peak, Milpitas, 408-946-9516

HIKING

If taking off for a hike away from the urban bustle is something that strikes your fancy you'll have many opportunities to indulge without straying too far from home. San Francisco offers plenty of hikes, including the famous Golden Gate Bridge walk (the Bridge is about a mile and a half long). Contact the folks at the Golden Gate Bridge Plaza, San Francisco 94129, 415-921-5858, for more details. Longer hikes can be found at **Presidio National Park** in San Francisco. Along the water, Crissy Field is a popular for walking and running. **Marin Headlands**, just beyond the northern end of the Golden Gate Bridge is nice. An enjoyable option for a long afternoon is to take the ferry to **Angel Island** to hike the island. **Mount Tamalpais** in Marin County and **Tilden Park** in the Oakland/Berkeley hills are great places to explore. Drive a little further north (about 90 minutes) to the popular **Point Reyes National Seashore** for exceptional hiking and views.

If you want to escape for more than a day, consider **Yosemite National Park**, located about a four-hour's drive to the east, in the Sierra Nevadas. Yosemite is a popular vacation destination for Bay Area residents, many of whom visit in the fall or early spring to avoid the summer tourist season. Despite what you may have heard about the crowds in the park though, the only consistently crowded part is Yosemite Valley; if you set out on foot for the high country you *can* leave the motor homes behind. Southern Yosemite Mountain Guides, 559-658-TREK, offer guided and catered backpacking adventures. For more park information contact Yosemite National Park, Wilderness Permits, P.O. Box 545, Yosemite, CA 95389, 800-436-7275. **Lake Tahoe** and the **Sierras**, which offer prime hiking and camping, are also about four hours away. Consult with the Forest Service for the best hikes: US Forest Service Information, Room 521, 630 Sansome Street, San Francisco, CA 94111.

HORSEBACK RIDING

Below is a list of some of the stables in the Bay Area.

SAN FRANCISCO/NORTH BAY
- **All Happy Horse**, Marin, 415-491-0623
- **Golden Gate Park Stables**, P.O. Box 22401, Golden Gate Park, John F. Kennedy Drive, San Francisco, 415-668-7360
- **Miwok Livery Stables**, 701 Tennessee Valley Road, Mill Valley, 415-383-8048

EAST BAY
- **Anthony Chabot Equestrian Center**, 14600 Skyline Boulevard, 510-569-4428
- **Grizzly Peak Stables**, 271 Loma Canada Street, Orinda, 925-254-8283
- **Wildcat Creek Stables**, 6102 Park Avenue, Richmond, 510-232-6344

PENINSULA
- **Mar Vista Stable**, 2152 Skyline Boulevard, Daly City, 650-991-4224
- **Palo Mar Stables**, 2116 Skyline Boulevard, Daly City, 650-755-8042
- **Sea Horse & Friendly Acres Ranches**, Half Moon Bay, 650-726-8550
- **Friendly Acres Ranch**, 2150 Cabrillo Highway North, Half Moon Bay, 650-726-9916
- **Portola Farms School**, 1545 Portola Road, Woodside, 650-851-0910
- **Sea Horse & Friendly Acres Horse Rentals**, Coast Highway, Half Moon Bay, 650-726-2362, ksshipley@aol.com

SOUTH BAY
- **Rosebank Equestrian Stables**, 17103 Hicks Road, San Jose, 408-927-0774
- **Bills Pony Ranch**, 5008 Alum Rock Avenue, San Jose, 408-259-0965
- **Brookside Stables**, 12100 Stevens Canyon Road, Cupertino, 408-255-9026
- **Hillcrest Ranch**, 5150 Sheridan Road, Fremont, 510-656-0692

KAYAKING

Sea kayaking is another way to enjoy the Bay. It's best to kayak early in the morning when the water is more likely to be calm.
- **California Adventures**, 2301 Bancroft Way, Berkeley, 510-642-4000
- **California Canoe & Kayak**, 409 Water Street, Oakland, 510-893-7833
- **Blue Waters Kayaking**, Point Reyes National Seashore, Inverness, 415-669-2600

- **Environmental Traveling Companions**, Fort Mason Center, Building C, 415-474-7662
- **Sea Trek Ocean Kayaking Center**, Schoonmaker Point Marina, Sausalito, 415-488-1000, all year

ROCK CLIMBING

To keep your finger muscles in shape, the Bay Area has a number of climbing gyms including:
- **Mission Cliffs**, 2295 Harrison Street, San Francisco, 415-550-0515
- **Berkeley Ironworks**, 800 Potter Street, Berkeley, 510-981-9900
- **Class 5 Climbing and Fitness Club**, 25B Dodie Street, San Rafael, 415-485-6931
- **Vertex Climbing Center**, 3358 A Coffey Lane, Santa Rosa, 707-573-1608
- **Planet Granite Rock Climbing Gym**, 2901 Mead Avenue, Santa Clara, 408-727-2777
- **Twisters Gym**, 2639 Terminal Boulevard, Mountain View, 650-967-5581

SAILING

According to aficionados, the sailing and windsurfing in San Francisco Bay is top-notch. The annual opening day on the Bay brings out hundreds of sailors and spectators each May. Although sailing is possible here year round, this event serves as the ceremonial, if not official, kickoff of the summer sailing season. Throughout the year the Bay is the place for various sailing regattas, from the casual Friday night beer can race to the competitive world championship.

Many of the local yacht clubs have summer sailing programs for children. Adults wanting to learn how to sail may want to consider the following outfits for instruction.

SAN FRANCISCO
- **Day on the Bay**, San Francisco Marina, 415-922-0227
- **Spinnaker Sailing San Francisco**, Pier 40, Beach Harbor South, San Francisco, 415-543-7333
- **St. Francis Yacht Club**, San Francisco Marina Small Craft Harbor, 415-563-6363
- **Golden Gate Yacht Club**, San Francisco Marina Small Craft Harbor, 415-346-2628

NORTH BAY
- **Cass Sailing School**, 1702 Bridgeway, Sausalito, 415-332-6789
- **Modern Sailing Academy**, 2310 Marinship Way, Sausalito, 415-331-8250
- **Club Nautique**, 100 Gate 6 Road, Sausalito, 800-343-7245

- **Sausalito Yacht Club**, 501 Humboldt, Sausalito, 415-332-5000
- **San Francisco Yacht Club**, 98 Beach Road, Belvedere, 415-435-4202
- **Board Sports**, 446 West Francisco Boulevard, San Rafael, 258-9283

EAST BAY
- **California Adventures**, 2301 Bancroft Way, Berkeley, 510-642-4000
- **California Sailing Club**, P.O. Box 819, Berkeley, 510-287-5905
- **Olympic Circle Sailing School**, #1 Spinnaker Way, Berkeley, 800-223-2984
- **Club Nautique**, 1150 Ballena Boulevard, Suite 161, Alameda, 800-343-7245
- **Berkeley Yacht Club**, One Seawall Drive, Berkeley, 510-843-9292
- **Berkeley Board Sports**, 1601 University Avenue, Berkeley, 510-527-7873

SOUTH BAY
- **Shoreline Aquatic Center**, 3160 North Shoreline Boulevard, Mountain View, 650-965-7474
- **Spinnaker Sailing School**, 451 Seaport Court, Redwood City, 650-363-1390, www.spinnakersailing.com
- **Helm Ski and Windsurf**, 333 North Amphlett Boulevard, San Mateo, 650-344-2711
- **ASD-Advanced Surf Designs**, 302 Lang Road, Burlingame, 650-348-8485

SCUBA AND FREE DIVING

Be prepared for chilly waters and otters when you scuba dive in Monterey Bay. Unlike Hawaii, Northern California's waters are not warm, so be sure you have a thick wetsuit. With the rich kelp forests in Monterey Bay you'll probably be underwater with the sea otters. If you have strong lungs try free diving (diving without a tank) for abalone in the Northern Coast of California by Mendocino. Make sure to get a fishing license if you are catching abalone or any fish. Also familiarize yourself with the rules regarding size and limits. Contact the Department of Fish and Game at 916-227-2245, www.dfg.ca.gov, for more information.
- **Any Water Sports**, 1130 Saratoga, San Jose, 408-244-4433
- **Bamboo Reef**, 584 4th Street, San Francisco, 415-362-6694
- **Cal. Dive and Travel**, 1750 6th Street, Berkeley, 510-524-3248
- **Diver Dan's**, 2245 El Camino Real, Santa Clara, 408-984-5819
- **Mistix State Park Reservation System**, Point Lobos, Bluefish Cove, Whalers Cove, and Monastery Beach (the latter is for experienced divers only), 800-444-7275
- **Monterey Bay Harbormaster**, 408-646-3950
- **Monterey Bay Dive Center**, 225 Cannery Row, Monterey, 408-656-0454
- **Scuba Unlimited**, 651 Howard Street, San Francisco, 415-777-DIVE; 517 East Bayshore Road, Redwood City, 650-369-DIVE

SKATING—ROLLER/IN-LINE/ICE

Every Friday night in-line skaters, sometimes more than 500 at a time, meet at San Francisco's Ferry Building to tour the City on wheels.

Roller-skating and in-line skating are both popular activities in San Francisco, especially on weekends in Golden Gate Park. If you don't own your own skates, head for Fulton Street along the northern end of the park in the morning and look for the brightly-colored rent-a-skate vans parked there. Alternatively, there are plenty of skate shops that will be more than happy to outfit you in the latest gear.

If you'd rather skate at an ice rink, you're in luck. After years without a regular indoor ice skating rink, the Yerba Buena Gardens in downtown San Francisco now offers an NHL-sized (200' by 85') hockey rink.

SAN FRANCISCO
- **Golden Gate Park Skate & Bike**, 3038 Fulton Street, 415-668-1117
- **CYCO SF**, 640 Stanyan Street 415-668-8016
- **Skates on Haight**, 1818 Haight, 415-752-8375
- **Yerba Buena Center Gardens Ice Skating and Bowling Center**, 750 Folsom Street, 415-777-3727
- **Bladium In-Line Hockey Rink**, 1050 3rd Street, 415-442-5060

NORTH BAY
- **Golden Skate**, 2701 Hooper Drive, San Ramon, 925-820-2525
- **Redwood Empire Ice Arena and Snoopy's Gallery and Gift Shop**, 1667 West Steele Lane, Santa Rosa, 707-546-3385

EAST BAY
- **Oakland Ice Center**, 519 18th Street, Oakland, 510-268-9000
- **Berkeley Iceland Ice Skating**, 2727 Milvia Street, Berkeley, 510-843-8800

PENINSULA/SOUTH BAY
- **Ice Centre of San Jose**, 1500 South Tenth, San Jose, 408-279-6000
- **Belmont Iceland**, 815 Country Road, Belmont, 650-592-0532
- **Ice Chalet**, 2202 San Mateo Fashion Island, San Mateo 650-574-1616
- **Ice Oasis**, 3140 Bay Road, Redwood City, 650-364-8090
- **The Winter Lodge**, 3009 Middlefield Road, Palo Alto, 650-493-4566, www.winterlodge.com
- **Rolladium Roller Rink**, 363 North Amphlett Boulevard, San Mateo, 415-342-2711

SKIING

Sierra Nevada ski resorts are about a four-hour drive east of the Bay Area, along Interstate 80 and Highway 50. If you don't own skiing equipment there are several local businesses that will rent everything you need to hit the slopes or cross-country ski trails in style, including the national chain, **Recreational Equipment Incorporated (REI)**: 1338 San Pablo Avenue, Berkeley, 510-527-4140; and 1119 Industrial Road, San Carlos, 415-508-2330. Other places to check: **FTC Sports**, 415-673-8363, and **Swiss Ski Sports**, 415-434-0322, both in San Francisco. For additional outfitters, try the Yellow Pages under "Ski Equipment-Retail."

SKYDIVING

Call one of the listings below for information about lessons, equipment, and getting connected with an instructor for this exhilarating sport:
* **A Thrillsource**, San Francisco, 415-474-4784
* **Skydive Cloverdale**, San Francisco, 415-584-6332
* **Skydive Cloverdale**, Petaluma, 707-765-2325

SOCCER: ADULT AND CHILD

Soccer is a popular sport in the Bay Area. If you are interested in organized games, contact your local parks and recreation department (see above). The **Palo Alto Adult Soccer League (PAASL)**, for men and women ages 25 and over, has an informative web site about local and international soccer, www.paasl.org. PAASL games generally take place at Jane Lathrop Stanford Middle School (next to Mitchell Park) in Palo Alto. Also listed on the PAASL web site is a list of pick-up games in the Bay Area. Many such pick-up games are now so crowded that participation may be limited to the first 20 players to arrive. Bring both a white and a colored t-shirt. Below is a partial list of games available:

SAN FRANCISCO
* **Lowell High School**, Winston Boulevard and Lake Merced Boulevard, Sundays, 10 a.m.
* **Lowell High School Gym**, Winston Boulevard and Lake Merced Boulevard, Tuesdays, 7 p.m.
* **Golden Gate Park**, Soccer fields at the west end of the park (between the windmills), Saturdays, 3 p.m.
* **Golden Gate Park**, Lincoln at 7th Avenue, Tuesdays and Thursdays, 5 p.m.
* **The Marina Green**, Saturdays, 9 a.m., Sundays, 10 a.m.
* **Glen Park**, Bosworth and O'Shaughnessy, Tuesdays, 8:30 a.m.

NORTH BAY

- **Pleasanton Sports & Recreation Park**, 5800 Parkside Drive, Pleasanton, Tuesdays, Wednesdays, and Thursdays, 12 p.m.
- **Town Park**, 498 Tamalpais Drive (1/2 mile west off 101), Corte Madera, weekdays, 4 p.m.
- **Hauke Park**, Roque Moraes Street and Hamilton Drive, Mill Valley, Tuesdays, 9 a.m. to 10 a.m.

EAST BAY

- **Ohlone Park**, Martin Luther King and Hearst, Berkeley, Tuesdays and Thursdays, 5 p.m. (12 p.m. in winter)
- **Kleeberger Field**, next to the University of California Memorial Stadium, Berkeley, Saturdays and Sundays, 2 p.m. to 3 p.m.

PENINSULA

- **Burlingame High School**, 400 Carolan Avenue, Burlingame, Sundays, 10 a.m.
- **San Mateo High School**, Delaware and Poplar, San Mateo, daily, 4 p.m. to 6 p.m., Sundays, 10 a.m. to 12 p.m.
- **Laurelwood Park**, Glendora Street, San Mateo, Tuesdays and Thursdays, 12 p.m.
- **Burgess Park**, 501 Laurel (off Ravenswood), Menlo Park, Mondays, Tuesdays, and Thursdays, 12:15 p.m.
- **El Camino Park**, Across El Camino Real from the Stanford Shopping Center, Palo Alto, Saturdays, 10 a.m.
- **Mitchell Park**, Middlefield Road, between Charleston and East Meadow, Palo Alto, Saturdays, 9:15 a.m., Thursdays, 6 p.m. (summer only)

SOUTH BAY

- **Fair Oaks Park**, Fair Oaks Avenue, where it splits with Wolfe, Sunnyvale, weekdays, 12:30 p.m.
- **Wilcox High School**, 3250 Monroe, Santa Clara, Saturdays, 9:30 a.m.
- **Homestead High School**, 21370 Homestead Road, Cupertino, Saturdays, 10 a.m.

SWIMMING POOLS

For those few days when it actually gets hot enough to swim outdoors in San Francisco there are a number of public pools. Hours vary, so the best bet is to call ahead. Below is a list of public pools in San Francisco, unless otherwise noted:

- **Angelo Rossi**, Arguello Boulevard and Anza Street, 415-666-7011
- **Balboa Park**, Ocean and San Jose avenues, 415-337-4715
- **Garfield Pool**, 26th and Harrison streets, 415-695-5010

- **Hamilton Recreation Center**, Geary Boulevard and Steiner Street, 415-292-2008
- **North Beach Playground**, Lombard and Mason streets, 415-274-0201
- **Alameda Swim Center**, 2256 Alameda Avenue, Alameda, 510-522-8107

Some private clubs have pools including the **Golden Gateway Tennis and Swim Club** (**GGTSC**), 370 Drumm Street, 415-616-8800, the **Bay Club** at 1 Lombard Street, 415-433-2550, and the **Presidio YMCA** at the Presidio, 415-447-9680.

Outdoors, **Lake Anza**, north of Berkeley, in Tilden Park has a sandy beach that is sheltered from the wind. Lifeguards are posted here during the swim season, April 15 to October 15. Picnic grounds are located nearby. There is an entrance fee to the swim area, which has changing rooms and a refreshment stand. The lake is open for fishing throughout the year.

Originally constructed as a storage lake for drinking water, **Lake Temescal**, next to the junction of highways 24 and 13 in Oakland, was opened to the public in 1936. Temescal is a popular urban oasis, with many coming for swimming, fishing, sunbathing, and picnicking. The swim area is open spring through fall. Lifeguards are on duty during posted periods. A snack stand is nearby, and many facilities are accessible to the disabled. There are picnic areas at both ends of the lake (several of them can be reserved for groups), and eight acres of lawn. For more information about Temescal, call 510-562-PARK.

People actually swim in San Francisco Bay, and some more than once. Many such intrepid souls belong to **The Dolphin Club**, 502 Jefferson Street, 415-441-9329 or the **South End Rowing Club**, 500 Jefferson Street, 415-776-7372. After a cold dip, you can enjoy the clubs' sauna and shower facilities.

TENNIS AND RACQUET SPORTS

There are 140 public tennis courts in San Francisco alone, most of which operate on a first come, first served basis. At the east end of **Golden Gate Park** there are 21 courts that may be reserved by calling 415-753-7100. There are also quite a few private clubs in and around San Francisco, including the **Golden Gateway Tennis and Swim Club**, 370 Drumm, 415-616-8800; **The Bay Club**, 1 Lombard Street, 415-433-2550; **San Francisco Tennis Club**, 645 5th Street, 415-777-9000; and the **California Tennis Club**, 1770 Scott Street, 415-346-3611. In addition, the **Presidio YMCA** has access to the numerous courts spread throughout the Presidio. Call 415-447-9622 for details. For more information about public tennis and lessons in San Francisco, call 415-751-5639. For courts outside San Francisco check with your local parks and recreation department (see above).

WINDSURFING

San Francisco Bay hosts some of the world's best windsurfing. The inexperienced should take instruction before heading out on the Bay, as understanding the ocean's tides and currents is key to staying safe. Check www.iwindsurf.com for updates on wind speed and direction on the Bay. (True windsurfing addicts can even get a pager called "call of the wind," that beeps in with updates on the Bay's wind and tide conditions.)

Area windsurfing outfitters include:

SAN FRANCISCO
- **CityFront Sailboards**, 2936 Lyon Street, 415-929-7873

EAST BAY
- **California Adventures**, Berkeley Marina, 510-642-4000
- **California Sailing Club**, P.O. Box 819, Berkeley, 510-287-5905
- **Berkeley Board Sports**, 1601 University Avenue, Berkeley, 510-527-7873

SOUTH BAY
- **Shoreline Aquatic Center**, 3160 North Shoreline Boulevard, Mountain View, 650-965-7474
- **Helm Ski and Windsurf**, 333 North Amphlett Boulevard, San Mateo, 650-344-2711
- **ASD-Advanced Surf Designs**, 302 Lang Road, Burlingame, 650-348-8485

THE SACRAMENTO DELTA
- **Windcraft Windsurfing**, 17124 East Sherman Island Levy Road, Rio Vista, 916-777-7007
- **Delta Windsurf Co.**, 3729 West Sherman Island Road, Rio Vista, 916-777-2299

YOGA

Yoga is popular in the Bay Area and many health clubs offer yoga classes. In addition, there are a number of studios devoted solely to the fine art of bending, stretching, and breathing. Here are a few:

SAN FRANCISCO
- **Integral Yoga**, 770 Dolores, 415-821-1117
- **Iyengar Yoga Institute of San Francisco**, 2404 27th, 415-753-0909
- **Global Yoga**, 2425 Chestnut, 415-292-9774
- **Mindful Body**, 2876 California, 415-931-2639
- **Yoga Society of San Francisco**, 415-285-5537

- **Yoga College of India San Francisco Branch**, 910 Columbus Avenue, 415-346-5400

NORTH BAY
- **Yoga Center of Marin**, 142 Redwood Avenue, Corte Madera, 415-927-1850
- **Yoga College of India**, 1295 2nd Street, San Rafael, 415-453-9642

EAST BAY
- **4th Street Yoga**, 1809C 4th Street, Berkeley, 510-845-9642
- **The Yoga Room**, 2640 College Avenue, Berkeley, 510-233-8470
- **Piedmont Yoga Studio**, P.O. Box 11458, Piedmont, 510-536-8996

PENINSULA/SOUTH BAY
- **Yoga Wellness Studio**, 105 East 3rd Avenue, San Mateo, 650-401-6423
- **Yoga Source**, 525 Alma Street, Palo Alto, 650-328-9642
- **Willow Glen Yoga**, 1188 Lincoln Avenue, San Jose, 408-289-9642
- **Stanford Yoga**, 700 Welch Road, #106, Palo Alto, 650-329-0400

HEALTH CLUBS

The Bay Area has no shortage of health clubs, so whether you're seeking the latest, most up-to-date exercise machine with a pulse-pumping soundtrack or the quietest, most peaceful yoga center, you can find it here.

SAN FRANCISCO
- **Bay Club**: 555 California Street, 415-362-7800; 50 Greenwich Street, 415-433-2200
- **Club One**: 1 Sansome Street, 415-399-1010; 60 Pine Street, 415-398-1111; Embarcadero Center, 415-788-1010
- **Crunch**, 1000 Van Ness, 415-931-1100
- **Gold's Gym**, 501 2nd Street, 415-777-4653
- **Golden Gateway Tennis and Swim Club**, 370 Drumm, 415-616-8800
- **Gorilla Sports**, 2324 Chestnut Street, 415-292-8470
- **Pinnacle**: 345 Spear Street, 415-495-1939; 61 New Montgomery Street, 415-543-1110
- **Strong Heart Strong Body**, 3366 Sacramento Street, 415-828-8818
- **Telegraph Hill**, 1850 Kearny Street, 415-982-4700
- **24 Hour Nautilus**, numerous locations, 800-24-WORKOUT
- **24 Hour Fitness**, numerous locations, 800-204-2400
- **YMCA**: 169 Steuart Street (Embarcadero), 415-957-9622; Presido, 415-447-9622; Stonestown, 333 Eucalyptus Drive, 415-242-7100; Chinatown (men only), 855 Sacramento Street, 415-576-9622; Central, 220 Golden Gate Avenue, 415-885-0460

- **YWCA**, 1830 Sutter Street, 415-775-6502

NORTH BAY
- **Mill Valley Personal Fitness**, 34 Sunnyside Avenue, Mill Valley, 415-381-4279
- **Recreate Personal Training**, 21 Tamal Vista Boulevard, Corte Madera, 415-927-0214
- **Gold's Gym**, 10 Fifer Avenue, Corte Madera, 415-924-4653
- **24 Hour Fitness**, 1001 Larkspur Landing Circle, Larkspur, 415-925-0333
- **Nautilus Of Marin**, 1001 4th Street, San Rafael, 415-485-1001

EAST BAY
- **Oakland Athletic Club**, 1418 Webster Street, Oakland, 510-893-3421
- **YMCA**, 2350 Broadway Oakland, 510-451-9622
- **World Gym**, 6101 Christie Avenue, Emeryville, 510-601-1141
- **Bay Island Gymnastics**, 2317 Central Avenue, Alameda, 510-521-1343
- **No Sweat Aerobic & Dance Studio**, 1831 Solano Avenue, Berkeley, 510-528-1958
- **Pulse Exercise Studio**, 233 El Cerrito Plaza, El Cerrito, 510-528-1312
- **In Forma**, 23 Orinda Way, #A, Orinda, 925-254-6877

PENINSULA/SOUTH BAY
- **Reach Fitness Club**, 707 High Street, Palo Alto, 650-949-3730
- **Prime Physique Fitness Specialists**, 3635 Union Avenue, San Jose, 408-558-1800
- **YMCA**, 4151 Middlefield Road, #211, Palo Alto, 650-856-3955
- **Studio Of Fitness**, 2624 Fayette Drive, Mountain View, 650-941-9148
- **Gym West**, 121 Beech Street, Redwood City, 650-364-0933
- **Callanetics Studio-Sunnyvale**, 1111 West El Camino Real, Sunnyvale, 408-739-6081
- **Right Stuff Health Club-Women**, 1145 South De Anza Boulevard, San Jose, 408-973-1088
- **Linda Evans Fitness Center**, 5278 Moorpark Avenue, San Jose, 408-366-8320

PARKS

Everyone knows about San Francisco's Golden Gate Park, and many have heard about the Presidio and Marin Headlands, but most newcomers are probably unaware of the profusion of little, gem-like parks scattered throughout the Bay Area. These little havens, some of them perched atop hillsides, are perfect for romping with the kids, taking in the views, and breathing in the misty morning air. In fact, in San Francisco alone there are 230 parks and recreation facilities; among them, you'll find six scenic golf courses and 52 playgrounds—not bad for a city of 48 square miles. And then there are the beaches...

SAN FRANCISCO

GOLDEN GATE PARK

The idea to create a large park in San Francisco first surfaced in the mid-1860s as city leaders strategized about how to wrest control of a large, sandy area occupied by squatters. Today this area spreads out about three miles from its eastern border of Stanyan Street to the Pacific Ocean, is about a half mile wide, and separates the Richmond district to the north and the Sunset to the south.

Visit Golden Gate Park and you will see that the rolling sand dunes of the 1800s have been transformed into rolling fields of green and wooded groves. The method for turning the land into the green space it is today was reportedly hit upon by accident. It seems William Hammond Hall, the park's designer and its first Superintendent (1871-1876), noticed a horse's barley nosebag fall to the sand and then sometime later the barley that spilled sprouted. Hall took note of this and decided to plant barley, grass, and other plants throughout the sandy areas needing to be reclaimed, and the rest is history. Hall is also credited with keeping traffic moving slowly through the park by insisting on the design of park roads that twisted and turned.

Hall appointed John McLaren as Assistant Superintendent, and by 1890,

McLaren, a native of Edinburgh, Scotland, became Superintendent. He went on to make a name for himself by continuing the reclamation process. With the advice of horticulturists from around the world as to what kinds of plants and trees might thrive in this region, word has it that he alone planted more than one million trees in the park. Following his death in 1943, "Uncle John," as he was lovingly known, was honored by City leaders who named the park's headquarters (his former home) after him, the McLaren Lodge.

Today Golden Gate Park is the City's 1,017-acre playground, seven days a week. It's huge—New York's Central Park comes in at a mere 750 acres. No matter what the weather, you'll find walkers, joggers, roller skaters and bike riders out using the trails. The meadows and groves are popular picnic sites. (The grills require reservations on weekends, see below.) The park also boasts numerous lakes and streams, baseball diamonds, soccer fields, tennis courts, playgrounds, an antique carousel, two art museums, a science museum and an aquarium, a Japanese tea garden and much more. Despite all the activity, Golden Gate Park also offers quiet places for those seeking a bit of solitude.

For further information or reservations visit www.parks.sfgov.org or call:
- **Asian Art Museum**, 415-668-8921
- **Baseball/softball diamonds**, 415-753-7024
- **Boating** (Stow Lake), 415-752-0347
- **California Academy of Sciences**, 415-750-7145
- **M. H. de Young Art Museum**, 415-863-3330
- **Equestrian**, 415-668-7360
- **Fly casting** (Angler's Lodge), 415- 386-2630
- **Football** (Polo Field), 415-753-7025
- **Golf** (nine hole course), 415-753-7259
- **Guided walks**, 415-221-1311
- **Horses** (stables), 415-668-7360
- **Lawn bowling**, 415-487-8787
- **Picnic/barbecue**, 415- 666-7027
- **Tennis** (21 courts), 415- 753-7100
- **Tea Garden**, 415-752-1171
- **Strybing Arboretum**, 415-661-1316

PRESIDIO NATIONAL PARK

Located at the northern tip of the San Francisco peninsula, the 1,480-acre Presidio is one of the City's biggest treasures. Only recently part of the National Park system, it was originally settled by the Spanish in 1776, and functioned as a military post. In 1847, under US rule, its military functions continued, serving as a training base for Union troops in the Civil War and, in the aftermath of the 1906 earthquake that destroyed much of San Francisco, as a refuge for displaced residents. During WW II, the Presidio functioned as command center for the Sixth Army Command. It wasn't until October 1,1994, when the National Park Service assumed control, that the US Sixth Army packed up and moved out. It is now part of the Golden Gate National Recreation Area and boasts some of the City's prime real estate, with more than one hundred miles of roads and wooded trails, ocean vistas, and a world-class golf course. Bikers and hikers enjoy the trails that meander through the eucalyptus groves; windsurfers and kite surfers head for Crissy Field. Fishermen look for crab, bass, perch, shark, or whatever else will bite at the pier near Fort Point.

Unique in the National Park System, the Presidio is run by the Presidio Trust, an independent federal agency, in combination with the National Park Service. The US Congress has mandated that the Presidio be completely self-sufficient by the year 2013, and to that end, the Presidio Trust has had to be creative about how to accomplish self-sufficiency. Finding big business tenants seems to be the way the Trust has decided to go, and in May 2000 George Lucas was approved to move Lucas Enterprises to the Presidio, much to the dismay of area environmentalists. Another incoming project may be a theater built by Robert Redford's Sundance Institute. Area organizations/businesses have offices here, including non-profits and some dot.coms, and the Presidio is also a residential area with houses and apartments—available primarily to those who work here. Regardless of the politics surrounding how best to manage the area, the Presidio is a San Francisco treasure, offering art, history, and cultural centers, a shorebird lagoon, and recreation space. For more information on what the park has to offer call the **Visitor's Center** at 415-561-4323. Military history buffs may want to visit the **Presidio Army Museum**, at Funston Avenue and Lincoln Boulevard, 415-561-4331. Golfers interested in teeing off at the **Golf Course** call 415-561-4663. Keglers can try out the park's 12-lane **Bowling Alley** in Building #93 (between Moraga and Montgomery Streets), call 415-561-2695 for more information. Visit the Presidio's web site at www.nps.gov/prsf and check the **Sports and Recreation** chapter for more details about these and other sports.

ADDITIONAL SAN FRANCISCO PARKS

- **Sigmund Stern Memorial Grove**, 19th Avenue and Sloat Boulevard, 415-252-6252
- **Harding Park**, Harding Drive off Skyline Drive, 415-753-1101
- **McLaren Park**, University and Woolsey Streets, 415-337-4700
- **Dolores Park**, Dolores and 19th Streets, 415-554-9529
- **Balboa Park**, Ocean Avenue and San Jose Street, 415-337-4715
- **Glen Canyon Park**, Bosworth Street and O'Shaughnessy, 415-337-4705
- **Crocker Amazon**, Moscow and Italy Streets, 415-337-4708

Most San Francisco neighborhoods have parks with playgrounds, tennis courts, various flora and fauna, views, and secluded sunbathing groves.

Washington Square Park in North Beach, **Alamo Square** at Fulton and Scott streets, **Lafayette Park** and **Alta Plaza** in Pacific Heights, and **Buena Vista Park** in the Haight are just a few. For more information about parks and recreational opportunities in your area call the **San Francisco Parks & Recreation Department**, 415-831-2700, or visit their web site at www.parks.sfgov.org.

BEYOND SAN FRANCISCO—BAY AREA PARKS

The park system throughout the rest of the Bay Area is vast and varied. Included here are city, county, and national parks. There are too many parks to list completely but the following will give you an idea of what to expect.

For information about additional parks in the western United States, call the **National Park Services' Pacific West Information line** at 415-556-0560.

NORTH BAY

Part of the Golden Gate National Recreation Area, **Marin Headlands** is located on the Marin side of the Golden Gate Bridge, and offers spectacular views of the City, the Bridge, and the ocean. Hiking, camping, and mountain biking are available, and it's only moments away from the City. Near Rodeo Beach you'll find the Marine Mammal Center, 415-289-SEAL, which provides shelter and medical assistance to elephant seals and sea lions. For more information about the Marin Headlands, contact the Visitors' Center in Sausalito at Bunker Road, 415-331-1540, or visit the Golden Gate National Recreation Area's web site at www.nps.gov/goga, telephone 415-556-0560.

Located in the center of San Francisco Bay is **Angel Island State Park**. People come here mostly by ferry, though a few arrive via sailboats. Ferries leave from Tiburon, San Francisco (at Pier 41, Fisherman's Wharf), and Vallejo. Once on the island, you can hike, bike, picnic, camp or enjoy a softball game or even climb the 750-foot Mount Livermore. For more information about Angel Island call 415-435-2131 or visit www.angelisland.org. For the San Francisco and Vallejo ferries, call the Blue and Gold Fleet at 415-773-1188. For information about the Tiburon Ferry, call 415-435-2131.

Mount Tamalpais (elevation 2,586 feet), in Mount Tamalpais State Park, has 50 miles of hiking and biking trails. On clear days, the views of San Francisco Bay and the City are stunning, especially by Trojan Point and Pantoll. You can even see the Farallon Islands, some 25 miles out to sea. In the spring the outdoor Mountain Theater presents plays. For information about Mount Tamalpais, call 415-388-2070. On your way to Mount Tamalpais, you'll pass **Muir Woods**, an eerily beautiful grove of ancient redwoods. Visit in the winter when there are fewer tourists, lots of greenery, and creeks that are running full blast. For more information call 415-388-2595 or visit the Golden Gate

National Park Recreation web site at www.nps.gov/goga.

Samuel P. Taylor State Park, fifteen miles west of San Rafael on Sir Francis Drake Boulevard, is fun. The groves of redwoods and Papermill creek make the area a popular camping spot. For more information call 415-488-9897. To reserve a campsite (there are 61 campsites), contact Reserve America at 800-444-7275.

Located between the towns of Bolinas and Tomales, **Point Reyes National Seashore** includes 30 miles of coastline and 70,000 acres of pristine wilderness. Amidst its rugged bluffs, wooded canyons, dense forests, and open meadows, you'll find spectacular hiking, biking, camping, bird watching, and whale watching. Mountain lions live here. If visiting with children, be sure to keep them nearby at all times. In 1995, a fire destroyed some 13,000 acres of the park, and though you can still see the effects of the fire, much of the area has recovered. For information about camping at Point Reyes contact the Visitors' Center at 415-663-1092. Make sure to reserve camping sites ahead of time.

To learn more about city parks in Marin County, contact the **Marin County Department of Parks and Recreation** at 415-499-6387, www.marin–countyparks.org.

EAST BAY

The East Bay has some spectacular parks, especially up in the Berkeley and Oakland hills. Call the **East Bay Regional Park District** at 510-562-7275 for information or visit their web site at www.ebparks.org.

In Berkeley, the Aquatic Park, at Seventh and Heinz Streets, 510-843-2273 is alive with the sounds of sculling teams and migrating birds. You can join a kite-flying contest at Berkeley Marina off University Avenue in Berkeley, 510-644-6376. Many would argue that the crown jewel here is **Tilden Park**. Located in North Berkeley, it has hiking trails, and Anza Lake for swimming (see **Sports and Recreation** for swimming details), a merry-go-round, miniature trains, golf course, a steam train and a petting zoo. For more information, call 510-635-0135.

Tucked away in Oakland are a number of lovely green havens. **Lake Temescal Recreation Area**, 510-635-0138, has a reservoir for swimming and trout or bass fishing. Only a few miles from downtown Oakland, **Redwood Regional Park**, 510-531-6417, offers stately redwoods, horseback riding, a swimming pool, and picnic areas. At **Anthony Chabot Regional Park** you can row along the 315-acre lake. No swimming allowed though. To reserve one of the 75 campsites (the cost is $15) call 510-636-1684. Another Oakland Park is the 425-acre **Joaquin Miller Park**, 510-238-7275, off Highway 13 on Joaquin Miller Road, where you'll find plenty of hiking trails. If you drive up Skyline Boulevard checkout the new **Chabot Observatory and Science Center**, 510-530-3480, with its high powered telescopes, planetarium and Dome IMAX theater.

In Richmond, **Wildcat Canyon** offers hiking trails that are less crowded than many other Bay Area trails.

In Alameda you can walk lazily along **Crown Memorial Beach**, Shoreline Drive, 510-521-6887, ext. 2200 or if you are energetic, try windsurfing or kitesurfing. The **Crab Cove Visitor Center** for tide pooling is another favorite recreation spot. Call 510-521-6887 for more details.

In Contra Costa County check out the 19,000-acrea **Mount Diablo State Park**, 925-837-2525, for hiking, camping, mountain biking, and incredible City views.

Located between Martinez and Lafayette is the hilly **Briones Regional Park**, 925-370-3020. Its 5,000 acres offer 45 miles of trails through meadows and wooded areas among lakes and waterfalls.

PENINSULA

In San Mateo County, along Highway 1 from Pacifica to Santa Cruz, you'll find stunning coastline, big waves and lovely beach combing. Beware of sharks; they have been known to chomp on surfboards.

Located about 55 miles south of San Francisco is the **Ano Nuevo State Reserve**, which hosts the world's largest breeding colony of northern elephant seals. Every year, the elephant seals mate and give birth to their 75 pound pups along the sand dunes. This is truly a remarkable area and if you are lucky, you may witness a female giving birth. Breeding season is from December to late March. For more information, call 650-879-0227.

On the San Francisco Bay, the **Coyote Point County Recreational Area**, Coyote Point Drive, 650-573-2592, has a well-visited Nature Museum along with swimming, boating, windsurfing and some kite-boarding. Windsurfing is also popular by **Candlestick Park State Recreation Area**, a few miles south of Coyote Point and near the San Francisco Airport. **Crystal Springs Reservoir**, located 13 miles south of San Francisco on Interstate 280, is another refuge as well as a source of water for San Francisco and the surrounding areas. Trails here are used for hiking, biking and horseback riding. The reservoir itself holds 22.6 billion gallons of Hetch Hetchy water for delivery to San Francisco and northern peninsula towns.

At **Huddart County Park** in Woodside, 650-851-1210, you'll find groves of second growth redwoods. The park also features a playground designed specifically for the physically challenged. Additional San Mateo County Parks are **Memorial Park** where you can fish for trout, plunge into a swimming hole, hike, bike, ride, or visit a nature museum; the 7,500-acre **Pescadero Creek County Park** with ridgetop ocean views and hiking and biking; and the **Sam MacDonald County Park** with 42 miles of hiking trails. Call 650-879-0212 for camping information at the above parks.

For more information on **San Mateo's County Parks** call the **Parks and Recreation Department** at 650-363-4020.

There are also many preserves and open spaces such as **Pulgas Ridge Open Space Preserve** in San Carlos and the **Thornewood Open Space Preserve** in Woodside. Call the **Mid-Peninsula Regional Open Space District Office** at 650-691-1200 to learn more.

SOUTH BAY

There are 28 parks in Santa Clara County; contact the **Santa Clara Department of Parks and Recreation** at 408-358-3741 or visit their web site at www.co.santa-clara.ca.us/parks. Below is just a sampling.

The 3,600-acre **Sanborn Skyline County Park**, nestled in the Santa Cruz Mountains between the city of Saratoga and Skyline Boulevard, is a steep and wooded area. It offers camping, an outdoor theater, and a youth hostel, call 408-867-9959 for more information. **Stevens Creek County Park**, in Cupertino, 408-867-3645, is great for riding or bicycling around its reservoir. Within the City of San Jose is **Alum Rock**, 408-259-5477, which has trickling mineral springs, as well as hiking, biking, and horseback riding trails.

Bird lovers from all over the country flock to **Palo Alto's Baylands Preserve.** Here, among the 2,000 acres of bird beckoning salt marsh, you'll find more than 100 species of birds, including white egrets, California clappers, and thousands of tiny shorebirds. In the fall and winter the tiny black rail makes its appearance. For more details call 650-329-2506 or check www.ci.palo-alto.ca.us. Remember to bring your binoculars.

With 80,000 acres, **Henry Coe State Park** is the largest state park in Northern California. People come to hike, mountain bike, backpack, camp, fish and ride horses. Located in Morgan Hill (south of San Jose), the park has blue oaks, ponderosa pines, wild pigs, deer, birds and much more. There is a $3 fee for day use. For more information, call the visitors center at 408-779-2728 or visit their web site at www.coepark.parks.ca.gov.

BEACHES

If you think all of California's beaches are like the ones seen on "Baywatch" erase that image from your mind. Those are Southern California beaches. Northern California beaches are much different than the miles-long oceanfront playgrounds seen on TV. Weather here is frequently foggy and cold, and the ocean's undertow is extremely dangerous. Although Bay Area beaches do host hardy surfers and sunbathers, you won't be out of place if you consider the beaches here more akin to the North Sea—places to walk with a stick and a dog and warm clothing.

Often socked-in by morning fog, temperatures along the shore rarely top the 70s, even by mid-afternoon. Nevertheless, there are a number of popular beaches in **San Francisco**. The appropriately named **Ocean Beach**, along the western edge of Golden Gate Park is popular for surfers and city strollers; hang-gliders, paragliders, and kite fliers. Dog walkers love the beach at **Fort Funston**, south of Ocean Beach, and nudists throw caution to the wind at **Land's End** (located on the northern edge of Lincoln Park). Families flock to the southern part of **Baker Beach**, which is along the western edge of the Presidio, were the views of the ocean, the Golden Gate Bridge, and the Marin Headlands to the north are spectacular. **China Beach** is a small, secluded stretch of sand adjacent to the upscale Sea Cliff neighborhood. Daring swimmers willing to endure the cold Bay water take the plunge at the beach in **Aquatic Park** near Fisherman's Wharf.

In **Marin County, Stinson Beach** is perhaps the Bay Area's most popular beach. As a matter of fact it is so popular that on summer weekends you should beware of the thousands of vehicles, and inevitable traffic jams, on Highway 1 along the coast north of San Francisco as city dwellers rev up their engines in search of peace and quiet. Keep in mind that the car trip there includes a winding road, which can make even the sturdiest stomach queasy. For clothing optional beaches in Marin try **Muir Beach** just before Stinson. Just past Stinson is the town of Bolinas, which has a small beach, popular for surfing.

There are much quieter beaches along the **San Mateo County** coastline so if you'd like to avoid the crowds, head south from San Francisco down Highway 1, through **Pacifica** and **Half Moon Bay** and keep your eyes peeled for a beach that fits the bill. Remember, though, that the water is cold, and the underwater currents are strong. For information on the beaches south of Pacifica, contact the San Mateo State Park District at 650-726-8819.

To find out more about area parks and to make camping reservations, call 800-444-7275 or log onto the National Recreation Reservation Service at www.reserveusa.com. The **National Park Service** is located in Fort Mason, Building 201, San Francisco, 415-556-0560.

WEATHER IN SAN FRANCISCO VARIES FROM NEIGHBORHOOD TO neighborhood. Often it can be foggy and cold in the Sunset and Richmond, but sunny and 20 degrees warmer in the Mission. Sometimes the entire City is blanketed in fog, and chilly, 60° temperatures, while outside the City it can be sunny and downright hot. This explains why weathermen have a forecast with a 30-degree variation—they're not trying to increase their odds at being accurate, it's just how weather works here.

Microclimates are a result of the Bay Area's sharp topography and the ocean bays. Surrounded on all three sides by year-round water temperatures of 56°, San Francisco keeps cool in the summer and warm in the winter. In fact, year-round air temperatures generally are between 50° and 60°, with rare forays outside this range. Summertime in San Francisco is typically foggy in the morning with clearing in the early afternoon and the fog returning by early evening. The fog is caused by the horizontal movement of cool marine air mixing with the hot air of the Central Valley. The hot air expands and rises giving room for the denser cool air from the ocean to blow back into the City. When the fog burns off, the cool air is denser, and thus heavier, bringing a strong afternoon breeze. The westerly winds blow fiercely through the Golden Gate Bridge, making the sailing and windsurfing challenging, wet, and fun. Typically, the winds will be between 20 and 30 miles per hour. This weather keeps the sweatshirt shops busy along Fisherman's Wharf and Sausalito as tourists think they're coming to sunny California, but quickly learn why Mark Twain's coldest winter was a summer in San Francisco.

Many find the best time to be in San Francisco is in the early fall or spring when the weather is clear and fog free. In fact some of the hottest days here are typically in September when the high pressure builds into the Pacific Northwest and Great Basin areas, and dry offshore winds replace the strong Pacific sea breeze.

During winter, the surrounding brown hills (referred to as "golden" in tourist brochures) turn lush and green from the welcome rains, which swell the rivers and fill the reservoirs. With a total yearly rainfall of 21.7 inches, San Francisco's wettest months are between November and March. Snow and hail have only been documented 10 times in the past 143 years. Winter temperatures are mild with highs between 55° and 60° and lows ranging between 45° and 50°. Often it's warmer along the coast than it is inland. The inland fog during the winter, especially in the towns near the Sacramento River Delta, is thick and dense, and known as tule fog. Avoid driving during the tule fog as it is extremely difficult to see in front of you, causing hazardous road conditions.

As for clothing, San Francisco is a casual city. If you are working and living in the City, your wardrobe will not change much with the seasons. However, if you are employed in the North Bay, South Bay or Peninsula, you may need lighter clothes for the summer and spring, as temperatures can be in the 90s, even the 100s. To fend off the winter rain, a raincoat is a must throughout the region. Don't get rid of that winter coat though. Even though winters here are notoriously mild, they are damp and there may be some windy days when 50 damp degrees feels like a 30° day, leaving you longing for a cozy parka.

WEATHER STATISTICS

According to Golden Gate Weather Services, www.ggweather.com, the average (mean) Fahrenheit temperatures in San Francisco are as follows:

```
January. . . . . 51.1°
February. . . . 54.4°
March . . . . . 54.9°
April. . . . . . . 56.0°
May . . . . . . . 56.6°
June . . . . . . . 58.4°
July. . . . . . . . 59.1°
August . . . . . 60.1°
September . . 62.3°
October . . . . 62.0°
November . . 57.2°
December . . 51.7°
Annual  . . . . 57.0°
```

The average (mean) rainfall in San Francisco from 1849 to 1999 is documented by Golden Gate Weather Services as follows:

```
January. . . . . 4.69 inches
February. . . . 3.69 inches
March . . . . . 3.08 inches
April. . . . . . . 1.48 inches
```

```
May . . . . . . . 0.60 inches
June . . . . . . . 0.15 inches
July. . . . . . . . 0.02 inches
August . . . . . 0.04 inches
September . . 0.27 inches
October . . . . 1.01 inches
November . . 2.64 inches
December . . 4.12 inches
```

For more information about Bay Area weather, visit the Golden Gate Weather Services web site at www.ggweather.com, the National Weather Service web site at www.nws.mbay.net, or the Weather Channel Connection, www.weather.com. If you are a sailor, kite boarder or windsurfer, consult with www.iwindsurf.com to obtain real time wind quotes. You can even order a pager that will update the wind conditions.

AIR POLLUTION

Like many metropolitan areas across the US, increased industry and automobile use has made air quality a problem. Air pollution is especially bad during the "ozone season" from June to mid-October, when emissions from cars and other sources interact with sunlight and heat to form ground level ozone, better known as smog. A serious public health problem, this toxic gas can cause chest pain, sore throats, shortness of breath, and long-term lung damage.

Air District meteorologists monitor and forecast Bay Area air quality by analyzing pollution levels and weather patterns. When their forecasts indicate that ozone concentrations for the next day will violate federal health standards, the **Bay Area Air Quality Management District** issues "spare the air advisories," requesting residents to leave their cars at home, take public transportation or better yet, bicycle or walk to work. Check for the spare the air notices on radio and television broadcasts, in the newspaper, or visit the spare the air web site at www.sparetheair.org. On average, spare the air advisories are issued about 20 times a year. See the Air Quality Index Table below for advisory details. The **Environmental Protection Agency** also issues up-to-the-minute ozone reports on their web site at www.epa.gov/airnow.

Here are a few things you can do on the spare the air days:
- Leave your car at home. Try a commute alternative!
- Don't use gas-powered lawn mowers and leaf blowers.
- Avoid using consumer spray products like hairspray and household cleaners.
- Ignite your barbecue with an electric or chimney starter. Don't use lighter fluids.
- Refuel your car after the sun has gone down —- and don't top off the tank.

AQI – AIR QUALITY INDEX

The table below may give you an idea of what to expect from the air quality reports.

INDEX VALUES	DESCRIPTOR	CAUTIONARY STATEMENT
0 to 50	Good	None
51 to 100	Moderate	Unusually sensitive people should *limit* outdoor exertion
101 to 150	Unhealthy for	People with respiratory problems should *limit* outdoor exertion
151 to 200	Unhealthy	People with respiratory problems should *avoid* prolonged outdoor exertion; active adults & children should *avoid* prolonged outdoor exertion; all other children and adults should *limit* prolonged outdoor exertion
201 to 300	Very Unhealthy	People with respiratory problems should *avoid* all outdoor exertion; active adults & children should *avoid* all outdoor exertion; all other children and adults should *limit* all outdoor exertion
Over 300	Hazardous	Everyone should avoid all outdoor exertion

(Condensed from *Measuring Air Quality: The Pollutant Standards Index*; Office of Air Quality Planning and Standards, US EPA; EPA 451/K-94-001; February 1994.)

A LL RIGHT, ALL RIGHT ... THE EARTH SHIFTS HERE EVERY ONCE IN awhile, but should you worry about earthquakes? Unfortunately, yes. But whether you should let the probability of seismic activity keep you from living here is questionable. Where on earth can you be totally safe? The flood-country of Johnstown, Pennsylvania? Hurricane-prone Miami or Galveston? Tornado-torn Kansas? Semi-arctic Minnesota? Sweltering Chicago or Houston? Each of those areas has experienced painful visits from Mother Nature in the recent past and probably will be visited again in the not too distant future. San Francisco has been victimized by major earthquakes twice, only twice in nearly 100 years—1906 and 1989. Glibness aside, in 1906 the 8.3 magnitude quake toppled buildings and sparked fires that destroyed much of the City, and killed 700 people. The 1989, 7.1 magnitude Loma Prieta temblor killed 67, brought down a section of a major East Bay freeway, dislodged part of the Oakland-San Francisco Bay Bridge, sparked fires in the Marina district, and brought the World Series to an abrupt, albeit temporary, halt. But it's only happened twice in nearly a century. You can be certain though that the San Francisco Bay area will be hit with more earthquakes, and in fact, a 5.2 tremblor shook Napa Valley in August 2000, which damaged over 2,000 buildings and left one child hospitalized. Many speak of the "Big One" that earthquake experts concede will come, although no one can predict when. Six million people live in the Bay Area today, and with all the public awareness programs underway one must assume that most of them know and accept the fact that they live in earthquake country.

DISASTER KITS

Aside from luck, the secret to surviving a major earthquake is found in the time-proven Boy Scout adage "be prepared." There are dozens of good books on the market about how to get ready for a seismic onslaught, and plenty of free information available from local, state and federal agencies. They all tell you that you need to be ready to be on your own for three to seven days, because it may take that long for emergency crews to restore power, water, and telephone service to affected areas. You should also have at least a basic disaster kit prepared. Remember to store your supplies away from areas likely to be damaged in a big earthquake. The kit should include the following:

- **Water** (at least one gallon per person, per day)
- **Food** for each family member *and* your pets (canned goods such as stews, beans, soups, evaporated milk, cereals, granola bars and nuts, dried fruit, cookies)
- **Non-electric can opener**
- **Flashlights and extra batteries**
- **Portable radio and extra batteries**
- **Blankets/sleeping bags/pillows**
- **Camping stove or your barbecue with plenty of appropriate fuel**
- **Swiss Army knife or similar tool**
- **Cooking and eating utensils, paper plates and cups**
- **Proper sized tent**
- **Water purification tablets**
- **Small bottle of chlorine bleach**
- **Toiletries, including toilet paper, feminine hygiene products, and contact lens supplies, diapers**
- **Waterproof matches**
- **Plastic garbage bags and ties**
- **Toys, games, cards, crosswords, paper and pencils, books**
- **Red lipstick** to scrawl a message on the front of the building door (or ruins) if you must leave
- **Sturdy shoes**
- **Rain gear**
- **Sunglasses and sunscreen**
- **Dust masks**
- **Cold weather clothing, gloves, scarves, hats**
- **Fire extinguisher**
- **Whistle**
- **Pet carrier and photos of your pets to identify them if they take off**
- **A basic tool kit with hammer, pliers, wrenches, etc., for minor repairs**
- **Cash** (bank ATMs may not work after a big temblor and merchants may not be accepting credit cards!)
- **First aid kit**, including the following:
  - **plastic adhesive strips**
  - **ACE bandages**
  - **gauze pads and tape**
  - **scissors**

- **tweezers**
- **safety pins**
- **chemical ice packs**
- **cotton balls or swabs**
- **aspirin or the equivalent**
- **antibiotic ointments**
- **hydrogen peroxide**
- **rubbing alcohol**
- **insect repellent**
- **thermometer**
- **over-the-counter medications for diarrhea and upset stomach**
- **First Aid Manual**
- **Prescription medications** that are not past their expiration dates

Once you've gathered everything together put it all in a container, such as a big plastic garbage can with a lid, and stash it in a place that's not likely to be buried in a quake. If you're living in a house, the backyard may be best. If you're living in an apartment building you'll have to be creative when it comes to protecting your kit.

Several Bay Area stores sell earthquake/disaster preparedness equipment and information. They also sell earthquake kits as well as individual components. These can be pricey, but when you consider that your life, following a major quake, may depend on how well prepared you are, it is probably worth the expense. Here are just a few of the stores specializing in quake supplies:

- **American Red Cross Bay Area Chapter Bookstore**, 3901 Broadway, Oakland 510-595-4420
- **The Beehive Country Store**, 5807 Winfield Boulevard, San Jose, 408-225-3531
- **The Earthquake Store**, 6251 Hollis Street, Emeryville, 510-655-6977
- **Earthquake Supply Center**, 615 B Street, San Rafael, 415-459-5500, www.earthquakesupplycenter.com
- **Earth Shakes**, 446 Cumberland Road, Burlingame, 650-548-9065
- **Health Plus**, call 415-469-7469 for their catalogue of earthquake supplies
- **Preparedness Outlet**, 1100 West El Camino Real, Mountain View, 650-965-2636
- **REI-Recreational Equipment Inc.**, 1338 San Pablo Avenue, Berkeley, 510-527-4140; 1119 Industrial Road, San Carlos, 650-508-2330

As you put your quake kit together you should also come up with a **family emergency plan**, in case the earthquake hits when you're not all in the same place. You can do the same thing with your apartment building neighbors. Emergency preparedness experts say you should:
- Agree on someone out of the area you can all call to check in, for example,

Aunt Mildred in Omaha. She'll want to know how you are as well, so let her be the clearinghouse for family information. Make sure each family member knows the number. The only chink in this armor is that telephones may not be working for a few days—keep trying, eventually they will be restored.

- Should your home suffer severe damage, create a planned meeting place, such as the local high school football field or a department store parking lot; someplace that is not likely to come tumbling down during the initial quake or any aftershocks.

- If you're inside when the earth shifts, remember these three words, *duck, cover* and *hold*. That means get down, get under something sturdy such as a table or desk, and stay there until the shaking stops. Get away from windows, mirrors, and anything else that could tumble down on you. If you are outside stay away from power lines, trees, buildings, and walls.

- There are a number of simple steps you can take prior to an earthquake that will make your home a bit safer. They include fastening computers, televisions and other big pieces of equipment to desks and counters so that they won't fall off during the quake. Large furniture items, such as bookcases, should be bolted to the wall. Small items, such as fragile collectibles, should be taped or glued to their shelves or stuck with clay. Strap the water heater and other large appliances to the wall. The folks in the earthquake supply stores will be more than happy to sell you what you need to do this or go to a hardware/home supply store and get the equivalent. Chances are it will be less expensive at the latter.

- One of the first things you should do following a quake is check to see if your natural gas line is leaking; if you detect a leak, and only if you detect a leak, turn the shutoff valve. Quake-prepared residents leave the appropriate tool for shutting off the gas valve right next to it at all times. Remember, don't turn the gas off if you don't think it's leaking. The gas company will no doubt be very busy fixing numerous emergency problems following the earthquake so it may be days before someone can get to those who shut things off unnecessarily. If your water supply is working fill the tub and sinks with water. Although the pipes are running now they may not later and you can use this water for washing. Outside check for downed utility lines, and turn on the radio for instructions and news reports.

- If you have to leave your residence and haven't found your pets or they have run off or hidden, remember to leave food and water. Leave the toilet seat up, fill the bathtub, open cans of food and tear open entire bags of dry food. They might be hanging around for several days before you are allowed to return.

Other **earthquake information sources**:
- **American Red Cross, Oregon Trail Chapter**, 503-284-0011, ext. 493
- **California Seismic Safety Commission** publishes *The Homeowner's*

Guide to Earthquake Safety as well as other materials on quake prepared-ness; 1900 K Street, Sacramento, CA 95814, 916-263-5506, www.seis-mic.ca.gov.

- **The Earthquake Preparedness Project** provides pamphlets and other materials on getting ready for a quake. Located at 101 8th Street, Oakland, CA 94607, 510-540-2713.
- **Federal Emergency Management Agency (FEMA)**, www.fema.gov
- **US Geological Survey**; this office helps to determine the size of the quakes and offers a treasure trove of information on all things seismic; 345 Middlefield Road, Menlo Park, CA 94025, 415-329-4390.

To get a free seismic assessment of your home call **SAFER**, the **State Assistance for Earthquake Retrofitting** at 877-723-3755. Available to homeowners in the Bay Area, they'll tell you what needs to be done to your home to make it safer and will give you information on contractors and financ-ing. *Peace of Mind in Earthquake Country* by Peter Yenev might offer some com-fort as well.

OTHER QUAKE-RELATED NOTES

If you're buying a home in California the seller is required by law to tell you if the property is in the vicinity of an earthquake fault line. Before buying you may want to engage the services of a civil engineer to give your prospective home the once-over, just to make sure it's as safe as it can be. Rental property owners are not required to disclose information about nearby faults to prospective tenants. To learn more about fault lines in the Bay Area and other quake-related information, log onto http://quake.abag.ca.gov.

Property owners are strongly advised to buy a homeowner's insurance policy that covers quake damage. The same is true for renters. The California Insurance Commissioner requires that companies that sell homeowners and renters policies in California must also offer earthquake insurance. While many policies are limited in what they offer for damage due to a quake, coverage is available. See the **Finding a Place to Live** chapter for more information.

Bolted wood frame buildings (such as Victorians) are quite safe and steel reinforced concrete buildings (such as downtown skyscrapers) are reasonably safe. The most dangerous building to be in during a quake is non-reinforced masonry. Many such buildings have warning plaques in their entryways. Dozens of San Francisco buildings are still being retrofitted following the 1989 earthquake. You might want to find out whether the building you live or work in has been retrofitted or bolted.

S AN FRANCISCO'S DIVERSITY IS MOST EVIDENT IN THE MULTITUDE OF churches, temples, ashrams, mosques, and other houses of worship to be found throughout the Bay Area. Below is a list describing just a few of the many religious organizations here. For more information about worship in the Bay Area talk to leaders or fellow congregants at your current place of worship. You'd be surprised at how many people across the US have ties to the San Francisco area. To find a place of worship close to your new home check the Yellow Pages under "Churches" or "Synagogues" or go online to www.qwestdex.com and do a key word search.

CHURCHES

BAPTIST

- **Ebenezer Baptist Church**, 275 Divisadero Street, San Francisco, 415-431-0200
- **First Chinese Baptist Church of San Francisco**, 1-15 Waverly Place, San Francisco, 415-362-4139; 3010 Noriega Street, San Francisco, 415-753-3950, www.fcbc-sf.org; serving San Francisco since its inception in 1880, the Waverly location is newly renovated and seismically retrofitted. The congregation is multi-generational, bilingual, and bicultural.
- **Third Baptist Church, Inc**. 1399 McAllister, San Francisco, 415-346-4426
- **Temple Baptist Church**, 3355 19th Avenue, San Francisco, 415-566-4080

EPISCOPAL

- **Grace Cathedral, and the Episcopal Diocese of California**, 1055 Taylor Street, San Francisco, 415-673-5015, perched atop Nob Hill, this is a lovely cathedral, complete with stained glass windows, murals, and lofty ceilings. Episcopalians come from all over the City to worship here. In particular, midnight mass on Christmas Eve, the Easter service which includes an egg roll at nearby Huntington Park, and the Evensong on Sundays are attended by members and non-members alike. The church also hosts concerts, indoor/outdoor art exhibits, offers an associated boy's school, a cafe, and a shop of religious items including music and Christmas cards. Just walking inside or strolling through the outdoor labyrinth offers a peaceful and meditative experience. There are a number of other Episcopal Churches throughout the City and the Bay Area; check the Yellow Pages under "Churches."

PRESBYTERIAN

- **Calvary Presbyterian Church**, 2515 Fillmore Street, San Francisco, 415-346-3832, located at the top of the hill in Pacific Heights, offers concerts, a preschool, and singles and elder groups.
- **Noe Valley Ministry**, 1021 Sanchez, San Francisco, 415-282-2317, holds popular concerts, including jazz, folk, classical, and religious music. It also offers community classes that range from belly dancing to ecology.
- The **Old First Presbyterian Church**, 1751 Sacramento Street, San Francisco, 415-776-5552, claims to be the oldest Presbyterian Church in the City.
- **Menlo Park Presbyterian Church**, 950 Santa Cruz Avenue, Menlo Park, 650-328-2340, www.mppc.org, is a popular church with loads of groups for singles and single parents, group activities, and outreach programs. Contact www.mppc.org.

LUTHERAN

- **St. Mark's Lutheran Church**, 1111 O'Farrell Street, San Francisco, 415-928-7770
- **St. Matthews Lutheran Church**, 3281 16th Street, San Francisco, 415-863-6371
- **West Portal Lutheran Church**, 200 Sloat Boulevard, San Francisco, 415-661-0242
- **Zion Lutheran Church and School**, 495 9th Avenue, San Francisco, 415-221-7500

METHODIST

- **Glide Memorial Methodist Church**, 330 Ellis Street, San Francisco, 415-771-6300, www.glide.org; the charismatic Reverend Cecil Williams, a prominent San Francisco figure, and his poet wife have instigated 52 programs at Glide including food giveaways, recovery meetings, classes, and housing programs. But what draws parishioners, the down and out, tourists, the movers and shakers of San Francisco society, and many others, at least once, is the lively music and singing at the services.

ROMAN CATHOLIC

There are 48 different Catholic parishes in San Francisco. For a comprehensive list, contact the **San Francisco Archdiocese** at 415-565-3600, or check their web site, www.sfarchdiocese.org. The office of the **Archdiocese of San Jose**, 900 Lafayette Street, Suite 301, 408-983-0100, www.dsj.org, can tell you about churches in the South Bay. Numerous churches in the Bay Area offer services in Italian, Chinese, Tagolag, French, Spanish, Latin, Vietnamese, Korean and more. Check the web sites listed previously to find one that may be of interest to you.

- In San Francisco, the main church of the diocese is the **Cathedral of St. Mary of the Assumption** at 1111 Gough Street, San Francisco, 415-567-2020; referred to as St. Mary's Cathedral, it is a bright and airy modern structure, completed in 1971 after the original cathedral burnt down.
- **Mission Dolores**, 3321 16th Street, San Francisco, 415-621-8203, is the oldest building in the City. Sunday services are at 8 a.m. and 10 a.m. for English speakers; there is a noon mass in Spanish.
- **St. Dominic's** at 2390 Bush Street in San Francisco, 415-567-7824, www.stdomincs.org, has a school for children, K-8.
- **St. Vincent de Paul Church** at 2320 Green Street, San Francisco, 415-552-9242, www.svdp-sfparish.org, has one of the largest and most active young adult groups, meets every second and fourth Monday of the month (not every other Monday), from 7:30 p.m. to 9 p.m.

EASTERN ORTHODOX

- **Russian Orthodox Church of Our Lady of Kazan**, 5725 California Street, 415-752-2502, is located in the Richmond District. The Church's glistening, onion-domed Cathedral with mosaics, icons, and frankincense is an exquisite place to visit, even if you aren't a member. The singing is spectacular. Several Russian bakeries and restaurants nearby offer mouthwatering breakfasts and lunches after services.
- **Greek Orthodox Diocese of San Francisco**, 372 Santa Clara Avenue, San Francisco, 415-753-3075, www.goaldsf.org
- **Greek Orthodox Cathedral of the Annunciation**, 245 Valencia Street, 415-864-8000
- **Greek Orthodox Cathedral of the Ascension**, 4700 Lincoln Avenue, Oakland, 510-531-3400; this Cathedral is known for its lovely stained glass. Overlooking the Bay Area from atop the Oakland hills, the church offers youth and senior programs and a choir.

UNITARIAN UNIVERSALIST

For a list of Unitarian Universalist centers in the Bay Area go to www.uua.org.
- **First Unitarian Universalist Church and Center**, 1187 Franklin, San Francisco, 415-776-4580

JEWISH CONGREGATIONS

The **Jewish Community Center** at 3200 California Street, San Francisco, 415-346-6040, www.jccsf.org, offers Jewish education classes and workshops, social and singles events, programs for interfaith couples and families, preschools, after-school programs, a teen center, summer and day camps, youth sports classes and leagues, dance, music, ceramics and art classes, and older adult programs. In Palo Alto, the **Albert L. Schultz Jewish Community Center**, 650-493-9400, www.paloaltojcc.com, also offers classes and community events. For a wealth of information log onto www.sfjcf.org, where you can find out about volunteer opportunities, trips to Israel for young people, and a great deal more. The **Jewish Community Information & Referral**, 415-777-4545, e-mail, JewishNfo@aol.com, should also be able to assist you. For more on Jewish congregations and organizations in the Bay area go to www.jewishsf.com where you can bring up information about cooking, personal ads, classifieds, entertainment, a calendar of events, etc.

There are at least twenty different Jewish congregations in the City. Below are just a few.

REFORM

- **Temple Emmanu-El**, 2 Lake Street, San Francisco, 415-751-2535, celebrated its 150th anniversary in 2000; a beautiful temple, it's one of the centers of reform Jewish life in San Francisco.
- **Temple Sherith Israel**, 2266 California Street, San Francisco, 415-346-1720

CONSERVATIVE

- **Beth Shalom**, 1301 Clement Street, San Francisco, 415-221-8736, is a traditional conservative congregation with more than 600 household members.

CONSERVATIVE REFORM

A conservative reform synagogue mixes conservative and reform traditions, and tends have more English and less Hebrew in the service.
- **Beth Israel** 625 Brotherhood Way, San Francisco, 415-586-8833; offers a

reform service on Fridays at 8 p.m., and a conservative service on Saturdays at 10 a.m. Parking is not a problem.

PROGRESSIVE REFORM

- **Sha'ar Zahav**, 290 Dolores, San Francisco, 415-861-6932, is a progressive reform synagogue for people of all sexual identities.

ISLAMIC

There are dozens of mosques, Islamic community centers, libraries, schools, and political and social groups in the Bay Area. For starters, in San Francisco contact the **San Francisco Moslem Community Center** at 415-563-9397 or the **Islamic Society of San Francisco** at 415-863-7997; in San Jose call 408-970-0647. You can reach the **South Bay Islamic Association** at www.sbia.net, which offers details about Bay Area mosque locations, schools, elder groups, restaurant listings, charities, and more.

FAR EASTERN SPIRITUAL CENTERS

HINDU

To find out more about the practice of Hinduism and its related yogic meditations, visit the **Sivanda Ashram Yoga Center**, 1200 Arguello Boulevard, 415-681-2731. There are a number of yoga centers sprinkled throughout the City. Voted one of the best place to practice yoga by the *San Francisco Bay Guardian* is the **Mindful Body**, 2876 California Street, 415-931-2639.

In Fremont try the **Hindu Temple and Cultural Center**, 3676 Delaware Drive, Fremont, 510-659-0655.

While not a religious organization, the **Vedanta Society of Northern California** at 2323 Vallejo Street, 415-922-2323, offers lectures, scripture classes, a bookshop, and library.

BUDDHISM

The **San Francisco Buddhist Center**, at 37 Bartlett Street, 415-282-2018, www.sfbuddhistcenter.org, is a good resource for newcomers wanting to contact other Buddhist centers in the Bay Area.

Bay Area Zen Buddhist centers offer peaceful and sheltered environments for ceremonies, meals, meditations, chanting, and more, to members and non-members alike. The old brick **Zen Center** at 300 Page Street, in San Francisco, 415-863-3136, and Marin County's **Green Gulch Farm Zen Center** in Sausalito, 415-383-3134, are just two of the many centers in the Bay Area.

(Vegetables grown at Green Gulch are used at Green's Restaurant in Fort Mason.) For more information and links to local centers, visit www.sfzc.com.

GAY AND LESBIAN

- **Congregation Sha'ar Zahav**, 290 Dolores Street, San Francisco, 415-861-6932, is a reform synagogue for people of all sexual identities.
- **Dignity San Francisco**, San Francisco, 415-681-2491, is for Catholic gay, lesbian, bisexual and transgender people and their friends. Services are held at the Seventh Avenue Presbyterian Church, 3129 7th Avenue.
- **Metropolitan Community Church**, 150 Eureka Street, San Francisco, 415-863-4434, www.mccsf.org, offers social activities, recovery groups, counseling. The Parishioners also serve meals to the homeless, provide showers for homeless, and tutor children at the Harvey Milk Civil Rights Academy.
- **Most Holy Redeemer Church**, (Catholic) 100 Diamond, San Francisco, 415-863-6259, offers services, reconciliation and confession, and AIDS support groups
- **Saint Francis Lutheran,** 152 Church Street, San Francisco, 415-621-2635; this entire church is excommunicated from the mainstream Lutheran Church. They offer over thirty self-help groups, senior meetings, and bingo.

RELIGIOUS STUDIES

- **The Graduate Theological Union**, 1798 Scenic Avenue, Berkeley, 510-849-8272, nicknamed Holy Hill, is on the north side of the University of California at Berkeley. It includes the Pacific School of Religion, the Bade Museum (of religious items), the Flora Lamson Hewlitt Library, at 2400 Ridge Road, 510-649-2500, as well as six schools of theology and six religious centers. Combined, these schools and centers offer seminars on every imaginable subject about any known religion. For more about lectures, presentations, and public prayer services call 510-649-2400.

THE MISSIONS

For California history buffs, Roman Catholics, or anyone who wants to get a sense of old California, a tour of some of Northern California's missions is a must. Spanish missionaries settled California during the 1700s and several mission sites are still in existence today. Some are active, consecrated churches, others exist only as crumbling remnants. Certainly the most well known and still operating mission is **Mission Dolores**, 3321 16th Street, 415-621-8208, in the heart of San Francisco. Little of Santa Clara's original mission remains, but a replication has been placed at the University of Santa Clara. **Carmel Mission**, 3080 Rio Road, 831-624-3600, in the Carmel Valley is still standing, and **Mission San**

Jose, 43300 Mission Boulevard, 510-652-1797, in Fremont has been reconstructed and re-consecrated. **Mission San Rafael**, 1104 5th Avenue, 415-456-3016, once a sanitarium for the California natives who were sickened by exposure to European diseases, is today a consecrated church. In outlying areas are **Mission San Luis Obispo**, 728 Monterey Street, 805-543-6850, **Mission Soledad**, 36641 Fort Romie Road, 408-678-2586, and **Sonoma Mission**, 114 East Spain Street, 707-938-1519. To find out more, visit www.ca-missons.com.

WHETHER YOU'D LIKE TO GIVE A LITTLE TO YOUR FELLOW MAN AND woman, you are looking to meet people in your new hometown, or you're interested in learning new skills that could be helpful in a job, volunteering your services to any of the organizations below is a great idea. Service agencies are always in need of help, and most will have no trouble finding something for you to do.

The agencies listed below can put you in touch with the many service organizations in the Bay Area in need of your assistance.

- **Bay Area Volunteer Information Center**, www.volunteerinfo.org
- **Contra Costa Volunteer Center**, 925-972-5760
- **Hayward Volunteer Center**, 510-538-0554
- **Marin Volunteer Center**, 415-479-5660
- **Oakland Volunteer Center**, 510-419-3970
- **Volunteer Center of San Francisco**, 415-982-8999, www.vcsf.org
- **Volunteer Center of San Mateo County**, 650-342-0801, www.vcsmco.org

If you already know which type of volunteer work suits you, try one of the agencies below.

AIDS

- **AIDS Foundation**, 415-863-2437
- **Face to Face**, 415-267-6121
- **Operation Concern**, 415-626-7000
- **Project Open Hand**, 415-447-2300
- **Restoration House**, 415-285-2302

ALCOHOL

- **Alcoholics Anonymous**, 415-621-1326

- **Glide Memorial Church**, 415-771-6300
- **Haight-Ashbury Free Clinic**, 415-487-5632
- **St. Vincent de Paul**, 415-621-6471
- **Women's Alcohol Center**, 415-282-8900

ANIMALS

- **Marine Mammals**, 415-289-7330
- **Pets Unimited**, 415-563-6700
- **Randall Museum**, 415-544-9600
- **San Francisco Society for the Prevention of Cruelty to Animals**, 415-554-3000
- **San Francisco Zoological Society**, 415-753-7100

ARTS AND CULTURE

- **Ansel Adams Center for Photography**, 415 495-7000
- **Asian Art Museum**, 415-668-8921
- **Cartoon Art Museum**, 415-227-8675
- **De Young Museum**, 415-863-3330; **Legion of Honour**, 415-863-3330
- **San Francisco Museum of Modern Art**, 415-357-4000

CHILDREN

- **Big Brothers/Big Sisters of San Francisco and the Peninsula**, 415-693-7700
- **Polly Klaas Foundation**, 800-587-4357
- **San Francisco Child Abuse Council**, 415-668-0494
- **San Francisco School Volunteers**, 415-749-3700

CRIME

- **San Francisco District Attorney Victim Services Unit**, 415-553-9049

SENIOR SERVICES

- **Catholic Charities**, 415-281-1200
- **Card & Visitor Association**, 209-269-1405
- **Friendship Line**, 415-752-3778
- **Legal Assistance**, 415-861-4444
- **Meals on Wheels**, 415-920-1111

DISABLED ASSISTANCE

- **Council of the Blind**, 800-221-6359
- **Crisis Line**, 800-426-4263
- **Hearing Society**, 415-693-5870
- **Recreation Center for the Handicapped**, 415-665-4100
- **Rose Resnick Lighthouse for the Blind**, 415-431-1481
- **United Cerebral Palsy Association**, 415-627-6939

DISASTER

- **American Red Cross**, 415-427-8000
- **United Way**, 415-772-4300

ENVIRONMENT

- **California Conservation Corps**, 800-952-5627
- **Nature Conservancy**, 415-777-0487
- **Sierra Club**, 415-977-5500

GAY AND LESBIAN

- **GLAAD (Alliance Against Defamation)**, 415-861-4588
- **Gay Youth Talk Line**, 415-863-3636
- **Metropolitan Church**, 415-863-4434

HEALTH

- **American Cancer Society**, 415-394-7100
- **American Heart Association**, 415-433-2273
- **Mental Health Association**, 415-82-6230
- **Irwin Blood Bank (central number for the Bay Area)**, 415-567-6400

HISTORY

- **California Historical Society**, 415-357-1848
- **San Francisco Maritime National Historic Park**, 415-556-9876

HUNGER AND HOMELESS

- **Glide Memorial Church**, 415-771-6300
- **Home Away From Home**, 415-561-5533

- **Meals on Wheels**, 415-920-1111
- **Project Open Hand**, 415-447-2300
- **St**. **Anthony's Dining Hall**, 415-241-2600
- **St**. **Vincent de Paul**, 415-626-1515
- **SF Food Bank**, 415-282-1900
- **Salvation Army**, 415-533-3500

LEGAL

- **ACLU**, 415-621-2488
- **Asian Law Caucus**, 415-391-1655
- **Legal Aid**, 415-864-8208
- **Legal Assistance for Children**, 415-863-3762

LITERACY

- **Project Read**, 415-557-4388

WOMEN'S SERVICES

- **NOW**, 415-861-8880
- **Women Against Rape**, 415-647-7273

BY CAR

C ALIFORNIA IS WIDELY KNOWN FOR ITS "CAR CULTURE." DESPITE THE best efforts of alternative transportation advocates, and the excellent public transportation options available, Bay Area freeways clog every weekday morning and afternoon, often to the point of gridlock. According to *Commute Profile 2000*, published by RIDES for Bay Area (www.rides.org), more than 3.5 million people in the Bay Area commute to work, and of these a whopping 67% ride alone in their cars. The remaining 33% choose to carpool, vanpool, or take the bus, train, ferry or bike.

For a comprehensive look at Bay Area transit options check out the latest edition of the *San Francisco Bay Area Regional Transit Guide*. Published by the Metropolitan Transportation Commission (MTC), the book is available at many bookstores for about $5. If you have trouble locating it, contact the MTC directly at 510-464-7700. To get the full range of Bay Area transit information and issues online, go to www.transitinfo.org.

TRAFFIC

In 1999 the Texas Transportation Institute ranked the San Francisco/Oakland area as the third most congested region in the country; San Jose was noted as the 15th worst city for commuting. If taking BART or some other form of mass transit is not feasible, the travel information line, 817-1717 (no area code needed), will give you up to the minute highway condition reports for the entire Bay Area. Or tune into KALW-FM at 91.7, KGO-AM at 810, and KCBS-AM at 740, during morning and afternoon commute hours. Real time traffic incidents are available at http://cad.chp.ca.gov.

CARPOOLING

Rides for Bay Area Commuters Inc. is a free carpool and vanpool matching service. To be matched with a fellow commuter, who is on a similar work schedule and lives and works close to you, call the service at 800-755-7665 or check www.rides.org. In the Bay Area you'll find carpool lanes, also called diamond lanes, on the major freeways. The number of passengers required to qualify as a carpool and the hours during which the lane may be used exclusively by buses, vanpools, and carpools varies. Call the above number for more details, or check your route for posted information. During commute hours, 5 a.m. to 10 a.m., and 3 p.m. to 7 p.m., the Bay bridges offer free tolls for those driving with three or more people in a vehicle. Commute hours for the Golden Gate Bridge are 5 a.m. to 9 a.m. and 4 p.m. to 6 p.m. There are also 150 Park & Ride lots throughout the area where you can leave your car to join a van or carpool. Contact Rides to join a van or carpool. There's no need to drive down that lonesome highway lonesome!

CAR RENTALS

All the big rental outfits are represented in the Bay Area, most with numerous locations. Here are a few numbers to get you started:
- **Alamo**, 800-327-9633, www.alamo.com
- **Avis**, 800-331-1212, www.avis.com
- **Budget**, 800-527-0700, www.budget.com
- **Dollar**, 800-800-4000, www.dollar.com
- **Enterprise**, 800-325-8007, www.enterprise.com
- **Hertz**, 800-654-3131, www.hertz.com
- **National**, 800-227-7368, www.nationalcar.com
- **Thrifty**, 800-367-2277, www.thrifty.com

TAXIS

The Bay Area is served by a number of cab companies, but they are not always easy to find and it almost always seems that once you sight a cab it's already full. Particularly on a rainy day, holidays (especially Halloween and New Years), and during rush hour, it is best to call ahead. If you are already out and about and need a cab, you might have better luck hailing one in front of a hotel, a department store, or a hospital.

SAN FRANCISCO
- **De Soto Cab**, 415-970-1300
- **Luxor Cab**, 415-282-4141
- **Veteran's Cab**, 415-552-1300
- **SuperShuttle**, 415-558-8500

NORTH BAY
- **Marin Cab**, 415-455-4555
- **Radio Cab**, 415-485-1234
- **Sausalito Taxi**, 415-332-2200
- **Yellow Cab**, 415-453-6030

EAST BAY
- **American Yellow**, 510-655-2233
- **Berkeley Yellow**, 510-528-9999
- **Contra Costa Cab**, 925-235-3000
- **Veteran's Cab**, 510-533-1900
- **Yellow Cab**, 510-317-2200

PENINSULA
- **A-One Airport Transportation**, 650-571-0606
- **Bubble Cab Co.**, 650-347-0743
- **Burlingame Rainbow Cab**, 650-344-6718
- **Hillsborough Yellow Cab**, 650-340-0330
- **Peninsula Cab Co.**, 650-344-2627

SOUTH BAY
- **American Cab**, 408-727-2277
- **Santa Clara Cab**, 408-773-1900
- **San Jose Taxicab**, 408-437-8700
- **United Cab**, 408-971-1111
- **Yellow Cab**, 408-293-1234

BY BIKE

Many Bay Area residents commute to work by bicycle. To find out everything you need to know about using your bike as transportation in the Bay Area call 817-1717 (no area code needed) and ask for the "RIDES Bicycle Resource Guide" or check www.transitinfo.org. At this site you can find out about bike racks at your place of work, track down a bike buddy, learn about bicycle routes and lanes, and find a bicycle club. If you choose this manner of commuting, make sure to purchase a bike light for the winter months, and wear a helmet! Bicycles are allowed on BART with the following restrictions: bikes are allowed on at the Embarcadero Station during morning commute hours (7:05 a.m. to 8:50 a.m.) and only for trips to the East Bay. For the evening commute (4:25 p.m. to 6:45 p.m.), bicycles coming from the East Bay, must exit at the Embarcadero Station. During non-commute times, bicyclists are allowed in any car, except for the first car. There is no extra cost for bringing your bike. Most buses (not all) and ferries also accommodate bikes.

For the latest about proposed bike routes, bicycle commuting initiatives, safety information, and bike laws go to California's Department of Transportation web site, www.dot.ca.gov/hq/tpp/bicycle. Another resource is the **San Francisco Bicycle Coalition** at 415-431-BIKE, www.sfbike.org. To learn more about recreational bicycling in the Bay Area consult the **Sports and Recreation** chapter.

A note of interest: on the last Friday of every month, Critical Mass, a large group of bike riders, gathers at the Ferry building in downtown San Francisco to ride together throughout the City. Their intent is to be noticed, particularly by city leaders and drivers, in the hope that more attention will be paid to biking as an alternative form of transportation. Take a look at their web site for more information, www.critical-mass.org.

PUBLIC TRANSPORTATION

BAY AREA RAPID TRANSIT (BART)

The king of local transportation systems is the Bay Area Rapid Transit, a high-speed, above- and below-ground train system that whisks travelers between San Francisco and the East Bay, through one of the world's longest underwater tunnels. BART transports about 350,000 people daily, and has a reputation for being clean, quiet, and on time.

Currently BART runs four lines between three dozen stations. It is also expanding service further into the East Bay, and is in the process of building track for four new stations, including one at San Francisco International Airport. Trains currently run weekdays from 4 a.m. to midnight, Saturdays, 6 a.m. to midnight, and Sundays, 8 a.m. to midnight. Fares are based on distance traveled, and range from $1.10 to $4.70, one way. Discount tickets (75% off) for senior citizens, children 5-12 years old, persons with disabilities who have proper identification, and students on a chaperoned field trip, are sold at participating banks, retailers, social service agencies and other community based organizations. These tickets are not sold at any of the BART stations.

BART stations are also connection points for local bus services, making it fairly easy to get just about anywhere in the Bay Area on public transit. You can purchase transfers from BART to AC Transit or to MUNI for $1.00 at all of the San Francisco stations, except for the Daly City Station, where transfers are free. Make sure to pick up your transfer before you exit the fare gates. All BART stations are wheelchair accessible. Bicycles are allowed on BART; see **By Bike** above for details. For schedule and fare information drop by the Customer Service window at the Lake Merritt BART station in Oakland, or at the Embarcadero or Montgomery Stations in San Francisco during normal business hours, or call 510-464-6000 or 650-992-2278; TDD/TTY, 510-839-2220. BART also has an informative web site, www.bart.gov.

SAN FRANCISCO MUNICIPAL RAIL (MUNI)

San Francisco's bus system or MUNI employs a variety of vehicles including diesel and electric buses, electric trolleys (some of them vintage), MUNI Metro light-rail-vehicles and the world-renowned cable cars. In total, MUNI operates 80 lines, 17 of them express, as well as special service to 3COM Park for 49ers games and other events. In general, service is available 24 hours, although not on all lines. The current adult fare is $1 one way, except on the cable cars which cost $2. Exact change is required on all MUNI vehicles, except for the cable cars. Transfers are available on all MUNI lines, as are discounts for seniors, youths and the disabled. A monthly pass costs $8.00 for seniors, youths and disabled people and $35.00 for everyone else. You can also buy a weekly pass for $9.00. The monthly pass is also valid on specific BART, CalTrain and SamTrans routes (routes 24B and 34 and only within San Francisco). If you are taking BART, you can buy a MUNI bus transfer for $1.00. Make sure you purchase your transfer before you exit the fare gates. You can also request a transfer to ride on another MUNI bus for free from the MUNI bus driver. Bus transfers are valid for 90 minutes and can be used for any direction.

For more information on MUNI service call 415-673-MUNI; TDD/TTY, 415-923-6366 or visit their web site at www.sfmuni.com. Call 415-923-6070 for information about services for passengers with disabilities.

ALAMEDA–CONTRA COSTA TRANSIT (AC)

AC Transit is the bus system connecting the East Bay to San Francisco, and serves Alameda and Contra Costa counties. Widely used are the commute-hour Transbay Express Routes from San Francisco to cities in the East Bay such as Oakland, Berkeley, Alameda, Emeryville, Richmond and more. AC Transit also connects with all East Bay BART stations. Ticket prices vary depending on distance traveled; they range from $1.35 to $2.50 down to sixty-five cents for seniors, the disabled, and those under twelve. You can purchase transfers for 25 cents. Transfers are valid for up to two and one half hours from the time of issuance.

For more information on AC Transit call 800-559-4636; TDD/TTY, 800-448-9790; or look at their web site at www.actransit.org.

SAN MATEO COUNTY TRANSIT (SAMTRANS)

SamTrans provides Peninsula residents with local bus service and offers routes to downtown San Francisco. It also links San Francisco International Airport (SFO) to the BART system at its Colma station with its 3X bus, and offers direct service from SFO to downtown San Francisco, making it possible for airline passengers to get to and from the airport entirely on public transit. The cost varies depending on distance traveled.

For more information on SamTrans call 800-660-4287; TDD/TTY, 650-508-6448 or visit their web site at www.samtrans.com.

GOLDEN GATE TRANSIT (GGT)

Golden Gate Transit provides local bus service for Marin County communities, as well as commute bus and ferry service between Marin and Sonoma counties and downtown San Francisco. The ferries depart for San Francisco from the Larkspur Ferry Terminal and a Sausalito dock located just off Bridgeway, the city's main street. There is plenty of free parking at the Larkspur facility and metered parking close to the Sausalito launch point. There is no more civilized or more relaxing way to commute than on the ferry, and more and more people are choosing to take the boat these days. Another added bonus about the scenic ferry is that numerous romances have blossomed on these morning and evening cruises. Drinks and snacks are served. The trip across the bay takes about 30 minutes. The cost varies depending upon distance traveled.

For more information on the bus and ferry service call 415-923-2000; TDD/TTY: 415-257-4554; also visit their web site at www.goldengatetransit.org.

ADDITIONAL BUS SERVICES

- **Contra Costa County Connection** provides local bus service in Contra Costa County, call 925-676-7500, TDD/TTY, 800-735-2929.
- **Santa Clara County Transit** or **Valley Transit Authority** offers bus and light rail service to the South Bay, call 800-894-9908; TDD/TTY, 408-321-2330.

FERRIES

ALAMEDA-OAKLAND-VALLEJO FERRY

Providing an aquatic link to downtown San Francisco for East Bay residents, this service is similar to **Golden Gate ferry service** outlined above. Those who use the boat regularly often develop friendships that continue on land and you can be sure there is plenty of professional networking taking place on board. The boats leave seven days a week from Oakland's Jack London Square, at the foot of Broadway, from Alameda's Main Street terminal, from Richmond, and from Vallejo. They dock at San Francisco's Ferry Building and at Fisherman's Wharf. Food and beverage service is available. One way fares range from $3 to $7.50. A number of new routes and terminals are under discussion by local planners. For more information call 510-522-3300.

HARBOR BAY ISLE FERRY

This ferry service takes riders from the San Francisco Ferry Building to Bay Farm Island (part of the City of Alameda) in the East Bay. Travel time is approximately 30 minutes. Fares are $4.50 for adults; $3.50 for seniors, disabled and military; $1.25 for children 6 to 12 years; children 5 and under ride free. Call 510-769-5500 for details.

ADDITIONAL FERRY SERVICE

- **Angel Island-Tiburon Ferry**, 415-435-2131
- **Blue and Gold Ferry**, 415-773-1188
- **Vallejo Baylink Ferry**, 707-648-4666

COMMUTER TRAINS

CALTRAIN

For Peninsula and South Bay residents the commuter rail option is CalTrain. This service runs between Gilroy in the South Bay and San Francisco's Fourth Street Station. Once you get to San Francisco you'll need to take a bus, cab, or walk to the Financial District. There is talk of extending CalTrain's tracks to the Transbay Terminal at First and Mission streets. Fares on CalTrain are based on distance traveled, and range from $2.00 to $5.25, and can be purchased at any CalTrain station. From San Jose, trains run Monday-Friday, 4:44 a.m. to 10:30 p.m., and from San Francisco, 5 a.m. to 11:59 p.m. Bikes are allowed. For more information call 800-660-4287, TDD/TTY, 415-508-6448.

AMTRAK

Amtrak trains don't board in San Francisco, instead you take the Amtrak bus at the Ferry Building, Pier 39 (near Fisherman's Wharf), or at Powell and Market, which will then drive you over the Bay Bridge to the Amtrak station in Emeryville. Or you can take BART, disembark at the Richmond station, and catch an Amtrak train one block away at 16th and MacDonald. For more information call the central line at 800-USA-RAIL or check www.reservations. amtrak.com. When visiting online, look for 'rail sale' entries where you'll find discounts of up to 60% on long-distance coach train tickets. Regional Amtrak information can be found at Amtrak California, www.amtrakcalifornia.com, which lists local specials and promotions.

ALTAMONT COMMUTER EXPRESS (ACE)

Altamont Commuter Express is a new commuter train service for those traveling between Stockton and San Jose, with additional stops in Lathrop/Manteca, Tracy, Livermore, Pleasanton, Fremont and Santa Clara. Currently, there are two morning and two afternoon trains. Fares depend on the distance traveled and range from $3 to $10 one-way. Monthly passes are available and range in price from $59 to $279. For more information, contact 800-411-RAIL or visit the ACE website at www.acerail.com.

GREYHOUND

Greyhound has numerous stations throughout the Bay Area. For more information, call 800-231-2222, or visit their web site at www.greyhound.com.

AIRPORTS & AIRLINES

SAN FRANCISCO INTERNATIONAL AIRPORT (SFO)

Located 15 miles south of downtown San Francisco, SFO sits just off Highway 101 near the Peninsula cities of Millbrae and San Bruno. The granddaddy of Bay Area airports, it seems to be under continuous construction. Presently a new international terminal is being built, and airport officials warn of increased traffic congestion and long-term and short-term parking shortages due to this construction.

There is no shortage of transportation options between the airport and San Francisco. A taxi or a limo will set you back about $40. One of the many shuttle vans, such as SuperShuttle, 415-558-8500, will cost about $13 and $8 for additional passengers in your party, but you may have to sit through a number of stops before you get to your destination (they claim no more than three stops per trip). If you've got time to kill and you need to conserve cash, catch a SamTrans bus outside the International or United Terminals for a ride directly into downtown San Francisco. (For more on SamTrans see above.)

For more information on SFO call 650-761-0800, or visit their web site at www.sfoairport.org; for SFO parking information call 650-877-0227 (24 hours).

Airlines serving SFO include:
- **American**, 800-433-7300, www.aa.com
- **British Airways**, 800-247-9297, www.british-airways.com
- **Continental**, 800-525-0280, www.flycontinental.com
- **Delta**, 800-221-1212, www.delta-air.com
- **Japan**, 800-525-3663, www.japanair.com
- **KLM Royal Dutch**, 800-374-7747

- **Northwest**, 800-225-2525, www.nwa.com
- **Qantas**, 800-227-4500, www.qantas.com
- **Scandinavian**, 800-221-2350, www.sas.com
- **TWA**, 800-221-2000, www.twa.com
- **USAir**, 800-428-4322, www.usairways.com
- **United**, 800-241-6522, www.unitedairlines.com

OAKLAND INTERNATIONAL AIRPORT

This East Bay airport is easier to use than San Francisco International for one simple reason: it is much smaller than its trans-bay Goliath. While SFO is serviced by many major US and international carriers, Oakland Airport focuses on commuter and low cost airlines, the most popular being Southwest and the United Shuttle. Oakland Airport is fairly easy to get in and out of by car, and is also served on a regular basis by a shuttle from BART's Coliseum station. Parking is usually available at Oakland Airport, even during peak holiday travel periods. The airport is located at the west end of Hegenberger Road, a clearly marked exit from Highway I-880.

- **Southwest Airlines**, 888-707-8279, www.swavacations.com
- **United Shuttle**, 800-748-8853, www.unitedairlines.com

For general information on Oakland Airport call 510-577-4000. For the latest on airport parking call 510-633-2571.

SAN JOSE INTERNATIONAL AIRPORT

Located just north of downtown, San Jose International Airport, like Oakland Airport, is relatively easy to navigate and to find parking. Large and small air carriers fly to San Jose International. For general information call 408-277-4759 or look at their web site at www.sjc.org. For parking information call 408-293-6788.

Some of the airlines serving San Jose include:

- **Alaska**, 800-252-7522, www.alaskaair.com
- **American**, 800-433-7300, www.aa.com
- **Continental**, 800-525-0280, www.flycontinental.com
- **Delta**, 800-221-1212, www.delta-air.com
- **KLM Royal Dutch**, 800-374-7747, www.nwa.com
- **Mexicana**, 800-531-7921, www.mexicana.com
- **Northwest**, 800-225-2525, www.nwa.com
- **Southwest**, 800-435-9792, www.swavacations.com
- **TWA**, 800-221-2000, www.twa.com
- **United**, 800-2416522, www.unitedairlines.com

ONLINE RESOURCES—AIR TRAVEL

There are a number of travel related web sites all touting great deals including Travelocity.com, Intellitrip.com, Expedia.com, Lowestfare.com, and Cheaptickets.com—take your pick. If cost far outweighs convenience, check Priceline, www.priceline.com, where you may be able to pin down a cheap fare at an inconvenient hour (often in the middle of the night). Some airlines post last minute seats at a reduced rate, usually online. Northwest, www.nwa.com, posts last-minute cybersavers on Wednesdays at 12:01 a.m. Check with other airlines' web sites for similar deals.

To register a complaint against an airline the Department of Transportation is the place to call or write: 202-366-2220, Aviation Consumer Protection Division, C-75 Room 4107, 400 7th Street SW, Washington, DC 20590.

Information about flight delays can be checked online at www.fly.faa.gov.

U NTIL YOU FIND YOUR FIRST BAY AREA HOME OR APARTMENT YOU'LL need an interim place to hang your hat. Besides hundreds of hotels, motels, and bed and breakfasts aimed at San Francisco's considerable tourist trade, there are old-fashioned, homey residential clubs in better neighborhoods that may be more economical. Also, although most of the hotels in the City are downtown or at Fisherman's Wharf, there are neighborhood hotels where you can get a sense of what it might be like to live in a particular area of San Francisco. If you are an adventurous and/or budget-minded newcomer, you may want to consider one of the single-room occupancy hotels, called SROs, that dot much of downtown. Keep in mind that these establishments typically offer just a small room with little more than a bed, dresser, chair, and a desk. They are popular because they are cheap and because they rent by the day, week or month. Unfortunately, these low-rent buildings are often located in the seedier parts of town, such as the southern half of Polk Street, the Fifth and Mission area south of Market Street, and the Tenderloin, which is just north of Market.

Reservations for bigger, more mainstream and chain hotels can be had by calling a hotel directly or through a reservation service such as **Central Reservation Service**, 800-548-3311, **Hotel Reservations Network**, 800-964-6835, **Quikbook**, 800-789-9887, or **San Francisco Reservations**, 800-333-8996. Or go online at the following web sites for similar information: www.quikbook.com, www.hoteldiscount.com, www.hotelres.com, www.reservation-services.com. Always ask about the cancellation policy when booking through discount sites, as charges may apply. Some companies ask for full payment upon making the reservation.

Low rates quoted below are for one person per night, and for the most part, high rates quoted are for two persons per night. Of course, prices are subject to change depending on the season. If you are a real bargain hunter try negotiating a lower price.

Unless otherwise noted all listed establishments are in San Francisco.

RESIDENCE CLUBS

Residence clubs offer secure housing, maid service, some meals, community rooms for television, videos, reading, games, message service, and the opportunity to meet dozens of people in the same situation as yourself. They are not the cheapest form of housing, but the pampering you receive while you search for something permanent may be worth the added expense.

- **The Gaylord Apartment Hotel**, 620 Jones Street, 415-673-8445, $350 weekly; a pretty, California Mission-style hotel.
- **Harcourt Residence Club**, 1105 Sutter Street, 415-673-7720, $150-$250 weekly
- **Kenmore Residence Club**, 1570 Sutter Street, 415-776-5815, $165-$275 weekly
- **Mary Elizabeth Inn**, 1040 Bush Street, 415-673-6768, $155 weekly for a minimum of two weeks; women only.
- **Monroe Residence Club**, 1870 Sacramento Street, 415-474-6200, $160-$235 weekly
- **San Francisco Residence Club**, 851 California Street, 415-421-2220, $330-$695 weekly

INEXPENSIVE HOTELS

- **Adelaide**, 5 Isadora Duncan Lane, 415-441-2261, $42-$64; basic, funky, full of budget-minded Europeans. Located in downtown San Francisco.
- **Amsterdam Hotel**, 749 Taylor Street, 415-673-3277, $99-$139; downtown
- **Comfort Inn**, 1370 Monument Boulevard, Concord, 925- 827-8998, $74-$89
- **Hotel Britton**, 112 -7th Street, 415-621-7000, $89-$149; downtown
- **Hotel Sheehan**, 620 Sutter Street, 800-848-1529, $99-$159; downtown; indoor swimming pool
- **Royal Pacific Motor Inn**, 661 Broadway, 415-781-6661, $84
- **San Remo**, 2227 Mason Street, 800-352-REMO, $50-$80; the San Remo is a charming old hotel (it has chain toilets) with odd-shaped rooms, a Victorian ambiance, a wine bar, and lots of European guests; located in North Beach.
- **Seal Rock Inn**, 545 Point Lobos, 415-752-8000, $98-$124; located in the Fog belt of the Richmond District, it's a good place to stay if you want to get a taste of the Richmond or Sunset districts.

MEDIUM PRICED HOTELS

- **Bedford Hotel**, 761 Post Street, 415-673-6040, $129-$179; downtown
- **Berkeley City Club**, 2315 Durant Avenue, 510-848-7800, $95
- **Berkeley Travelodge**, 1820 University, 510-843-4262, $80-$98

- **Canterbury Hotel**, 750 Sutter Street, 415- 474-6464, $129-$200; downtown
- **Chancellor Hotel**, 433 Powell Street, 415-362-2004, $145; downtown
- **Claremont Resort and Spa**, Ashby and Domingo, Berkeley, 510-843-3000; a rambling Victorian spa
- **Hotel Boheme**, 444 Columbus Avenue in North Beach, 415-433-9111, $139-$159; an ode to the beatniks
- **Hotel Juliana**, 590 Bush Street, 415-392-2540, $149-$170; downtown, houses the famous restaurant Masa's
- **King George Hotel**, 334 Mason Street, 415-781-5050, $140-$170; downtown, an interesting, skinny, green building with a popular tea room.
- **The Maxwell**, 386 Geary Street, 415-986-2000, $149-$225; downtown
- **Oakland Marriott**, 1001 Broadway, 510-451-4000, $99-$144
- **Courtyard by Marriott**, 2500 Larkspur Landing Circle, Larkspur Landing, 800-321-2211, $115-$199
- **Madison Street Inn**, 1390 Madison Street, Santa Clara, 408-249-5541, $75-$125
- **Hotel California**, 2431 Ash Street, Palo Alto, 650-322-7666, $70-$85
- **San Ramon Marriott**, 2600 Bishop Drive, San Ramon, 925-867-9200, $99-$189
- **York Hotel**, 940 Sutter Street, 415-885-6800, $109-$220, downtown, houses the Plushroom, a cabaret venue

LUXURY HOTELS

- **The Archbishop's Mansion**, 1000 Fulton Street, 415-563-7872, $139-$419; located in the Western Addition/Alamo Square, the decor of each room is based on a different opera
- **Casa Madrona**, 801 Bridgeway, Sausalito, 415-332-0502, $168-$300
- **The Clift**, 495 Geary Street, 415-775-4700, $255 on up; located downtown, considered to be one of the best in the City. It houses the elegant Redwood Room, an ever-popular piano bar.
- **Cupertino Inn**, 10889 North De Anza Boulevard, Cupertino, 408-996-7700, $174-$375
- **Dockside Boat and Bed**, 489 Water Street, Oakland, 510-444-5858, $115-$300
- **El Drisco,** 2901 Pacific Avenue, 800-634-7277, $220-$325; in Pacific Heights, an old gem with great views.
- **The Fairmont**, 950 Mason Street, 415-772-5000, $289 on up; in Nob Hill, it's one of the City's opulent, old-world hotels.
- **The Fairmont**, 170 South Market Street, San Jose, 408-998-1900, $229-$329; located at the top of Nob Hill.
- **Garden Court Hotel**, 520 Cowper Street, Palo Alto, 650-322-9000, $250 on up

- **The Grand Hyatt**, 345 Stockton Street, 415-398-1234, $199-$284; downtown
- **Hotel Sausalito**, 16 El Portal, 888-442-0700, Sausalito, $135-$270
- **The Mark Hopkins**, 1 Nob Hill Circle, 415-392-3434, $260-$350; in Nob Hill, what a view!
- **The Palace**, 2 New Montgomery Street, 415-512-1111, $205-$375; downtown, with a Palm Court reminiscent of days gone by.
- **Ritz-Carlton**, 600 Stockton Street, 415-296-7465, $365-$425; in Nob Hill, luxurious
- **Stanford Park Hotel**, 100 El Camino Real, Menlo Park, 650-322-1234, $260-$300

SHORT-TERM APARTMENT RENTALS

Short-term apartment rentals are usually not cheap. Generally, these residences cater to corporations not individuals.

- **Bridgestreet**, 482 Mercury Drive, Sunnyvale, 800-944-7966; junior one-bedrooms start at $2,300. They'll provide you lodging for short term or longer term.
- **California Suites/Suite America** (short-term rentals nationwide), 800-367-9501, Bay Area rates: one-bedroom, one-bathroom, $117-$125 per day; two-bedroom, two-bathrooms, $105-$170 per day; rates south of San Jose run as little as $88-$105 per day.
- **ExecuStay**, 800-500-5110, is a nationwide service that offers fully furnished apartments. They also can accommodate pets and children.
- **Fox Plaza**, 1390 Market Street, 415-626-6902; a prime example of high-rise temporary apartments, you'll find one- and two-bedroom units, each with a panoramic view of San Francisco. The building has 24-hour security, a fitness center, underground parking and restaurants in the building. Cats are the only pets allowed, provided you pony up a $500 deposit. A studio runs $1,585-$1,885 per month, and a one-bedroom, $2,850.
- **Key Housing Connections**, 800-989-0410, www.keyhousing.net, offers furnished accommodation Bay Area wide for a minimum of 30 days, up to three months, depending on availability.
- **Oakwood Corporate Apartments**, 800-888-0808, www.oakwood.com; this company owns the buildings they lease to renters all over the South Bay and Peninsula. Fully furnished apartments are customized to suit your needs. The minimum stay is 31 days. Prices vary depending on location. At the Oakwood/San Jose South location, 700 South Saratoga in San Jose, a 31 day stay in a studio apartment costs $3,098, a one-bedroom, $3,874; a stay at the Oakwood/Mountain View location, 555 West Middlefield Road in Mountain View, costs $3,253 for a studio, and a one-bedroom, $4,029 (these prices do not include maid service).

- **Trinity Plaza**, 1169 Market Street, 415-861-3333: studio, $885 per month; one-bedroom, $1,200 per month. Trinity Properties offer numerous short-term rentals around San Francisco but none such a bargain as at Trinity Plaza. Call 415-433-3333 or 474-0330 for information about others.

BED & BREAKFASTS

There are hundreds of B&Bs in the Bay Area, ranging in price from as low as $65 per night for a simple room in a private home to as much as $200 per night for an opulent unit in an historic Victorian or a self-contained carriage house or private cottage. **Bed and Breakfast International** has been providing information and reservations about local B&Bs since 1978 and boasts connections to more than 300 B&Bs and similar lodgings. Call Bed and Breakfast International at 408-867-9662 or find them on the web at www.bbintl.com. Their mailing address is P.O. Box 2247, Saratoga, CA, 95070.

HOSTELS/YMCAS

SAN FRANCISCO/NORTH BAY

- **AYH Hostel Union Square**, 312 Mason Street, 415-788-5604, $18
- **AYH Hostel Fort Mason**, Fort Mason, Bldg, #240, 415-771-7277, $18
- **Globetrotters Inn**, 494 Broadway, 415-346-5786, $13-$26
- **HI Marin Headlands**, 941 Fort Berry, Sausalito, 415-331-2777, $13 for a dorm, $39 for a private room—must have at least two people in your party to stay in a private room.
- **YMCA**, Administrative Office, 44 Montgomery Street, 415-391-9622
- **YMCA Hotel**, 220 Golden Gate Avenue, 415-885-0460, $27-$81
- **YMCA Hotel**, 855 Sacramento Street, 415-576-9622, $31

SOUTH BAY

- **Hidden Villa Hostel**, 26870 Moody Road, Los Altos Hills, 650-949-8648, (closed for renovations until September, 2001).
- **Sanborn Park Hostel**, 15808 Sanborn Road, Saratoga, 408-741-0166, $8.50 for hostel members, $10.50 for non-members

To find out further information on local youth hostels try www.hostel-web.com or www.hiayh.org.

ACCESSIBLE LODGING FOR THE DISABLED

Hilton Hotels, 800-445-8667, TDD 800-368-1133, **Hyatt Hotels**, 800-233-1234, **ITT Sheraton**, 800-325-3535, **Marriott Hotels**, 800-288-9290, and **Microtel Inn and Suites**, 888-771-7171, offer rooms specializing in the needs of the disabled.

AS WONDERFUL AND DIVERSE AS THE BAY AREA IS, EVERYONE LIKES TO get away from city living now and again. Whether it's skiing, water sports, scenery, gambling, historical tours, wining and dining, or just rest and relaxation, there are dozens of nearby destinations to suit most anyone. Interesting possibilities abound outside the immediate Bay Area; in fact, you can go skiing on Saturday and sailing on Sunday, and be back to work by Monday. Following are just a few of the many quick getaways Northern California has to offer.

NORTH OF SAN FRANCISCO

If you don't want to drive far and you want to keep an eye on San Francisco, **Angel Island** may be the ticket. Located in the middle of San Francisco Bay, Angel Island is a short jaunt, either by ferry or sailboat and a good place to picnic, barbecue, join a softball game, bike, kayak, hike the scenic trails, and camp. Call 415-435-1915 or visit www.angelisland.org for more information. For the San Francisco and Vallejo ferries, contact the Blue and Gold Fleet at 415-773-1188; the Tiburon Ferry information is at 415-435-2131.

In Marin County a stay in a cedar lodge with meals included is available at **Green Gulch Farm Zen Center**, 1601 Shoreline Highway, Sausalito, 415-383-3134. Here you can witness a Japanese tea ceremony, join in classes and meditation and even learn about organic gardening. Most of the fruits and vegetables grown at Green Gulch end up as a vegetarian meal at Greens Restaurant in Fort Mason. If this kind of getaway appeals to you get a copy of *Sanctuaries, the Complete United States: A Guide to Lodging in Monasteries, Abbeys, and Retreats* by Jack and Marcia Kelly.

On a hot summer day, you may want to drive windy Highway 1, past the Green Gulch Farm Zen Center, and venture to **Stinson Beach** for sunbathing, body surfing, swimming or just exploring the shore. Beware that you may not be the only one with this plan; traffic can be horrible. Another great beach getaway is **Point Reyes National Seashore**, which includes 30 miles of coastline and 70,000 acres of pristine wilderness. Amidst its rugged bluffs, wooded canyons, dense forests, and open meadows, you'll find spectacular hiking, biking, camping, bird watching, and whale watching. For information about camping at Point Reyes contact the Visitors' Center at 415-663-1092. Make sure to reserve camping sites ahead of time. If you don't want to camp and pine for an upscale romantic lodge, the Manka's Inverness Lodge, 415-669-1034, is lovely. While you are in the area try some oysters at Hog Island Oyster Company, 415-663-9218.

One of the most popular Bay Area getaways is a journey to **Napa** and **Sonoma counties** for fine wines and steaming mud. If you're a gourmand these areas offer dozens of world-renowned **vineyards** and **wineries**, most with tours, tastings, and some with fine restaurants. Connoisseurs recommend Auberge du Soleil, 180 Rutherford Hill Road, Rutherford, Tra Vigne, 1050 Charter Lane, Saint Helena, and The French Laundry, 6640 Washington Street, Yountville. You can even take a wine train to eat, drink, and view the gentle landscape all the way from St. Helena to Napa, without having to designate a driver. For information about the train call 800-427-4124.

In addition to touring the wineries, Napa and Sonoma counties host numerous **spa-type resorts**. Facilities range from the funky to the glamorous. Most of the spas are in the town of Calistoga. Below is a list of some of the spas, many which have indoor and outdoor pools, mineral baths, steamrooms, dirty but oh so cleansing mud baths, salt scrubs, massage and more. This list is far from comprehensive:

- **Dr. Wilkinson's Hot Springs**, 1507 Lincoln Avenue, Calistoga, 707-942-4102, www.drwilkinsons.com
- **Calistoga Indian Springs Resort**, 1712 Lincoln Avenue, Calistoga, 707-942-4913, www.indianspringscalistoga.com
- **Nance's Hot Springs**, 614 Lincoln Avenue, Calistoga, 707-642-6211
- **Lavender Hill Spa**, 1015 Foothill Boulevard, Calistoga, 707-942-4495
- **White Sulphur Springs**, 3100 White Sulphur Springs Road, St. Helena, 707-963-8588, www.whitesulphursprings.com
- **Calistoga Spa Hot Springs**, 1006 Washington Street, Calistoga, 707-942-6269, www.calistogaspa.com.
- **Sonoma Mission Inn**, 18140 Sonoma Highway, Boyes Hot Springs, 707-938-9000, www.sonomamissioninn.com

If all this isn't enough, you can ride a hot air balloon, take a tram up a mountainside, sail through the air on a glider, hike, bike, horseback ride, picnic, or shop at posh designer outlets. For further information about the entire region contact www.co.napa.ca.us or www.sonoma.com.

Another North Bay getaway is a visit to the old logging region of **Russian River**. In the 1920s and '30s, the area was a working class summer resort.

During and after the Depression it suffered from neglect and overuse, and was quite deteriorated by the 1970s when entrepreneurs, many from the gay community, arrived and began restoring the old buildings. Today Russian River is again a resort destination with lodging, fine restaurants, wineries, camping, hiking, horseback riding, and more. The natural environs of the Russian River, with its sandy beaches, redwood groves, and placid river, make it a pleasant place to spend a day or even a weekend. Canoeing down the river is a popular way to explore the area. Begin in Forestville and the local canoe company will meet you and your canoe 10 miles down river in Guerneville. After canoeing, take a trip down the Russian River Wine Road (www.wineroad.com) to sample fine wine. For more information about the many things to do here contact the Russian River Visitors Bureau at 800-253-8800 or visit www.rrvw.org.

Moving toward the coastline around **Mendocino**, located about three and half-hours north of San Francisco, is simply breathtaking. The town of Mendocino reminds some of fishing villages on the East Coast. Here you can watch for whales, wade in the tide-pools, hike in Mendocino Headlands State Park, 707-937-5397, or camp among redwoods at Van Damme State Park, 707-937-4016. At the **Jug Handle State Reserve** you can view tectonic uplifts and pygmy forests. If riding horses along the beach appeals to you, take a trail ride at Ricochet Ridge Ranch, 707-964-7669. Many opt to explore the area by train, allowing the engineer of the Skunk Train to do the driving through forty miles of redwoods and gulches. Call 800-777-5865 for more information.

The community of **Sea Ranch**, located 100 miles north of San Francisco on Highway 1, offers house rentals with ocean views and nearby trails. Abalone diving, kayaking, horseback riding, and swimming are only some of the activities, not to mention the golf course. For more details go to www.searanchvillage.com or call 707-785-2468.

Fort Bragg, about four hours north of San Francisco on Highway 1, was built to protect the peace-loving Pomo Indians from less peaceful settlers, though the actual fort hasn't been the here since the 1860s. These days Fort Bragg is a lumber town, and during the annual Paul Bunyan Days you can watch lumberjacks test their skill in a number of competitions. Contact the Mendocino Coast Fort Bragg Chamber of Commerce at 707-961-6300 or visit www.mendocinocoast.com for more information.

PENINSULA/SOUTH BAY

The coastline from San Francisco all the way south to Santa Cruz offers a scenic getaway with bluffs, beaches, and great surfing spots. In Half Moon Bay, you can pick pumpkins at any of the numerous pumpkin patches along the highway. Sixty miles south of San Francisco brings you to **Ano Nuevo State Reserve**, home to large numbers of northern elephant seals. The reserve offers memorable tours during breeding season from December to March. Call 800-444-7275 for more information.

Monterey/Carmel is also known as John Steinbeck country, as he based many of his novels here, including *Cannery Row*, *Of Mice and Men*, and *The Grapes of Wrath*. Now the canneries are closed, and resorts and tourist sites stand in their stead. Another attraction is the Monterey Bay Aquarium, where you can come eye to eye with strange-shaped sunfish or marvel at the elegant jellyfish. For more information call 800-756-3737, www.monterey.com.

These days, Carmel is tourist oriented—full of restaurants, art galleries, gift shops, inns and hotels, and is an easy place for children and elderly folks to get around. The scenery is spectacular, with sea lions and coves, rocky beaches, wind whipped cypress trees, and well-maintained indigenous gardens. Nor can we forget to mention the famous Pebble Beach Golf Course, where Tiger Woods etched his name into the golfing record books, winning the 100th US Men's Open by 15 shots. The Carmel Mission on Rio Road and Lasuen Drive, 831-624-3600, dates from 1797. The missionaries assigned here must have counted their blessings to be in such a scenic place and gentle climate. In the early 1900s, Carmel-by-the-Sea became a mecca for artists and writers. Robert Louis Stevenson, Ansel Adams, Sinclair Lewis, Edward Weston, Upton Sinclair, and Mary Austin settled at one time in Carmel. Poet Robinson Jeffers' home has been made into a museum; contact Tor House at 831-624-1813 for details. The Henry Miller Library, with memorabilia from that famous author, is located nearby in Big Sur. Call 831-667-2574, or check www.henrymiller.org for more details. Residents and tourists alike gather to watch the sunset at Nepenthe Restaurant along the cliffs of Big Sur.

Those looking for a more spiritual outing may want to drive to Big Sur to the famous **Esalen Institute/Hot Springs**, 831-667-3000. The institute, designed to foster personal and social transformation, offers seminars, lodging, dining, hot springs, a pool, massages and awesome views of the California coastline.

On the northern part of Monterey Bay sits **Santa Cruz**, a striking contrast to the more conservative town of Carmel. The bohemian-hippie enclave of Santa Cruz is as lovely as any beach town, with wind-swept trees, rolling hills, and ocean vistas, though most outsiders come here for the Santa Cruz Beach Boardwalk, 400 Beach Street. Here you can ride the wooden roller coaster, the merry-go-round and experience an old style amusement park. The University of California at Santa Cruz, with its laid-back student body adds to the beachy feel of this friendly town—despite its many resident panhandlers. Visit the Santa Cruz Municipal Wharf for the Santa Cruz Surfing Museum on West Cliff Drive, 831-420-6289. Come in the summer and sit on the beach to listen to Summertime Summer Nights Concerts, or attend an opera at the Capitola Theatre, 120 Monterey Avenue Capitola, 831-462-3131. If thrift shopping is your thing, junkstores on Capitola Avenue are quite popular; they even offer a guide and map for your convenience. Call 800-833-3494 to order one. For a perfect place to watch the sunset or build a fire on the beach after dusk, try New Brighton, Seacliff, Rio del Mar, or Manresa State Beaches. There are fire rings for barbecues and roasting marshmallows. For more information, contact the Santa Cruz County Traveler's Guide, 800-833-2494 or check www.ci.santa-cruz.ca.us.

Amateur and professional geologists alike flock to the epicenter of the 1989 Loma Prieta quake at what's known as the **Earthquake Trail** in **Nicene Marks State Park**. Located 80 miles south of San Francisco, just a few miles outside of Santa Cruz, the area is lovely, sheltered by pines and oaks with gentle streams running through. There are 10,000 acres of forest here, so plenty of non-geology folk visit as well. Call 831-763-7064 for more information. Call the Aptos Chamber of Commerce at 831-688-1467 for further sightseeing and hotel ideas.

SIERRAS AND GOLD COUNTRY

Twenty-five miles north of Auburn in the **Sierra Nevada foothills** is **Gold Country**. View what the '49ers experienced when they flocked here from around the world in search of their fortunes. In this old mining territory you can pan for gold, swim, or sun on a rock while being sprayed by the cooling foam of the Yuba River. Bird watching is popular, or if you're a homesick Northeasterner, come in the autumn to take in the brilliantly colored maple and aspen leaves. In summer and fall you can fish for trout or bass. Hiking is possible at Buttermilk Bend, Independence Trail, or if you're up to it, try the steep Humbug Trail. Call 800-655-6569 for information or go to www.nevadacityinns.com to find a place to stay. Some of the best white water rafting and kayaking can be had along the American, Stanislaus, Tuolumne and Merced rivers, all weaving through the Sierra foothills.

In winter, many head north on I-80 to ski in the Sierras. There are dozens of choices in **Lake Tahoe** for downhill or cross-country skiers. You can also ice-skate, snowboard, or sled. Lake Tahoe is loads of fun in the summer too. That's when folks go water-skiing in the icy waters of Lake Tahoe. You can also kayak, river raft, or even try inner tubing the chilly Truckee River. Camping, rock climbing, and hiking in the Sierras are first rate. If you want to reserve a roof over you head, contact Lake Tahoe Central Reservations at 800-824-6348 or on the web at www.tahoe.com.

NATIONAL PARKS

To learn about the camping and tour reservation system for the National Park system contact www.reservations.nps.gov or call 800-365-2267. The National Park Service Office for the Bay Area is located at Fort Mason, Building 201, 415-556-0560.

YOSEMITE NATIONAL PARK

Beloved by Californians and out-of-state tourists alike, Yosemite is a popular destination for many, though most Bay Area visitors come in the fall, after the summer crowds have gone. President Theodore Roosevelt called Yosemite "the most beautiful place on earth," and it seems photographer Ansel Adams and naturalist John Muir were equally awestruck, having spent years here documenting the incredible natural beauty, including Half Dome, El Capitan and Nevada Falls. Yosemite has gotten much more popular and crowded since Muir and Adams made their way around the valley. The valley floor is often packed with tourists, and many try to avoid it preferring to head to the backcountry hiking trails. Intrepid folks hike 17 steep miles to the top of Half Dome, while rock climbers finesse their way up El Capitan. There's a hut system for luxury backcountry camping, but the permits for these are issued by lottery and therefore can be difficult to obtain. Wilderness permits are required for any overnight travel into the park's backcountry, call 209-372-0740 for more details about hut and wilderness permits. For more details about Yosemite, contact the Yosemite National Park, P.O. Box 577, Yosemite, CA 95389, 209-372-0200 or check www.nps.gov/yose or www.yosemitepark.com.

NATIONAL FOREST SERVICE

If you are planning a camping trip, call the National Forest Service's toll free reservation line at 877-444-6777, TDD, 877-833-6777. You can reserve up to 240 days in advance. You can also make your reservation online at www.reserveusa.com.

GETAWAYS WITH YOUR KIDS

In addition to the above-mentioned getaways, many of which would be perfectly suitable for children, there are a number of places in the Bay Area specifically designed for kids. In the Sierras many of the ski resorts cater to children. Head north or south to vast agricultural areas for apple and berry picking or to find the perfect pumpkin or Christmas tree. For amusement parks, try Vallejo's Marine World, 2001 Marine World Parkway, 707-556-5200, Paramount's Great America amusement park on Highway 101, Santa Clara, 408-988-1776, or the Santa Cruz Beach Boardwalk (see above). There are also a bunch of museums specifically geared to children. Below is just a sampling of the various getaways.

NORTH BAY

For a short overnight, camp at **Kirby Cove** in the Marin Headlands. Camp sites cost $20 per night. Bring a warm sleeping bag. Call 415-561-4364 for reservations. The **Miwok Stables** in Tennessee Valley has horseback riding lessons. For more information call 415-383-8048. Also in Marin, **Slide Ranch** has an educational center geared for children. Located on Highway 1, two miles north of Muir Beach, at Slide Ranch you can explore the tide pools, meditate in a *yurt*, or pet goats. Up in Napa and Sonoma counties there are farms open to the public where visitors can pick fruit off the vine or the tree. For more information, contact farm trails at 800-207-9464, www.farmtrails.org

EAST BAY

Tilden Park in Berkeley has a merry-go-round, miniature steam train and golf course, and a petting zoo. For more information call 510-525-2233. **Oakland's Children's Fairyland** at the corner of Grand and Bellevue avenues, 510-452-2259, www.fairyland.org, brings the fairytale world to life, from Alice in Wonderland's world to Captain Hook's pirate ship.

SOUTH BAY

Kids love picking ollalie berries (a cross between a blackberry, loganberry and youngberry, with a tangier taste than a boysenberry) from thick vines all over Northern California, including **Coastways Ranch** in Santa Cruz County, 650-879-0414, and the **Phipps Ranch**, 650-879-0787, located one mile east of the town of Pescadero, along the coast. When you are not picking berries (their season is May through July), you can pick pumpkins in October, and kiwi fruit in November and December. Christmas trees are available at Coastways as well. During pumpkin season, you'll find a number of Pumpkin Patches along Highway 1 near Half Moon Bay. **The Prusch Farm Park**, 647 South Kind Road, San Jose, 408-926-5555, is an educational center where you can learn about gardening, fruit orchards, and farm animals. Also along the coast is the **Roaring Camp and Big Trees Railroad**, located in the Santa Cruz mountains not far from San Jose, which has 1,500 year old redwoods, a steam train, and an old west town for young'ns where they can pan for gold. Call 831-335-3509 or contact www.roaringcamper.com. Another steam train in the South Bay is at the **Billy Jones Wildcat Railroad and Carousel** in Oak Meadow Park, Los Gatos, 408-395-RIDE, where kids can ride a 1905 miniature steam engine or be whirled around on a restored carousel.

A few of the **Bay Area museums** for children include:
- **Burlingame Museum of Pez Memorabilia**, 214 California Drive, Burlingame, 650-347-2301, www.spectrumnet.com/pez; this museum is devoted to Pez candy dispensers.
- **Chabot Space and Science Museum**, 10902 Skyline Boulevard,

Oakland, 510-530-3499; perched on top of Joaquin Miller Park, the new museum has an enormous telescope, a planetarium, and an IMAX dome theater. Definitely worth the trip up the hill.

- **Children's Discovery Museum**, 557 McReynolds Road, Fort Baker, Sausalito, 415-487-4398
- **Children's Museum of San Jose**, 180 Woz Way, San Jose, 408-298-5437, www.cdm.org; this children's museum is one of the largest in the US and has many interactive exhibits for children under 13 years old.
- **Exploratorium**, 3601 Lyon Street, San Francisco, 415-563-7337, www.exploratorium.edu, is a hands-on science museum which includes the tactile dome, a labyrinth of different textures to be explored in the dark.
- **Habitot Children's Museum**, 2065 Kittredge Street, Berkeley, 510-647-1111, is designed especially for infants, toddlers, and preschoolers.
- **Lawrence Hall of Science**, Centennial Drive, Berkeley, 510-642-5132
- **Monterey Bay Aquarium**, 886 Cannery Row, Monterey, 408-648-4888; here, you can be eye-to eye with sharks, sunfish, jelly fish and more and stay dry at the same time.
- **Randall Museum**, 199 Museum Way, San Francisco, 415-554-9600, www.randall.mus.ca.us; run by the San Francisco Parks and Recreation Department, the museum has classes and events for children plus an animal room with birds, snakes, lizards, and more reptiles.
- **Winchester Mystery House**, 525 Winchester Boulevard, San Jose, 408-247-2000, www.winchestermysteryhouse.com; a 160-year-old Victorian mansion with 47 fireplaces, designed by the Winchester Rifle heiress, Sarah L. Winchester. Among other oddities is a set of stairs that lead to the ceiling!
- **Zeum Museum and Yerba Buena Center**, 221 Fourth Street, 415-777-2800, www.zeum.com, is an art and technology center for kids eight to 18 years old. Also in the center, an ice-skating rink and a carousel.

ALMOST EVERY DAY OF THE YEAR THERE IS SOMETHING SPECIAL TO DO or see in this culturally rich region. Many local events take place on an annual basis so you can look forward to them year after year. Here are just a few of the celebrations and events you may want to experience for yourself. Specific dates are not provided as they may change depending on the particular year. Locations are provided when possible although they too sometimes change from year to year. If none is given, then assume San Francisco and call for details.

JANUARY

- **Chinese New Year Celebrations** begin, toward the end of the month in Chinatown, San Francisco, 415-982-3000
- **East-West Shriners Football Game**, Stanford University, 650-372-9300
- **Martin Luther King, Jr. Birthday Celebration**: Alameda, 510-748-4505; El Cerrito Community Center, El Cerrito, 510-215-4370; Regional Shoreline Park, Oakland, 510-562-1373; in San Francisco call for location, 415-771-6300; MLK Jr. Community Center, San Mateo, 650-377-4714
- **Orchid Show**, Red Morton Community Park, Redwood City, 650-780-7250
- **San Francisco Sports and Boat Show**, Cow Palace, Daly City, 415-469-6065
- **San Jose International Auto Show**, McEnery Convention Center, San Jose, 408-277-3900
- **Tet Festival**, Vietnamese New Year (sometimes in February), in San Francisco at the Civic Center and Tenderloin District, 415-391-8050; Santa Clara County Fairgrounds, San Jose, 408-494-3247
- **Whale Watching** (through March), Point Reyes National Seashore, 415-669-1534

FEBRUARY

- **American Indian Art Show**, Marin Center, San Rafael, 415-472-3500
- **Black History Month Celebrations**, Oakland Museum of California, Oakland, 510-2338-2200; Oakland Public Libraries, Oakland, 510-238-3134
- **Black History Month Celebrations**, Westlake Park, Daly City, 650-991-8001; MLK Jr. Community Center, San Mateo, 650-377-4714
- **Chinese Community Street Fair**, Chinatown, 415-982-3000
- **Chinese New Year Golden Dragon Parade**, Chinatown, 415-982-3000
- **Golden Gate Kennel Club Dog Show**, Cow Palace, Daly City, 415-469-6065
- **Japanese Cultural Festival**, Community Center, Rohnert Park, 707-584-5978
- **Pacific Orchid Exposition**, Fort Mason, 415-546-9608
- **Russian Festival**, Sutter and Divisadero streets, 415-921-7631
- **Tet Festival**, Vietnamese New Year (sometimes in January), Civic Center and Tenderloin District, 415-391-8050; Santa Clara Country Fairgrounds, San Jose, 408-494-3247
- **Tribal Folk and Textile Art Show**, Fort Mason, 415-455-2886.
- **Valentine's Day Walk**, benefits American Heart Association, Lake Merritt, Oakland, 510-632-9606

MARCH

- **Bay Area Music Awards**, "The Bammies," Bill Graham Civic Auditorium, 510-762-2277
- **Farm Day**, celebration of National Agriculture Day, Marin Center, San Rafael, 415-456-3276
- **International Women's Day Celebration**, call San Francisco location, 415-431-1180
- **Russian River Wine Barrel Tasting**, local wineries strut their stuff; call for locations in Sonoma County, 800-723-6336
- **Saint Patrick's Day Celebration**, Happy Hollows Park & Zoo, San Jose, 408-295-8383
- **Saint Patrick's Day Parade**, Market Street, San Francisco, 415-661-2700
- **San Francisco Asian American Film Festival**, Japantown, San Francisco, 415-252-4800
- **Sonoma County Home and Garden Show**, Sonoma County Fairgrounds, Santa Rosa, 800-655-0655
- **White Elephant Sale**, benefits Oakland Museum of California, call for location, Oakland, 510-536-6800

APRIL

- **Berkeley Bay Festival**, Berkeley Marina, Berkeley, 510-644-8623
- **Britain Meets the Bay**, celebration for Anglophiles in San Francisco, through early June, call for location, 415-274-0373
- **Cherry Blossom Festival**, Japantown, 415-563-2313
- **Christmas in April**, volunteers restore homes for seniors and disabled, call for locations in San Francisco, 415-905-1611
- **Earth Day Events**, Center Street Park, Berkeley, 510-548-2220, call for locations in Oakland, 510-238-7611
- **Flower and Earth Day Festival**, Marin Center, San Rafael
- **Opening Day on the Bay**, kicks off the local yachting season, San Francisco Bay, 415-381-1128; Tiburon and Sausalito, 415-435-5633
- **Palo Alto Asia-Pacific Film Festival**, call for locations, Palo Alto, 650-329-2366
- **San Francisco International Film Festival**, call for theater locations in San Francisco, Berkeley, Larkspur, 415-992-5000
- **Spring flower Festival**, Marin Art & Garden Center, Ross, 415-454-5597
- **Youth Arts Festival**, Berkeley Arts Center, Berkeley, 510-644-6893
- **Whole Life Expo**, a must for New Age aficionados, Fashion Design Center in San Francisco, 415-721-2484
- **Zoo & Aquarium Month**, Happy Hollow Park & Zoo, San Jose, 408-295-8383

MAY

- **Arboretum Plant Sale**, San Francisco County Fair Building, 415-661-3090
- **Bay to Breakers**, a seven-mile, cross-city, run/walk, with incredible sights and costumes, in San Francisco, 415-808-5000, ext. 2222
- **Carnava**, Latin street party in San Francisco, 24th and Mission streets, 415-826-1401
- **Charmarita Pentecost Festival**, Portuguese extravaganza, IDES Hall, Half Moon Bay, 650-726-2729; IDES Hall, Pescadero, 650-726-5701
- **Cherry Festival**, Marin Center, San Rafael, 415-456-3276
- **Cinco de Mayo Parade**, in San Francisco, 24th and Mission streets, 415-826-1401
- **Cinco de Mayo Celebration**, Stanford University, Palo Alto, 650-723-2089; downtown San Jose, 408-923-1646
- **Civil War Memorial & Re-Creation**, San Jose Historical Museum, San Jose, 408-287-2290
- **Grecian Festival**, Zorba would feel welcome, Nativity of Christ Church, Novato, 707-883-1998

- **Greek Festival**, Greek Orthodox Cathedral, Oakland, 510-531-3400
- **Hometown Days**, local arts & crafts, Burton Park, San Carlos, 650-594-2700
- **Jack o' the Green Spring Faire**, Old English celebration, Bodega Bay, 707-875-3704
- **Marin a la Carte**, gourmet treats, Marin Center, San Rafael, 415-472-3500
- **Maritime Day**, a nautical observance, Jack London Square and Waterfront, Oakland, 510-814-6000
- **Nikkei Matsuri Japanese Festival**, Japantown, San Jose, 408-277-3900
- **Polish Spring Festival**, San Francisco County Fair Building, 415-285-4336
- **Stanford Pow-Wow**, massive gathering of Native Americans, Stanford University, Palo Alto, 650-725-6944
- **Tiburon Wine Festival**, Point Tiburon Plaza, Tiburon, 415-435-5633
- **Youth Arts Festival**, M.H. de Young Museum, Golden Gate Park, 415-759-2916

JUNE

- **Alameda County Fair**, Alameda County Fairgrounds, Pleasanton, 925-426-7600
- **Art & Wine Festival**, call for location, Sunnyvale, 408-736-4971
- **Black & White Ball**, open to the public, this glamour symphony fundraiser is held every other year in San Francisco, call for locations, 415-864-6000.
- **Cherry Festival**, call for location, San Leandro, 510-577-3462
- **Gay Pride Celebration & Parade**, Guadalupe River Park, San Jose, 408-277-3900
- **Haight Street Fair**, fun and frolic at the free love flash point, Haight and Ashbury streets, San Francisco, 415-661-8025
- **International Lesbian & Gay Film Festival**, call for locations, 415-703-8663
- **Juneteenth Celebration**, marking Lincoln's Emancipation Proclamation: Berkeley, 510-655-8008; Lakeside Park, Oakland, 510-238-3866; Evergreen Valley College, San Jose, 408-292-3157; San Francisco, Fillmore Street, 415-928-8546, call for locations
- **Lesbian Gay, Bisexual & Transgender Celebration & Parade**, numerous San Francisco locations, 415-864-3733
- **Midsummer Mozart Festival**, call for locations, 415-392-4400
- **Mill Valley Wine & Gourmet Food-Tasting**, Lytton Square, Mill Valley, 415-388-9700
- **North Beach Festival**, an Italian blowout, North Beach, 415-403-0666
- **Novato Art, Wine & Music Festival**, Old Town, Novato, 707-897-1164
- **Puerto Rican Festival**, Santa Clara County Fairgrounds, San Jose, 408-742-1204
- **Race Unity Day**, Pickleweed Convention Center, San Rafael, 415-454-8689

- **San Anselmo Art & Wine Festival**, San Anselmo Avenue, San Anselmo, 415-454-2510
- **San Francisco Jazz Festival summer sessions**, call for locations, 415-398-5655
- **Shakespeare on the Beach**, call for location, Stinson Beach, 415-868-9500
- **Silicon Valley Concours d'Elegance**, fine wine and vintage cars, Guadalupe River Park, San Jose, 408-277-3900
- **Sonoma-Marin Fair**, Petaluma Fairgrounds, Petaluma, 707-763-0931
- **Stern Grove Midsummer Music Festival**, through August, Stern Grove, 415-252-6252
- **Summer Concert Series**, through August, call for locations, Milpitas, 408-942-2470
- **Trips for Kids Bike Swap**, huge bicycle event, San Rafael High School, San Rafael, 415-458-2986
- **Twilight Concerts in the Park**, Tuesday nights through July, call for locations, Palo Alto, 650-329-2121
- **Union Street Festival**, Cow Hollow event with music, art, and gourmet food, Union and Fillmore streets, San Francisco, 415-346-9162

JULY

- **Berkeley Kite Festival and West Coast Kite Flying Championships**, Cesar Chavez Park, Berkeley, 510-235-5483
- **Chinese Summer Festival**, Kelly Park, San Jose, 408-842-1625
- **Festa Italia**, plenty of pasta and pesto, B Street, San Mateo, 650-312-0730
- **Fourth of July Celebrations**, call for locations: Alameda, 510-748-4545; Albany, 510-524-9283; Berkeley, 510-644-6376; El Cerrito, 510-215-4370; Milpitas, 408-942-2470; San Jose, 408-274-4000; San Francisco, 415-777-8498; Oakland, 510-8140-6000; Santa Clara, 408-988-1776
- **Gilroy Garlic Festival**, a pungent party, Christmas Hill Park, Gilroy, 408-842-1625
- **Jazz and All That Art On Fillmore**, Fillmore and California streets, 415-346-9162
- **Jewish Film Festival**, through August, UC Theatre, Berkeley, 510-548-0556; call for locations in San Francisco, 510-621-0556
- **Los Altos Art & Wine Festival**, downtown Los Altos, 650-949-5282
- **Marin County Fair**, Marin County Fairgrounds, San Rafael, 415-499-6400
- **Marin Shakespeare Festival**, Dominican College, San Rafael, 415-499-1108
- **Mill Valley Chili Cook-off**, Blithedale Plaza, Mill Valley, 415-380-0042
- **Obon Festival**, Buddhist Church, San Jose, 408-293-9292
- **San Jose American Festival**, Guadalupe River Park, San Jose, 408-457-1141
- **San Jose International Mariachi Festival**, Guadalupe River Park, San Jose, 408-292-5197

- **San Francisco Jazz Festival summer sessions**, call for locations, 415-398-5655
- **Santa Clara County Fair**, Santa Clara County Fairgrounds, San Jose, 408-494-3100
- **Scottish Highland Games**, Dunsmuir House, Oakland, 510-615-5555
- **Shakespeare in the Park**, through October call for locations, 415-422-2221
- **Summer Festival & Chili Cook-off**, Mitchell Park, Palo Alto, 650-329-2121
- **Tahiti Fete**, island music and delicacies sure to please, Plaza de Cesar Chavez, San Jose, 408-486-9177

AUGUST

- **Berkeley Farmers' Market Cajun Festival**, MLK Jr. Park, Berkeley, 510-548-3333
- **California Small Brewers Festival**, microbrew beer bash, Franklin and Evelyn streets, Mountain View, 888-875-273
- **Chinatown Street Festival**, Chinatown, Oakland, 510-893-8979
- **Cupertino Art & Wine Festival**, Memorial Park, Cupertino, 408-252-705
- **Nihonmachi Street Fair**, a celebration of Japanese culture, Japantown, 415-771-9861
- **Old Adobe Festival**, Adobe State Historic Park, Petaluma, 707-762-4871
- **Palo Alto Festival of the Arts**, University Avenue, Palo Alto, 650-324-3121
- **Park Street Art & Wine Faire**, Park Street, Alameda, 510-523-1392
- **Renaissance Pleasure Faire**, journey back to Elizabethan England, call for locations, 800-523-2473
- **Reptile Festival**, Coyote Point Museum, San Mateo, 650-342-7755
- **San Francisco Jazz Festival**, summer series continues call for locations, 415-398-5655
- **San Jose International Beer Festival**, Guadalupe River Park, San Jose, 408-293-4373
- **San Jose Jazz Festival**, Plaza de Cesar Chavez, San Jose, 408-288-7557
- **San Jose Reggae-Blues Festival**, Guadalupe River Park, San Jose, 408-277-3900
- **San Mateo County Fair**, San Mateo County Expo Center, San Mateo, 650-574-3247
- **Sausalito Art Festival**, Bay Model Visitors Center and Marinship Park, Sausalito, 415-332-3555
- **Stern Grove Midsummer Music Festival**, in San Francisco, Stern Grove, 415-252-6252
- **Street Jam and Filipino Festival**, Plaza de Cesar Chavez, San Jose, 408-259-2164
- **West Marin Music Festival**, call for locations, 415-663-9650

SEPTEMBER

- **A la Carte a la Park**, gourmet food in the park, Sharon Meadows, Golden Gate Park, 415-383-9378
- **American Indian Trade Fest**, Miwok Park, Novato, 707-897-4064
- **Armenian Food Festival**, Saroyan Hall, 415-751-9140
- **Art in the Park**, Memorial Park, Cupertino, 408-777-3120
- **A Taste of Chocolate**, a chocoholic's dream come true, Ghirardelli Square, 415-775-5500
- **Black Filmworks**, honoring African-American films and filmmakers, call for locations, Oakland, 510-465-0804
- **Blues & Art on the Bay**, call for locations, 415-346-4446
- **Fall Arts Festival**, Old Mill Park, Mill Valley, 415-381-8090
- **Folsom Street Fair**, Folsom between 7th and 12th streets, 415-861-3247
- **Italian Festival**, Jack London Square, Oakland, 510-814-6000
- **Harvest Faire**, Marin Center, San Rafael, 415-456-3276
- **Latino Summer Festival**, 24th Street, 415-826-1401
- **Mexican Independence Day Celebration**, downtown, San Jose, 408-923-1646
- **Mid Autumn Festival**, Guadalupe River Park, San Jose, 408-277-3900
- **Mountain View Art & Wine Festival**, Castro Street, Mountain View, 408-968-8378
- **Opera in the Park**, free arias, Sharon Meadows, Golden Gate Park, 415-864-3330
- **Pacific Coast Fog Fest**, clearly a good time in the fog, Palmetto & Salada Avenues, Pacifica, 650-359-1460
- **Sandcastle Classic**, architects vs. amateurs in sandcastle building, Aquatic Park, 415-861-1899
- **San Francisco Blues Festival**, Great Meadow, Fort Mason, 415-979-5588
- **San Francisco Fair**, parking space race included, Civic Center Plaza, 415-434-3247
- **San Francisco Fringe Festival**, a celebration of the offbeat, call for locations, 415-931-1094
- **Santa Clara Art & Wine Festival**, Central Park, Santa Clara, 408-984-3257
- **Sir Francis Drake Kennel Club Dog Show**, Marin Center, San Rafael, 415-472-3500
- **Solano Stroll**, massive street fair, Solano Avenue, Albany and Berkeley, 510-527-5358
- **Summer Festival**, call for location, San Jose, 408-971-0772
- **Tiburon Chili Festival**, Main Street, Tiburon, 415-435-5633

OCTOBER

- **Black Cowboys Parade**, call for location, Oakland, 510-531-7583
- **Castro Street Fair**, Castro Street, 415-467-3354
- **Classic Car Show**, Park Street, Alameda, 510-523-1392
- **Days of the Dead Community Festival**, Oakland Museum of California, Oakland 510-238-3818
- **Fall Festival**, call for location, Milpitas, 408-726-9652
- **Fleet Week**, celebrating San Francisco's long relationship with the US Navy, call for locations, 415-705-5500
- **Grand National Rodeo**, for the cowpoke inside us all, Cow Palace, Daly City, 415-469-6065
- **Great Halloween & Pumpkin Festival**, Polk Street, 415-346-9162
- **Half Moon Bay Pumpkin Festival**, Main Street, Half Moon Bay, 650-726-9652
- **Halloween Celebration**, Jack London Square, Oakland, 510-814-6000
- **Halloween Night**, no holds barred party, Civic Center, 415-777-5500
- **Halloween at the Winchester Mystery House**, a sprawling, 160 year-old Victorian mansion, San Jose, 408-247-2000, www.winchestermystery-house.com
- **Italian Heritage Day**, honoring, among others, Christopher Columbus, North Beach, 415-434-1492
- **Mill Valley Film Festival**, call for locations, Mill Valley, 415-383-5256
- **Milpitas Main Street USA Parade**, a flag-waving good time, Main Street, Milpitas, 408-942-2470
- **Novato Harvest Festival**, Farmers Market, Novato, 415-456-3276
- **Open Studios**, a citywide, month-long tour of artists studios, 415-364-1629
- **Pacific Fine Arts Festival**, Santa Cruz Avenue, Menlo Park, 650-325-2818
- **Potrero Hill Festival**, a neighborhood favorite, call for location, 415-826-8080
- **Pumpkin Festival**, Marin Center, San Rafael, 415-456-3276
- **Reggae in the Park**, Sharon Meadow, Golden Gate Park, 415-383-9378
- **San Francisco International Accordion Festival**, can you stand it? Fisherman's Wharf, 415-775-6000
- **San Francisco Jazz Festival**, twelve days of jazz around the city, call for locations, 415-398-5655
- **Sequoia Auto Show**, Sequoia High School, Redwood City, 650-368-8218
- **Sunny Hills Grape Festival**, Larkspur Landing, Larkspur, 415-256-3276
- **World Pumpkin Weigh Off**, big gourds and big fun, Ferry Building, 415-346-4561

NOVEMBER

- **American Indian Film Festival**, Palace of Fine Arts, 415-554-0525
- **Bay Area Book Festival**, Concourse Exhibition Center, 415-908-2833
- **Christmas Crafts Fair**, Strawberry Recreation Center, Mill Valley, 415-383-6494
- **Christmas Tree Lighting**: Ghirardelli Square, 415-775-5500; Golden Gate Park, 415-831-2700; Pier 39, 415-981-8030; Jack London Square, Oakland, 510-814-6000
- **Festival of Lights Parade**, downtown, Los Altos, 650-948-1455
- **Harvest Festival**, Concourse Exhibition Center in San Francisco, 707-778-6300; McEnery Convention Center, San Jose, 707-778-6300
- **Holiday Faire**, Santa Clara County Fairgrounds, San Jose, 408-298-2644
- **Holiday Food & Art Fair**, Marin Center, San Rafael, 415-456-3276
- **Native American Culture Day**, Oakland Main Library, Oakland, 510-238-3134
- **San Francisco International Auto Show**, Moscone Center, 415-673-2016
- **Thanksgiving Farmers Market**, Marin Center, San Rafael, 415-456-3276
- **Veterans Day Parade**: Market Street, 415-467-8218; downtown San Jose, 408-277-3900

DECEMBER

- **Celebration of Craftswomen**, Fort Mason, 415-252-8981
- **Christmas in the Park**, Plaza de Cesar Chavez, San Jose, 408-277-3303
- **Christmas Revels**, Scottish Rite Temple, Oakland, 510-452-9334
- **Christmas at Sea**, holiday fair with a nautical bent, Hyde Street Pier, 415-561-6662
- **Festival of Lights**, Union Square, 415-362-6355
- **Hanukkah Family Celebration**, Marin Jewish Community Center, San Rafael, 415-479-2000
- **Kwanzaa Celebration**, MLK, Jr. Community Center, San Mateo, 650-377-4714
- **Kwanzaa Gift Show**, Oakland Convention Center, Oakland, 510-644-2646
- **Lighted Yacht Parade**, Jack London Square & Waterfront, Oakland, 510-814-6000
- **Messiah Singalong**, Center for Performing Arts, San Jose, 408-246-116
- **Our Lady of Guadalupe Fiesta**, Mission Dolores, 415-621-8203
- **San Jose Holiday Parade**, downtown, San Jose, 408-277-3303
- **Santa Claus Comes to Town**, train station, Menlo Park, 650-325-2818
- **Sing-it-yourself Messiah**, Davies Symphony Hall, 415-431-5400

- **Tour de Noel**, Christmas house tour, lunch and crafts, Saint John's Episcopal Church, Ross, 415-456-1102
- **Victorian Christmas**, San Jose Historical Museum, San Jose, 408-287-2290
- **Winterfest**, Oakland Museum of California, Oakland, 510-238-3818

THERE ARE HUNDREDS, IF NOT THOUSANDS, OF BOOKS ABOUT SAN Francisco and the Bay Area. Below is a small selection of guides, works of fiction, and historical books that will help you get acquainted with your new home.

ART

- *Art in the San Francisco Bay Area: 1945-1980* by Thomas Albright
- *Artful Players: Artistic Life in Early San Francisco* by Brigitta Hjalmarson
- *Bay Area Wild: A Celebration of the Natural Heritage of the San Francisco Bay Area* by Galen Rowell; captures the natural beauty of the Bay Area with the author's photographs and insightful text.
- *San Francisco Album* by George Robinson Fardas; early photographs of the City

FICTION

- *The Best of Adair Lara* by Adair Lara
- *Eyes of a Child* by Richard North Patterson
- *Jack London's Golden State*, edited by John Miller
- *The Joy Luck Club* by Amy Tan
- *The Maltese Falcon* by Dashiell Hammet
- *San Francisco Stories*, edited by John Miller
- *Tales of the City* by Armistead Maupin

FOOD

- *Bay Area Consumers' Checkbook Guide to Bay Area Restaurants* by Sue Remick
- *Bread and Chocolate: My Food Life in San Francisco* by Fran Gage
- *Eat this San Francisco* by Dan Leone

- *The Eclectic Gourmet Guide to San Francisco* by Richard Sterling
- *Patricia Unterman's Food Lover's Guide to San Francisco* by Patricia Unterman
- *San Francisco in a Teacup* by Ulrika Hume; where to find tea, accoutrements, and afternoon teas.
- *Zagat Survey, San Francisco Bay Area Restaurants*

HISTORY

- *Baghdad by the Bay* by Herb Caen
- *Historic San Francisco* by Rand Richards
- *The Mayor of Castro Street*: *The Life and Times of Harvey Milk* by Randy Shilts
- *Reclaiming San Francisco History, Politics, Culture*; a City Lights Anthology edited by James Brook, Chris Carlsson, and Nancy J. Peters
- *Tales of San Francisco* by Samuel Dickson
- *The World of Herb Caen* by Herb Caen

KIDS

- *Best Hikes with Children*: *San Francisco North Bay* by Bill McMillon with Kevin McMillon
- *The City by the Bay, A Magical Tour* by Tricia Brown
- *Fun Places to go with Children in Northern California* by Elizabeth Pomada
- *A Kid's Golden Gate* by Michael Elsohn Ross
- *San Francisco* by Barbara Kent

LIVING HERE

- *Connecting in San Francisco* by Diane de Castro; once you've found your job and your home, this'll help you find friends.
- *How to Get a Job in San Francisco* by John Bailey

OUTDOORS

- *101 Great Hikes of the San Francisco Bay Area* by Ann Marie Brown
- *Adventuring in the San Francisco Bay Area* by Peggy Waybarn; information about camping, hiking, fishing, area wildlife and weather.
- *Bay Area Backroads* by Doug McConnell
- *East Bay Trails*: *Outdoor Adventures in Alameda and Contra Costa Counties* by David Weintraub

- *Inside/Out Northern California: A Best Places Guide to the Outdoors* by Dennis J. Oliver
- *Roaming the Backroads of Northern California* by Peter Browning
- *Sailing the Bay* by Kimball Livingston; about sailing on San Francisco Bay.
- *San Francisco at Your Feet* by Margot Patterson Doss; offers a selection of walking tours rated for their difficulty.
- *San Francisco Running Guide: the 45 Best Routes in the Bay Area* by Bob Cooper
- *Short Bike Rides San Francisco* by Henry Kingman

SAN FRANCISCO GUIDES

These off-beat and theme-oriented guides to San Francisco will get you out and exploring, but away from the hordes of tourists

- *The Dog Lover's Companion to the Bay Area* by Maria Goodavage; the name says it all—amongst the concrete walls of the City, there are places for your dog.
- *Get Lost! The Cool Guide to San Francisco* by Claudia Lehan; a hip guide to the Bay Area
- *Romantic Days and Nights in San Francisco: Intimate Escapes in the City by the Bay* by Donna Peck; with this book, you can truly leave your heart in San Francisco.
- *San Francisco as You Like: 20 Tailor-made Tours*; there's an old hippie tour, a tour for gourmet lovers, kids tours, and others.
- *San Francisco Secrets* by John Snyder; full of little known information about the City for lovers of trivia and history.
- *Underground Guide to San Francisco* by Jennifer Joseph; if you need a new tattoo or an unusual museum to show a visiting friend here's the guide for you.

SHOPPING

- *Bargain Hunting in the Bay Area* by Sally Socolich
- *Cheapskates Guide to San Francisco* by Connie Emerson
- *Mr. Cheap's San Francisco* by Mark Waldstein

O NCE YOU ORDER PHONE SERVICE, WITHIN TWO WEEKS PACIFIC BELL will deliver the White and Yellow Pages to your door. To get them faster, call Pacific Bell at 800-248-2800 and have them deliver the books to you by UPS—this will take three to five days—or you can purchase a phone book at any Safeway grocery store. To obtain a phone book from outside your county you will have to order by mail and pay the additional cost. The prices vary considerably from county to county, although counties other than your own, but within your area code generally are free. You can access Pacific Bell's online Yellow Pages at www.smartpages.com. Although not as extensive as the print Yellow Pages, the list below should be of some assistance:

AMBULANCE, all areas, 911

ANIMALS

- Animal bites, 911
- Animal Control, 415-554-6364
- Humane Society of Contra Costa County, 925-279-2247, www.cchumane.org
- Humane Society of East Bay, 510-845-7735, www.behumane.org
- Humane Society of Marin County, 415-883-4621, www.marinhumane.org
- Humane Society of Peninsula, 650-340-8200, www.peninsulahumanesociety.org
- Humane Society of Santa Clara, 408-727-3383, www.scvhumane.org
- Humane Society of Sonoma County, 707-526-5312, www.humanesocietysonomaco.org
- Pets Unlimited, 415-563-6700, www.petsunlimited.org
- San Francisco Lots Pet Services, 415-567-8738
- Silicon Valley Friends of Ferals, www.svff.org

- SPCA (Society for the Prevention of Cruelty to Animals), 415-554-3000, www.sfspca.org

AUTOMOBILES

- American Automobile Association (AAA), 800-AAA-HELP; 415-222-4357
- BBB Auto Line, 800-955-5100
- Bureau of Automotive Repair, 800-952-5210
- California Department of Motor Vehicles, 800-777-0133, www.dmv.ca.gov
- California State Automobile Association, 800-922-8228, www.csaa.com

SAN FRANCISCO
- Abandoned Automobiles, 415-781-5861
- City Tow, 415-621-8605
- DMV, San Francisco, 415-557-1170

PARKING AND TRAFFIC
SAN FRANCISCO
- Web Site, www.ci.sf.ca.us/dpt
- Information, 415-554-7275
- Complaints, 415-553-1631
- Parking Permits, 415-554-5000
- Citation Division, 415-255-3900; Pay Traffic/Parking Citations with Credit Card, 415-255-3999, 800-531-7357
- Towed Vehicles, 415-553-1235

NORTH BAY
- DMV, Corte Madera, 415-924-5560
- Marin County Traffic Authority—Parking, 800-281-7275

EAST BAY
- DMV, El Cerrito, 510-235-9171
- DMV, Hayward, 510-728-2174
- DMV, Oakland, 510-450-3670
- Oakland Parking Bureau, 510-238-3099
- Traffic Division of the Superior Court, 510-268-7673

PENINSULA/SOUTH BAY
- DMV, San Mateo, 650-342-5332
- DMV, Daly City, 650-994-5700
- DMV, Gilroy, 408-842-6488
- DMV, Mountain View, 650-968-0610
- DMV, Redwood City, 650-368-2837

- DMV, San Jose, 408-277-1301
- DMV, Santa Clara, 408-277-1640
- San Mateo, Parking Permits, Residential & City Parking Facilities, 650-522-7326

BIRTH/DEATH CERTIFICATES

- Alameda County, 510-628-7600, www.co.alameda.ca.us/PublicHealth
- Marin County, 415-499-6094, www.marinorg/comres/records
- San Francisco County Health Department, Birth: 415-554-2700; Death: 415-554-2710, www.dph.sf.ca.us
- San Mateo County, 650-363-4712, www.smhealth.org
- Santa Clara County, 408-299-2481, www.co.santa-clara.ca.us

CITY/COUNTY GOVERNMENT—SAN FRANCISCO

- Board of Supervisors, 415-554-5184, www.ci.sf.ca.us./bdsupvrs
- California Governor, SF office, 415-703-2218, www.governor.ca.gov
- Assessor's Office, 415-554-5421, www.ci.sf.ca.us/assessor
- City Attorney, 415-554-4748
- City Clerk, 415-554-4267
- City Hall, 415-554-4000
- District Attorney, 415-551-9595
- Health Department, 415-554-2500, www.dph.sf.ca.us
- Marriage Licenses, 415-554-4150
- Mayor's Office, 415-554-6141
- Parking Commission, 415-554-9800, www.ci.sf.ca.us/dpt
- Residential Parking Permits, 415-554-5000
- Public Utilities Commission, 415-923-2400, www.ci.sf.ca.us/puc
- Public Schools Office, 415-241-6000
- Parks and Recreation, 415-831-2700
- California Registrar of Voters, 800-345-8683
- Recycling Program, www.sfrecycle.org
- Rent Stabilization Board, 415-252-4600, www.ci.sf.us/rentbd

CITY OF SAN FRANCISCO—ONLINE

- www.bayarea.com
- www.bayinsider.com
- www.ci.sf.ca.us
- www.citysearch7.com
- www.sanfrancisco.sidewalk.com
- www.sanfran.com

- www.sfbay.yahoo.com
- www.sfbayarea.com
- www.sfgate.com
- www.sanfranciscoonline.com

NORTH BAY—ONLINE

- Corte Madera, www.ci.corte-madera.ca.us
- Fairfax, www.mo.com/Fairfax
- Marin County, www.marin.org
- Mill Valley, www.cityofmillvalley.org
- Napa County, www.co.napa.ca.us
- Novato, www.ci.novato.ca.us
- San Rafael, www.cityofsanrafael.org
- Sausalito, www.ci.sausalito.ca.us
- Santa Rosa, www.ci.santa-rosa.ca.us
- Sonoma County, www.sonoma-county.org
- Tiburon, www.tiburon.org

EAST BAY—ONLINE

- Alameda City, www.ci.alameda.ca.us
- Alameda County, www.co.alameda.ca.us
- Albany, www.albanyca.org
- Antioch, www.ci.antioch.ca.us
- Berkeley, www.ci.berkeley.ca.us
- Concord, www.ci.concord.ca.us
- Contra Costa County, www.co.contra-costa.ca.us
- Fremont, www.ci.fremont.ca.us
- El Cerrito, www.el-cerrito.ca.us
- Emeryville, www.ci.emeryville.ca.us
- Hayward, www.ci.hayward.ca.us
- Livermore, www.ci.livermore.ca.us
- Martinez, www.cityofmartinez.org
- Oakland, www.oakland.ca.us
- Pinole, www.ci.pinole.ca.us
- Pittsburg, www.ci.pittsburg.ca.us
- Pleasanton, www.ci.pleasanton.ca.us
- Richmond, www.ci.richmond.ca.us
- San Leandro, www.ci.san-leandro.ca.us
- Union City, www.ci.union-city.ca.us
- Walnut Creek, www.ci.walnut-creek.ca.us

PENINSULA/SOUTH BAY—ONLINE

- Atherton, www.ci.atherton.ca.us
- Belmont, www.ci.belmont.ca.us
- Brisbane, www.ci.brisbane.ca.us
- Burlingame, www.burlingame.org
- Campbell, www.ci.campbell.ca.us
- Cupertino, www.cupertino.org
- Daly City, www.ci.daly-city.ca.us
- Foster City, www.fostercity.org
- Half Moon Bay, www.half-moon-bay.ca.us
- Hillsborough, www.hillsborough.net
- Los Gatos, www.los-gatos.ca.us
- Menlo Park, www.ci.menlo-park.ca.us
- Millbrae, www.ci.millbrae.ca.us
- Mountain View, www.ci.mtnview.ca.us
- Pacifica, www.ci.pacifica.ca.us
- Palo Alto, www.city.palo-alto.ca.us
- Redwood City, www.ci.redwood-city.ca.us
- San Carlos, www.ci.san-carlos.ca.us
- San Jose, www.sjliving.com, www.sanjose.org, www.ci.santa-clara-ca.us
- San Mateo City, www.ci.sanmateo.ca.us
- San Mateo County, www.co.sanmateo.ca.us
- Santa Clara City, www.ci.santa-clara.ca.us
- Santa Clara County, www.co.santa-clara.ca.us
- Saratoga, www.saratoga.ca.us
- South San Francisco, www.ci.ssf.ca.us
- Sunnyvale, www.ci.sunnyvale.ca.us
- Woodside, www.ci.woodside.ca.us

CONSUMER AGENCIES

- Alameda County Bar Association, 510-893-7160
- Better Business Bureau, 415-243-9999, www.bbb.goldengate.org
- California Agencies Directory, 916-657-9900
- California Attorney General, 800-952-5225, 415-703-1958, http://caag. state.ca.us
- California Department of Consumer Affairs, 800-952-5210, 510-785-7554, www.dca.ca.gov
- California Public Utilities Commission, 415-703-1282
- Department of Consumer Complaints, 800-952-5210, www.ci.sf.ca.us/casf
- Federal Communications Commission, 888-225-5322, www.fcc.gov

- Federal Consumer Information Center, 800-688-9889, TTY, 800-326-2996, www.pueblo.gsa.gov
- Federal Trade Commission, 202-382-4357, www.ftc.gov
- Financial Consumer Information, www.moneytalks.org
- Marin County Bar Association, 415-453-8181
- San Francisco Bar Association Lawyer Referral Service, 415-989-1616
- San Francisco District Attorney, 415-553-1814
- San Francisco Public Utilities Commission, 415-554-3155, www.ci.sf.ca.us/puc
- San Mateo County Bar Association, 650-369-4149
- Santa Clara County Bar Association, 408- 287-2557
- State Bar of California, 415-538-2000
- Telecommunications and Research Action Center, www.trac.org
- The Utility Reform Network (TURN), 415-929-8876, 800-355-8876, www.turn.org
- United States Consumer Product Safety Line, 800-638-2772

CRISIS LINES

- Gay Youth Talk Line, 415-863-3636
- Suicide Prevention, 415-362-3400
- Suicide Prevention, Marin, 415-499-1100
- Westside Crisis Services, 415-353-5055

ALCOHOL AND DRUG DEPENDENCY
- Alcoholics Anonymous, 415-621-1326, www.aa.org
- Cocaine Anonymous, 415-821-6155
- Community Substance Abuse Services, 800-750-2727
- Contra Costa County AA, 925-939-5371
- Drug Crisis, 415-362-3400, TDD 415-781-2224
- East Bay AA, 510-839-8900
- Marin County Alcoholics Anonymous, 415-499-0400
- Napa County AA, 707-255-4900
- Narcotics Anonymous, 415-621-8600
- San Mateo County Alcoholics Anonymous, 650-342-2615
- Santa Clara County AA, 408-374-8511
- SOS (Save Our Sobriety), 415-255-1622
- Smoker's Hotline, 800-662-8887

CHILD ABUSE/PROTECTION
- Domestic Violence Hotline, 800-540-5433
- Alameda County Child Protective Services, 510-259-1800
- Child Abuse Council of Santa Clara County, 408-293-5450
- San Francisco Child Abuse Council, 415-668-0494
- San Francisco Child Abuse Emergency Response, 415-554-5184

- Marin Child Abuse Prevention Council, 415-472-7164
- Marin Child Protective Services, 415-499-7153

RAPE/DOMESTIC VIOLENCE
- Casa de Las Madres, 877-503-1850 (offers shelter and advocacy to battered women and children)
- Domestic Violence Hotline, 800-540-5433
- Marin Rape Crisis Center, 415-924-2100
- East Bay Rape Crisis Line, 510-845-7273
- San Jose Rape Crisis Line, 408-779-2115
- Victim's Resource Center, 800-842-8467
- Women against Rape, 415-647-7273

CULTURAL LIFE

- San Francisco Events, 415-391-2001
- www.culturefinder.com
- www.sffringe.com
- www.sfgate.com
- www.sfstation.com
- www.sftoday.com
- Tix Bay Area (discount tickets), 415-433-7827
- BASS Tickets, 510-762-2277; 408-998-2277; 707-546-2277, www.tickets.com/BASSOutlets
- Ticketmaster, 415-421-8497, www.ticketmaster.com

MOVIES
- www.sfgate.com
- 408-777-FILM, San Jose

MUSEUMS
SAN FRANCISCO
- Ansel Adams Center, 415-495-8517, www.friendsofphotography.org
- Asian Art Museum, 415-379-8800, www.asianart.org
- California Academy of Sciences, 415-750-7145, www.calacademy.org
- California Historical Society, 415-357-1848, www.calhist.org
- Cartoon Art Museum, 415-227-8666, www.cartoonart.org
- De Young Museum, 415-750-3600, www.thinker.org
- Exploratorium, 415-397-5673, www.exploratorium.edu
- Fort Mason Complex, 415-441-3405, www.fortmason.org
- Haas-Lilienthal House, 415-441-3004, www.sfheritage.org
- Jewish Museum of San Francisco, 415-591-8800, www.jewishmuseumsf.org

- Mexican Museum, 415-202-9700
- Palace of the Legion of Honor, 415-750-3600, www.thinker.org
- San Francisco Cable Car Museum, 415-474-1887
- San Francisco Maritime Museum, 415-556-3002
- San Francisco Museum of Modern Art, 415-357-4000, www.sfmoma.org
- Yerba Buena Center for the Arts, 415-978-2787, www.yerbuenaarts.org
- Zeum, 415-777-2800, www.zeum.org

EAST BAY
- Berkeley Art Museum, 510-642-0808, www.bampfa.berkeley.edu
- Blackhawk Automotive Museum, 925-736-2277, www.blackhawkauto.org
- Judah L. Magnes Museum, 510-549-6950, www.jfed.org/mentry
- Lawrence Hall of Sciences, 510-642-5132, www.lhs.berkeley.edu
- Oakland Museum, 888-625-6873, www.museumca.org

PENINSULA/SOUTH BAY
- Children's Discovery Museum of San Jose, 408-298-5437, www.cdm.org
- Intel Museum, 650-765-0503, www.intel.com/go/museum
- Palo Alto Art Center, 650-329-2366
- Rosicrucian Egyptian Museum, 408-947-3636, www.rosicrucian.org
- San Jose Historical Museum, 408-287-2290
- San Jose Museum of Art, 408-294-2787, www.sjmusart.org
- San Jose Museum of Quilt and Textiles, 408-971-0323, www.sjquiltmuseum.org
- Tech Museum of Innovation, 408-294-TECH, www.thetech.org

MUSIC
- San Francisco Symphony, 800-696-9689, www sfsymphony.org
- San Francisco Opera, 415-864-3330, www. sfopera.org
- San Jose Symphony, 408-288-2828, www.sanjosesymphony.org
- Opera San Jose, 408-437-4450, www.operasj.org
- Palo Alto Chamber Orchestra, 650-856-3848
- Peninsula Civic Light Opera, 650-579-5568
- Peninsula Symphony Orchestra, 650-574-0244
- Pocket Opera, 415-575-1102
- Stanford Symphony Orchestra, 650-723-3811
- West Bay Opera, 650-843-3900

THEATER & DANCE
- American Conservatory Theater, 415-749-2228
- American Musical Theater of San Jose, 408-453-7100, www.amtsj.org
- Beach Blanket Babylon, 415-421-4222

- Berkeley Repertory Theater, 510-845-4700
- Curan Theater, 415-776-1999
- Eureka Theater, 415-788-SHOW
- Exit Theater, 415- 673-3847
- Magic Theater, 415-441-8822
- Marin Shakespeare Company, 415-499-1108, www.marinshakespeare.org
- Marin Theater Company, 415-388-5200, www.marintheater.org
- Mountain View Center for the Performing Arts, 650-903-6000
- Palo Alto Players, 650-329-0891
- San Francisco Ballet, 415-865-2000
- San Jose Repertory Theatre, 408-291-2255, www.sjrep.com
- Theater Artaud, www.theaterartaud.org
- Theatre Rhinoceros, 415-861-5079

EARTHQUAKE INFORMATION

- American Red Cross, Oregon Trail Chapter, 503-284-0011, ext. 493
- Bay Area Quake Information, http://quake.abag.ca.gov.
- California Seismic Safety Commission, 916-263-5506, www.seismic.ca.gov
- Earthquake Preparedness Program, 510-540-2713
- Federal Emergency Management Agency (FEMA), www.fema.gov
- US Geological Survey, 415-329-4390

EDUCATION

- Alameda County Unified School District, 510-887-0152, www.alamedacoe. k12.ca.us
- Berkeley Unified School District, 510-644-6147 or www.berkeley.k12.ca.us
- California Department of Education, www.cde.ca.gov
- Contra Costa County Office of Education, 925-942-3388, www.cccoe.k12. ca.us.
- Cupertino Union School District, 408-252-3000, www.cupertino.k12.ca.us
- Fremont Unified School District, 510-657-2350, www.fremont.k12.ca.us.
- Hayward Unified School District www.husd.k12.ca.us
- Institute for Childhood Resources, www.ggcbs.com
- Marin County Office of Education, 415-472-4110, www.mcoeweb. marin.k12.ca.us
- Novato Unified School District, 415-897-4201, www.novato.ca.us/nusd
- Oakland Unified School District, 510-879-8100, www.oakland.k12.ca.us.
- Palo Alto Unified School District, 650-329-3700, www.pausd.palo-alto.ca.us
- Pleasanton Unified School District, 925-462-5500, www.pleasanton. k12.ca.us.
- San Francisco Unified School District, 415-241-6000, www.sfusd.k12.ca.us

- San Jose Unified School District, www.sjusd.k12.ca.us
- San Mateo County Office of Education, 650-802-5300, www.smcoe. k12.ca.us
- Santa Clara County Office of Education, 408-453-6500, www.sccoe. k12.ca.us
- Santa Clara Unified School District, 408-983-2000, www.scu.k12.ca.us
- Sonoma County Office of Education, 707-524-2600, www.scoe.k12.ca.us
- West Contra Costa Unified School District, 510-234-3825, www.wccusd. k12.ca.us

HEALTH AND MEDICAL CARE

- American Board of Medical Specialties-Board Certification Verification, 800-776-2378
- Berkeley Drop-in Center, 510-653-3800
- Berkeley Free Clinic, 510-548-2870
- Cancer Care, 800-813-4673
- Dental referral, 800-DENTIST
- Lead Poisoning Prevention Program, www.aclppp.org
- Marin Community Clinic, 415-461-7400
- Marin County Department of Health and Human Services, 415-499-7397
- Medical Board of California, 800-633-2322
- Medi-Cal information, 415-558-1955
- Poison Control, 800-876-4766
- Public Health Department, San Jose, 408-299-6120
- San Francisco General Hospital, 415-206-8000
- San Francisco Department of Public Health, 415-502-5700, www.dph.sf.ca.us
- Sexually Transmitted Disease, 415-487-5500
- Suicide Prevention, 415-781-0500

HIV-TESTING
- AIDS/HIV Nightline, 415-434-2437
- AIDS Hotline, Marin, 415-499-7515
- AIDS Hotline, Oakland, 510-271-4263
- AIDS Hotline, San Francisco, 415-502-8378
- AIDS Hotline, San Jose, 408-885-7000
- San Francisco AIDS Foundation, 800-367-2437

HOUSING

- Berkeley Rent Stabilization Program, 510-644-6128, www.ci.berkeley.ca.us/rent
- California State Fair Employment and Housing Department, San Francisco, 415-703-4175, 800-884-1684, www.dfeh.ca.gov

- California Tenants Association, www.catenants.com
- Contractors State License Board, 800-321-2752
- Franchise Tax Board, 800-852-5711, www.ftb.ca.gov
- East Palo Alto Rent Stabilization Program, 650-853-3109
- Eviction Defense Collaborative, San Francisco, 415-986-9586
- Eviction Defense Center, Oakland, 510-452-4541
- Housing Rights Committee, San Francisco, 415-398-6200
- Housing Rights, Inc., Berkeley, 510-548-8776, www.housingrights.com
- Project Sentinel, specializes in landlord/tenant disputes in Sunnyvale, 408-720-9888
- St. Peter's Housing Committee, San Francisco, 415-487-9203
- San Francisco Rent Board, 415-252-4600
- San Francisco Tenants Union, 415-282-5525, www.sftu.org
- San Jose Rental Dispute Program, 408-277-5431
- San Jose Housing Counselor Program, 408-283-1540
- San Jose Community Legal Services, 408-283-3700

KIDS' STUFF

- Bay Area Children's Discovery Museum, 415-487-4398
- Burlingame Museum of Pez Memorabilia, 650-347-2301, www.spectrumnet.com/pez.
- Casa de Fruta Orchard Resort, 408-842-971-0323
- Chabot Space and Science Museum, 510-530-3499
- Children's Discovery Museum of San Jose, 408-298-5437, www.cdm.org
- Great America, 408-986-5855, www.pgathrills.com
- Habitot Children's Museum, Berkeley, 510-647-1111
- Monterey Bay Aquarium, 408-648-4888
- Oakland's Children's Fairyland, 510-452-2259, www.fairyland.org
- Randall Museum, 415-554-9600, www.randall.mus.ca.us.
- San Francisco Zoo, 415-753-7061, www.sfzoo.org
- Six Flags Marine World, 707-643-6722, www.sixflags.com
- Winchester Mystery House, 408-247-2101, www.winchestermystery-house.com
- Youthline Programs and Services, 415-777-3399
- Zeum, 415-777-2800, www.zeum.org

LEGAL MEDIATION OR REFERRAL

- AIDS Legal Referral Panel, 415-291-5454, www.alrp.org
- Alameda County Bar Association, 510-893-7160
- American Civil Liberties Union of Northern California, 415-621-2488, www.aclunc.org

- Berkeley Dispute Resolution Service, 510-428-1811
- California Courts, www.courtinfo.ca.gov
- California Community Dispute Service, 415-865-2520
- Community Boards of San Francisco, 415-552-1250
- Conciliation Forums of Oakland, 510-763-2117
- Legal Aid San Jose, 409-998-5200
- Legal Aid of the North Bay Area, 800-498-7666
- Marin County Bar Association, 415-453-8181
- San Francisco Bar Association Lawyer Referral Service, 415-989-1616
- San Francisco State University Legal Referral Center, 415-338-1140
- San Mateo County Bar Association, 650-369-4149
- Santa Clara County Bar Association, 408- 287-2557
- State Bar of California, 415-538-2000

SMALL CLAIMS COURTS
See **Consumer Protection** section in the **Helpful Services** chapter.

LIBRARIES

- Berkeley Central Branch, 510-644-6100, www.infopeople.org/bpl
- Marin County Library, 415-499-6057, www.countylibrary.marin.org
- New Main, San Francisco, 415-557-4400, www.sfpl.lib.ca.us
- Oakland Public Library, Main Branch, 510-238-3134, www.oaklandlibrary.org
- Peninsula Library System, 650-780-7018, www.plsinfo.org
- San Jose Public Library, 408-277-4846, www.sjpl.lib.ca.us
- Santa Clara County Library System, 408-293-2326, www-lib.co-santa-clara.ca.us

MARRIAGE LICENSES

- San Francisco City and County, 415-554-4950
- Alameda County, 510-272-6363
- Contra Costa County, 510-646-2956
- Marin County, 415-499-3003
- San Mateo County, 650-363-4712
- Santa Clara County, 408-299-7310

PARKS

- East Bay Regional Park District, 510-562-7275 , www.ebparks.org
- Golden Gate National Recreation Area, 415-556-0560, www.nps.gov/goga
- Golden Gate Park, 415-831-7200

- Marin County Department of Parks and Recreation, 415-499-6387, www.marincountyparks.org
- San Francisco Recreation and Parks Department, 415-831-2700, www.parks.sfgov.org
- San Mateo County Parks and Recreation Department, 650-363-4020, www.co.sanmateo.ca.us
- Santa Clara Department of Parks and Recreation, 408-358-3741, www.co.santa-clara.ca.us/parks

POST OFFICE, 800-275-8777, www.usps.com

SANITATION—GARBAGE & RECYCLING

CALIFORNIA
- California Integrated Waste Management Board, 800-CLEAN-UP
- The California Department of Conservation, 800-732-9253

SAN FRANCISCO
- Golden Gate Disposal, 415-626-4000, www.goldengatedisposal.com
- Household Hazardous Waste, 415-554-4333
- San Francisco League of Urban Gardeners (SLUG), 415-285-7585
- San Francisco Recycling Program, 415-554-3400
- Sunset Scavenger, 415-330-1300, www.sunsetscavenger.com
- Recycling Hotline, 415-544-7329

NORTH BAY
- Marin Recycling Center, 415-485-6806
- Marin Sanitary Services, 415-456-2601

EAST BAY
- Alameda County (north), Waste Management, 510-430-8509 www.stop-waste.org
- Alameda County (south), BFI, 510-657-3500
- Alameda County Home Composting Education Program, 510-635-6275
- Pleasanthill Bayshore Disposal, BFI, 925-685-4711
- Tri Cities Waste Management, 510-797-0440
- Recycle America of Northern California, 510-638-4327, ext. 308

PENINSULA/SOUTH BAY
- San Mateo County, BFI, 650-592-2411
- Santa Clara County, BFI, 408-432-1234
- South Bay, USA Waste Management, 408-451-0520, recycle@green-team.com

SENIORS

- AARP California, 916-440-2277, www.aarp.org
- Alameda County Area Agency on Aging, 800-510-2020
- Alameda County Adult Protective Services, 510-567-6897
- Elder Care Locator, 800-677-1116
- Health at Home, 415-753-8116
- Legal Assistance for Seniors, Oakland, 510-832-3040
- Legal Assistance to the Elderly, San Francisco, 415-861-4444
- Marin Adult Protection Services, 415-499-7118
- Richmond District Senior Central, 415-752-2815
- San Jose Senior Information Line, 800-255-3333
- San Francisco Adult Day Services Information and Referral, 415-773-0111

SHIPPING SERVICES

- Airborne Express, 800-247-2676, www.airborne.com
- DHL Worldwide Express, 800-225-5345, www.dhl.com
- Federal Express, 800-238-5355, www.fedex.com
- US Postal Service Express Mail, 800-222-1811, www.usps.com
- United Parcel Service, 800-742-5877, www.ups.com

SPORTS

- www.sfgate.com
- Golden State Warriors, 888-479-4667, www.warriers.com
- Oakland A's, 510-638-0500, www.oaklandathletics.com
- Oakland Raiders, 510-638-0500, www.raiders.com
- San Francisco 49ers, 415-468-2249, www.sf49ers.com
- San Francisco Giants, 800-5-GIANTS, www.sfgiants.com
- San Jose Earthquakes, 408-985-4625, www.sjearthquakes.com
- San Jose Sharks, 408-287-7070, www.sj-sharks.com
- Women's United Soccer Association, www.wusaleague.com

TAXES

- Internal Revenue Service, 510-839-1040, 800-829-1040, www.irs.gov
- San Francisco Tax Collector, 415-554-4400
- State Franchise Tax Board, 800-338-0505, www.ftb.ca.gov
- State of California Department of Finance, www.dof.ca.gov

TELEPHONE

- AT&T, 800-222-0300, www.att.com
- Excel, 800-875-9235
- Frontier, 800-482-4848
- GTC Telecom, 800-486-4030, www.gtctelecom.com
- IDT, 800-438-7964, www.idt.com
- Matrix, 800-282-0242
- MCI-World Com, 800-444-3333, www.mci.com
- Pacific Bell, 800-303-3000, www.pacificbell.com
- Qwest, 800-860-2255, www.qwest.com
- Sprint, 800-746-3767, www.sprint.com
- Utility.com, www.utility.com
- Verizon, 800-483-4000, www.verizon.com
- Working Assets, 800-363-7127, www.workingforchange.com

DIRECTORY ASSISTANCE—ONLINE
- www.smartpages.com
- www.555-1212.com
- www.altavista.com
- www.anywho.com
- www.bigbook.com
- www.people.yahoo.com
- www.switchboard.com
- www.whowhere.lycos.com
- www.worldpages.com
- www.zip2.com

TICKETS

- BASS Tickets, 510-762-2277; 408-998-2277; 707-546-2277, www.tickets.com/BASSOutlets
- Ticketmaster, 415-421-8497, www.ticketmaster.com
- TIX Bay Area, 415-433-7827

TIME, 415-POPCORN

TRANSPORTATION

- Bay Area Public Transportation, go to www.transitinfo.org or call 817-1717 (no area code needed—be prepared to hold).

- Carpool and Vanpool Services, www.rides.org , 800-755-7665
- Real Time Traffic Updates, http://cad.chp.ca.gov

TRAINS AND BUSES
- AC Transit, 510-839-2882, 800-559-4636; TDD/TTY 800-448-9790, www.actransit.org
- Altamont Commuter Express, 800-411-RAIL, www.acerail.com
- Amtrak, 800-USA-RAIL, www.amtrak.com, www.amtrakcalifornia.com
- BART (Bay Area Rapid Transit), www.bart.gov, 650-992-2278; TDD/TTY, 510-839-2220
- CalTrain, www.caltrain.com; 800-660-4287; TDD/TTY, 415-508-6448
- Contra Costa County Connection, 925-676-7500; TDD/TTY, 800-735-2929
- Goldengate Transit, www.goldengatetransit.org; 415-923-2000; TDD/TTY, 415-257-4554
- Green Tortoise Bus, 415-956-7500
- Greyhound, 800-231-2222, www.greyhound.com
- SamTrans, www.samtrans.com; 650-817-1717, 800-660-4287; TDD/TTY, 650-508-6448
- San Francisco Municipal Rail, www.sfmuni.com; 415-673-MUNI, TDD/TTY 415-923-6366
- Santa Clara County Transit, 800-894-9908, TDD/TTY, 408-321-2330
- Sonoma County Transit, www.sctransit.com
- SuperShuttle, 415-558-8500
- Valley Transit Authority, www.vta.org; 800-894-9908, TDD/TTY 408-321-2330

AIRPORTS
- Oakland International Airport, 510-577-4000; parking, 510-633-2571
- San Francisco International Airport, 650-761-0800, www.sfoairport.com; parking, 650-877-0227
- San Jose International Airport, 408-277-4759, www.sjc.org; parking, 408-293-6788

FERRIES
- Alameda Oakland Ferry, 510-522-3300
- Angel Island-Tiburon Ferry, 415-435-2131
- Blue and Gold Ferry, 415-773-1188
- Golden Gate Transit Ferry, San Francisco County, 415-923-2000; Marin County, 415-455-2000;
- Harbor Bay Isle Ferry (Alameda-SF), 510-769-5500
- Vallejo Baylink Ferry, 707-648-4666

TAXIS, see **Transportation** chapter.

UTILITIES

- City of Palo Alto Utilities (CPAU), 650-329-2161
- Pacific Gas and Electric, 800-743-5000; TTY, 800-652-4712, www.pge.com
- Santa Clara County Municipal Utilities, 408-984-5111
- Green Mountain Energy, 888-461-9929, www.greenmountain.com
- See **Water** in the **Getting Settled** chapter for water district numbers and web sites.

UTILITY EMERGENCIES
- Pacific Gas & Electric, 800-743-5002
- Pacific Bell Repair, 611

WEATHER, Regional Weather Reports, http://iwin.nws.noaa.gov/iwin/ca

A NATIVE SAN FRANCISCAN, RUTH RAYLE GREW UP IN THE RICHMOND District, was bused around to five different elementary schools in four years, even home-schooled for a bit before she donned the green plaid uniform and rode her bicycle to Katherine Delmar Burke's School for Girls. After Burke's, Ruth went to San Francisco University High School and then crossed the Bay to Berkeley, where she majored in Rhetoric and wrote for *The Berkeley Voice*. A desire to improve the world through law brought her to UC Davis Law School. Her first case, *Cal-NOW v. California State University System*, helped level the playing field for California State University Women's Athletic Teams. In addition to practicing law, Ruth loves to write and hopes that this is the first of many books to come.

A NATIVE OF Oxford, England, Michael Bower moved to California in 1967, and has been there ever since. He has lived in the San Francisco Bay Area for over 20 years, in the City itself, as well as in the North Bay, on the Peninsula, and now in the East Bay. If it weren't for the trees in front of his house he'd be able to see the Golden Gate Bridge from his living room window. He's an award-winning broadcast journalist. There's nowhere else in the United States he'd rather live than the Bay Area. This is Michael's first book.

READER RESPONSE FORM

We would appreciate your comments regarding this second edition of the *Newcomer's Handbook® for Moving to San Francisco and the Bay Area.* If you've found any mistakes or omissions or if you would just like to express your opinion about the guide, please let us know. We will consider any suggestions for possible inclusion in our next edition, and if we use your comments, we'll send you a *free* copy of our next edition. Please send this response form to:

Reader Response Department
First Books
3000 Market Street N.E., Suite 527
Salem, OR 97301

Comments:

_____

_____

_____

_____

_____

_____

_____

_____

Name: _____

Address _____

_____

_____

Telephone (   ) _____

3000 Market Street N.E., Suite 527
Salem, OR 97301
503-588-2224
www.firstbooks.com

NEWCOMER'S ORDER FORM HANDBOOK®

THE ORIGINAL, ALWAYS UPDATED, ABSOLUTELY INVALUABLE GUIDES FOR PEOPLE MOVING TO A CITY!

Find out about neigborhoods, apartment and house hunting, money matters, deposits/leases, getting settled, helpful services, shopping for the home, places of worship, cultural life, sports/recreation, vounteering, green space, schools and education, transportation, temporary lodgings and useful telephone numbers!

	# COPIES	**TOTAL**
Newcomer's Handbook® for Atlanta	_____ x $17.95	$_____
Newcomer's Handbook® for Boston	_____ x $18.95	$_____
Newcomer's Handbook® for Chicago	_____ x $18.95	$_____
Newcomer's Handbook® for London	_____ x $18.95	$_____
Newcomer's Handbook® for Los Angeles	_____ x $17.95	$_____
Newcomer's Handbook® for Minneapolis-St. Paul	_____ x $20.95	$_____
Newcomer's Handbook® for New York City	_____ x $18.95	$_____
Newcomer's Handbook® for Philadelphia	_____ x $16.95	$_____
Newcomer's Handbook® for San Francisco	_____ x $20.95	$_____
Newcomer's Handbook® for Seattle	_____ x $18.95	$_____
Newcomer's Handbook® for Washington D.C.	_____ x $18.95	$_____
	SUBTOTAL	$_____
POSTAGE & HANDLING (*$7.00 first book, $1.00 each add'l.*)		$_____
	TOTAL	$_____

SHIP TO:

Name _____

Title _____

Company _____

Address _____

City _____ State _____ Zip _____

Phone Number (_____) _____

FIRST BOOKS

Send this order form and a check or money order payable to:
First Books

First Books, Mail Order Department
3000 Market Street N.E., Suite 527, Salem, OR 97301

Allow 1-2 weeks for delivery

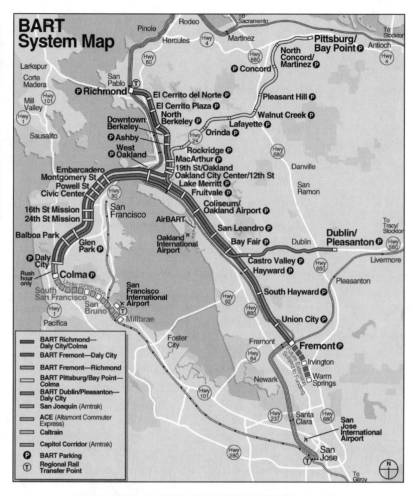

BAY AREA RAPID TRANSIT SYSTEM MAP

THE NEWCOMER'S HANDBOOK® SERIES

Newcomer's Handbook® for Atlanta

Newcomer's Handbook® for Boston

Newcomer's Handbook® for Chicago

Newcomer's Handbook® for London

Newcomer's Handbook® for Los Angeles

Newcomer's Handbook® for Minneapolis-St. Paul

Newcomer's Handbook® for New York City

Newcomer's Handbook® for Philadelphia

Newcomer's Handbook® for San Francisco

Newcomer's Handbook® for Seattle

Newcomer's Handbook® for Washington D.C.

Visit our web site at
www.firstbooks.com
for a sample of all our books.